Banished to the
Great Northern Wilderness

Contemporary Chinese Studies

This series provides new scholarship and perspectives on modern and contemporary China, including China's contested borderlands and minority peoples; ongoing social, cultural, and political changes; and the varied histories that animate China today.

A list of titles in this series appears at the end of this book.

Banished to the Great Northern Wilderness

Political Exile and Re-education in Mao's China

NING WANG

UBC Press • Vancouver • Toronto

25 24 23 22 21 20 19 18 17   5 4 3 2 1

Printed in Canada on FSC-certified ancient-forest-free paper
(100% post-consumer recycled) that is processed chlorine- and acid-free.

Library and Archives Canada Cataloguing in Publication

Wang, Ning, 1964-, author
   Banished to the great northern wilderness : political exile and re-education in Mao's China/
Ning Wang.

Includes bibliographical references and index.
Issued in print and electronic formats.

ISBN 978-0-7748-3223-6 (hardback). – ISBN 978-0-7748-3225-0 (pdf)
ISBN 978-0-7748-3226-7 (epub). – ISBN 978-0-7748-3227-4 (mobi)

1. Zhongguo gong chan dang – History – 20th century.   2. Intellectuals – China – Beijing – History – 20th century.   3. Political persecution – China – Beijing – History – 20th century.
4. Exiles – China – Manchuria – History – 20th century.   5. Labor camps – China – Manchuria – History – 20th century.   6. Forced labor – China – Manchuria – History – 20th century.
7. Manchuria (China) – History – 20th century.   8. China – History – 1949–1976.   I. Title.
II. Series: Contemporary Chinese studies

HD4875.C62W35 2017   331.11'730951809045   C2016-903866-1
                                                          C2016-903867-X

Canadä

UBC Press gratefully acknowledges the financial support for our publishing program of the Government of Canada (through the Canada Book Fund) and the British Columbia Arts Council.

This book has been published with the help of a grant from the Canadian Federation for the Humanities and Social Sciences, through the Awards to Scholarly Publications Program, using funds provided by the Social Sciences and Humanities Research Council of Canada.

Financial support from the Chiang Ching-Kuo Foundation and the Brock University Faculty Fund.

Printed and bound in Canada by Friesens
Set in Garamond by Marquis Interscript
Copy editor: Joanne Richardson
Proofreader: Alison Stroebel
Indexer: Margaret de Boer
Cartographer: Eric Leinberger
Cover designer: Gabi Proctor

UBC Press
The University of British Columbia
2029 West Mall
Vancouver, BC V6T 1Z2
www.ubcpress.ca

To those whose spirits never died under Mao

Contents

Acknowledgments

There are many ways to tell the story of Mao's China. From among myriad possibilities, one might favour recounting the Communist Party's campaigns to facilitate regime consolidation, the effects of court politics on social life, or the persecution of dissidents. In the traditional narratives, however, the plight of the victims of the Anti-Rightist Campaign (1957-58) has often been overshadowed by the human tragedies caused by the Great Leap Forward and the grand turmoil of the Cultural Revolution. Yet, that Campaign brought tremendous suffering to China's educated elites through a combination of political suppression and psychological manipulation, paving the way for further purging of both intellectuals and communist cadres during the Cultural Revolution.

A significant portion of the sources for this book comes from personal interviews. I am deeply indebted to my interviewees in China, the majority of whom were victims of that Anti-Rightist persecution. Some sent me memoirs but, faced with my obstinate requests, many graciously opened the floodgates of their memory for me. My heartfelt appreciation also goes to those who helped me obtain valuable archives, local gazetteers, and unpublished memoirs; to those who offered their precious private collections of sources; and to those who helped arrange interviews. Their bravery and generosity cannot be overstated. While their names cannot be recorded here for their protection, their contributions to this book are carved into my consciousness.

As the flow of time wears down human memory, and the Chinese state attempts to neutralize its troubled past by suppressing public discourse and monopolizing the interpretation of its history, many victims of the Anti-Rightist Campaign – and certainly most of those featured in this research – would have otherwise carried their stories of suffering and redemption to the grave. So, I present this book not only to add another colour to the incredibly complex tapestry of Mao's China but as a tribute to those who suffered, perished or survived, to offer some measure of peace and healing to their grieving souls, and so that the silence and misinterpretation around their experience can at last be shattered.

In writing this book, I am deeply grateful to two of my mentors. During the book's formative stages, Diana Lary provided much-needed inspiration and encouragement in her characteristically supportive way. Her insightful ideas, seasoned advice and nurturing care guided me in my approach to this sensitive topic, and drove me forward in the most strenuous years of my research. Timothy Cheek gave unselfishly of his time and energy in methodological guidance, challenging me to rethink many parts of the manuscript, as well as introducing me to a broad academic dialogue. His input improved not only the quality of this book, but my general expertise in researching Chinese intelligentsia under Mao. Both mentors carefully watched over my progress, rightfully reminded me of any shortcomings, and enthusiastically cheered my every success.

I have been fortunate to have Norman Smith as my colleague and loyal supporter from the very beginning. Throughout the years, he has offered me tireless and unending assistance, from critiquing the very first draft to suggesting a possible cover image for this final published book. For as long as I live, I will forever remain indebted to Norman. My thanks also go to Alexander Woodside, Glen Peterson, Wu Guoguang, Leo Shin, Josephine Chiu-Duke, Victor Zatsepine, and Gu Xiong, who have lent either general advice or specific help. Particular gratitude is due to Frank Dikötter and Jeremy Brown. Both pushed me to delve even deeper in my research and suggested a great deal of additional sources; Jeremy provided incredibly specific and detailed advice on how to revise the manuscript. This book is not wholly my own; some part of it belongs to each of these learned and enthusiastic minds. Of course, I take full responsibility for any remaining deficiencies.

This book in its current form would not have been possible without the support of several individuals and foundations: the Social Sciences and Humanities Research Council of Canada, which provided generous funding, and my two remarkable editors at the University of British Columbia Press. As editors for a crotchety, non-native English speaking old man, Emily Andrew and Megan Brand displayed astonishing dedication, patience, and magnanimity.

Finally, my special thanks go to my daughter Ivy. As she grew up, she became more and more involved in my project, pouring countless hours of her time and life into the effort. In addition to simple copyediting and imaginative translations from Chinese, she painstakingly edited the entire book, correcting many stylistic issues and adding colour to prosaic paragraphs. Her efforts greatly enhanced the coherence and readability of the final draft. Debating the finest nuances of my ideas with her and watching her intellectually engage in my field made for many of the happiest moments of my life.

Banished to the
Great Northern Wilderness

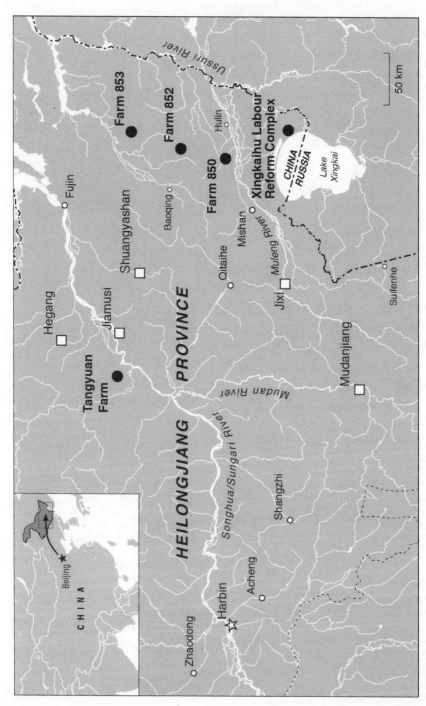

Eastern Heilongjiang featuring the labour farms covered in this book. *Source: Adapted by Eric Leinberger.*

Introduction

Countless hearts,
Prisons for countless wronged souls.
Theirs is the fate
Of convicts in a primeval forest.
Axes and saws to cut the year-rings of life.
O, the endless ploughing in the fields!
Ploughshare to crush their shining youth.
The suffering is great, very great,
But there are no sighs, no groans.

—Tang Qi

A train winds its way through the silent, snow-laden forest, bearing its weary burden to the Great Northern Wilderness. The year is 1958; the cargo, the human collateral of yet another Maoist campaign. Over half a million Chinese, mostly intellectuals, suddenly became "rightists," "ultra-rightists," and "counter-revolutionaries" under the Anti-Rightist Campaign of 1957 and 1958. The governing Chinese Communist Party (CCP, or the Party) grossly mistreated these individuals, meting out prison sentences, forced manual labour, and, in many cases, banishment to the countryside or distant frontier regions. For some, nearly a quarter of a century passed before they were allowed to return home and pick up the broken fragments of their lives; many others died of starvation, disease, and overwork, sometimes leaving behind sick and uncared for young children. Tang Qi's poem captures the essence of the massive banishment of political offenders to the labour reform centres in China's northeastern borderlands, known as *Beidahuang* – the Great Northern Wilderness. Their experiences, together with the unique labour reform regime, form an important chapter in the global history of concentration camps in the twentieth century.[1]

The Anti-Rightist Campaign has long attracted academic attention throughout the world, but the post-campaign experiences of those persecuted (including their banishment) has not received proportionate treatment by either Chinese or Western historians.[2] My research aims to examine the operation of political banishment in the post-1957 period; to show how political offenders exiled from Beijing fared, collectively and individually, in the Great Northern Wilderness; and to investigate the behavioural patterns and the psychological world of the Chinese intellectuals in exile. I also explore the techniques of physical and psychological control that state agents employed at the local level in exile communities as well as some of their efforts to "remould" the exiles.

Conventional wisdom mostly presents Chinese intellectuals as victims, CCP labour camp policy as oppressive, ideological remoulding as powerful and effective, and so on. Whereas I do not dispute that this was often the case, I argue that political exiles to the Great Northern Wilderness were not necessarily real or even potential opponents of Mao's government; rather, they were often "loyal dissidents" and faithful followers of the CCP. Some of them were receptive to ideological remoulding and worked hard to achieve self-redemption. This struggle for redemption was self-imposed and was significantly compounded by mental and physical distress. In addition to Party politics (e.g., the desire to reform state enemies), the conditions in the camps (e.g., modes of manipulation, temperament of camp managers, etc.) also contributed to the suffering of exiles. We shall see both admirable resistance and subversion of state efforts to subdue these exiles on the one hand, and regrettable infighting and service to those same dark forces on the other. While these people were, indeed, victims of a Maoist political campaign, some of them were also victims of (and victimized) their fellow exiles.

Although this research focuses on what happened in the Beidahuang borderlands in the 1950s and 1960s, its findings may show us a way of analyzing the experiences of political exiles in Mao's China as a whole. Standing at the intersection of Maoist persecution, banishment, and the ideological remoulding of Chinese intellectuals, and contributing to a nuanced understanding of China's labour camps, banishment, and the ruling style of the CCP, my research seeks to complicate the picture of Chinese intellectuals in general and the exile community in particular.

Why focus on those banished from Beijing? And why focus on Beidahuang? There are four reasons. First, the northeastern borderland, with its difficult natural environment and isolated geographical location, was long regarded by China's imperial rulers as an ideal place to banish various offenders. The CCP government followed suit, raising banishment to a new height in terms of both the exiles involved and the exile settlements established. Second, the mass persecution in Beijing in 1957–58 coincided with an ambitious state program of land reclamation in the northeast, so the tragic experiences of the purged were exacerbated by a government that, in the pursuit of economic growth, wanted to use them as cheap labour. Third, the political exiles from Beijing were among China's best-educated elite, therefore an examination of their experiences in one of the country's harshest regions will help illuminate the fates of Chinese intellectuals in the Mao era.[3] Finally, the political exiles from Beijing, many of whom were journalists and writers, have left a wealth of valuable memoirs and other biographical materials. Official sources (untapped archives, local histories, gazetteers, etc.) are also quite satisfactory.

Readers should bear in mind that the stories about Beidahuang cannot be considered to be typical of banishment in the Mao era. Hundreds of labour camps existed in China, in the interior and on the frontier, and informal labour reform settlements were numerous. Each of them had different stories to tell about its inmates and their experiences. Such diversity and complexity can only be appreciated through rich and varied case studies. I am convinced that the experiences of the persecuted Chinese in exile and the actual operation of various labour camps/settlements can only be understood through such case studies – each specified according to time, group, and locale.

POLITICAL EXILES IN BEIDAHUANG:
A GENERAL PICTURE AND CHAPTER DESCRIPTIONS

The term "political exiles" refers to those banished by the government of the People's Republic of China (PRC) for political reasons, although the CCP denies the existence of political offenders or political prisoners. In particular, the term refers to "rightists" (including "ultra-rightists") and "counter-revolutionaries" who were sent to various labour reform centres in Beidahuang.

Beidahuang, or the Great Northern Wilderness, generally refers to the northern borderland of northeast China (Manchuria). Although far from well defined (see Chapter 2), Beidahuang was widely agreed to be the geographical region north of Harbin and Mount Yilehuli, extending to the Russian border and encompassing the Three River Plain (bounded by the Amur, Ussuri, and Sungari Rivers) and the Mudan River Plain. Although arable land was abundant and soil fertile, its frigid northern climate, primitive physical conditions, and distance from China proper made it an undesirable place for human habitation. Within Beidahuang, four counties – Mishan, Hulin, Baoqing, and Raohe – as well as the area east of Lake Xingkai are particularly relevant to this work as the army farms and labour camps located there received a large number of exiles.

During the late 1950s and early 1960s, the political offenders banished to Beidahuang could be roughly broken down into the following categories:

(1) Beijing rightists on the army farms

With the conclusion of the Anti-Rightist Campaign in 1958, more than fourteen hundred rightists from various government agencies, press media, research institutes, and military units in Beijing were sent to army farms in the name of "labour under supervision" (*jiandu laodong*), or "tempering through labour" (*laodong duanlian*). According to incomplete statistics, their ages ranged from seventeen to fifty-four.[4] Their former occupations ranged from research assistants and scientists to writers and artists, from junior office clerks to Party officials and veteran revolutionaries. In Beidahuang, they worked on the same farms with demobilized soldiers and convicted criminals under the surveillance of demobilized military officers. The majority of them stayed there for close to three years. In the early 1960s, massive deaths from starvation propelled the central government to return them to less physically difficult areas (such as Beijing and Hebei).

(2) Counter-revolutionaries in the labour reform (*laogai*) camps of Xingkaihu[5]

Many of those accused of being counter-revolutionaries during the Anti-Rightist Campaign, if sentenced, were sent to Xingkaihu labour reform camps. Their numbers, by conservative estimation, amount to around two thousand. These people included university students, young teachers, scientists, and government employees as well as those who were considered to have been historically disloyal to the CCP and to have committed new offences in 1957. The major difference between them and the rightists sent to the army farms was that they had voiced relatively strident criticisms of the Party and/or tried to flee China to avoid arrest. As well, those who were at first labelled rightists but denied their guilt or appealed for redress invited harsher penalties and, thus, were elevated to counter-revolutionary status. Most people in this category who were rounded up in Beijing were sent to Xingkaihu (the focus of Chapter 3), but some were sent to other labour farms in northern or northeastern China.

(3) Ultra-rightists (*jiyou pai*) in the labour re-education (*laojiao*) camps of Xingkaihu

Ultra-rightists were those at the top of the rightist scale. They were considered to have committed serious offences, and thus the punishment they received was more severe than that meted out to other rightists. For some, family background and overseas connections, in addition to their criticisms of the Party, contributed to their arrest. Although they did not receive a formal trial and thus, due to the Party's "leniency," were not subject to term-sentencing, they were still seen to be in need of being disciplined by the police. Labour re-education camps were thus considered to be appropriate places for them to go. A considerable number of them were arrested in universities, colleges, and research institutes. In Xingkaihu, they were distributed into four labour re-education camps.

These three types of political outcasts constituted the majority of the anti-rightist victims banished from Beijing to Beidahuang. They were deployed as agricultural labourers, lumber workers, construction workers, and so on. They were valuable forced labour in the great wilderness. Their banishment and enslavement coincided with the most serious famine (1959–62) in modern Chinese history. Their food supplies were low, and this was compounded by demanding labour, lack of medical care, and physical abuse. The death rate was high, in some camps up to 20 to 30 percent. Discussions of their suffering – hardship, hunger, death, escape, physical abuse, and psychological torment – and the politics of this suffering form the bulk of this book.[6]

One of the fundamental questions with which China specialists are confronted concerns how to define rightists. Are they political dissidents who posed real threats to the governing party and, thus, logically invited harsh treatment? If the answer is negative, or the number of dissidents was insignificant, this leads to a second question: How does one explain the mass persecution? In Chapter 1, I argue that, although some intellectuals were labelled rightists because of their sharp criticism of Party policies and cadre officials (for their abuse of power) or because of their advocacy of greater intellectual freedom, many others were so labelled due to factional conflicts, personal animosity, grudges, and/or the mishandling of interpersonal relations. Furthermore, labelling quotas set by higher authorities forced local Party chiefs to frame innocent people. I suggest that, although the CCP launched the Anti-Rightist Campaign to punish opponents of the state, intellectuals and officials took advantage of it to attack their peers and competitors.

It is important to look at the role of daily politics in Maoist persecution. In authoritarian states, daily politics, generally understood as the way a person manages relations with the state, its agents, and other individuals, is central to one's life. In the PRC context, as Party bosses and heads of work units had the power to interpret state policies and to determine a person's fortune, those individuals who did not truly display dissent but simply failed to adequately manage their relations with these power holders, inevitably suffered in politically motivated campaigns. While they were the de facto victims of daily politics and were sacrificed to the machinations of state crackdowns, state ideology (e.g., the theory of class struggle) provided legitimacy to such crackdowns. Correspondingly, forced "labour reform" and banishment, the purpose of which was seemingly to ensure the ideological renewal of offenders, often ended up transforming how these individuals handled daily politics – that is, how they altered their behaviour and attitude when dealing with lower-level state agents in order to improve their lots.

In Chapter 2, I focus on the experience of Beijing rightists on the army farms of Beidahuang. Some rightists, not silenced by the Anti-Rightist Campaign, continued to articulate their criticisms and expressed abhorrence of Beidahuang; many others, however, were willing to be sent down in order to ease the political pressure placed upon them or to display their commitment to self-redemption. Heavily indoctrinated by Party norms or overwhelmed by the mass condemnation in 1957, a considerable number of the persecuted admitted their "crimes" and their need to go through labour reform to cleanse their "reactionary" minds and to achieve spiritual growth through trial and tribulation. Despite the official rhetoric pertaining to "thought reform," however, they were essentially used as forced labour on the army farms. Some farms exercised specific regimens in order to make their "thought work" effective, but others reduced political indoctrination (if such existed) to rebukes and psychological abuse. Life on these farms was generally difficult, but experiences varied depending on location and camp managers. Personal connections with influential officials were important for the rightists, even in banishment, and their former prestige and expertise often made their lives easier.

In Chapter 3, I examine the life experiences of counter-revolutionaries and ultra-rightists in the Xingkaihu labour reform complex. I argue that it was the mass persecution of the 1950s and the subsequent shortage of prison facilities that prompted the boom of labour camps in the northeast, including the establishment of Xingkaihu, a colony directly administered by the Beijing Public Security Bureau. In Xingkaihu, student inmates who were mentally or ideologically unyielding were more assertive than others in articulating their opinions, resisting thought reform, and refusing to entirely submit to camp cadres. Their Xingkaihu experience, including their access to officially allowed readings, heightened their dissidence and prompted them to move from a position of "loyal opposition" to the Party to real alienation. The CCP practice of mixing political prisoners with criminal prisoners in labour camps turned out to be quite insidious, enabling the police to use the latter to monitor and discipline the former. I also discuss various remoulding techniques used in Xingkaihu as well as the relationships among camp officials, political inmates, and criminal inmates.

Analysis of the physical suffering – hunger, death, physical abuse, and suicide – of the exiles constitutes the major part of Chapter 4. I demonstrate that, although the adventurous Great Leap Forward (GLF) and the subsequent great famine formed the general background of the camp experience, the hyper-activism of labour camp authorities (e.g., submitting excessive amounts of grain to state granaries, setting high production targets, etc.) and their self-profiteering manoeuvres led to severe food shortages and heavy workloads for the exiles, which, in turn, led to a massive death toll. The impact of local politics upon the actual lives of these exiles was no less severe than was the impact of high politics. I also show how the dignity and moral integrity of intellectuals were damaged. Due to difficult life conditions, reprehensible behaviour (such as stealing and fighting) became commonplace in the daily lives of political exiles, exacerbating the physical abuse meted out by camp authorities. Intellectuals were forced by circumstances in which they found themselves to make some very difficult moral compromises.

In Chapter 5, I tap into the psychological world and behavioural patterns of political exiles. I show that many of them, especially the rightists, still identified with Party ideology and accepted the notion of ideological remoulding through labour; many worked hard in order to show repentance and achieve self-redemption. Some, although not all, of the political exiles transformed the Party's ideological battle into self-affliction.

Chapter 5's most important theme is the ultra-activism of the exile community. Both on the army farms and in the Xingkaihu labour camp complex, some of the intellectual inmates attacked others in order to advance themselves and to show their loyalty to the authorities. They reported and denounced their fellow inmates and used trivial issues to launch scathing attacks. This was a matter not only of personality but also of survival: incriminating others was a strategy of self-protection. Those who succeeded in creating good images of themselves were often assigned lighter work and were even appointed as group leaders and entrusted to monitor others. Those deemed to be politically backward or to have poor work performances suffered not only at the hands of labour camp cadres but also at the hands of their fellow inmates. Some of the victims of political persecution turned into perpetrators.

In Chapter 6, I discuss the suspension of banishment to the Great Northern Wilderness and the post-banishment experiences of political exiles. I show that the mass deaths in the borderlands and countryside prompted the central government to evacuate rightists. In the early 1960s, the majority of Beijing rightists were allowed to leave the army farms, and the ultra-rightists in Xingkaihu were also transferred to the interior. These ex-inmates, however, still bore the stigma foisted upon them as a result of consciously designed state policies; consequently, they were discriminated against and were unable to resume their normal lives until they were finally rehabilitated in the post-Mao political thaw.

PUNITIVE EXILE IN A COMPARATIVE PERSPECTIVE

The CCP's deployment of convicts to labour camps had deep roots: it did not start with the Party's takeover of China. In 1932, the redemption-through-labour reformatories (*laodong ganhua yuan*) were formally instituted in the Jiangxi Soviet base area to "redeem" prisoners through persuasion while forcing them to engage in economic production. The inmates were mostly counter-revolutionary elements from such ideologically reprehensible backgrounds as the landlord, rich peasant, and capitalist; however, poor peasants and hired labourers who had committed crimes were also incarcerated there. This was the forerunner of the modern *laogai* system.[7] In the 1940s, as Frank Dikötter shows, certain local communists, such as those in Shandong Province, abandoned the concept of using prisons to confine convicts and, in order to confront the organizational problems and scarce resources caused by the unstable military situation, moved instead towards a system of mobile labour teams and camps that were dispersed throughout the countryside. This practice later spread to other communist areas and was adopted by CCP headquarters at Yan'an.[8]

Nevertheless, exiling offenders to cultural and economic peripheries or moving undesirable elements to rural locations is not the invention of the Chinese communists; rather, it is a centuries-old form of punishment used by various states in the East and in the West. Well-known cases include the British deportation of convicts to Australia, the French expulsion of offenders to "Devil's Island" in French Guiana, the Russian banishment of Decembrists to Siberia, the labour camp regimes (Gulags) across the Stalinist Soviet Union, and the Taiwanese internment of convicts on Green Island, to name but few. The motives for these practices ranged from the removal of disruptive elements to the rehabilitation of offenders, from the colonization of frontiers to the assimilation of ethnic minorities. In this book, I focus on the internal and external influences on the CCP's post-1949 operation of banishment, among which the imperial state's practice of *liufang*, the Guomindang's employment of convict labour in agricultural colonies, and the Soviet Gulag are of special relevance.

In China, the practice of banishing political and criminal offenders to frontiers is of ancient origin. Starting as early as the Qin dynasty (3rd century BCE), imperial rulers have been deporting convicts, disgraced officials, and those in political disfavour to border locations or insalubrious mountain regions in Yunnan, Guangxi, Guangdong, and Hainan to perform military service or manual labour in such state programs as land reclamation, road construction, and/or river projects. This is the practice of *liufang*.[9] In the eighteenth century, the Qing court successively used Manchuria (the Northeast) and Xinjiang (the Northwest) as banishment destinations. In the early years, the offenders banished to Manchuria were mostly common criminals (such as robbers, counterfeiters, and smugglers) as well as lesser figures who had participated in popular rebellions. "Traditionally, such crimes ranked among the most serious." "Many of these exiles had originally been sentenced to death but had had their sentences commuted."[10] Disgraced scholars and officials as well as their families were also banished. In 1759, after the Qing's conquest of what is now Xinjiang, tens of thousands of criminals and the disfavoured were sent there as labourers and managerial personnel.[11]

The extent to which the PRC banishments drew upon the imperial legacy warrants interrogation. Both sent offenders away from the main centres of China and made extensive use of exiles as a source of labour for state projects. The CCP claim that it treats the guilty with leniency and its alleged stress on ideological remoulding resembles the imperial focus on benevolent rule and moral regeneration.[12] If we consider the fact that the leadership of the CCP, especially Party chairman Mao Zedong, was familiar with imperial history and ruling tactics, it is reasonable to presume that the imperial style of banishment influenced the CCP style. Mao was known to habitually flaunt his knowledge of Chinese history on important occasions, gushing about "making the past serve the present (*gu wei jin yong*)." However, there were clear distinctions between the CCP form of banishment and that of its imperial predecessors. Qing exiles in Xinjiang, for instance, were provided with enough food and were allocated sufficient farmland to support themselves, whereas PRC exiles were often threatened with hunger while almost all their agricultural produce flowed to state barns. In the Qing's Manchurian frontiers, ideological and physical control were flexible, and literati exiles were granted various job options, working as teachers, river patrollers, and postal workers. Some were even allowed to conduct business: banished scholars were employed as secretaries or assistants to local officials, their learning and expertise highly appreciated.[13] In the PRC period, however, political exiles, many of whom were well schooled, were subjected to strict physical control in the labour camps and were nearly exclusively used as manual labourers. Only a small portion of them were recruited part time for local magazines, art troupes, and so on after performing a period of physical labour. Compared with their counterparts in the imperial period, the PRC exiles were treated with little respect by camp cadres and fared even worse in the borderlands.

In the twentieth century, the Guomindang (GMD, or Nationalist) government also used convict labour in state-run projects. According to Frank Dikötter, during the Japanese War, in order to deal with financial crisis the GMD's Ministry of Justice ushered in the practice of employing prisoners to reclaim wasteland in Sichuan, Guizhou, and Guangxi. A number of agricultural colonies were established in remote and inhospitable areas, where prisoners were sent to support themselves by cultivating land and to receive moral instruction.[14] But the projects encountered a lot of "practical administrative difficulties." For instance, the output of the farmlands was not sufficient for the prisoners' own sustenance, many of those sent to the colonies were too old or sick to work in the fields, prisoners were difficult to supervise out in the open, and the projects were plagued by shortages of funds. For these reasons, the GMD's agricultural convict colonies "were never developed in any systematic way."[15] This probably taught the CCP to strengthen its administration and physical control over inmates as well as to reclaim relatively fertile land.

It should be noted that the CCP banished a fairly large number of political prisoners, including those who had previously served the GMD and those who had criticized the CCP. Those who committed criminal offences were considered less dangerous to the state than were those who committed political offences. In this respect, the Mao's China was more similar to the Soviet Union than to Imperial China.

The Soviet practice of sending offenders to exile settlements and labour camps has been intensively researched over decades. It is held that this practice originated in the Tsarist banishment of offenders to Siberia and to the deserted island of Sakhalin. In October 1922, the Soviet government set up a permanent exile commission to deal with "socially dangerous persons and active members of anti-Soviet parties."[16] The Gulag thus developed as a formidable exile and labour reform regime that interned a variety of people, from rich peasants and common criminals to counter-revolutionary offenders. According to a socialist principle propounded by Vladimir Lenin – namely, "he who does not work shall not eat" – in 1929, the Soviet government established an elaborate system of exile and imprisonment in conjunction with forced labour, in which the *zeks* (inmates of forced labour camps) had to earn what was needed to feed and clothe themselves and to increase national production.[17] Upon the proclamation of the PRC, the CCP government, driven to borrow wholesale from the Soviet experience, enthusiastically followed the Soviet model of combining exile and forced labour. Mao Zedong and military commander-in-chief Zhu De both actively advocated learning from the Soviets about setting up labour camp facilities and using convict labourers for state projects. Soviet advisers were invited to share their counsel on matters such as prison construction, prison rules, and inmate administration.[18]

Distinctions between the Soviet system and the CCP system can be identified, however. In the Gulag, political offenders were kept separate from criminal offenders: "Camps were for more 'socially dangerous elements' such as political offenders, while colonies had more common criminals."[19] But the CCP system typically put political offenders among the criminal and made use of the latter to monitor and discipline the former. When Gulag authorities administered the construction of railways,

canals, and roads, their disciplining of inmate labourers was relatively
lax and the number of escapes large. By contrast, in the early PRC period, as I show in the case of Beidahuang, labour farms/camps were built
in remote, isolated regions, disciplinary and preventive measures were
strong, and the chance of escape limited.[20] Furthermore, as Harry Wu
notes, "the purpose of the Soviet labor camps is suppression and punishment – not the systematic, complete 'thought reform' emphasized by
the PRC camps."[21] The available sources on the Soviet camps (such as
Aleksandr Solzhenitsyn's *The Gulag Archipelago* and Anne Applebaum's
Gulag: A History) all point to the fact that Gulag administrations rarely
forced inmates into political study sessions or compelled them to preach,
to listen to propaganda, or to write self-criticism. In Mao's China, however, indoctrination sessions were usually taken seriously, and thought
reports were required from all inmates. Last, some Chinese ex-prisoners
believe, based on their own experience and their knowledge of Soviet
cases, that the treatment they received in the Chinese labour camps was
worse than the treatment that prisoners received in the Soviet Gulag.[22]
Comparing the labour camp regimes in the two major communist states
shows that, although the Soviets exerted significant influence upon the
Chinese labour reform system, and banishment in both countries was
an important way of economizing state resources, the Chinese practices
reflect the CCP's unique, and probably more sophisticated, approach to
dealing with the socially and politically disfavoured. The CCP leadership
was also more ambitious than was the Soviet leadership with regard to
controlling and "reconfiguring" inmates' minds.

HISTORIOGRAPHIC CONSIDERATIONS

On the whole, China scholars in the English-speaking world have paid a
great deal of attention to communist politics, the political campaigns and
purges in the Mao era, and the relationships between intellectuals and
the state. The works of Roderick MacFarquhar, Frederick Teiwes, Merle
Goldman, Jonathan Spence, Timothy Cheek, and nearly all general treatments of PRC political history pay considerable attention to investigating the causes and the implementation of the 1957 persecution and its
impact on China and Chinese intellectuals. It seems, however, that the
studies of intellectuals under communism have been integrated into a
discussion of grand political history – how intellectuals were involved in,

and committed to, China's political changes; how their life trajectories were affected by these changes; and how their fortunes were inextricably intertwined with the course of twentieth-century China. In this process, the individual experiences of persecuted intellectuals, including those sent to labour camps or other exile settlements, have received little focused treatment but, rather, are incorporated into the general account of the long history of the social catastrophes and human tragedies associated with the CCP rule.

In Western scholarship that touches on the persecuted, the limelight often falls on a limited number of famous writers, scholars, and scientists. Ding Ling, Fei Xiaotong, Liu Binyan, and Fang Lizhi, for instance, are given special attention due to their literary fame and scholarly achievements or to their reputations as political dissidents and human rights campaigners.[23] What awaits further investigation is the post-1957 experiences of a broader spectrum of rightists – including lesser known professionals, media workers, schoolteachers, students, and government employees – in terms of how they suffered during the campaign, how they survived or perished in the exile settlements, and how their mental life evolved. It is through exploring their stories, supplemented by various archival sources, that we gain a more nuanced understanding of the complex world of those who suffered during the Anti-Rightist Campaign and subsequent banishment.

Another important issue is the PRC labour camp. Fuelled by a growing interest in this, Western scholarship and narratives have been flourishing for the past two decades, beginning with Jean-Luc Domenach's comprehensive and well-researched account of Chinese labour camps and Harry Wu's painstaking work disclosing the vast system of labour farms and factories that produced a wide range of goods for export.[24] These are echoed by some of the finest pieces of scholarly work, such as that by Philip Williams and Yenna Wu, James Seymour and Richard Anderson, Kate Saunders, and others.[25] The most gripping Chinese narrative so far is the collection of interviews, *Gaobie Jiabiangou* (with its English version *Women from Shanghai*), gathered by Yang Xianhui, who spent many years of his life searching for stories of camp survivors and assembling them into a captivating work on rightists who suffered and perished in a dreadful northwestern labour re-education camp. Both Harry Wu and Bao Ruo-Wang (Jean Pasqualini) enrich us with stories of their personal experiences in the different camps of northern China. These works range from the daily routine in the labour camps to heart-wrenching human suffering, from brainwashing to physical abuse, from individual stories to collective experiences. Nevertheless, virtually all of them omit a specific group of rightists that was banished from Beijing to the harsh north-eastern borderlands, and none of them investigate an alternative labour reform regime – the little known army farms that interned countless political outcasts. Nor do they adequately address the internecine strife and complex psychological world of the banished intellectuals.[26] All of this leaves room for, and necessitates, this book.

I

The Anti-Rightist Campaign and Political Labelling

1957, a year of savageness and gloom, was saturated with the blood of the Chinese intelligentsia and youth.
— Lin Zhao, a student rightist, written using her own blood

The frontier banishment of the politically suspect in the late 1950s was the direct result of a political crusade – the Anti-Rightist Campaign. During this campaign, sizable numbers of Chinese intellectuals, including writers, teachers, professionals, and university students as well as CCP cadres and government employees were labelled "rightists" or "counter-revolutionaries," lost or were suspended from their jobs, and were sent to labour camps. The campaign negatively affected the lives of millions of Chinese, and the governing party seemingly achieved its agenda of state consolidation by effectively crushing its opposition (real or imagined) and imposing political conformity.[1] For this reason, an examination of political banishment must account for the Anti-Rightist Campaign of 1957 and investigate the general process of political labelling. I focus on three questions: Why did the campaign happen? Who were the rightists? Why were they labelled?

Received opinion has it that the misfortunes of rightists (those singled out for persecution during the campaign) had political causes: they were labelled and then punished because they protested CCP control over intellectuals and pursued intellectual freedom, they criticized Party officials for their abuse of power, they demanded liberal political and cultural reform as well as institutional changes, they questioned the relevance of Mao Zedong thought to academia, they challenged CCP domination in the spheres of literature and art, and so on. Although recognizing that their chief motivation was to rectify rather than to displace the Party, Western scholars emphasize that the political, ideological, and literary stance of intellectuals was the root cause of their persecution.[2] This is in accordance with a Chinese observation that intellectuals, in pursuing scientific truth, were bound to be at odds with Marxist ideology and to come into conflict with the CCP. This falls within a well-received explanatory framework, which holds that the purpose of the Anti-Rightist Campaign was to suppress democratic intellectuals.[3]

This Party–intellectual relation model is, in fact, only applicable to a small number of victims, such as well-known student rightist Lin Xiling and democratic party leader Zhang Bojun.[4] To the vast majority, however, the purge (including political labelling) was random and unpredictable, not something that was caused by their actions. Frederick Teiwes, in his monumental work *Politics and Purges in China*, argues that during the political campaigns of the early PRC, sanctions meted out to individuals were based on the seriousness of their offences, and a cadre "could assess his vulnerability on the basis of past actions."[5] Teiwes's thesis is built on his observation of the CCP's purge of the middle- to high-level elite between 1950 and 1965. Recent scholarship, however, shows that the identification of rightists could have been "an overt conspiracy" engineered by local Party leaders. Cao Shuji, for instance, indicates that, in rural Henan, where the Rectification Movement started in the fall of 1957, county Party leaders who were fully aware of the Anti-Rightist Campaign intentionally set traps and administered hidden plans, encouraging rural cadres and village schoolteachers to air their criticism in order to create a sufficient number of "rightists."[6] In this chapter, I analyze the experiences of both well-known intellectuals (such as Ding Ling and Dai Huang) and lesser known ones (schoolteachers, college students, office clerks, etc.) during the Anti-Rightist Campaign in order to demonstrate that, in terms of their arbitrariness, absurdity, and unpredictability, lower-level political campaigns could be conducted in ways that differed dramatically from those conducted at the elite level.

I argue that the majority of those labelled and banished were not political dissidents, that many of them were dedicated CCP members/ followers, and that many others were not politically engaged. While acknowledging that some activists, especially university students, boldly condemned the CCP's abuses of power and advocated political and intellectual freedom, or adopted the stance of "loyal opponents," I argue that the majority of intellectuals and government employees were persecuted not for political reasons but, rather, due to factional conflict, poor relations with Party bosses, personal animosity, grudges, jealousy, and so on. Furthermore, labelling quotas, set by higher authorities, forced local Party committees to frame innocent people. These people were victimized by both high politics and local politics. Whereas the higher-ups waged the Anti-Rightist Campaign in order to consolidate the regime, and their anti-rightist directives provided the crackdown with political legitimacy, to a great extent the conduct of the campaign deviated from what they had initially intended. I also maintain that, although the CCP launched the campaign to deal with real (or what it imagined to be real) threats, both intellectuals and Party officials took advantage of it to attack their respective rivals.

THE CAMPAIGN AND ITS ABSURDITY

Scholars view the Anti-Rightist Campaign through different lenses. Frederick Teiwes sees the campaign as a "defensive" measure to restore CCP control over educated elites; Merle Goldman considers the campaign to be a manifestation of the Party's "anti-intellectual stance"; and Roderick MacFarquhar characterizes it as an important step towards the Cultural Revolution.[7] These scholars primarily focus on how the upper echelon of the CCP engineered the campaign, leading to the massive purging of intelligentsia and Party cadres. In this section, I provide a brief overview of the campaign in order to clarify the basic context within which the political manoeuvres of the Party leaders evolved into a disaster for the general public.

In early 1956, the CCP leadership intended to win the cooperation of intellectuals and, in so doing, to facilitate economic and social progress. Brandishing the slogan "let a hundred flowers bloom and a hundred schools of thought contend," the elite leaders, especially Party chairman Mao Zedong, promised to grant intellectuals a degree of freedom to express their opinions on literature, arts, and the sciences.[8] This initiative may be seen as the origin of the Hundred Flowers Movement. The following spring, Mao pushed this campaign to the "Party rectification" stage in order to enlist intellectuals' criticism of bureaucracy and the Party.[9]

In the beginning, most intellectuals did not respond to Mao's call; instead, they held back, instinctively cautious about getting involved in politics.[10] Unhappy with the tepid reaction of intellectuals, Mao reaffirmed his demand for critique. In the speeches he delivered on March 12 and 20, 1957, for instance, Mao made extraordinary efforts to call on "all people to express their opinions freely, so that they dare to speak, dare to criticize, and dare to debate." He insisted that, "as long as they are not counter-revolutionaries, people should have the freedom to speak not only on pure scientific and artistic issues, but also on matters of a political nature in terms of right and wrong."[11] Moved by Mao's seemingly sincere promise to protect their freedom of expression and pressured by Party functionaries, intellectuals, professionals, students, and leaders of the democratic parties began to speak out. They criticized the CCP's monopoly of power, demanded real participation in policy making, and complained about the Party's ideological straitjacketing of literary creation and its interference in academia. They also condemned the Party for its privilege, abuse of power, alienation from the masses, and economic corruption.[12] Those who had suffered unfair treatment in previous campaigns demanded rectification and rehabilitation. Encouraged by Mao, and considering his promise a sign of a political thaw, the educated elites let loose a flood of criticism of the governing party. In the later part of 1957, some Party cadres and government employees went so far as to criticize Party policies and Party leadership.

Shocked by this torrent of criticism, the CCP leadership found that the Hundred Flowers Movement was getting out of hand and that criticism of specific Party policies and instances of abuse of power had led to attacks not only upon high Party leaders but also upon the political system itself. Even Mao became the target of sharp criticism.[13] Workers strikes and student protests were under way in this increasingly politicized climate. The Party line shifted with the political winds, and Mao, the chief architect of "blooming and contending," made a dramatic move to the side of the hardliners.[14] On June 8, with the *People's Daily* announcing a counter-attack, the political climate abruptly reversed, and the Anti-Rightist Campaign was set in motion.[15] The major phase of the campaign lasted from June 1957 to the end of that year, and an additional round of "supplementary labelling" was applied in 1958. Although the campaign chiefly targeted the members of democratic parties and other non-communist intellectuals, CCP members and officials also fell victim to it. Sources released by the CCP Central Organization Department indicate that the total number of people labelled "rightists" was over 550,000.[16]

The CCP called the primary targets of the campaign "bourgeois rightists" (*zichan jieji youpai*) or "rightists" (*youpai*). The term "rightist" is dubious and amorphous. During the course of the Communist Revolution, although the CCP frequently denounced any political force that did not favour the Party as "nationalist right wing" (*guomindang youyi*) or as a "bourgeois rightist force" (*zichanjieji youyi shili*), the term "rightist" was mainly applied to the social elite associated with foreign "imperialist forces," those who had been urban capitalists or rural landlords, or who were strongly anti-communist.[17] During the campaign of 1957, Mao first used the term "bourgeois rightist" in his May 15, 1957, article "Things Are Going to Change," an inner-Party document in which he held that 1 to 10 percent of non-Party intellectuals were rightists whose agenda was to get rid of the Party's leadership.[18] In various anti-rightist onslaughts after June 8, whoever was thought to have disagreed with Party policies, to have questioned Chinese socialism, or to have taken issue with Party officials was branded a rightist. For example, vice-chairman of the Chinese People's Political Consultative Conference, Zhang Bojun, was given a rightist hat for criticizing the CCP's monopoly of power, as was a young clerk for evincing concern about declining agricultural production.[19]

Officially, the CCP central leadership retained the power to define a rightist; however, in most cases, actual labelling fell to lower-level Party officials. Among the various speeches the high leaders delivered regarding rightists, the most comprehensive was that of Deng Xiaoping, the general secretary of the CCP. In his "Report on the Rectification Campaign," given at the third plenum of the Eighth Congress of the CCP, rightists were assigned the following characteristics:

- opposing socialist economic and political systems and socialist culture in favour of bourgeois ones
- opposing the fundamental policies of the state
- denying the achievements of the people's democratic revolution, the socialist revolution, and socialist construction
- opposing the leadership of the Chinese Communist Party in governmental frameworks, particularly in cultural, educational, scientific, and technological organizations.[20]

This sweeping and overarching definition, broad enough to net anyone who was considered problematic, was made public on September 23, 1957, three and a half months after the Anti-Rightist Campaign had been launched. It was not until October 15 that the CCP Central Committee finally provided the criteria for the labelling of rightists.[21] From early June to mid-October, therefore, it was essentially the leaders of local Party committees (or branches) or the heads of various urban work units who administered the campaign and decided who needed to be condemned and singled out, based on their understanding of the anti-rightist speeches of Party leaders, their reading of the tone of Party media, and their personal observations of their work units.[22] It is not presumptuous to say that, during this time period, the mandate to purge people was in the hands of local Party bosses and the heads of various work units and that they had no formal guidelines for issuing the rightist label.

IMAGES OF RIGHTISTS

Since the late 1950s, two contrasting images of rightists have emerged. The first, which prevailed during the Mao era, was mainly generated by Party propaganda in 1957 and the officially sponsored literature that sprang up in its wake. Within this political culture, rightists were portrayed as an evil force: they attacked the beloved Party and socialism; they agitated the masses, turning them against collectivization; they colluded with the GMD in Taiwan and with American imperialists in order to make China a semi-colony of the Western powers and to plunge China into the fire of hell. All of this warranted severe punishment by the "government of the people."[23] The rhyme "Rightists, rightists, demons and ghosts" (*youpai youpai, yaomo guiguai*) floated constantly from loudspeakers in the streets and was even adapted for popular children's songs during that hectic anti-rightist period. Starting in 1958, rightists began to be categorized as one of the "five black elements" (*heiwulei*) – coming right after landlords, rich peasants, counter-revolutionaries, and criminals – and were thus deeply demonized. This propaganda regime had a considerable impact upon members of the general public, who, for a long time, were led to discriminate against rightists, shunning them as they would have a disease.[24] This ostracizing of rightists was seen as perfectly normal in a highly politicized China.

After Mao died in 1976, another image of rightists surfaced as a result of the post-Mao political thaw and the subsequent rectification of the cases of those falsely accused rightists. These people have come to be regarded as heroic figures who courageously condemned the abuses of the Maoist regime and pursued political democracy and social justice. They underwent untold suffering but loved the motherland, being its sons and daughters. In the literature and movies of the immediate post-Mao period – such as *Tianyunshan chuanqi* (The legend of Tianyun Mountain) by Lu Yanzhou, *Muma ren* (Herdsman) by Zhang Xianliang, and *Kulian* (Unrequited love) by Bai Hua – rightists were portrayed as fearless, devoted, and patriotic, having lofty political ideals and being spiritually committed. They were the backbone of the nation and true heroes.[25] Beginning in the mid-1980s, a considerable number of ex-rightists and other victims of the Anti-Rightist Campaign, such as Fang Lizhi, Liu Binyan, and Wang Ruowang, either excelled in their respective fields and/or became famous campaigners for political reform and human rights in China, thus greatly boosting the image of rightists among the intelligentsia.

A close examination of the term "rightist" shows that it refers to a diverse group of individuals and thus resists any simple unitary analysis. First of all, among more than half a million people labelled rightists, democratic parties leaders, scientists, writers, professors, and student activists – that is, those who offered relatively sharp criticism of the Maoist regime – accounted for merely one-fifth to one-fourth of the total: the rest were elementary school teachers (18 percent), Party cadres (7 percent), and media workers (12 percent), along with government clerks, medical workers, police officers, high school teachers and students, and military personnel.[26] In other words, they represented a cross-section of Chinese society. Although, being the recipients of various political charges, all of them wore the rightist hat, many were not in fact persecuted for political reasons, as was claimed by Party authorities. There were great differences among these people in terms of their political awareness and involvement, the reasons they were purged, and their individual experiences afterwards. Dai Huang, who was interned in post-1957 labour camps for seventeen years, comments:

> The rightists were not an integrated whole. Many did not have in their minds national affairs, but instead entirely personal affairs. They were labelled rightists mostly because of complaints against their superiors over the issues of salaries, ranks, living conditions, or other trivia, or because of their head-on arguments with their leaders, which resulted in their being victimized by the political line that "attacking leaders means attacking the Party."[27]

Dai's observation opens a new window onto the martyrs of 1957. It is inappropriate for us either to stigmatize or to excessively honour them.

Although the CCP was indeed sharply criticized during the spring and summer of 1957, resulting in the Party's fierce counterattack and nationwide purge, the vast majority of its victims were not its true opponents. As I show below, most rightists were "accidental dissidents." Many were revolutionaries or devoted followers of the CCP, who firmly identified themselves with the Party and its ideology. Lu Gang, a former college head in Harbin, recounts what happened when he was labelled a rightist: "I never meant to take a stand against the Communist Party. I joined the revolution when I was sixteen years old during the Anti-Japanese War, and I followed the Party line step by step. How could I suddenly turn an anti-Party element? I was just outspoken, raising criticism against certain Party leaders."[28] Disgraced senior revolutionaries were numerous, including Sha Wenhan (provincial governor of Zhejiang), Chen Yi (the cultural director of the People's Liberation Army's General Political Department), Ding Ling (the Party secretary of the Chinese Writers Association), and so on. Many other victims were young intellectuals who were fervently dedicated to the communist cause. As described by Yue Daiyun, young students were quite supportive of the CCP when it took over China and were willing to follow the Party to serve the nation.[29] As Fang Lizhi recalls: "Almost all the youths that I had known back then [the early-mid 1950s], as well as myself, were surely supporters of Mao Zedong and the CCP, to the extent of being staunch, if not fanatical. The so-called backward elements were by no means the ones displaying political dissent."[30]

If we look carefully at the criticism that sprang up in 1957, it is apparent that many strident voices (including those seemingly expressing political dissent) were those of loyal followers of the CCP. It was their faith in the Party that led them to be so straightforward about speaking out regarding what they believed to be good for the Party, attempting to help the Party improve itself. Dai Huang's letter to Mao during the Hundred Flowers helps us to understand this. As a People's Liberation Army (PLA) veteran and a senior military correspondent, Dai condemned the emergence of a "privileged class" in post-1949 China and criticized the corruption of Party officials and the Party's tendency to alienate the masses. He even blamed the CCP Central Committee for widespread bureaucratic malpractice. In the meantime, however, he swore his unswerving allegiance to the Party, reiterating "our Party is correct and our cause great" and insisting that the purpose of his criticism was "to help the Party cure its diseases" and help it to "draw closer to the masses" and so regain their support.[31] The relationship between criticism and allegiance is also manifested in Wang Meng's much-celebrated novel *Young Newcomer in the Organization Department*. While Wang revealed that the Party establishment had become increasingly arrogant, inert, and bureaucratically rigid, his novel's overarching tone endorsed Party norms and revolutionary values.[32] Like those of Dai and Wang, many well-known "anti-Party writings" that, on the surface, appeared to be provocative and subversive, actually pushed for political renovation and advocated the revitalization of the governing party.

There is no denying that some critics were bold enough to attack the autocracy of the CCP and to call for a way of holding its governing power to account. Zhang Bojun, for instance, strongly suggested that the National People's Congress, the People's Political Consultative Conference, and various democratic parties should function as the chief designers of China's governing framework by forming a "political design institute" that would share power with the CCP. As a consequence of this, Mao accused him and his comrades of trying to "eliminate the Communist Party."[33] University campuses were thriving centres of dissent. Professors such as Chen Shiwei requested that Party committees withdraw from universities and proposed that universities be governed by professors.[34] With their liberal journal *Guangchang* (Public square) as a platform, Peking University students spearheaded their attack on the Party establishment, condemning the existing system, especially the monopoly of power by the top leaders. Some of them claimed that "the bureaucratism, subjectivism and sectarianism that the CCP claimed to rectify have roots firmly placed in the existing social system" and that "there is no real democracy in current China ... due to the political heavy-handedness and [the people's] absolute subservience to Party leaders."[35] Lin Xiling, a law student at the Chinese People's University, claimed that all Chinese should be entitled to show their disapproval of the government because Chinese socialism was not real socialism.[36] During the spring of 1957, some students even attempted to form new political parties. For instance, Li Jiangxin, a student at the Northeastern People's University, criticized the CCP for its ruthless exploitation of the working class and proclaimed his intention to establish a "Socialist Labour Party of China," for which he was arrested.[37] These students came to question various Party policies and to reassess political institutions and social reality under the Party, something that logically led to a demand for political reform. Eddy U is correct in saying that the reforms (especially competitive elections) proposed by the students "would have reduced the CCP's role in governance dramatically." "Their goal was to promote democratic values and institutions, so as to prevent socialist development from being ravaged by political despotism and state violence."[38] In this sense, students did pose a challenge to the legitimacy, credibility, and orthodoxy of the CCP.

Sharp and confident as they were, however, the majority of critics persisted in endorsing Party rule and Marxist ideology (which they believed to be original and authentic) and called for "real socialism." In order to clarify his stance, Tan Tianrong, the "No.1 rightist" at Peking University, declared, when criticizing the Party's "bureaucratism": "I don't doubt the Communist Party will rid itself of its black sheep for its own good, I don't doubt Marxism will rid itself of dogmatism in the course of its development, and I don't doubt Chairman Mao will back us up forever."[39] According to Lin Xiling: "What we need is a real socialism ... The Communists should be those who sincerely serve the people and strive for the Communist cause."[40] Their agenda was, apparently, not to push the CCP off the scene but, rather, to revitalize the Party and make it into something that they believed would be more "Marxist." It was their faith in the CCP that made them unwilling to remain silent when they saw certain things as undesirable and when the Party leaders called for rectification. As Wang Meng points out in an interview in October 2002: "Deeply committed to the Party's cause, they were fearless in speaking up to defend whatever they regarded as being morally or politically correct and logically reasonable, even at the risk of offending their direct superiors. Bookish and naïve, they had no hesitation in raising criticism against that with which they disagreed and thus were easily singled out in the campaign."[41]

Furthermore, the leaders of democratic parties, who became the chief targets in 1957, were far from what the CCP portrayed as "anti-Party elements" or the "agents of imperialists." Some, such as Zhang Bojun, had been Communist Party members in the 1920s and 1930s, while others, such as Luo Longji, had long collaborated with the CCP in fighting the GMD government. Chu Anping was a staunch believer in Mao when the "New China" was established.[42] These were "higher intellectuals and notables," who, as Eddy U points out, had close relationships with the CCP leaders and often drew upon Mao's speeches to express their concerns: "They pressed for participation, voice and authority under the existing political system." They "wanted to use law to establish structural constraints on Party and state behavior, to realign governance away from cadre management and abuse, from campaign-style violence and justice and from institutionalized discrimination"; however, they "did not challenge CCP reign but only protested against state practices."[43] While advocating for the independence of democratic parties and for power-sharing with the CCP, these critics wished to build the sound political framework for which they had long struggled and that, before 1949, the CCP had promised. They treated the CCP's abuse of power and governmental malfunctioning as cancers in the body of the New China. If the tumours were removed, they believed, socialism would be truly realized and the nation would reassume its vitality.[44] In other words, the CCP elite miscalculated the political nature of these critics and exaggerated the menace they posed. During the Hundred Flowers Movement, the voices of a relative few sounded strident and dissenting and were echoed by thousands of others. This led the CCP to assume that those who spoke out were political opponents who posed a grave threat and so needed to be dealt with firmly.

It seems that the Party leadership did not have a clear idea regarding how many critics truly posed a menace to the CCP. On June 29, 1957, Mao estimated that there were probably four thousand rightists across the country who needed to be publicly condemned.[45] With the Anti-Rightist Campaign gathering strength, the number of individuals who needed to be singled out sky-rocketed. By early October 1957, around sixty-two thousand had been labelled, and the CCP expected some 150,000 rightists to be further uncovered during the campaign. On April 6, 1958, Mao updated his estimate of the number of rightist to 300,000, but this was not the end. In September 1959, the CCP Central Committee disclosed that 450,000 rightists had been seized.[46] The dramatic increase in the number of rightists being identified indicates the Party's uncertainty regarding the size and potential of its opponents; it also suggests that, with the escalation of the campaign, a sizable number of Chinese who might not have been critics were netted for other reasons. Due to the volatile atmosphere generated by a campaign run wild, political persecution spilled beyond the initially designated targets to a broader population.

As mentioned above, it was not until October 15, four more months after the launch of the Anti-Rightist Campaign, that the Party issued a document entitled "Criteria for the Labelling of Rightists." According to this document, those who "oppose[d] the socialist system and fundamental socioeconomic policies of the Party," who "oppose[d] proletarian dictatorship and attack[ed] the foreign policies of the government," who "[took] a stand against Party leadership in the nation's political life, viciously attack[ed] the organizations and personnel of the Party and government, defame[d] worker-peasant cadres and revolutionary activists," and who "participate[d] in anti-Party, anti-socialist cliques" must all be labelled "rightists."[47]

Extensive as these dictates are, the yardstick against which one's political stance and behaviour were measured was often variable, obscure, and thus subject to interpretation and manipulation. While Party leaders might truly aim at punishing political offenders, those at the lower levels could use party politics as a reason to label people to suit their own agenda. As I show below, principles were often manipulated to meet practical purposes, and interpersonal relations took on the appearance of following the Party line. Under the guise of political necessity, the real reasons for persecuting individuals could be multifarious. As Keith Forster notes in his work on Zhejiang, in the daily process of labelling, practical reasons for doing so were often more crucial than were political reasons.[48] Likewise, Frederick Teiwes argues that a "mechanical struggle" in early CCP history allowed questions of a purely practical nature to reach the level of principle: "In this form of struggle the goal of ideological reform is cast aside; rectifying mistakes degenerates into attacks on individuals. Personal grievances and factional differences come to the fore and instead of strengthening the party unity such struggles deepen already existing rifts."[49] When testing these arguments in the context of the Anti-Rightist Campaign, we find that the mechanical struggle and the over-emphasis on pragmatic considerations evolved into a variety of low-level politics. Factional differences and group conflicts that stretched back for decades, personal dislikes and grudges that survived from past campaigns, old love affairs, jealousy, labelling quotas, and so on all played a role in the persecution, and all had a part in the growing severity and viciousness of the Anti-Rightist Campaign.

Reasons for the Labelling and Purge

In this section, I show that, under high-flying political rhetoric, the following elements were among the most important reasons for massive purges and extensive labelling.

Factional Conflict and the Resulting Personal Feuds

Factional conflict and its resulting personal feuds are the most common reasons that a considerable number of Party writers, cadres, and even senior revolutionaries fell into disgrace. Throughout CCP history, factional differences were widespread, both at higher levels of leadership and at local levels.[50] During the Anti-Rightist Campaign, faction-related feuds made political struggles extremely intense as groups and/or individuals seized the chance to eliminate rivals and competitors. For example, Chen Yi, the cultural director of the PLA's General Political Department, was charged as a rightist due to his long-time feud with a conflicting faction within the department. He was sent to Heilongjiang for thought reform. It is also well known that Yuan Yongxi, vice-Party secretary of Qinghua University, was labelled due to his inability to get along with Party secretary Jiang Nanxiang.[51]

Factional struggle was also deeply rooted in left-wing literary circles. Since the 1930s, Chinese left-wing writers had largely split into two factions based on whether they were aligned with Lu Xun (the head of the League of Left-Wing Writers) or Zhou Yang (the CCP's literary watchdog and the president of the Chinese Writers Association) respectively.[52] After the communist takeover of China, the discord persisted even though Lu Xun had long since died: the purging of writers and artists in 1957 and 1958 was more or less related to factional divisions and conflicts in the upper echelon of the PRC's cultural bureaucracy.

The experience of Ding Ling (a protégé of Lu Xun) provides a good example of how a prestigious Party writer could be violently victimized due to factional struggle. It was not her criticisms during the Hundred Flowers Movement but, rather, her long-standing discord with Zhou Yang that sealed her fate. As early as 1955, she was internally condemned for allegedly belonging to the "Ding Ling–Chen Qixia Anti-Party Group." When the CCP Central Propaganda Department was about to redress her case in 1957, the anti-rightist struggle occurred, enabling Zhou Yang to obstinately question her party loyalty in the pre-1949 period. Without having spoken a single word regarding the Hundred Flowers Movement, Ding Ling was labelled a rightist and lost her Party membership of twenty-five years standing.[53] The victims of Ding Ling's case were numerous. Many of her associates and friends, including Ai Qing, Lo Feng, and Bai Lang, were also attacked as they were considered to be in "Ding Ling's line." Feng Xuefeng, another one of Lu Xun's disciples and Zhou Yang's long-term rivals, was given a rightist hat on the grounds that he was trying to establish an anti-party magazine. Party cadre Li Xin contends that almost all the purgings of senior Party writers in 1957 were more or less related to factional struggles.[54] Although this is difficult to verify, at least for Ding Ling, Feng Xuefeng, and Zhou Yang, historically rooted tensions provided fodder for renewed trouble when the situation became such that those who occupied higher seats were able to speak on behalf of the Party and thus purge their foes.

A prominent feature of factional tensions was that antagonists used every pretext to attack their rivals for "principle divergence" or on other such political grounds. Family backgrounds and personal histories (such as having been associated with the former GMD government) provided perfect excuses. As a case in point, the accusations against Ding Ling were partially based on her arrest by the GMD in 1933 and her inability, at that time, to prove her allegiance to the CCP. Charges against Sha Wenhan and his three associates were based on the assumption that they were all from "non-proletarian" families and continued to espouse bourgeois ideology.[55]

From the aforementioned cases, it is apparent that the CCP's attempt to silence dissent was exacerbated by factional strife and its resulting feuds. Tragically, when persecution threatened, some people remained unwilling to stop their internal feuding. When Zhang Bojun and Luo Longji, two chief leaders of the China Democratic League, were groundlessly accused by Mao of being part of the "Zhang-Luo Anti-Party Coalition," they continued their long-term rivalry, discrediting each other in public. And other China Democratic League leaders joined the chorus of accusations against the two.[56]

Fabrication and Framing

Teiwes notes that, in the CCP's political campaigns, the basic approach to dealing with individuals at the elite level "has been selective and surgical rather than arbitrary" and that the "rectification movements prior to the Cultural Revolution were generally under strict Party control with targets carefully chosen, models of deviant behavior widely propagated, and sanctions meted out according to the seriousness of offenses."[57] Stressing the rationality of the campaign's methods, Teiwes's thesis may be valid with regard to specific cases in the higher echelons (such as the case of Gao Gang and Rao Shushi in 1954), but its relevance to broader spheres may be questioned. At the local level and for ordinary individuals, the methods deployed in the Anti-Rightist Campaign (and those similar to it) were arbitrary, irrational, and even preposterous. Thus, the picture is far more complex than that presented by Teiwes. Stories repeatedly show that people were incriminated for wrongdoings that they never committed and for critiques that they did not make – all so that those who labelled them could accomplish certain political or personal goals.

Ge Peiqi, widely known for the threatening phrase "kill the Communists," was a university lecturer in Beijing. During the Hundred Flowers Campaign, he was repeatedly urged to speak up and contribute to the rectification of the Party. According to his memoir, what he said in a blooming-and-contending meeting was that non-professional cadres were incapable of managing universities, that Party leaders should not look

down upon intellectuals, and that Party members should not disassoci-
ate themselves from the masses by seeking personal gain. When printed
in an internal circular for the university, however, parts of his speeches
were misquoted, resulting in his saying: "Do not distrust intellectuals ...
It is fine if the Communist Party runs China well; otherwise, the masses
are entitled to get rid of the Party, or even to kill the Communists."[58]
Realizing his speech had been tampered with, Ge immediately requested
that the university correct these mistakes. Nothing was done, however,
and, on June 8, his distorted speech was published in the *People's Daily*,
together with the editorial comment: "Ge Peiqi airs his anti-communist
declaration." This version of Ge's speech further suggested: "The masses
have always been wishing to overthrow the Communist Party and kill
Party members; if you Communists refuse to correct your wrongdoings
or discontinue your corruption, you will meet your doom."[59] Ge was well
aware of the enormity of this issue and wrote to the newspaper asking for
a correction. Far from being granted a correction, Ge faced a torrent of
denunciations. Newspapers published masses of critical articles in which
Ge was portrayed, among other things, as a careerist, an arch-reactionary,
and a murderer. Based on this fabricated speech, Ge was identified as
an ultra-rightist and, in June 1959, subjected to a life sentence for his
"counter-revolutionary crimes." His attempt to defend himself in court
was entirely ignored.[60]

Another person who was framed was playwright Wu Zuguang. Having
shared interests and hobbies, Wu and several friends formed an arts club
that met regularly for the enjoyment of poetry, drama, calligraphy, and
painting. With the Anti-Rightist Campaign in full swing, the club was
inexplicably attacked as a "small counter-revolutionary clique." Wu and
most members of the club were labelled rightists, and none were given
the chance to explain the club's real purpose.[61]

Ge and Wu were certainly not the only victims of fabrication.[62] Due to
the need to foster an anti-rightist climate, Party bosses of work units often
did not hesitate to invent any kind of case that could transform innocent
people into rightists. In Ge's case, the inside story of the manipulation he
suffered has thus far not been fully disclosed. However, it is safe to presume that, with "politics in command" and to enliven the campaign, the
People's University (Ge's employer) and the *People's Daily* closely collaborated to concoct a case that would result in Ge's being labelled a rightist.
It is apparent that, when those in a position of power were determined to
apply the rightist label to someone, whether to satisfy their superiors or
their own desires, "facts" could be conjured out of nothing.

At the time, the Party claimed that it did not wish to see the Anti-Rightist Campaign go astray. On October 15, 1957, the CCP Central Committee instructed provincial authorities to avoid falsely labelling people and to correct any cases that had been mishandled. In the meantime, however, it also stated: "In the units where labelling was overdone and rectification necessary, the enthusiasm and commitment of the masses and activists must be protected. Avoid giving the wrong impression that the Anti-Rightist struggle is excessive ... There is no need to publicly acknowledge the mistakes."[63] The chiefs of various party organizations had no difficulty in reading the tone of such instructions. Lu Gang indicates that, in the atmosphere of 1957–58, there was a general understanding among the Party secretaries of various work units that the campaign had been initiated by the Party Central Committee and, thus, was an epochal event; even though some individuals were unfairly treated, major rectifications were to be avoided for the sake of maintaining the campaign's momentum and protecting the revolutionary zeal of the anti-rightist activists.[64] In times of political necessity, it was considered justifiable to treat the lives of common people as collateral damage.

In discussing the "coercive disciplinary measures" used in the political campaigns of pre-Cultural Revolution China, Teiwes argues that, "in cases where cadres persist in deviant behavior despite repeated educational efforts, the most severe disciplinary measure of expulsion is invoked. Thus the purge is regarded as an extreme action taken only when rectification fails."[65] Findings from my analysis of the Anti-Rightist Campaign show that it was not comparable to the purges Teiwes describes. At least at the local and work-unit levels, an absence of "educational efforts" – and even of a willingness to verify basic facts or to rectify wrongs – indicates that mistreatment was meted out both arbitrarily and crudely. As rightist writers such as Liu Binyan and Dai Huang show, it was mass condemnation rather than educational efforts (or thought work) that formed the prelude to purging and labelling. When evidence was twisted to provide proof of condemnable thoughts, it was not the victims' political thoughts that mattered but, rather, the labellers' need to complete their work.

Questioning Previous Political Campaigns and Asking for Redress

All too often, people were persecuted for requesting the redress of past wrongs. Those who demanded the redress of Hu Feng's case, for instance, were particularly subject to attack. In 1954, renowned writer

Hu Feng delivered to the Politbureau of the CCP Central Committee a lengthy letter criticizing the current cultural bureaucracy and the CCP's policy of imposing Marxist doctrines and Maoist ideas upon writers. The letter infuriated Mao and triggered a vicious attack upon Hu as well as a nationwide campaign to eliminate counter-revolutionaries. Hu was arrested in 1955, and around twenty-one hundred people were eventually implicated.[66]

In the spring of 1957, a considerable number of young students rose to advocate for the redress of Hu's case. Lin Xiling argued that "Hu Feng's opinion about literature [was] correct" and that "the grounds on which to accuse him [were] ridiculous." Lin's subsequent persecution was closely connected with her defence of Hu.[67] Liu Qidi, a physics student at Peking University, put up a wall poster that called for the immediate release of Hu. The poster indicated that Hu Feng was a progressive writer rather than a counter-revolutionary, that the charges against him were groundless, and that his arrest was illegal.[68] Liu gained warm support from university students across the country. Not only was Hu Feng's case not rectified at this time but Liu was charged as a counter-revolutionary and sent to a *laogai* camp in Xingkaihu, where he died before the completion of his term. Lin and Liu were among the many who suffered for their defence of Hu Feng.[69]

Closely related to Hu Feng's case was the demand for rectification of the wrongs committed in the "Elimination of Counter-Revolutionaries Campaign" of 1955. At the time, the CCP estimated that approximately 5 percent of those working in the Party and the government were "hidden counter-revolutionaries." Approximately 1.4 million Chinese experienced various kinds of persecution during the campaign, with eighty-one thousand being labelled counter-revolutionaries, out of which thirty-eight hundred were determined to be "active counter-revolutionaries" and were imprisoned. Countless innocent people suffered false accusations and physical abuse, and some were wrongly executed.[70] In 1957, with the devastating impact of the campaign still fresh in their memories, a considerable number of intellectuals and leaders of democratic parties asked for rectification of the abuses of 1955. For this, they were labelled rightists when the anti-rightist onslaught began. Luo Longji, a vice-chairman of the China Democratic League, was designated a leading rightist due to his ardent calls for the establishment of a "rehabilitation committee" to redress the cases of those who had been falsely accused in 1955.[71]

Party cadres also suffered for their petitions to redress the cases of those who had been falsely accused. Li Xin, an associate Party secretary of the CCP Central Propaganda Department, recounted the reasons for his labelling:

> During that period, I complained about the consequences of the Elimination of the Counter-Revolutionaries Campaign, and I questioned the cases of labelling Hu Feng's friends Shu Qun and Luo Feng as "anti-Party elements," all of which displeased my superiors. As a result, I was degraded to a minor post in Hubei Province. The next year, I was deprived of Party membership and labelled a rightist. The irony is that when the campaign got started, I was a member of the Anti-Rightist committee in my work unit, while in the end I myself became a rightist.[72]

It is uncertain whether Li's disgrace was due solely to his wish to rectify past wrongs or whether there were other reasons. Seen in the context of CCP history, advocating the redress of wrongs would not necessarily lead to a purge as the Party itself sometimes did this in order to salvage its tarnished reputation (e.g., in the case of the Yan'an Rescue Movement and the Anti-Trotsky Elements Campaign).[73] However, it was considered offensive for lower-level Party members to raise questions of such enormity or to join in the mass outcry for rectification via political campaigning. Apparently such actions posed a threat to the authority of the CCP's central leadership. Given the context of 1957, such actions could be interpreted as opposing the Party policy of "eliminating counter-revolutionaries" and as undermining the prestige of the Party leaders who implemented it. Li Xin's call for the rectification of the cases associated with Hu Feng at least partially explains his purge.

At the grassroots level, people suffered for demanding the redress of wrongful accusations that had been brought against their families, friends, or themselves. Harry Wu complained about his elder brother's being charged as a "spy suspect"; Hu Qiya vented his grievance relating to the execution of his father during the land reform of 1951; and Liu Meng disputed his own unfair treatment in 1955. In the end, all were identified as either rightists or ultra-rightists.[74]

Criticizing Party Members

In many cases, impeachment and labelling occurred when individuals were accused of "disregarding Party organization," "defying Party leadership," or "orally abusing Party members." The purported goal of such purging was to prevent assaults on the authority of Party organizations and Party members during the Anti-Rightist Campaign. However, careful analysis of individual cases reveals that almost all those so charged were actually those who criticized, or showed insufficient deference to, the Party secretaries or Party members of their work units. For non-Party people, criticizing individual Party members during the Hundred Flowers Campaign was invariably seen as anti-Party in nature as it was assumed that disregarding or defying any individual Party member (particularly a Party leader) was equivalent to opposing the Party organization and, thus, to opposing the Party as a whole.[75] The story of journalist Yin Jiliang exemplifies this problem.

> During that [Hundred Flowers] period, I was rather active and straightforward ... I bluntly condemned the abuse of power by the Party secretary of my work unit and his rudeness in treating comrades, which greatly irritated him. When the Anti-Rightist Campaign began, I was immediately labelled by him. While I complained that this was his revenge against me, he said that it was to defend the Party branch. My repeated petitions brought no desirable results. The more I appealed, the worse things became. Eventually I was labelled an active counter-revolutionary in November 1957. The secretary hated me to my bones.[76]

In Yin's narrative we see that the Hundred Flowers Movement was exploited by the Party boss of Yin's work unit to vent his personal vengeance on a defenceless victim. When political monopoly and executive high-handedness are used to settle personal scores, any discord with, or criticism of, individual Party leaders or members could be interpreted as opposing a Party branch or committee. Even non-political issues were raised to the level of, and under the disguise of, "struggles of principle," thus ensuring that the targets would always be knocked down.

The experience of Yan Xueli, a middle school teacher, is similar to those recounted above:

> Two issues that I raised during the Hundred Flowers [Movement] sent me to the labour camp. One was my discussion of the Hungarian Incident.[77] I said in a political study session that it was the mismanagement of the Hungary Communists Party that caused the riots in that country rather than Western imperialist agitation. But the main reason was, I believe, that I had a terrible experience with a Party member in my school, someone who was in a strong position to label rightists. If you rubbed him the wrong way, he would always find a chance to get you into trouble. When

he insisted on labelling me rightist, other party members did not bother to argue against him. Furthermore, because I consistently refused to acknowledge this charge, I was labelled ultra-rightist in the end.[78]

Discord between political cadres and professional leaders in a work unit often took on a political hue. When a professional leader (in many cases a non-Party member) resisted the intervention of a Party head with regard to such administrative issues as a work plan or the appointment of an employee, an accusation of "defying the Party's leadership" would likely follow. He Shanzhou, the head of the Chinese Literature Department of the Northeastern Normal University, was branded a rightist mainly because he disagreed with the Party secretary over a new hiring. The Chinese Literature Department Party branch interpreted his dissent as a political offence.[79]

Jealousy, Petty Resentment, and Poor Interpersonal Relationships

Tani Barlow, in discussing Ding Ling's involvement in communist politics, comments that antagonisms between rival individuals were often "not really ideologically motivated, [but] had in many cases developed on the basis of jealousy or personal dislike."[80] In a work unit, interpersonal relations, including relations with colleagues and bosses, were particularly important during political campaigns. This issue is too intricate and extensive to discuss in detail here, but a couple of examples help show the pattern by which the personal (and, in most cases, the trivial) became political in Mao's China.

Young He Ying, for one, was brought down for rising too fast and eclipsing his co-workers:

> It is difficult to imagine how I became a rightist at nineteen years old. Before that year [1957] I had been the youngest editor at a literary journal in Jilin and was well known in the literary circle of the province. I got higher pay than many of my colleagues, and I became the focus of public attention. So sometimes I was over-confident and arrogant. Many of my colleagues were jealous of me and wanted to see me brought down ... I said nothing about politics during the Hundred Flowers, but they put the Party secretary up to label me when the Anti-Rightist Campaign started.[81]

The story told by student rightist Yin Jie is strikingly similar to that of He Ying:

When I was studying at a college in Dalian, I got a higher allowance than many of my fellow students because I was a "cadre student" [i.e., those who began to work for the communist government before attending school]. I got paid RMB27.5 *yuan* monthly and lived a better life than many. In addition, I did not study hard but always got good marks. Therefore, I became a target of jealousy. Some students really hated me. When the campaign came up, some urged the head of my department to label me.[82]

One may ask whether these ex-rightists over-emphasized the role of jealousy and personal grudges in their purging while omitting elements of a political nature. It is possible that they were unable or unwilling to discuss all the factors that contributed to their labelling. It is safe to say, however, that the social context at the turn of the century (when these interviews were conducted) posed no barrier to, and was actually conducive to, these elderly survivors of the Maoist purge discussing any factors, including political ones, that had affected their lot. My impression is that many interviewees readily acknowledged both the political and the personal elements that led to their purge. Their narratives recapture the agitated social atmosphere of 1957, recall their political involvement and consciousness, and invoke their personal lives (even touching on love affairs). They avoided mentioning the names of people who played roles in their cases, and their memories of some details may be hazy. It is unlikely, however, that interviewees He Ying and Yin Jie chose to highlight the interpersonal elements of their purging to the exclusion of other elements. It is not presumptuous to say that, during the Anti-Rightist Campaign, there was a sharp divergence between, on the one hand, the political rhetoric and purported agenda of the higher-ups and, on the other, the personal impulses that drove the campaign, especially at the grassroots level. While upper-level leaders aimed to liquidate "anti-Party and anti-socialist" forces in order to consolidate state power, those singled out for purging were often the victims of lower-level politics. Non-political and even trivial issues anchored in interpersonal relationships did play a part in political persecution – at times an important one.

Labelling as a Means of Meeting Designated Quotas

The story told in the movie *My Father and Mother* (*Wode fuqin muqin*) by Zhang Yimou is more than mere fiction. A young teacher in a rural elementary school is asked by the principal to fill the labelling quota set for the school and thus suffers for life. A similar experience is presented in *The Blue Kite* (*Lan fengzheng*) by Tian Zhuangzhuang: the Party boss of Lin Shaolong wanted to have more rightists in his work unit and so held a political meeting, at which participants were reluctant to openly accuse their colleagues. When Lin came back to the meeting from the washroom, however, he found that he had been identified as a rightist.[83] These stories dramatize what is probably the most preposterous aspect of the Anti-Rightist Campaign, making the tragic events inflicted upon countless Chinese look like black comedy.

In numerous political campaigns during both the pre- and post-1949 periods, the Party arbitrarily established labelling, purging, and/or execution quotas in order to determine class lines, net a sufficient number of antagonists (both real and imagined), and set the number of executions. Yang Kuisong argues that the CCP practice of determining the proportion of landlords and rich peasants among the rural population in 1947, of setting quotas for the execution of counter-revolutionaries in 1951, and of estimating the ratio of "pro- and anti-socialist elements" among intellectuals in 1957 all indicate its intent to control purges and executions and to formulate an effective way of carrying out campaigns. All this led to the inadvertent magnification of persecution.[84] I would say that the problems here involve more than directing the class struggle through establishing a premeditated quota or making guidelines for a campaign by designing labelling targets. For one thing, the quotas set in various campaigns were not based on a careful investigation of the actual situation but, rather, on the Party elite's habitual conviction that less than 10 percent of the entire population were likely political opponents of the CCP (and, later on, of socialism), among which the die-hard constituted approximately 2 to 3 percent. This notion dated back to Mao's 1927 "Report on an Investigation of the Hunan Peasant Movement," which declared that around 10 percent of landlords and rich peasants opposed the revolutionary movement in rural China. This mindset hardened over time and became the Party's modus operandi for decades. This quantitative approach seemed to provide the CCP with a concrete idea of the class composition of Chinese society and, in so doing, made it possible for "enemy identification" and purging to be carried out on what was presented as a scientific basis. However, the problem was that, when announcing quotas, the Party leaders hardly provided either a rationale or a statistical basis for them. As a Party senior publicly admitted: "We [the CCP leaders] did not have a realistic or reliable estimate of the situation of rightists ... but mechanically designated [a] labelling percentage and made up the number if there were not enough targets ... Such estimates were, to a great extent, subjective and haphazard, rather than built upon solid facts."[85]

Making quotas for rightists started on May 15, 1957, when Mao formally announced that the proportion of rightists might range from 1 to 3 to 5 to 10 percent in different urban work units.[86] Although this estimate was not always treated as a compulsory guideline, its gist was repeated in Mao's subsequent speeches and Party directives and thus acquired power. On June 10, 1957, the CCP Central Committee stated: "In the Democratic League, the proportion of rightists and reactionaries is relatively larger, accounting for around 10 percent of the whole." As the Anti-Rightist Campaign continued, in October 1957 Mao estimated that "those who uphold socialism account for approximately 90% of the whole population [of China] while those who take a stand against socialism account for 10%, among which the die-hard elements account for 2%."[87] The statistics cited in these documents, although they fluctuated, functioned as a ground rule for the campaign, and the heads of work units gradually accepted them as mandatory. Each work unit – including universities, middle schools, elementary schools, hospitals, research institutes, and government agencies – were obligated to single out a certain number of employees as rightists, regardless of the real state of affairs. Labelling quotas set for various units ranged from 5 to 10 percent, while implementation depended on the activism of Party secretaries or heads of work units.[88] Where local or work unit enthusiasm and official commitment were high, more than 10 percent were labelled rightists. For example, 8.5 percent of Fudan University's professors were branded as rightists, while 13.8 percent of professors were so branded in Beijing.[89]

Teiwes correctly notices the destructive role of "poorly educated officials lacking a clear grasp of the ideological and policy goals of the Party" as well as that of those "who [fell] into routinized bureaucratic patterns of behavior" during Maoist campaigns.[90] In the case of labelling rightists, two elements may be discerned. First, labelling was decreed by the CCP Central Committee and so had to be fulfilled: it was the state that imposed bureaucratic patterns of behaviour. Party secretaries and heads of work units had to provide scapegoats to fill the labelling quota; otherwise, they themselves risked being condemned either as having rightist tendencies or simply as being rightists.[91] Second, labellers at the work unit level tried not to fall behind those at other work units and so needed to be creative with regard to finding enough targets. Consequently, mislabelling was commonplace, and those who had little involvement in the Hundred Flowers Movement fell victim to this type of malpractice.

Ye Songtao, an ex-doctor who died in the late 1970s in Dandong, Liaoning Province, was one of many anti-rightist victims. His story was told by his colleague Wang Zhiliang.

When Ye came back from his vacation in the late summer of 1957, the anti-rightist struggle was almost over in our hospital. The heads of the hospital had already decided who were to be rightists, except for one rightist space that needed to be filled ... Ye, as well as everyone else, was asked to say something at a mass meeting to condemn rightist Zhang. "Comrade Zhang," Ye began to say, "I thought you were a good guy before. How could you come to take a stand against the Party?" Right at this moment, the chairperson of the meeting, the Party secretary, declared the conclusion of the meeting. An announcement was made soon: Ye was designated a rightist because, first of all, he had called Zhang "comrade," and secondly, he said Zhang had been a good person before. This way, that rightist space was filled and Ye was instantly deprived of his position as doctor and degraded to that of sanitation worker.[92]

If we take Wang's account at face value, it would appear the Party secretary used the meeting to trap someone into inadvertently saying something inappropriate and thus becoming the last to be labelled a rightist. With the labelling quota in place, the Anti-Rightist Campaign became a matter of machination and conspiracy at the local and work unit levels, losing sight of its original goal of purging political opponents.

In some cases, party secretaries or heads of work units chose to exceed the quota to show their dedication to the campaign. While the Harbin Foreign Language Institute labelled 11 percent of its teachers and students, the heads of the Ministry of Justice labelled 16 percent of their employees, and the New China News Agency labelled 18 percent of its journalists and news editors.[93] As the CCP Central Committee suggested that ultra-rightists should comprise 20 to 25 percent of all rightists, the university authorities in Beijing seized 1,115 ultra-rightists in total, accounting for 23 percent of all 4,874 rightists.[94]

Lu Gang, a senior Party official at Harbin Foreign Language Institute, believed that one of the reasons for his purge was his criticism of his superior. "However," recalled Lu,

raising criticism was not the only reason for my labelling. Another important cause [was] that I was a high-ranking cadre in my institute though only twenty-nine years of age. I was thus classified as a "senior cadre of young age," the group from which a representative needed to be singled out to attack. So I was designated as the representative of this type of person.[95]

In cases where it was difficult to find scapegoats to meet the quota, some work unit heads chose to assign rightist labels by drawing lots. This was how "lot-drawing rightists" (*zhuajiu youpai*) were produced. A movie theatre was allocated a rightist quota, and the head of the work unit could find no way to meet it. Finally, he made his employees draw lots, by which method a box cashier was eventually selected.[96] This "soft" approach to labelling rightists enabled work unit heads to meet Party demands without laying undue blame on the masses. To work unit officials, the implementation of political labelling was often simply a matter of meeting a quota rather than unearthing political opponents or suspects.

Disengagement and Non-Cooperation as Reasons for Being Labelled

In his discussion of Maoist political labelling, Cai Wenhui describes a bizarre phenomenon: "People could also be labelled deviants simply because they said nothing at the meeting. The term *you du bu fang* or having poison but not releasing it ... applies to this situation."[97] In 1957, charges were sometimes brought against those who remained silent during, or kept aloof from, political sessions. Remaining silent during the Hundred Flowers Movement, when the Party encouraged criticism, could be interpreted as *you du bu fang* when the political wind reversed. Accusations could also be made against those who refused to show support for the Party's anti-rightist initiatives. In both situations, non-activists became targets.

During the Hundred Flowers Movement, some, due to their uncertainty of the CCP's intentions regarding rectification, adopted the strategy of "acting wisely by playing it safe" (*ming zhe bao shen*). They kept silent during blooming-and-contending meetings; indeed, some, due to a lack of political interest or "consciousness," simply had nothing to say. This strategy was not always effective, however. Silence could be taken as a sign that someone was holding a grudge against the Party – "nursing a grievance in the heart" or "burying hatred inside" (*huai hen zai xin*). "The rationale was that non-speech revealed your refusal to show support for the Party, an indication that you had anti-Party tendencies."[98] In this situation, one was not immune to attack if a Party secretary needed someone to fill his or her labelling quota. Lu Wencai, a Chinese literature professor, recalled:

> I had a friend named Wang Deyu, a genius in foreign languages. He did not say anything during the rectification period, but merely put his opinions in his diary. After the diary was seized in a sudden house search, he was labelled a rightist, even though he constantly refused to admit his "fault."[99]

On the surface, it would seem that Wang Deyu was persecuted for the anti-Party contents of his diary. However, upon closer analysis, based on the context of the Hundred Flowers Movement, it would seem that it is just as probable that he was considered guilty for the outrageous act of secretly keeping a diary while publicly remaining silent.

People were labelled for remaining silent during the Party's anti-rightist counterattack and/or for being reluctant to expose their friends or colleagues. After Chen Yi was labelled, three of his assistants were also persecuted because they had all remained silent during the meeting in which he was condemned, despite being repeatedly prodded to speak against him.[100]

During the labelling period, individuals could be implicated simply for associating with rightists. In Beijing, more than 170 students, teachers, and others were implicated in Lin Xiling's case.[101] One might also be purged simply for having family members or relatives who were rightists. Chen Ming was labelled primarily because his wife, Ding Ling, was "the No.1 rightist" in literary circles; opera star Xin Fengxia was labelled because of her obstinate refusal to divorce her husband Wu Zuguang.[102] Friends or work relations might also be a source of trouble. Qian Xinbo, a journalist in the Central People's Broadcasting Service, was confronted by his boss: "You once worked in a bourgeois newspaper, and you also have some friends who have become rightists now; so what do you think if we name you as rightist?" Qian answered: "It's up to the Party." He was then pronounced a rightist.[103] According to Wang Li: "My main fault was that some people I had recruited into a democratic party, the 'September 3 Society,' became rightists, so I had to take the blame and join them."[104] Although the CCP leadership and theoreticians acknowledged that implicating innocents was a "feudal practice," and they condemned the ex-GMD for using unsubstantiated rumours to arrest and execute the "revolutionary masses," this practice was prevalent in the daily operations of CCP politics, especially when Party bosses found it necessary to locate targets during particular campaigns.

Political labelling in 1957–58 China was a bizarre and grotesque phenomenon, its perpetrators having various motives and sharing certain characteristics, including: (1) interweaving high politics with low politics,

(2) raising mundane issues to the level of inviolable principles and using political campaigns to facilitate personal ends (e.g., defending prestige, pursuing grudges, etc.), (3) victimizing people not so much for their offensive politics but for their poor interpersonal relations or simply because the Anti-Rightist Campaign needed a victim. As a result, the actual exercise of labelling often went beyond the use of standard categories:

- A school principal wanted to have an affair with the wife of his employee. During the Anti-Rightist Campaign, he found an excuse to label this employee, send him to a labour camp, and get involved with his wife.[105]
- Dai Juying was a seventeen-year-old office typist when the campaign started. Deemed guilty of making the casual comment "shoe polish made in the United States is really good," and her refusal to acknowledge anything wrong with it, she was eventually accused of "having a blind faith in foreign imperialist things" and was sent to Beidahuang for labour reform.[106]
- The top Party journal *Red Flag* invited artist Li Binsheng to draw a cartoon to satirize those who were too cautious to speak out during the Hundred Flowers. When the political climate changed, Li was accused of "using cartoons to release anti-Party poison."[107]
- Movie director Ba Hong was identified as both a rightist and a "historical counter-revolutionary" because he had worked for an American intelligence agency in 1944. Though he was approved by an underground CCP cell leader, his former work was still considered to be a serious blot on his "political history."[108]
- Party intellectual Xie Hegeng was labelled for suggesting that the CCP Central Committee should end its occupation of Zhongnanhai in order to make way for a public resort.[109]
- Middle school teacher Chen Dongbai was accused of committing a serious offence when he opposed the program of simplifying Chinese characters and lamented a PLA garrison's failure to protect historic sites.[110]

It is worth noting that one was rarely labelled for a single reason. Artist Ding Cong, for example, was persecuted for three reasons. First, as the executive editor of the *People's Pictorial*, which was chiefly published for overseas readers, Ding argued for less political hue and a greater emphasis on Chinese social and cultural life. For this he was accused of "using bourgeois tastes to run the *Pictorial*." Second, at one time Ding took issue with a Soviet adviser regarding management of the *Pictorial*. For this he was accused of being anti-Soviet. Third, he and several friends formed an artists' salon. For this he was condemned for "forming a counter-revolutionary clique similar to the Petofi Circle."[111] To the labellers, multiple reasons seemed to make the purging both more necessary and more solidly grounded. If, upon screening, fault was found with one reason, there were always others.

One of the reasons that junior police officer Wang Hongren was labelled a rightist was that he attempted to leave his job to attend college, which his supervisor interpreted as a lack of commitment to the work assigned by the Party. On top of this, Wang had composed a poem, "The Tree and the Grass," which was thought to have anti-Party undertones. Wang's supervisor commented:

> You described how the grass had difficulty surviving under the tree. That obviously implies that you are the grass, and the Party is the tree. How could our beloved Party cause you difficulty to survive? This is absolutely an anti-Party poem.[112]

It is ironic that the people who took a leftist stance during the high tide of the Anti-Rightist Campaign in 1957 were not immune from "supplementary labelling" in 1958. In several cases, when activists attempted to show their strong allegiance to the Party, they went to the extreme of attacking the heads of their work units for their lack of revolutionary initiative and/or for their alleged administrative failures. When supplementary labelling came about in 1958, the purpose being to net "escaped rightists" (*louwang youpai*), many people were rounded up by their grudge-bearing bosses on the grounds of "anti-Party leadership." A typical case was that of Hou Fang, a philosophy teacher at the Northeastern People's University, whose revolutionary aggression during the Anti-Rightist Campaign resulted in the suffering of many of his colleagues. When the campaign concluded, it seemed that Hou had secured his place in the work unit. However, too confident and aggressive to know where to stop, Hou, in December 1957, waged a sudden attack on the university president, Kuang Yaming, for his alleged "bureaucratism." As a result, Hou was soon labelled, dismissed from his teaching job, and sent to a road construction project.[113] In this case, a leftist stance led to a rightist hat, and the perpetrator quickly became the victim.

Similarly, there were people who tried to show their devotion to the Party by making a "clean breast" of their "unhealthy thoughts," but this often ended in disgrace. A Party document indicates that "in the recti-fication and 'Opening One's Heart' movement, some individuals were punished or labelled as rightists based on the materials they voluntarily submitted."[114] The official source of this information is supported by per-sonal recollection. A female cadre in Beijing tried to demonstrate her fidelity by handing the Party secretary her diary, which recorded her frus-tration over her personal life. Unexpectedly, the diary was condemned and likened to "anti-socialist poisonous weeds." The woman was kicked out of the Party and banished to Beidahuang.[115] Her sincerity and fidel-ity were her undoing as the Party boss was more interested in completing his labelling work than in appreciating her making a "clean breast" of it.

From the foregoing, one can see that, although the CCP leadership deemed rightists to be "anti-Party, anti-socialist reactionaries" and for this reason loosed upon them a campaign of mass persecution, the majority of these rightists were labelled for reasons other than those officially stat-ed. While some did criticize Party officials and/or policies, and an even smaller number challenged the legitimacy and credibility of the CCP, the majority of these people were victimized for reasons that were far from political. At the national level, they were victimized by the CCP's desire to eliminate real and potential threats and by its strategy for gaining and maintaining political control. At the local and work unit level, they were victimized for administrative expediency and to serve the personal hid-den agendas of Party bosses. The actual process of labelling bore little resemblance to the ideological goals proclaimed by the CCP leadership.

ENVISIONING PUNISHMENT

By early 1958, the CCP had seemingly achieved success on the political front. Critics were largely silenced, the press was under strict control, the vast majority of the labelled confessed their crimes, and the working class was mobilized to condemn the rightists and to express its support for the Party.[116] The CCP seemed to have achieved an unprecedented conformity.

Along with political labelling, the Party envisaged a set of policies for the treatment of rightists. Although insisting that the enmity between the CCP and rightists was like a "contradiction between ourselves and the enemies," the Party leadership also opened the door to a solution, which it wanted to resemble that solution used to handle the "contradiction among the people."

This was meant to be a sign of the Party's leniency and willingness to "save" those who had gone astray but wished to repent. At the conferences in October and December 1957, for instance, Mao stated: "We need to take disciplinary action against those rightists, but we should not be too harsh." He continued: "[We need to] criticize them seriously but treat them leniently."[117] Teiwes believes that, in most circumstances, Mao argued against punishing rightists and favoured treating their problems with magnanimity. For those who were treatable, Mao advocated traditional rectification measures, reasoning, and "curing the illness to save the patient."[118] One of Mao's "magnanimous treatments" was to "give [rightists] a way out" by sending them to various labour reform centres in the borderlands and making them engage in "ideological remoulding" through manual labour.

In January 1958, the CCP Central Committee issued guidelines for the treatment of the various grades of rightists (see Chapter 2). It seems, however, that it did not enact any specific directive with regard to banishing those so labelled;[119] rather, it treated the banishment of ordinary rightists to rural areas as part of its general plan for sending down cadres for manual labour. On February 28, 1958, the Party issued a directive entitled "Instruction of the CCP Central Committee on Sending down Cadres to Manual Labour," which addresses manual labour as a crucial measure for ensuring that cadres cultivate a "proletarian outlook" and "draw close to the masses." The portion that concerns the rightists reads:

> All those who were condemned to "labour under supervision" due to a serious offence are to be sent to agricultural cooperatives to perform manual labour, overseen by cooperative members and cadres; others, who committed a minor offence, showed acceptable repentance, and were punished by "being kept on probation" can be sent down after their problems are solved, providing that their physical condition allows.[120]

This instruction, together with Mao's preference for remoulding through labour, constituted a formal basis for post-1957 banishment.[121]

However, rightists were not banished immediately. First of all, they had to be ejected from the Communist Party or the Communist Youth League (if they had been members) then most were stripped of their posts, dismissed from their offices, and told to await further instructions. The waiting period ranged from a couple of months to half a year, during which time they were told to study anti-rightist documents and to write self-criticisms. In the meantime, with the exception of a limited

number of disgraced senior revolutionaries and the leaders of democratic parties, the majority of rightists were required to perform physical
labour within their work units, on local collective farms, or on nearby
construction sites.[122]

For the rightists labelled in Beijing, industrial and agricultural sectors
around the city provided plenty of places for their labour reform. Many
student rightists were removed from campus and taken to these places.
Lin Xiling, for instance, was sent to a university farm to perform supervised physical labour. Some student rightists at Peking University, such
as Yan Tunfu, worked in a textile mill, but most were sent to Mentougou
Coal Mine or worked on the nearby farms.[123] Some were able to retain
their status as students, albeit under strict surveillance. Before being sent
to a labour camp, Harry Wu was allowed to attend class. He could go to
the library in the evening but only after informing his keeper. He lost
the privilege of asking questions or making comments in his classroom,
could not eat with other students in the dining hall, and was banned
from school-related recreational activities. His tasks included catching
rats, flies, and maggots to improve campus hygiene.[124] It was considered
lenient to allow a rightist student to retain her/his status and to work in
Greater Beijing.

As for the thousands of rightists gleaned from various central government agencies and press circles, working near Beijing was the first phase
of their forced labour experience. Many were sent by their work units to
the mountain villages of the western suburb or to the construction site
of the Ming Tombs Reservoir, a well-publicized state project north of
Beijing. Normally, they were allowed to return home on weekends and
received a limited stipend (from RMB 28 *yuan* to 32 *yuan* per month).[125]
Waiting to redeem themselves, they passed the gloomy winter of 1957
being apprehensive of the next spring, when the large-scale banishment
commenced.

Having discussed the background of the Anti-Rightist Campaign and
the major characteristics of political labelling, in the following chapters I move on to investigate the experiences of the banished, especially
those who were sent from Beijing to army farms and labour camps in
Beidahuang, the Great Northern Wilderness.

2

Beijing Rightists on the Army Farms of Beidahuang

Arriving at Qianmen railway station, I found that many people were lining up along the sidewalk close to the old dilapidated city wall. Most of them were wearing heavy cotton-padded clothes and cumbersome winter shoes, some with coarse sheepskin overcoats under their arms. They seldom talked to each other, with seriousness on their faces and sadness in their eyes. I joined in at the end of the waiting line, gathering that this would probably be the line for rightists coming from various central organizations ... When I got on board, I came to realize that this train was an "express" specified to deliver more than one thousand rightists. Its destination was Mishan, eastern Heilongjiang.

—Yin Yi, banished rightist on Farm 850

The spring of 1958 saw a heavy flow of humanity through the Qianmen railway station, which had been used for half a century before the new Beijing railway station was completed in 1959 to celebrate the tenth anniversary of the People's Republic. Priority was given to the transportation of a wide variety of migrants (including demobilized People's Liberation Army soldiers and newly recruited young farmers) to northeast China. Among these migrants, the most conspicuous were thousands of political exiles who had been labelled rightists and were being sent to the Beidahuang borderlands. Yin Yi was one of the witnesses and participants in this human movement.

Among the rightists punished in 1957, those sent from Beijing to Beidahuang were noteworthy due to their background and political standings, the harsh physical conditions they encountered, and the terrible suffering they endured. In this chapter, I look at the origin of their banishment and how it was implemented. I also address their perceptions of Beidahuang, their daily work and lives, their attitudes towards ideological remoulding, and the measures and strategies used by the army farm authorities. I further show that, although banishment was a penalty and was abhorred by the majority, a considerable number of Beijing rightists looked at it in a positive light during the early part of their stay in Beidahuang.

THE DISPOSAL OF THE RIGHTISTS

At the end of 1957 and the beginning of 1958, while the Anti-Rightist Campaign was drawing to a close, the Chinese Communist Party's central authorities had on their agenda the disposal of half a million rightists. According to a Party directive issued in January 1958, the rightists needed to be broken down into six categories and punishment meted out correspondingly. Those in the first category, the ultra-rightists, were to be removed from their jobs and sent to labour re-education camps; those in the second category were to be removed from their jobs and made to perform "labour under supervision"; those in the third category were to be removed from their jobs and sent to perform physical labour with reduced salaries; those in the fourth category were allowed to keep their jobs on probation; those in the fifth category were punished with lowered rank and reduced salary; and those in the sixth category were merely given rightist "hats" or "caps" without other punishment.[1] This directive constituted the formal guidelines according to which hundreds of thousands of rightists were sent to various locations: factories, mines, countrysides, and borderlands. However, the actual implementation of these penalties was far more complex than what might be implied by the rules. For instance, those sent to Farm 853 in Heilongjiang Province to perform "labour under supervision" included not only rightists of the second category but also those of other categories (i.e., 57 first category, 47 third category, 71 sixth category, 54 unclassified rightists, and 59 historical counter-revolutionaries).[2]

Even with the general disposal guidelines in place, however, it seems that the elite leaders of CCP command did not make any clear plan regarding how to effectively dispose of the rightists taken from the central government organizations in Beijing (referred to as "Beijing rightists" in this book). As mentioned in Chapter 1, these rightists were at first arranged by their work units to perform temporary labour around Beijing for several months. It was not until February 1958, when Wang Zhen, the minister of land reclamation, proposed his enlarged plan for land reclamation in eastern Heilongjiang and asked for more labourers that the central government decided to send the Beijing rightists to Beidahuang.

Land reclamation in eastern Heilongjiang started in 1954, when seventeen thousand demobilized soldiers were transported to the counties of Mishan, Hulin, Baoqing, and Raohe under the former PLA general Wang Zhen and established dozens of army farms.[3] In the early spring of 1958, within the heated climate of the Great Leap Forward, the CCP Central Committee decided to accelerate the development of army farms, and thus more demobilized soldiers were forcibly relocated to Beidahuang, followed by young peasants recruited from interior provinces (mostly Shandong and Hebei), and convicts from northern and eastern China. Agricultural, construction, and forestry labourers were still in great demand at this stage, however, prompting Minister Wang Zhen to ask the State Council to supply more workers, including the rightists from Beijing. His request was approved in February 1958.[4] The great demand for labour in Beidahuang coincided with the purging of rightists and the authorities' wish to dispose of them.

Little is known about how the CCP leadership made the decision to send Beijing rightists down; it is also unclear how the various central ministries coordinated the process of mass relocation. The recollections of rightists, however, provide us with valuable perspectives on this issue. Ding Ling recalled the experience of her husband Chen Ming:

> A couple of days after the [Chinese] New Year, the Beijing Movie Studio of the Ministry of Culture informed Chen Ming of his verdict: while he could keep his job post, he was to be deprived of his rank and sent to "labor under supervision" in Mishan, Heilongjiang. Three days were given to him to report to a meeting place in an eastern suburb.[5]

Other recollections (such as those of Yin Yi) provide similar accounts: the rightists, after being stripped of their posts and/or ranks and undergoing a period of manual labour in Greater Beijing, were ordered to designated meeting places (e.g., Qianmen) where they were to board trains for Beidahuang. Who was to go was mainly decided by the heads of their work units, and cadres from these units supervised their departure. Some trains were "rightist expresses" (*youpai zhuanlie*) that had been reserved by the Ministry of Land Reclamation, but many went to Beidahuang in small groups.[6] There is no official source to tell us how the banishment was coordinated. From the recollections of political exiles, which largely concern their own experiences, we can tell that the banishment was loosely managed by work units, which operated under the general instruction to send people down. Not all Beijing rightists were banished to Beidahuang, of course, as vast territories in north and northeast China provided numerous destinations for internal exiles. The rightists from the Beijing Forestry Institute, for instance, were sent to the Great Xing'an Mountains in Heilongjiang Province as lumber workers, and those from the *Beijing Daily* went to road construction sites in the western mountains of Greater Beijing.[7] Journalist Liu Binyan (a renowned political dissident in the post-Mao period) was banished to a Shanxi village with his colleagues, and writer Liu Shaotang was allowed to return to his home village in Hebei. Some were allowed to choose their banishment destination, but most were not.[8]

The rightists exiled to Beidahuang came from various agencies of the State Council, institutions of higher learning, news media, and so on. They ranged from senior revolutionaries to members of the non-Party elite, from college graduates to office clerks. Whereas many of them, such as Liu Meng and Dai Juying, were unknown, others included prestigious figures who held important posts in managerial, economic, cultural, and literary fields. Figures such as Ding Ling, Ai Qing, Wu Zuguang, and Ding Cong were well known in literary and artistic spheres, while Wang Zuoru (director of the Protocol Department of the Foreign Ministry) and Xie Hegeng were revolutionary veterans.[9] Nor were military personnel immune from banishment: of around seven thousand PLA officers, cadets, and technicians who were labelled rightists, more than a hundred were sent to Beidahuang.[10]

The severity of the punishments meted out to rightists did not necessarily match the severity of the denunciations they received during the Anti-Rightist Campaign. Those who had attained high political rank before being labelled usually received moderate punishment. For example, Zhang Bojun and Luo Longji, who were both harshly condemned by Mao, were not sent to labour camps but remained in Beijing, retaining their membership in the Chinese People's Political Consultative Conference and living a relatively easy life, albeit isolated and ostracized. Zhang Bojun even continued to enjoy subsidized housing and a car.[11] Ding

Ling, whose official position had been Party secretary of the Chinese Writers Association, was designated a rightist of the sixth category and was thus allowed to continue her work in Beijing before she voluntarily went to Beidahuang.[12] We can see, therefore, that, although banishment encompassed a considerable number of famous intellectuals, those with high official rank or a significant role in the "united front" were not put on the list. It was thought that the treatment of well-known rightists should show the Party's benevolence and its policy of "tempering justice with mercy" in order to win over the majority of intellectuals and ensure the continuing support of other social elites.[13]

BEIDAHUANG: AN IMAGINED WORLD

The term "Beidahuang," the Great Northern Wilderness, was first used by the Han Chinese during the Qing dynasty (1644–1912). Considering Manchuria their homeland, late seventeenth-century Qing rulers started implementing an "exclusion policy" in the territory north of Shanhaiguan. Two lines of willows – the Willow Palisades – were planted in southern Manchuria to prohibit Han Chinese migration, to preserve the Manchu way of life, and to retain control over the valuable products of that region.[14] The Han who lived south of the Willow Palisades called the boundless northern land (probably including eastern Siberia) Beidahuang.[15] With the Qing's lifting of the ban on migration to Manchuria in the second half of the nineteenth century, and the massive influx of Han migrants, the imagined world of Beidahuang was reduced in scope. By the time of the communist takeover, the term "Beidahuang" referred to the vast plains north of Harbin and Yilehuli Mountain, encompassing the Three River Plain (*Sanjiang pingyuan*, an alluvial plain formed by the Amur, Ussuri, and Sungari Rivers) and the Mudan River Plain (*Mudanjiang pingyuan*). The ecology of these areas was still in a primitive state in the 1950s. As one folk song has it, it was a place for "hunting roe deer with club, netting fish with gourd ladle, and watching pheasants fly into the kitchen."[16]

During the massive land reclamation of the mid-1950s, four counties – Mishan, Hulin, Baoqing, and Raohe in the eastern frontier region of Heilongjiang Province – came to be the location of a dozen army farms, some of which received Beijing rightists.[17] In later years, especially during the Cultural Revolution, Beidahuang, as the destination of hundreds of thousands of sent-down youths, was the generic name for the Heilongjiang borderlands.

Beidahuang had long been considered an undesirable area in which to live. Although arable land was abundant and the soil fertile, its climate (minus thirty degrees Celsius on average during the winter), its isolation from China proper, and its transportation difficulties made people wince at the sound of the name. Lack of trade and amenities, a diet based on coarse grains (corn, sorghum, etc.), and a shortage of vegetables during winter were also deterrents. Even after the Qing lifted its exclusion policy, the Han Chinese, except for Shandong and Hebei migrants, preferred to stay away from this desolate land.[18] In the 1930s, Japanese colonizers attempted to reclaim this area, but this ended in failure.[19]

Historically, the northeastern borderland provided a perfect place for late imperial rulers to send undesirable elements (e.g., criminals, disgraced officials and scholars, etc.).[20] Its harsh physical environment and difficult living conditions generated considerable fear in those sent there, including those sent in 1957. When told that they would be sent to Beidahuang, many Beijing rightists were overwhelmed by sadness and distress. As many of them were literati, they instinctively linked their fate to that of their imperial predecessors who had been banished there hundreds of years ago. Wu Yongliang, Yin Yi, and Ni Genshan all expressed deep sorrow, lamenting their misfortune and the uncertainty of their future lives.[21] Many of them did not know how long they would be away or how their families would carry on without them. Some appealed to remain in Beijing due to their poor health or family obligations, but they were harshly declined.[22]

A perplexing phenomenon, however, is that a considerable number of Beijing rightists did not fear being sent to Beidahuang and that some literati volunteered to go even though they were offered other options. According to a directive from the central authorities (the State Council's "The Stipulations on Disposal of the Rightists among State Employees and University Students," issued on January 29, 1958), only those rightists assigned to the first and second categories of punishment were to be sent to labour camps or farms for labour re-education and/or to perform labour under supervision. But some rightists of other categories, such as writers Ding Ling and Nie Gannu, asked to go to Beidahuang.[23] The reasons for their request are multiple and complex.

Some rightists were impressed by the landscape of the northeast and sought spiritual enjoyment from it. With the tidal wave of land reclamation, media coverage of the landscape and local culture of Heilongjiang Province had dramatically increased; this contributed to people's knowledge of the province and led to their having an idealized image of an aesthetically pleasing Beidahuang. Ding Ling was among the many who were interested in the beauty of the Heilongjiang forests pictured in some of the books she had collected.[24] Journalist Cong Weixi was also fascinated by the boundlessness, the picturesque scenery, and the fertility of Beidahuang. Cong believed that, to people who did not have families to care for, Beidahuang was an oasis far from mundane life – a place to purify the human soul. He also wrote: "I was infatuated with the northeast, especially in winter when it was dressed up by the white snow, so I went to this silvery white world twice in the fall of 1956 and the spring of 1957."[25] To these idealists, life in this great wilderness seemed like something that would lead to enjoyment and spiritual purification. Thus was generated a romantic view of Beidahuang.

The second reason to go to Beidahuang, especially for some revolutionary writers, had to do with looking for literary inspiration in "ordinary people." Taking to heart Mao's injunction in the Yan'an Talks, some writers sincerely believed that it was important to go to the grassroots to find fresh sources for their writing on the masses.[26] Ding Ling, for instance, insisted that a revolutionary writer should enthusiastically descend to the world of rural people and observe and learn from their lives, even though the writer himself/herself lived in adversity. She presumed that "living close to the earth" would nourish her literary creativity and that her writing should depict the epic transformation of heaven and earth in the northeast.[27] Another example of this enthusiasm is found in essayist Nie Gannu. With his record as a revolutionary veteran, Nie, after being labelled a rightist, was offered the option of either retiring or working at a lower rank at the People's Literature Press, but he declined both options. "Life is the source of writing," he said: "As a writer, I should experience all kinds of life. Now that I have become a rightist, I would like to lead the real life of the rightists."[28] In an effort to find literary inspiration and to lead a "real life," what these intellectuals sought was, in fact, self-banishment.

The third reason that some rightists wanted to go to Beidahuang was a desire for self-redemption through manual labour. Party functionaries told artists such as Ding Cong and Huang Miaozi that they had committed serious crimes against the Party and the nation and that they needed to redeem themselves through hard labour in the most difficult regions. Beidahuang, with its promise of physical hardship and its unprecedented revolutionary changes since 1949, was an ideal place to go and work. They were also told that, through hard labour and physical suffering, they could transcend their past faults and their deep-seated bourgeois ideology.[29] Showered by such propaganda, these intellectuals were willing to go to Beidahuang and display their commitment to self-reform and self-redemption.

For most rightists, this forced-fed revolutionary indoctrination did not make the desolate Great Northern Wilderness appear more attractive. However, Beidahuang did offer them an escape. Having been demonized and having experienced attacks and insults, rightists were notorious among their colleagues and neighbours, and they could not pass their friends on the street without lowering their heads in shame. Wu Yongliang recalls that, with Party instructions to isolate rightists, "there was no nodding, no hello, no smile from the friends, who began to treat us as strangers and shunned us as a contagious disease." Even their families were persuaded to condemn them and to draw a political line around them.[30] The social isolation of rightists was tremendous and often unbearable. Given these circumstances, leaving for Beidahuang seemed, to some, to offer relief. Many rightists assumed that in an exile community established in a remote location everybody would be equal, there would be no discrimination, and the smell of the black earth would bring hope.[31] When their fate as rightists was sealed, many wished to seek refuge in the wilderness in order to free themselves from political pressure, interpersonal coldness, and social ostracism.

Arrival in Beidahuang

When they first arrived at their places of banishment – Farm 850 and Farm 853, the chief concern of Beijing rightists was the length of their stay. Things did not seem so grim at this point. Before leaving Beijing, some rightists were led to believe by the heads of their work units that, as long as they did well, they might be recalled in one or two years.[32] There were other signs that remoulding through labour in Beidahuang would likely be a short-term experience: the bosses of many work units advised rightists not to let their professional expertise get rusty. The rightists from the Beijing Central Orchestra, for instance, were allowed to take their musical instruments with them, while journalists from the New China News Agency were encouraged to take English books and English-Chinese dictionaries.[33] Many exiles, therefore, expected that their frontier banishment would be neither harsh nor long. As long as they sincerely engaged in the process of remoulding through labour, they assumed, the Party would rehabilitate them and allow them to resume normal life at their previous posts in Beijing. Journalist Dai Huang recalls: "Taking the journey with my box filled with books, I was full of confidence in pursuing a bright future in the wilderness." Yin Yi, too, admits that he did not feel so bad after having heard an encouraging speech from the minister of culture.[34] Even though it is not possible to definitively state that Dai's and Yin's mentalities were typical, it seems that at least some political exiles were not feeling hopeless during the early period of their banishment.

From early March 1958, thousands of Beijing rightists arrived in successive waves at various farms in Beidahuang. Ding Ling was assigned to Tangyuan Farm; Ai Qing, a famous poet, and his family were sent to Farm 852; and the vast majority of Beijing rightists were sent to Farms 850 and 853.[35] Senior revolutionaries Nie Gannu and Xie Hegeng, artists Ding Cong and Huang Miaozi, as well as journalists Dai Huang, Wu Yongliang, Yin Yi, and Liu Meng were sent to Farm 850, the first army farm established in Beidahuang. English literature specialist Huang Wu, playwrights Wu Zuguang and Wang Zheng, and journalists Zheng Xiaofeng and Sun Zhanke were sent to Farm 853, as was Chen Ming (before being allowed to join Ding Ling in Tangyuan).[36] In sum, the 925 rightists placed in Farm 850 were from twenty-seven organizations located in Beijing, and the 486 rightists in Farm 853 were from fifty-four such organizations.[37] In these farms, Beijing rightists worked with demobilized soldiers and convicts but formed separate labour teams. Local annals; the Farm 853 Archives; the memoirs of Dai Huang, Wu Yongliang, Yin Yi, and Ni Genshan; and the recollections of Zheng Xiaofeng all mention the different kinds of involuntary migrants that constituted the major labour force in these army farms. Still, the number of Beijing rightists was relatively small in comparison to other kinds of labourers. For instance, there were 925 Beijing rightists on Farm 850, but there were 5,074 convicts and approximately 12,800 demobilized soldiers.[38]

For most of the rightists on Farm 850, the first months were manageable. Their formal status on the farm was "agricultural worker" (*nonggong*) rather than "rightist," and this considerably relieved the political pressure they had suffered in Beijing. The farm authorities designated 120 demobilized officers to supervise their daily life and to organize their work.[39] Administrative and ideological control was relatively loose in the first few months; political slogans, which permeated Beijing, were rarely heard, and political study sessions loosely organized, all of which gave rightists ample freedom to read, talk, and relax after work. They sang Peking opera, practised painting, played bridge, conducted research, and read foreign-language texts.[40] While living conditions were poor – they lived in ramshackle sheds or thatched, mud-walled barracks

– and the physical work heavy, they led acceptable lives. This came to an end when the Rectification Movement in Beidahuang, initiated in the fall of 1958, intensified the political atmosphere. The situation was similar on Farm 853, where, as Zheng Xiaofeng recalls, the exiles did not feel much political or administrative pressure. The demobilized PLA officers on Zheng's labour team treated the rightists quite politely, addressing them as "sent-down cadres" (*xiafang ganbu*) rather than referring to them in insulting or derogatory terms. Except for the strenuousness of daily work, the lives of the rightists were not badly affected, and discrimination was kept at a minimum. Huang Wu and his friends believed that on Farm 853 people treated each other equally, although the living conditions were difficult: there was no discrimination of the kind they had encountered in Beijing. So the rightists felt "psychologically much relieved,"[41] and the army farms seemed to offer a temporary refuge for those in dire straits.

Some of the state officials in charge of land reclamation adopted a moderate attitude towards the rightists. Minister Wang Zhen seemed rather sympathetic towards the labour forces that he recruited from Beijing. He visited the rightists in Farms 850 and 853 shortly after they arrived, gave warm speeches, and tried to cheer them up by suggesting that they would have a "bright future" if they took a positive attitude towards land reclamation. What most delighted them was that Wang addressed them as "comrades," which seemed to help momentarily remove the humiliation they had suffered during the Anti-Rightist Campaign.[42] They saw Wang Zhen's message as a sign of the Party's benevolence towards banished intellectuals. Under Wang's instructions, army farm authorities took efforts to improve the living conditions of rightists (for instance, providing electricity) and reassigned a limited number of them to work part-time on local literature magazines, in art troupes, and so on. Satisfied with these arrangements, many rightists on Farm 850 went so far as to refer to their experience as "civilized banishment,"[43] and they assumed that this would remain the normal state of affairs.

Rightists were allowed to bring family members with them. Although few of them had the heart to make their families experience hardship, some wives voluntarily accompanied their husbands to this desolate world, and vice versa. Han Yuan, an office clerk in the Ministry of Culture, accompanied her rightist husband, following the example of the heroic wives of Russian Decembrists whom she had seen depicted in Soviet movies.[44] On Farm 850, Nie Gannu worked alongside several wives who willingly left Beijing in order to be with their husbands. For a period, they were accommodated with other men in a newly built shed that housed approximately ninety rightists. "At night, the wives slept at both ends of the wide *kang* (northern style bed), with their husbands close to them, and the rest of the men jammed together on the other side of the husbands. With women about, the men tried to show better manners, and the dirty jokes that used to go around among the men completely disappeared."[45] Couples in such surroundings were certainly unable to enjoy conjugal life, but they felt and appreciated the warmth and kindness of the exile community.

Most rightists, however, left their wives or husbands behind. In cases where both spouses were labelled and banished, their children were left in Beijing, mostly to the care of grandparents. Although divorce due to political disgrace was not as common as it was during the Cultural Revolution, there were cases in which one spouse tried to avoid being implicated by drawing a political line between him- or herself and the once beloved spouse who had now become an "enemy of the people." While there are touching stories about unwavering commitments to marriage (e.g. Wu Zuguang, Huang Miaozi, and Ding Cong), sometimes spouses of rightists showed their fidelity to the Party by asking for a divorce (e.g. Xu Zimei and Dai Huang).[46] A Ministry of Culture inspection panel noticed that some rightists on Farm 853 were disturbed by family crises, especially by requests for divorce, and that this "negatively affected their thought reform."[47] Some, however, willingly filed for divorce once they were labelled rightists, or publicly announced a break with their families, in order not to bring trouble to their loved ones. Many broke off engagements.[48]

Manual Labour

The early, relaxed stage of life in Beidahuang turned out to be transitory. It was not long before rightists realized just how harsh their conditions were and that things would not work out as they had expected. During 1958–59, the nationwide economic adventure known as the Great Leap Forward featured the huge and wasteful use of labour and resources. In Beidahuang, the state's agenda to establish a national grain base meant daunting manual work in agriculture and construction.

Difficulties resulted from both physical conditions and official pressure. Beidahuang was considered to be located in the harshest region of Manchuria. When rightists, together with other involuntary migrants, gathered there in the late 1950s, as far as the eye could see they faced a vast stretch of swamp and boggy grassland.[49] The land was marshy, the weather cold and volatile, and the roads essentially non-existent. Since the level of mechanization was low in the early stages, most of the newly reclaimed farmland had to be tilled, sowed, and reaped manually. Put into separate labour teams, rightists had to do all kinds of work, including cultivating the land, harvesting crops, building reservoirs, cutting wood, excavating earth, making bricks, erecting barracks, building roads, and raising livestock.[50] The work was particularly backbreaking for intellectuals, who were used to engaging in academic or managerial duties. Dai Huang provides us with examples of daily work at the Yunshan Branch of Farm 850:

> Right after the soybean harvest in the early winter of 1958, dozens of us went into the Wanda Mountains to cut hard oak trees ... Less than a month afterward [December 1, 1958], we were transferred to the grassland for an irrigation project ... The people in our platoon had to strive to finish the assigned work quotas. We used pickaxes to break the frozen topsoil, sometimes close to one meter thick, then dug out the unfrozen layer ... It was still dark when the reveille was sounded in the early morning. We had to leave our barracks and rush for dozens of *li* to work, and then have breakfast at the worksite. That winter, we usually slept for no more than four hours a day.[51]

On average, work hours ranged from twelve to sixteen hours a day in the busy seasons – sowing, harvesting, and building reservoirs – and lasted from three or four o'clock in the morning until dark. On some branch farms, thanks to the GLF, weekends were cancelled in the summer of 1958.[52] It was explained that, when the whole nation was going all out for Chinese communism, farm workers should not stick to a regular schedule and that rightists, in particular, should take the opportunity to make more contributions. In this way, rightists were driven to ceaseless physical exertion, which, together with severe food shortages, resulted in massive deaths in 1959 and 1960 (see Chapter 4).

The army farm authorities also used rightists as lumber workers. When agricultural work stopped, most rightists were organized into lumbering teams. In the winter of 1958, around fifteen hundred workers, including almost all rightists, were mobilized from Farm 853 to cut trees in the mountains.[53] As Huang Wu recalls:

> In the winters of 1958 and 1959, we rightists were twice ordered to go into the Wanda Mountain to cut wood. We entered the mountain in

September and left in March the next year, which was the coldest time in this remote border area ... The valleys were deep and the forests dense, without a trace of human habitation, and we had to co-exist with wolves, bears and wild boars day and night ... Sorghum, corn flour and dry cabbage were our daily diet.[54]

They lived in the forests, worked in pairs with handsaws, and struggled to meet work targets (eight cubic metres per day in most cases). As some farm chiefs adopted a "shaving-the-mountain" policy to produce as much wood as possible in support of the "ten major constructions" in Beijing, rightists were forced to engage in the excessive lumbering of the primeval forests. This policy led to an immense waste of natural resources. Many rightists were pained to witness how large amounts of felled wood, stained with their sweat and blood, were discarded to rot by the mountainside due to lack of transportation.[55]

Rightists were also used in charcoal making. Both Farm 850 and Farm 853 established "charcoal teams" in the winter. In order to produce charcoal of good quality, rightists were obliged to enter kilns to take out the charcoal while the kilns were still filled with hot smoke and ash. Physically strong people could manage to get this done quickly, but those in poor physical condition often fainted inside. Some were rescued by their fellow workers, but others died covered in charcoal ash.[56]

Rightists, like demobilized soldiers and convicts, were organized according to a quasi-military system, being put in regiments, companies, platoons, squads, and so on. Demobilized officers (now farm cadres with different titles) headed these units above company level. Some officers, such as those with whom Nie Gannu worked at Branch 4 of Farm 850, displayed a degree of compassion for the physical fitness of the rightists, assigning the elderly and the weak to lighter work, such as collecting fuel, fixing tools, and weaving baskets.[57] Other officers, driven by work targets set from above and enmeshed in the fanatical fervour of the GLF, treated rightists as slaves, even requiring them to engage in labour competitions with demobilized soldiers and convicts. The screw was tightened during the busy seasons – particularly planting and harvesting – when unreasonable work targets were established (e.g., reaping an untenable number of acres of wheat or soybeans by the end of the day). Although Dai Huang's comment, "the cadres wanted to wring every ounce of sweat and blood out of us," may sound overly emotional, others, such as Yin Yi and Ni Genshan, concur that designated work quotas often had to be completed within a specific time period, regardless of the weather conditions or whether the team had enough capable labourers. When work quotas were not filled, rightists would be denied rest and food.[58]

During their banishment, despite their status as *nong'gong* (seemingly equal to other farm workers), the Beijing rightists were treated worse than were demobilized soldiers in terms of living conditions, work assignments, and even labour safety. On Farm 850, while demobilized soldiers were provided with makeshift sheds when they worked far away from their barracks, rightists had to sleep in the open air. On Farm 853, while demobilized soldiers could refuse work due to food shortages in the famine years, rightists could not. And, for more than two years, two of the three rightist labour teams on Farm 853 had no fixed accommodations. When working in the mountains, demobilized officers were allowed to carry firearms to deal with beasts, but rightists could only bring clubs.[59] The rationale for the different treatment was that the farm cadres considered demobilized soldiers to be one of them ("ourselves") but considered the rightists to be "others." Whenever rightists on Farm 850 lodged complaints, the cadres would respond with comments such as: "Don't you want to get your label removed?"; "You are rightists! You are here to remould yourselves"; or "If you don't behave yourself, I will not allow you to leave here but make you suffer more hardships."[60] The status of rightists as "political pariahs" was constantly highlighted, and the threat to prolong their internment was a useful tool for muffling their complaints.

The harsh natural environment caused rightists much physical difficulty. We need to remember that state policy specified sending political offenders to geographically harsh areas, which would inevitably cause them tremendous suffering. Official sources tend to gloss this, but the memoirs of the exiles provide rich descriptions of the land in which they had to survive.

One of the major problems was the freezing cold winter. As early as mid-October, the cold wind would begin to slice through the mountains and plains of eastern Heilongjiang. Between December and March, when the land was frozen solid, any agricultural activity was impossible. Rural northeasterners customarily stayed indoors, drinking, gambling, gossiping, and occasionally emerging to hunt roe deer. Essentially, they spent their time "hiding from the winter" (*mao dong*). After the communist takeover, however, the winter season was a time to complete state projects, such as hydraulic works, road construction, and forest work, and this is exactly what rightists experienced in Beidahuang. They were often exposed to temperatures as low as minus twenty to thirty degrees Celsius during the day, and at night they slept in makeshift shacks made of birch logs, willow twigs, and thatched roofs, with wheat straw for beds. The temperature outside could go down to minus thirty degrees Celsius, and indoors, where wind and snow could blow in, was not significantly better.[61] The Party committee of the Mudanjiang Land Reclamation Bureau admitted that farm labourers often lived in dormitories whose temperature could be minus twenty or thirty degrees and that this was ignored by cadres who lived in well-heated homes.[62] Many rightists, such as Yin Yi and his fellow campmates, would drink alcohol to warm up before going to bed and wear cotton-padded hats to keep warm at night. Having meals outdoors was not easy. The food (typically corn or sorghum bread) sent to the worksites was often frozen solid and people had to cut it into pieces with an axe before eating it.[63]

In the summertime, insects, especially mosquitoes, posed a maddening problem. Nourished in the grassy marshland to an abnormally large size, mosquitoes tortured everyone in Beidahuang. Wang Zheng recalls: "Once wakened from the grass, these vicious creatures would swarm those of us who worked in the field, and would try to get into our noses, eyes, ears and mouths ... They were hard to repel when we were working. People would almost become mad in this situation."[64] Exposed skin led to instant bites. Insect-proof suits being in short supply, the exiles had to keep moving – to work nonstop – to try to hold the mosquitoes at bay. For many political exiles, mosquitoes were a nightmare during their time in Beidahuang.[65]

DIFFERENT ATTITUDES TOWARDS IDEOLOGICAL REMOULDING

Ideological remoulding (or thought reform) of offenders is considered to be an important characteristic of the People's Republic of China's prison-camp system. Some Western observers tend to emphasize the effectiveness of Mao-era ideological remoulding and re-education techniques when applied to labour camp inmates, seeing them as being in sharp contrast to Soviet techniques. Academics also assume, though this is not uncontested, that the thought work anchored in political study, moral teachings, and mass condemnation sessions (or "struggle sessions") that were an integral part of the CCP's remoulding regimen was quite successful in remaking human minds.[66] This argument is in accordance with the CCP's well-known ability to reconfigure offenders through its elaborate thought-reform repertoire, with some Chinese intellectuals accepting and even endorsing the Party's ideological grounding. In this chapter, however, I show the complexity of Beidahuang army farms, indicating that, while some rightists were sincere in their attempt to achieve "ideological renewal," others resisted officials and continued to air their dissent. I also show that, within a given time period (such as the GLF) or within a specific location (such as Farm 850), the agenda of ideological remoulding could be relegated to the background or significantly compromised by local-level cadres.

First of all, in the early stages (i.e., spring and summer of 1958), authorities on Farm 850 and Farm 853 had not developed clear ideas about how to treat and ideologically remould Beijing rightists. When they were sent down to the farms to engage in "labouring under supervision," their formal title, *nong gong* (agricultural worker), did not resolve the ambiguity of their political status. For this reason, farm leaders sometime addressed them as "sent-down cadres" while internally referring to them as "rightists." Farm 853 leaders were aware that "rightists [were] reactionaries" but had the somewhat perplexing idea that "they [were] still state cadres who [kept] their public offices."[67] The term "comrade," used by Minister Wang Zhen, added to this confusion. In these circumstances, the authorities on Farms 850 and 853 did not, probably *could* not, envisage a clear, consistent plan or political guide for remoulding these rightists, especially in the first year of the Great Leap Forward. Consequently, the decision of how to deal with those who had committed political errors in Beijing and needed to be re-educated on the farms was, to a great extent, left to low-level farm cadres.

For their part, the Beijing rightists had different attitudes towards ideological remoulding through labour. When they first arrived in Beidahuang, some were earnest about their desire to engage in remoulding. While many resented their mistreatment during the Anti-Rightist Campaign and lamented their banishment to the "wilderness," they nevertheless recognized that physical labour in combination with political study could play a role in their spiritual growth and in cleansing them of their "bourgeois ideologies." As mentioned earlier, Ding Ling and Nie Gannu looked at Beidahuang as an opportunity to learn from the working class, cast off their old selves, and achieve ideological renewal and spiritual regeneration. Nie Gannu wrote in his thought report:

I was born into a non-working class family, and thus had neither experience of physical labour nor access to working people. Therefore, I am glad to go to the countryside or the mountain area, join working people and participate in physical labour, or work at the grassroots level, in order to change my worldview ... I am now well prepared for long-term self-remoulding anywhere.[68]

This self-portrait should not simply be treated as play-acting as it is consistent with Nie's ardent requests to go to Beidahuang as well as with his serious engagement in physical labour while there. Others, such as Huang Miaozi and Dai Huang, also had a positive attitude towards political study and the role of physical work, and they expected to achieve ideological renewal.[69]

The letters of Huang Miaozi to his wife illustrate this point. So far, the autobiographies of rightists such as Dai Huang, Wu Yongliang, and Yin Yi are based mostly upon their memories as their post-banishment recollections, diaries, notes, and other writings were lost or destroyed in the years before their rehabilitation.[70] Huang Miaozi's biography *Ren zai xuanwo* by Li Hui, however, contains nine letters Huang wrote in Beidahuang to his wife Yu Feng from March to July 1959. These are among the rare sources that reveal the mental state of a rightist as described during this period: Huang earnestly repented his "sin" and offence, and he struggled to attain ideological renewal. Besides discussing his daily work and life (reservoir construction, daily meals, etc.), these letters reveal several aspects of his mental state. First, he expressed his deep gratitude to the Party and his appreciation of its policy to "save" rightists who committed political offences; he even felt guilty for "failing to meet the Party's expectations" of him. Second, the letters reveal his piety as he attempted to "dig deep to the very soul." In a political session involving "opening one's heart to the Party," Huang confessed his "dirty and vile thoughts" (e.g., hoping to return to Beijing soon, lacking interest in learning agricultural techniques, holding grudges against certain farm cadres, etc.). Third, he criticized his fellow rightists' "bourgeois behaviour." For instance, when Huang found that a rightist had "begged" the farm kitchen to sell him powdered milk, he considered this to be shameless and selfish bourgeois behaviour, and he expressed his deep disgust. Fourth, he expressed his confidence in thought reform. Huang told his wife: "I have always achieved ideological gains through political study. It is worthwhile to engage in introspection and self-criticism, although I feel somewhat bitter when going through it." He also said in his letters that, in the early months of his stay in Beidahuang, he seriously studied *Red Flag* (a leading Party journal) articles, the works of Karl Marx and Friedrich Engels, and the Party newspapers.[71]

These letters are valuable not only because they are primary records – composed by Huang during his banishment and recording his frame of mind during that period – but also because, after being rehabilitated, Huang frankly admitted that his self-effacing writing "came from my heart indeed, the real mindset of a rightist."[72] One may wonder if these letters were censored or monitored by farm cadres, given the post-1957 context. However, if we consider the fact that none of the rightists ever mentioned censorship on the army farms, a situation that differed from that in Xingkaihu labour camp (See Chapter 3), it is not presumptuous to suppose that Huang had no need to use hyperbolic language in his letters to his wife. Furthermore, if he had realized in 1959 that the farm cadres were monitoring his letters and so censored them himself, Huang would almost certainly have indicated this in 1997. These letters reveal the longing for ideological reconfiguration that an "old" member of the elite could experience when ostensibly given a chance to engage in it.

Other rightists demonstrated a similar earnestness in their desire to undergo ideological renewal. Many brought political readings with them to the farms and tried to read during work breaks.[73] Some wrote poems and songs describing their enthusiasm and job satisfaction and expressing their willingness to make a new start through labour reform. A very popular song entitled "Let's Build Our Beautiful Beidahuang" was composed by a rightist on Farm 850.[74] Perhaps such political piousness surfaced because among these rightists were a considerable number of artists, writers, and journalists who were relatively eager to engage in "soul-searching" activities and because, in their early time on these army farms, which were euphemistically portrayed as the focus of border development rather than as institutionalized labour reform camps, the atmosphere was relaxed.

However, army farms were complicated places. There were many cases in which Beijing rightists not only verbally resisted the concept of labour reform but also defied the remoulding arrangements. The Farm 853 Archives provide rich and novel sources on these phenomena.

Some rightists clearly articulated their abhorrence of Beidahuang banishment and their dislike of physical labour. According to a farm document dated 1959, Chen Shonglin claimed: "Beidahuang is a prison, and being sent to Beidahuang is just like being exiled to Russian Siberia." Fang Zixun wrote to the Farm 853 leadership: "It is unnecessary to come here for thought reform; one can go back to his original work unit to do so … Physical labour is not the only way for such reform; other work can also help achieve it."[75] Wang Xiuxian simply asserted that workers and peasants were incapable of remoulding intellectuals as they could not understand the latter's inner world. Someone complained that the makeshift sheds in army farms constituted a "living hell."[76] Such remarks stand in sharp contrast to those who held a favourable view of Beidahuang and its role in thought reform. It is apparent that, after spending a certain amount of time on the army farms, a number of rightists developed grievances.

Other rightists were outspoken in their criticism of the CCP's socioeconomic policies as well as of the policies implemented on the army farms. According to Li Kegang: "The General Line, the Great Leap Forward, and the People's Commune are not the result of economic development but mass forced labour ... [T]he GLF has destroyed the rustic life of rural China and damaged family happiness. People become estranged from each other under socialism." Li Tao comments: "The current policy over grain is what makes people starve. If you manage to get your stomach filled, you will be deemed to have violated the policy. Some bad elements [actually committed theft] due to such policy, due to hunger."[77] Wang Qingbin contended that the lives of ordinary people were now too difficult and that this could lead to mass grievances. Gu Ansheng wrote to Minister Wang Zhen, sharply criticizing Farm 853's GLF programs.[78]

A small number of Farm 853 rightists actively resisted the labour reform arrangements. According to a report from Farm 853, Zhao Zhendong once stated outright: "I just don't want to work anymore. You [farm cadres] can do whatever you want with me. I don't fear anything." Fang Shi stated: "I had expected to meet everything, good and evil, in Beidahuang ... I don't fear any demons or ghosts (*yaomo guiguai*)." After two years of being at the farm, Zhou Aihua still refused to write a thought report; Xiong Huisan seized an opportunity to flee the farm.[79] This Farm 853 document does not provide the context within which such resistant "words and deeds" transpired. It is reasonable to assume, however, that they were the manifestation of long-term resentment due to work pressure and/or oral abuse. Some may have reached the point of thinking: "I have already been banished here and reached the absolute bottom; I cannot sink any lower."[80] Their nerve was remarkable, and farm authorities considered their acts as the "outright resistance of reactionaries to thought reform."

Even after a period of manual labour, study sessions, and political lectures, some rightists still maintained their ideological stance, continued to espouse differing opinions, and sometimes even criticized some of the fundamental tenets of PRC society. The most well-known figure was Wang Qingbin. According to a Farm 853 document, Wang provided a host of reflections upon the main flaws of the PRC and the problems of Party teachings. His theoretical points may be summarized as follows:

(1) Fierce struggle makes it hard for people to speak their minds and this unavoidably forces them to lie, thus honest people are disappearing in the new society; (2) the logic behind "letting a hundred flowers bloom and a hundred schools of thoughts contend" should be truly followed, otherwise it is impossible to convince people of the Party's honesty when Marxism has a monopoly over all other positions; (3) Strict Party discipline hinders the growth of genius as, if there is no freedom to choose one's occupation, one cannot give full play to one's talents; (4) idealism and religious freedom should be truly allowed: "Now that freedom of religion is officially allowed, why is thought reform necessary?" and (5) "It remains to be seen whether and when the proletarian revolutions will occur in the capitalist countries ... thus co-existence [with capitalist countries] will be a long-term issue."[81] Although Wang was repeatedly condemned for these incisive and jarring observations, he maintained his "reactionary standpoint" and refused to change. The case of Wang, as well as those of other Farm 853 rightists (such as Li Kegang) resonates with Cao Shuji's research on rural rightists in the Province of Henan, who insisted on voicing their opinions even though they knew they would be punished for doing so.[82]

Such strong voices show that not all Beijing rightists were silenced by the Anti-Rightist Campaign or subdued by subsequent punishment. To some, subjugation during the mass condemnation was transient and probably strategic, and their dissent would revive depending on their milieu. On Beidahuang army farms, where rightists faced terrible working and living conditions, where they were maltreated by farm cadres, and where official efforts at ideological indoctrination were sometimes repulsive, dissent and defiance would not be surprising.

Another issue concerns how accurately dissent is portrayed in official documents – periodical reports on the ideological reformation of rightists. Official documents often distort or misrepresent the "words and deeds" of the targeted victims of a political campaign (see the case of Ge Peiqi, Chapter 1) or the "crimes and blunders" of the rivals of certain Party leaders. Those found in the archives of Beidahuang's army farms are no exception. Bearing this in mind, it is more than likely that the speech and comments of some rightists were tampered with or distorted by the farm cadres who collected them. If we consider that some material came from informants or was secretly reported by rightists who wanted to earn credits, we must admit that the risk of misrepresentation is indeed high. For instance, according to two official archival documents ("The Work Summary of the Ideological Remoulding of the Rightists in the Past One Year and Six Months" and "Report on the Thoughts of the Rightists in the Year 1960"), Huang Wu and a couple of his fellow rightists were guilty of trying to establish a "rightist kingdom" in Beidahuang to confront the people's government. It seems that this alarming charge was made purely for shock value. According to Huang Wu and a third-party narrative, these people had merely been having a casual conversation in which they joked about gathering all the country's rightists in Beidahuang to work on the farmland. This joke was distorted and reported by the rightist Pan and, in the process, was transformed into a serious political incident.[83] Clearly, the accuracy of some archival sources needs to be carefully appraised.

However, the value of these sources should not be underrated. Informants might misrepresent some of what their campmates say but not everything. Farm authorities wanted to know what rightists were really saying and doing, and they normally checked the veracity of reported information. Furthermore, some dissenting ideas were difficult to concoct. For instance, Wang Qingbin's thesis was elegantly constructed when presented to the farm leaders. His arguments concerning religious freedom and worldwide proletarian revolution, and his criticism of the monopoly of Marxism seemed to be the result of careful contemplation, and his refusal to give up his "reactionary stance" after being repeatedly condemned for it attests to his commitment to his theories. As well, Gu Ansheng's letter to Wang Zhen regarding the GLF programs on Farm 853 and Fang Zixun's letter to Farm 853 leadership regarding labour reform were both put on file. Thus, the official farm archives are indispensably valuable sources for determining the thoughts of these intellectuals, even though we need to bear in mind the issue of accuracy.

DEALING WITH RIGHTISTS: THE REMOULDING REGIMENS OF THE FARM AUTHORITIES

When Beijing rightists first arrived at the army farms in the spring of 1958, farm authorities viewed them in a largely negative light. A Farm 853 document states: "When these rightists were gathered at Shuangqiao in March, the main characteristic of their minds was grievance at being labelled rightists, and some of them even wanted to reverse their cases. Only a small number admitted to their crimes; others came to Beidahuang with their anti-Party reactionary stance already entrenched and thus had no intention to reform themselves."[84] Although the document indicates that various branch farms made "administrative and ideological efforts" to cope with this situation, it seems that little was actually accomplished. Managerial rules were loose, farm cadres treated rightists with courtesy (according to the rightist memoirs), and rightists at certain branches of Farm 853 did not work hard (at least in comparison to those on Farm 850). This situation remained unchanged until October 1958, when the belated Anti-Rightist Campaign was waged in the land reclamation regions and was quickly followed by the Rectification Movement.[85] Although, in Beidahuang, these two campaigns chiefly targeted demobilized officers, the attempt to rectify "unhealthy trends" among farm employees (such as reluctance to engage in long-term work in the borderland) also affected Beijing rightists. Discipline was tightened, workloads were escalated, rightists' complaints resulted in a higher state of alert, and rightists became more vulnerable to mass condemnation. Most important, farm leaders developed relatively sophisticated measures for dealing with and remoulding rightists.

Farm 853 Archives include a considerable number of Party documents issued in 1959 and 1960, involving curricula and strategies for ideologically reconfiguring rightists. The most important are the Farm 853 Party Committee's "Dui youpai fenzi yinian ling liugeyue gaizao de gongzuo zongjie" (The work summary of the ideological remoulding of rightists in the past one year and six months) and "1960 nian yinian lai youpai fenzi sixiang qingkuang huibao" (The report on the thoughts of rightists in the year 1960), which also cover important but scattered ideas from other documents. A number of points stand out.

First, farm authorities adopted a policy of "combining severity and leniency," which involved launching struggles against the unyielding rightists while encouraging the more submissive ones to expose and condemn the former. It also involved isolating and targeting "a small group of diehards" in an attempt to win over the majority. Most ordinary rightists were subjected to the method of "criticism and education," while "commendation and encouragement" was given to those who truly admitted their offences and accepted reform measures. Farm cadres also encouraged altercations among rightists.[86] Such policies formalized different treatments for rightists based on their state of thought and behaviour, as determined by farm authorities. The document claims that, after more than one year of reform, the majority of rightists tended to draw close to the Party organization and to express their eagerness to remould themselves through labour.

Second, farm authorities provided regular educational sessions on domestic and international affairs, especially on such topics as Party policies regarding the GLF, the long-term plan of Beidahuang, Yugoslavian revisionism, anti-rightist conservatism, and the superiority of socialism.[87] The most common measure involved a two-hour per day newspaper reading and discussion session for all rightists on the farm (though this was not guaranteed, especially during the GLF period).[88]

Third, farm authorities claimed to strengthen labour management – setting labour quotas, tightening workplace discipline, establishing rules related to performance, and institutionalizing competitions among various labour teams. The purpose was, apparently, to raise the work efficiency of the rightists and to increase crop yield. Farm cadres had allegedly found that the performance of rightists was unsatisfactory in the summer of 1958 and, specifically, that "most of the rightists in Team Six [a rightist team] dawdled over work, refused to work on the pretext of illness, or disobeyed instructions." Farm headquarters took measures to deal with these issues: branch farm leaders made decisions on labour tasks, production targets, and work discipline, and farm cadres would enforce these as well as "comparison and appraisal sessions" and would require rightists to supervise each other. Assessment methods were also formulated: "make a comparison and assessment every day, an examination once every ten days, a brief summary every month, and a comprehensive appraisal every half a year."[89] When going through comparison and assessment, participants were obliged to conduct thought examination and self-appraisal as well as to criticize others in order to build "correct attitudes towards labour reform." Such high-handed measures, according to the farm documents, brought in positive, even "amazing," results not only for that problematic rightist team – work efficiency of each rightist in weeding increased from half a *mu* to seven *mu* per day – but also "facilitated farm-wide development of healthy trends and brought down bad trends." It was said that people worked harder than before and that the amount of accomplished farmwork increased; some rightists learned a lesson and improved their performance from being unable to meet the labour quota to exceeding it. It is difficult to verify such optimistic narratives. As far as the archives reveal, however, the farm leadership was convinced that it was successful in "conducting ideological remoulding by strengthening labour administration" and that, in this way, "labour under supervision [could] be realized, and thought reform ... achieved."[90]

Fourth, farm leaders took a firm stand in dealing with "reactionary and subversive actions" such as "instigating farm workers against cadres," "spreading rumors," "undermining production," and/or refusing to work. Actually, farm cadres sought to work with the relatively docile rightists, encouraging them to disclose and condemn those rightists who formed a "reactionary backbone." According to a farm document, when half of the rightists (the document does not indicate whether it is referring to half the rightists on all of Farm 853 or only on a certain branch farm) refused to work, farm authorities decided to seize some key rightists, such as Chen Xingui and Wu Zuguang, and pitted other rightists against them until they were rendered notorious.[91] For these "die-hard reactionaries," punishment was not limited to mass condemnation but could manifest itself in instant arrest. Li Kegang was one of the victims of such excess. According to the farm document, he and his friends suggested to farm leaders that they should be allowed to form a "rightist association of self-rule," and they advocated the unity and mutual support of rightists. Li said, according to the document, that if he got a chance to leave the mainland, he would go cry in front of the Statue of Liberty and write a book about what was happening inside China. He also said that the more campaigns he experienced, the further he distanced himself from the Party.[92] Even when undergoing mass condemnation at a struggle session, Li Kegang stood firm and refused to make any self-criticism. He was immediately arrested and sent to a detention centre – a decision that, according to the document, "was applauded by all the attending rightists." It seems that such policies were successful deterrents. Whereas some, such as Wang Qingbin and Li Kegang, continued to refuse to recognize their crime, others eventually expressed repentance or, at the very least, displayed caution. Wu Zuguang, who was guilty of "poisoning others with the aid of petty economic enticements" and was thus relentlessly "rectified," privately admitted that "the Communist Party [was] really tough." Qin Zhengtang, an ex-military officer who had constantly asked to leave the farm and who refused to work, said: "The rectification here on the farm is much harsher than in the army." He began to work after being condemned as a rightist. Farm documents indicate that some "stubborn elements" began to behave properly after rectification.[93]

One of Farm 853's critical strategies was to "work with some of the key rightists who [had drawn] close to the organization and make them provide routinized or un-routinized reports." According to one document:

> [Farm authorities are aware that] it is relatively easy for these people to be familiar with the thoughts of other rightists. Therefore, we use these activist-backbone elements to help understand the rightists and push them to play roles in bringing along the middle elements and reforming the backward. However, leaders must carefully check the materials that they

report in order to be sure that they are reliable and trustworthy ... Make use of the conflicts among them, combat poison with poison, and uncover hidden problems ... All of these are good ways to keep abreast of their reactionary minds and acts. For example, when crashing the anti-Party small group headed by Zhang Dunyi in Branch 2 last year, we obtained from others' reports useful information regarding the reactionary thoughts of the group members.[94]

This paragraph indicates that farm authorities were shrewd about exploiting useful resources within the target group, taking advantage of their internal strife and manipulating their psychological need for "advancement" in order to exercise ideological control. By "encouraging the rightists to disclose and condemn the reactionaries and targeting the small group of diehards," the farm leadership seemed to know very well how to use the CCP's "divide-and-rule" tactics, although its implementation depended on farm cadres.

Along with heavy-handed measures, the farm also used "soft approaches" in dealing with rightists. Farm leaders periodically went down to labour teams and talked with rightists, trying to understand their work, life, and state of mind; answering their questions; giving edifying speeches; and pointing out the "correct direction of their progress." In addition, the farm attempted to "make use of the talent of those who behaved well" by giving them technological postings and making them schoolteachers.[95] Such soft approaches were designed to manifest leniency towards these individuals. It is not known how farm cadres actually carried out these initiatives. The memoirs of Farm 853 rightists, however, contain far fewer complaints about the managerial style of farm cadres than they do about the labour reform regimen and their living conditions.

Farm 853 leadership boasted about its success in ideologically remoulding rightists. An October 1959 document claims that, after more than one year of reform, especially after going through the Rectification Movement, "most rightists have developed deeper repentance over their offences and are willing to remould themselves and make a fresh start in life."[96] The August 1960 document states that, after waves of "reform work," the disintegration of the rightist group became obvious; more people pursued progress, and a small number of "reactionary elements" were isolated; ideological chaos came to an end, and the minds of most rightists had come round to accepting an entirely new state, all of which helped prepare them for long-term reformation and facilitated the completion of designated production targets.[97] Concrete examples from the documents include: the drop in number of those "behaving in a reactionary way" from twenty-eight in November 1959 to sixteen in August 1960; the progress of rightist Ling Ling, who, originally in the depth of despair and unable to work, "ha[d] attained high political spirit through our education and a rapidly growing work efficiency"; and the case of Liu Si: "After rectification, the gastritis of rightist Liu Si is healed; he works actively and often reports to the organization the thoughts of himself and others."[98] These stories aside, the documents offer a number of other cases in which rightists purified "their vile and foul minds," wrote confessions in their thought reports, and expressed their determination to achieve thorough ideological remoulding. A small number of "stubborn reactionaries" were forced to acknowledge their crimes. The officially optimistic tone of these documents notwithstanding, the real effects of these reform regimens are open to question. Due to pressure from cadres and the pragmatic consideration of rightists themselves, it is more than possible that some thought reports were not honestly composed but that the authorities were satisfied with the mere appearance of their having accomplished their thought work. In later years, none of the rightists on Farm 853 recalled any consequential ideological change. However, the farm authorities, or at least the authors of these farm documents, were confident that their remoulding regimens and strategies were successful.

Archival sources for Farm 850's strategies for remoulding rightists are not available to outside researchers. Local annals (*Bawuling nongchangshi*) only mention that, "in May 1959, the Political Department of the farm convened a forum attended by counter-revolutionaries, bad elements, and rightists in order to understand their trends of thought about labour reform."[99] Nevertheless, rightists' memoirs to some extent compensate for the lack of official documents.

As I have shown in the preceding section, a considerable number of Farm 850 rightists were eager for ideological renewal or at least expected to benefit spiritually from their Beidahuang experiences. With time, however, they found that their Farm 850 cadres were more interested in using them as cheap labour than in purifying their hearts and minds. Rightists did not feel that farm authorities had a systematic plan to reform them. After twelve to fourteen hours of back-breaking labour in the fields, forests, or on road construction, any form of study or reading session was an empty shell. Yin Yi recalls that, during the GLF "the repertoire of daily life was reduced to an endless cycle of working, eating, and sleeping, plus the strident morning call of a cadre. There was nothing more than that."[100] (Farm 853 had made a seemingly suitable plan – a two-hour political study session per day – but admitted that it was not assured during the GLF.) As long as the work assignments were completed, farm cadres were likely to be satisfied. At times, rightists were asked to submit "thought examination" papers (*sixiang jiancha*) discussing their ideological gain through physical labour. Furthermore, rightists needed to fill out certain self-appraisal forms to address their "progress and shortcomings." But cadres often used these materials, so painstakingly composed, as wrappers or toilet paper.[101] The much-trumpeted ideological remoulding curriculum gave way to practical considerations related to economic growth, and exalted rhetoric decayed into little more than window dressing.

On Farm 850, there was indeed some sort of reformation effort, and it often took the form of political indoctrination. Rightists discovered, however, that their spiritual and ideological renewal translated into a handful of feeble and often demeaning attempts at their being remoulded. Wu Yongliang recalls that, at times, Zhu, a farm cadre at the Yunshan Branch of Farm 850, arranged newspaper readings at breakfast in an attempt to update rightists on national politics, especially regarding the allegedly high crop yields, record-breaking nationwide steel production, and other such myths. Demobilized soldiers were brought in to give political talks to these well-schooled yet "bourgeois" elements. When some rightists expressed their doubts about the alleged high crop yield, Zhu angrily pointed out that this was a clear indication that rightists were suspicious of what could be achieved in socialist China and thus truly needed to be re-educated.[102]

The most common political lecture given by Farm 850 cadres was known as *xunhua* – "rebuking," or "dressing down." *Xunhua* normally occurred in two situations. The first situation occurred whenever cadres found that rightists had failed to finish designated work quotas or had displayed a less than positive attitude towards work. In this case, *xunhua* would be delivered, likely followed by a denial of food or the imposition of extra work hours. The language used was insulting, including phrases such as *tufei* (bandits), *chunzhu* (stupid pigs), *laomianyang* (old sheep), and *fulu* (captives).[103] The second situation occurred when camp cadres felt the need to maintain pressure on rightists. Topics would include their "bourgeois taste," their ignorance of agriculture, and their lack of physical strength. Rightists were also constantly reminded of their inferiority to "the working people" and of their need to engage in long-term labour reform.[104] Aiming to make rightists deferential and to encourage them to work harder, the *xunhua* was normally given before breakfast and at evening roll call, although it could be given at other times if deemed necessary. With *xunhua*, political lecturing was essentially reduced to reprimand, and thought reform through labour to forced labour.

This kind of political lecturing had a negative rather than a positive effect as it not only deepened the sense of humiliation and frustration among rightists but also undermined the confidence of those who truly sought a "positive experience" in Beidahuang. Often dressed down, and treated solely as forced labourers, many rightists on Farm 850 came to realize that Beidahuang was far from a refuge and that getting involved in the land reclamation project involved little more than physical and psychological punishment. As Yin Yi puts it, the maltreatment meted out in his branch made his fellow exiles realize that thought reform was little more than a veneer and that the ill-concealed reality was punishment through labour.[105]

In assessing the remoulding regimen of farm officials and the experiences of Beidahuang exiles, the relationship between rightists and their supervisory officers (farm cadres) merits discussion. Although rightists were unfairly treated and experienced hardship throughout most of their exile, their lot was to a great extent in the hands of individual cadres – that is, branch directors (*fenchang zhang*), brigade leaders (*duizhang*), and political instructors (*zhidaoyuan*), whose attitudes and managerial styles were by no means identical or uniform, but rather individual and situational, varying according to location and time. Generally speaking, the cadres on Farm 853 treated rightists in a less heavy-handed manner, though with stronger and more formal disciplinary measures, than did the cadres on Farm 850. On Farm 850, the rightists at Branches 1, 2, 4, and 5 fared better than did those at the Yunshan Branch (no rightists were assigned to Branch 3); Ding Ling on Tangyuan Farm and Ai Qing on Farm 852 received favourable treatment in comparison to those on other army farms.[106]

It is difficult to provide details about farm cadres because adequate sources are lacking. Rightist's recollections about cadres are fragmentary, dealing only with their work relations. Although some of their names are mentioned, most are not. So our picture of these people is partial at best.

Most of the cadres had to follow the directives of farm headquarters regarding how to deal with sent-down rightists, organize their work, and, in theory, help them with their thought reform. Nonetheless, they had enough leeway to manipulate arrangements so that they could favour (or disfavour) rightists regarding such issues as food, sick leave, and living conditions, or simply by taking a laissez-faire attitude towards their daily activities. At Branch 4 of Farm 850, when Nie Gannu was struggling to meet his soybean sowing quota, two farm cadres often came to help him with his work – something that deeply impressed Nie and his fellow rightists. On Farm 853, brigade leader Li Fuchun worked together with the rightists that he supervised, treated them as friends, and helped them with food supplies. When Yin Yi was transferred from the Yunshan Branch to Branch 5 of Farm 850, he was surprised by the "nearly benevolently relaxed attitude of the branch director – no work target, no rebukes, fairly good food supplies during the famine, and so on.[107] Political instructor Liu Wen at the Yunshan Branch of Farm 850 was sympathetic towards and considerate of the rightists (and was demoted as a result). Under these compassionate officers, the rightists felt respected, were deeply grateful, and were highly motivated to work, even though their workloads remained heavy and the cold wind chilled them to the bone. To some extent, these farm officers acted as a buffer between the demanding state and the disadvantaged political pariahs.

Anne Applebaum's observation on the Soviet Gulag – "Life in a camp headed by a relatively liberal boss was not the same as life in a camp led by a sadist" – seems to have been true of Beidahuang.[108] At the Yunshan Branch of Farm 850, the same group of rightists fared well or miserably, depending on their farm cadre. When the sympathetic officer Liu Wen was dismissed, their situation dramatically deteriorated under the newly appointed officers Zhu and Lu, who treated them harshly and reprimanded them frequently. They prolonged the working hours, cancelled holidays, disallowed people from talking while working, and enforced extra workloads on those who were considered less than dedicated. They not only used *xunhua* to dress down rightists but also applied physical punishment, such as denying food and rest to those who could not complete their work targets.[109] These disastrous changes were related to the Rectification Movement in the land reclamation region, but it also had to do with the individual personalities of cadres.

Rightists tried to determine why some cadres treated them so badly. In the case of cadre Lu, Yin Yi believes that, due to his "working-class" background (of which he often boasted) and long service in the People's Liberation Army, Lu's class consciousness and military indoctrination rendered him instinctively hostile towards anyone condemned by the Party. Furthermore, since he was not particularly well schooled, he looked upon the banished rightists as the pre-1949 "capitalist masters" who "exploited and oppressed" the working class. As for cadre Zhu, Wu Yongliang believes that, as a veteran soldier, Zhu had identified with those in power for so long that he was accustomed to scolding those whom he viewed as socially and politically inferior.[110] These observations offer useful lenses through which to view the mentality and behaviour of abusive farm cadres and partly explain why rightists fared better on some farms than on others (although, of course, it would be a mistake to interpret their treatment solely according to the class or military backgrounds of the cadres).

Few rightists recall how they handled their relations with the farm cadres. Perhaps they do not see this as an important aspect of their Beidahuang experience when compared to their physical and psychological sufferings, or perhaps they feel that to discuss this would be embarrassing as it would reveal how they used every means possible to alleviate their position. Many memoirists mention that some rightists tried to curry favour with farm cadres by, for instance, sending "small reports"; however, they avoid talking about themselves. An exception is Yin Yi, who courageously confesses that he seized a chance to cement relations with his political instructor. When Yin heard that this cadre wished to buy his sheepskin overcoat, he immediately offered it as a gift.[111] This anecdote reveals that some rightists, at least, realized the importance of properly handling their personal relations with farm cadres, aside from showing their political progress.

Fortunate Exiles: Ding Ling, Ai Qing, and Others

While a large number of political exiles began to face increasingly heavy workloads on the army farms, a small number of them, for various reasons, led relatively easier lives. Compared to those who laboured on Farms 850 and 853, Ding Ling fared rather well, thanks to the patronage of Minister Wang Zhen, her friend from the Yan'an period. Jonathan Spence provides a commentary on Ding's experience in post-1957 Beidahuang:

> During this period Ding Ling was assigned to duty in the chicken coops of Tang Yuan. She has recorded that she grew absorbed in the task of raising the fowl and expert at looking after the ailing chickens, some of which she nursed back to health on the heated *kang* in her own hut ... She began to take a genuine interest in the problems of developing the best methods for raising a healthy flock, and during her spare time even built models of an ideal chicken complex, using the cardboard from old toothpaste containers or any other materials she could find.[112]

With the limited sources available right after Ding's rehabilitation, Spence does a remarkable job of vividly portraying her life at the grass-roots level and her seeming ability to adapt to her surroundings. Later sources, including her 1987 memoir and the interviews with her husband, provide a more comprehensive picture of her experience. When assigned to Tangyuan Farm, Ding lived in a chicken run with her husband. Because of her health problem (osteomyelitis), she was assigned light work – selecting eggs for hatching and feeding chickens that were raised around her dormitory. At times, when her husband was sent to work on road construction during the winter, she was asked to engage in literacy programs for the benefit of the local community. Due to the patronage of Wang Zhen, she did not lack for stationery and special food and medicine during the famine years. The good relationships she enjoyed in the village actually made her hesitate to return to her job in Beijing when the opportunity arose.[113] It seems that living in Beidahuang did not bother her at all and that she was content to be a chicken run worker and to perform light physical labour. "Why should a writer not raise chickens when common people can do this?" she said: "There is nothing to complain about working in a chicken run. Why should a writer be distinguished from the commoners?"[114] In a thought report delivered in August 1960, Ding warmly extolled the effect of performing physical labour with farm workers. While condemning her own individualism of an anti-Party nature, she claimed: "The only correct pass is to thoroughly reform myself by learning from workers and peasants ... In the past two years I lived and worked with them and thus strongly felt their noble qualities – seeing labouring as duty and taking labouring as glory ... [This] is what I should learn from them. Engaging in physical labour with them, I have moved from [doing so] reluctantly to [doing so] naturally and happily."[115] For Ding, its seems, the love of labour should not only be internalized but also recognized as a virtue. Furthermore, physical labour, such as feeding chickens, provided her with the chance to integrate with, and learn from, the masses and thus cultivate a proletarian point of view. The extent to which Ding's report reveals regret for her "anti-Party crime" is hard to determine. However, due to her dedication to the idea of "labouring with the masses and treating labour as glory," it is apparent that Ding did not consider her years in Beidahuang to be a form of political banishment.

This intentional integration with the "common people" is closely related to Ding's effort to distance herself, as well as her husband Chen Ming, from other exiles. It seems that Ding and Chen did not consider themselves to be rightists as the term was generally understood. Although it is undeniable that Ding and Chen were victims of the Anti-Rightist Campaign, Chen contends that they were purged not because of their political position but because of Ding's rivalry with other leaders of the Chinese Writers Association. When interviewed, Chen insisted: "We [he and Ding] were different from those rightists; so we wished to keep our Party membership and to be treated as an inner-Party struggle." He continued: "Our situation was not the same as theirs, so we never associated ourselves with them; we went to the farms voluntarily, not in exile."[116] Ding, too, insisted that she and Chen were "true revolutionaries in dire straits" and that they suffered for different reasons than did other exiles.[117] To Ding, staying and labouring with the working class was a good way of distancing herself and Chen from those "real" rightists and to show their revolutionary commitment. With this self-aggrandizing attitude, Ding Ling (and probably Chen Ming as well) attempted to craft a different identity.

Like Ding Ling, poet Ai Qing was also fortunate in his treatment as a political exile. Due to his long-term friendship with Wang Zhen, Ai Qing received favourable treatment on Farm 852. He was appointed deputy director of a forestry centre and offered a single detached house, which was rare on the farm.[118] Together with the demobilized soldiers, Ai Qing engaged in various forms of physical work – lumber-work, raising seedlings, building barracks, and so on. For him, however, physical labour was only symbolic as his major task was to write poetry in praise of labour heroes and the success of land reclamation. A farm leader publicly commended him as "our great poet," which significantly enhanced his prestige, and he responded by making a generous donation (RMB 5,000 *yuan*) to the farm. The experiences of Ding and Ai attest to the importance of personal networking. Party writers with long revolutionary roots were still able to invoke their influence and connections to make their life easier, even while in political disgrace.

As for artists, playwrights, and professionals who did not have personal connections with important figures, their expertise did, to some extent, improve their lots. After working for several months on reservoir construction, Ding Cong, thanks to his ability to draw cartoons, was transferred to a part-time job editing a magazine entitled *Beidahuang wenyi* (Literature and art in Beidahuang). On Farm 853, in the winter of 1958, playwright Wu Zuguang succeeded in changing his fortune: he was asked to serve in an army farm art troupe writing plays in praise of land pioneers. Although these people still had to perform some physical labour, their new posts provided them with benefits other rightists could hardly dream of – better living conditions, freedom to travel to county towns, the chance to display their expertise, and, most important, better food.[119] In the difficult years, less manual labour and better food meant a greater chance of survival.

The political exiles granted favourable treatment were few in number. Of more than fourteen hundred Beijing rightists and other "problematic elements" in Beidahuang, no more than twenty were transferred to less strenuous work before December 1959.[120] For the vast majority, the only chance of leaving lives mired in hardship and starvation rested with the periodic "removal of the hat (or label)," which began in the fall of 1959. In August 1959, the CCP high leadership proposed the conditional removal of rightist labels from those who were deemed to have behaved well during labour reform, and it stipulated that the proportion of rightists to benefit from this policy was to be around 10 percent per annum.[121] When the first round of this removal project was completed on the Beidahuang army farms in 1959, only around 8 percent of rightists had their labels removed and were able to leave.[122] The rest remained there until the early 1960s, when mass starvation and deaths (see Chapter 4) forced the central authorities to remove all Beijing rightists from the borderlands.

Conclusion

The Beidahuang army farms, as newly invented border settlements accommodating various involuntary immigrants, constituted an alternative labour reform regime outside the regular PRC penal system – the camps "without walls." In the late 1950s and early 1960s, it was to these farms that more than one thousand rightists were sent down from Beijing as land reclamation labourers. Although heavy workloads were a major problem and life was hard for these people, their freedom was not as harshly restricted as was that of those interned in formal *laogai* organizations. Their attitudes towards Beidahuang varied: some wished to make Beidahuang a refuge from political pressure; others wanted to make a new start there or even achieve a degree of ideological renewal; still others were critical of the labour reform policy and resisted work arrangements. The Beijing rightists' attitudes depended on various elements – the extent to which their minds had been affected by the Anti-Rightist Campaign, what they saw, how they fared on the army farms, and so on.

Although the farm authorities formulated plans and rules for administering and remoulding the political exiles, lower-level cadres, who performed the day-to-day administration of farm life, were left with some leeway. Their actual handling of rightists was based on the political climate, the need for production, and personal style. Given these circumstances, the experiences of Beijing rightists varied considerably, depending on their location, the work requirements, the farm cadres, and their personal connections.

The experience of Beijing rightists can also be seen through three other lenses. To the CCP elite, putting these political undesirables under the supervision of demobilized soldiers was a suitable solution as it was necessary for them to receive appropriate discipline and ideological indoctrination. To the army farm authorities, rightists were seen more as a precious labour force than as faulted people who needed to be ideologically remoulded (this resulted in remoulding efforts being focused on facilitating production), and some of them resorted to political lecturing and rebukes largely as a means of getting the exiles to work harder. As for the rightists, whereas some of them simply wanted to survive and return to Beijing and be reunited with their families, many started by embracing their stay in Beidahuang as a chance to achieve "self-renewal." Their seemingly lenient treatment by the land reclamation authorities in the early stages of their banishment added to their illusion. However, when their internment became prolonged and the harshness of the conditions became manifest, rightists eventually became disillusioned and demoralized. The conflicting goals of those involved in the Beidahuang banishment resulted in both physical and mental suffering for Beijing rightists.

3

Political Offenders in Xingkaihu
Labour Camp

Starting in late 1957, many prisons and pre-trial detention centres in metropolitan Beijing saw an increasing intake of suspects of various kinds. Following the heated climate of the Anti-Rightist Campaign, the Chinese Communist Party government waged a renewed battle against counter-revolutionaries: thousands of so-called "historical counter-revolutionaries" and "active counter-revolutionaries" were arrested across the country and filled existing prison facilities to capacity. On August 3, 1957, the State Council issued "The Resolutions on Re-Education through Labour," under which various elements that were thought to want to foster political and social instability were to be sent to newly established labour re-education camps.[1] In Beijing, the Public Security Bureau heightened its crackdown by rounding up "social undesirables," street hooligans, pickpockets, and tramps who had previously not been dealt with harshly. Villagers in suburban Beijing were picked up for petty theft or vagrancy. By December 1957, the police had arrested 2,044 people in Beijing for labour re-education.[2] Prior to further disposal, all of these detainees were held in various detention centres, such as Caolanzi, Banbuqiao, and Beiyuan. Those who received term sentences were sent to prisons and nearby labour camps, such as Beijing Prison, Tongzhou Prison, and Qinghe Farm.[3] The political campaign escalated social tension and resulted in a broader crackdown and an increasing number of victims.

This large-scale arrest stressed the holding capacity of Beijing's labour reform regimes. For instance, Caolanzi Detention Centre, which was

notorious for its confinement of CCP offenders during the Guomindang
period, was terribly crowded due to new inmates: each cell held around
forty inmates, and the space in which each had to sleep was fewer than
ten inches – inmates had to lie on their sides at night rather than on their
backs.[4] According to Harry Wu, who was placed in Beiyuan Detention
Centre, the problem of crowding was still unresolved in 1960: "The *kangs*
[traditional brick sleeping platforms in north and northeast China] were
clogged with bodies. No longer did we have two feet of space, but we lay
on our sides, pressed tightly together. Twice each night the duty prisoner
gave orders for everyone to turn over, and we shifted to the other side
in a collective movement because the kang was too crowded for us to
move individually."[5] In early 1958, pressured by the fact that existing
prison facilities were unable to accommodate so many alleged opponents of the "proletarian dictatorship," Bejing's Public Security Bureau
decided to transfer a portion of the inmates (both political and criminal)
to the northeastern frontier regions, in particular to the Xingkaihu labour farm (please note that hereafter "labour farm" and "labour camp"
are used interchangeably) in Heilongjiang Province, in order to make
room for newcomers.[6]

The Xingkaihu labour farm is crucial to the study of the PRC *laogai*
regime and the phenomenon of political banishment because (1) it was
the most notorious labour reform complex established by the Beijing
police authority in the northeastern borderlands; (2) its growth was the
direct result of the mass persecutions in the late 1950s; and (3) its inmates endured tremendous suffering in its harsh physical environment.[7]
Unlike the army farms discussed in Chapter 2, Xingkaihu was an institutionalized labour reform regime, and its camp cadres seemed more "professional" than did the army farm cadres. While Xingkaihu held various
types of offenders, in this chapter I am concerned with those charged
with political offences (hereafter referred to as political prisoners, political offenders, or political inmates – all of whom, of course, are rightists or
counter-revolutionaries of one degree or another), although the real reasons for their sentencing and confinement might be far from political. In
particular, I discuss the stories of the ultra-rightists in labour re-education
branch camps and the counter-revolutionaries in labour reform branch
camps. Where relevant, I occasionally discuss other inmates of Xingkaihu
as well as political inmates in other labour camps in northeastern and
northern China.

Since few official documents or camp records relating to the political
inmates of Xingkaihu have been released, it is difficult to obtain an official

version of their work, lives, and deaths. Officially sanctioned local gazetteers and histories, such as *Gazetteer of Heilongjiang Province: The State Farms Volume*; *Gazetteer of Mishan County*; and *The History of Xingkaihu Farm*, are valuable in that they provide official farm histories – economic records (especially regarding agricultural growth), demographics, and the farm/camp structure as well as information on the efforts made to ideologically remould the inmates. Yet information on how the inmates were managed, how they laboured, lived, and died in Xingkaihu, is insufficient. However, this chapter greatly benefits from the memoirs and short recollections of former inmates – publications by Chen Fengxiao, Wu Ningkun, and Liu Naiyuan (Peter Liu) as well as unpublished manuscripts by and interviews with inmates Tan Tianrong, Han Dajun, Yin Jiliang, Ba Hong, Hui Peilin, and police officer Liu Junying. In addition, I found relevant individual recollections in *Allegorical Words* by Hu Ping, *Everlasting Beidahuang* by Huang Zhan, and *Bitter Winds* by Harry Wu.

<h2 style="text-align:center">XINGKAIHU LABOUR FARM</h2>

Xingkaihu labour farm, its name taken from nearby Lakes Xingkai (Little Xingkai Lake in the north and Great Xingkai Lake in the south), is located in the southeastern corner of Heilongjiang Province. Its geographical position ranges from E 132°35" to 133°08," N 45°02" to 45°23." In the mid-1950s, it was still a vast stretch of desolate marshland surrounded by rivers and lakes, with little trace of human habitation. During the rainy season (from April to August), when the Little Xingkai Lake frequently overflowed, this region was terribly waterlogged, with thousands of square kilometres being inundated.[8]

Geographical considerations contributed to the selection of Xingkaihu as a desirable site for a labour camp. When the massive military colonization of Heilongjiang began in the mid-1950s, the Ministry of Public Security instructed the Beijing Public Security Bureau to use heavily sentenced convicts (*zhongxingfan*) from Beijing to establish a labour farm in the Heilongjiang borderlands, the purpose of which was to both facilitate grain production and to promote convict rehabilitation.[9] The Xingkaihu area was given preference because of its geographical location, physical environment, and the state's need to confine inmates. In August 1955, with a document signed by Zhou Enlai, the premier of the People's Republic of China, the Xingkaihu labour reform complex was formally acclaimed under the official title of Xingkaihu State Farm of Heilongjiang.[10]

The administrative features of Xingkaihu differed from those of other labour camps that sprang up throughout China. From the date of its founding to January 1967, when it ceased to be a labour farm, Xingkaihu was a de facto colony of the Beijing police establishment: its inmates were customarily transported from Beijing; all Xingkaihu personnel, from police cadres and managerial staff to inmates, retained their Beijing household registration (*hukou*), used Beijing food coupons, and had their farm produce (grain, pork, poultry, and dairy) shipped to Beijing. The Beijing Public Security Bureau selected "well qualified" police cadres to run the farm, regularly sent inspection teams to screen farm work, and imposed sanctions on aberrant cadres.[11]

Xingkaihu's early development involved the intensive use of inmate labour. Infrastructure construction commenced in winter 1955, when more than two thousand convicts (former GMD soldiers labelled counter-revolutionaries, leaders of secret societies, various kinds of criminal offenders, etc.) were delivered there by train and truck. Upon arrival, these convicts were assigned to numerous projects, the purpose of which was to change the physical landscape of this area. The construction work they undertook included: (1) a main dyke to separate Little Xingkai Lake from the surrounding marshland; (2) a flood relief channel that was used to discharge flood water from Little Xingkai Lake to Great Xinkai Lake; (3) a set of drainage networks leading to the nearby Songacha River to secure land reclamation; and (4) a fifty-kilometre-long trunk canal, which was used to irrigate rice paddies.[12] These massive undertakings were accomplished by the use of spades, shovels, and picks. While official media warmly acclaimed the development of this formidable area, only limited credit was accorded to the convict labourers.[13] By early 1958, when hordes of political offenders – victims of the Anti-Rightist Campaign – arrived, the irrigation projects had been largely completed: rice, wheat, and soybean cultivation remained the major work of the camp inmates.

The years 1958 and 1959 saw a massive deportation of political offenders to Xingkaihu as well as an influx of camp cadres (police officers) to supervise them.[14] By the end of 1959, the total population (inmates, camp cadres, supporting workers, etc.) numbered 20,435; in the following year it numbered 25,694.[15] By 1960, at its peak holding capacity, Xingkaihu consisted of ten branch farms that utilized forced labour: Branches 1 to 5 were labour reform camps for sentenced convicts; Branches 6 to 8 were labour re-education camps that interned those who were punished through "administrative" sanction; Branch 9 held "resettled workers" (i.e., those who were forcibly retained in the labour reform system after the completion of their terms); and the livestock farm accommodated all female offenders. There was also an affiliated prison for those who committed new offences during the course of their term.[16] With these elaborate institutions and a few industrial enterprises (a coal mine and a paper mill) that also involved the partial use of convict labour, Xingkaihu came to be recognized as one of the most comprehensive labour reform complexes in China.

THE LABOUR REFORM FRAMEWORK AND
CATEGORIES OF POLITICAL OFFENDERS

Beginning in August 1957, when the labour re-education system was invented, the PRC's labour reform regime typically consisted of three distinct types of camps: (1) camps for "reform through labour," or "labour reform" (*laogai*), which held those who had been legally sentenced; (2) camps for "re-education through labour," or "labour re-education" (*laojiao*), which held those who had not been formally sentenced but who were subjected to "administrative discipline" by police authorities; and (3) camps for "forced job placement" (*jiuye*), which held those who had completed their sentence but were not allowed to leave the labour camps. All of these camps involved the intensive use of inmate labour and ideological indoctrination, and all are generally referred to as labour reform camps.[17] Since those incarcerated in detention centres and prisons were overwhelmingly transferred to *laogai* or *laojiao* camps and, if they were lucky enough to survive, eventually ended up in *jiuye* camps, *laogai*, *laojiao*, and *jiuye* comprised the major part of China's forced labour reform regime in the Mao era. The Xingkaihu labour farm, with its well-established facilities, interned and employed all three kinds of inmate labourers.[18] Its structure precisely embodied the characteristics of the PRC's labour reform framework.

In the 1950s, a significant portion of Xingkaihu inmates were political offenders. Although inaccurate, *Xingkaihu nongchang shi* provides useful information on the number of political offenders: "During the early period (1955–57), one-third of the convicts were counter-revolutionaries, out of more than two thousand in total."[19] Despite the massive influx from 1958 to 1960, it seems that the proportion of political offenders remained little changed. According to Yin Jiliang, a former journalist who was labelled a counter-revolutionary, throughout his five years of imprisonment there were three or four people who were sentenced for political reasons in his twelve-person squad at Branch 1.[20] Tan Tianrong, an ultra-rightist, estimates that political offenders roughly accounted for 30 per-cent of the inmates in his labour team.[21] It is unknown whether the camp authorities intentionally maintained this percentage for all labour units. If this percentage does represent the average, then Xingkaihu might have incarcerated at least six thousand political inmates at its high point in the early 1960s.[22]

Political inmates in Xingkaihu could be broken down into three cat-egories: the ultra-rightists, the historical counter-revolutionaries, and the active counter-revolutionaries.

Ultra-rightists (*jiyou pai*)

The ultra-rightists, such as Tan Tianrong from Peking University and Han Dajun from the Chinese Academy of Sciences, were sent to the labour re-education branches of Xingkaihu. They were considered to have committed serious offences – criticism of the Party and/or lack of deference to Party cadres – and they received punishment that was harsher than that meted out to rightists sent to army farms but less severe than that meted out to those sent to labour reform camps. Although they had not undergone any legal procedure and were thus free from term-sentence, police authorities still saw them as in need of discipline and they were sent to labour re-education camps. According to the "Resolution on Re-Education through Labour" promulgated by the State Council on August 3, 1957, re-education through labour was an administrative rather than a judicial penalty, and it was used to deal with various "anti-socialist elements" and those discharged by their work units. Both criteria applied to ultra-rightists who, after be-ing labelled, lost their jobs.[23] Ironically, however, they had to sign ap-plication forms before they were sent to the *laojiao* camps, indicating that they voluntarily applied for re-education through labour, as well as accede to any disciplinary arrangements demanded by the police.[24]

Historical counter-revolutionaries (*lishi fangeming* or *lifan*)

Offenders in this category mainly included those who had been em-ployed by the GMD government (which was overthrown by the CCP in 1949), those who collaborated with the Japanese and colonial govern-ments during the Japanese occupation, and those who did military ser-vice for these regimes. Ringleaders of secret societies that existed before the communist takeover were also put into this category. Relatively older than other inmates and lacking any vested interest in the New China, the *lifan* normally had little political commitment, admitted to their crimes, and were deferent towards camp authorities. Although historical counter-revolutionaries were invariably considered as class enemies, Xingkaihu camp cadres generally treated them with a degree of leniency.[25]

Active counter-revolutionaries (*xianxing fangeming* or *xianfan*)

This group received the worst treatment among political prisoners and, indeed, among prisoners as a whole. Under weighty charges such as "trying to overthrow the People's government" and/or "sabotaging socialism," they underwent formal trials, were sentenced for relatively long terms,[26] and were sent to labour reform camps. Many of the *xianfan* in Xingkaihu were young and energetic, assertive in their political opinions, and less subject to ideological influence and administrative discipline than other prisoners. For this reason, camp authorities deemed them to be the most subversive elements. As shown below, they were the prime targets of various forms of maltreatment and discrimination.

These three types of inmates constituted the majority of the political outcasts sent from Beijing to Xingkaihu.

It is often assumed that people who were put into labour reform camps had committed more serious offences than had those who were put into labour re-education camps because the former were sentenced convicts while the latter were merely subject to "administrative discipline." Accounts of Xingkaihu inmates, however, complicate this picture: some of those sent to labour reform camps under frightening political charges had not actually done anything that could be reasonably referred to as "political" or even "criminal";[27] however, given the context of the 1950s, their actions were considered offensive and were punished as political offences. Han Chuntai, a Beijing construction worker, never expressed any dissent towards state powers; rather, it was his oral reprimand of a Soviet engineer that got him sent to a Xingkaihu labour reform camp. When one day he found a Soviet giving a Chinese woman a hug in public, he was upset and scolded them both: "Shameful (*buyaolian*)!" The judges before whom he appeared found it difficult to declare him guilty of being either counter-revolutionary or rightist. Eventually, he was sentenced to fifteen-year imprisonment on the grounds of "insulting a Soviet expert and sabotaging the Sino-Soviet friendship."[28] According to Klaus Mühlhahn, due to the fact that the Party defined crime as a consciously or unconsciously rebellious act against the social order, "all crime [was] thus politicized" in socialist China and "ha[d] a political meaning."[29] During the Sino-Soviet honeymoon, particularly, Han's verbal abuse of a member of the CCP's ally unquestionably constituted a serious political issue. An interesting but perplexing contrast is that Tan Tianrong, a leading member of the student dissidents at Peking University, received no formal sentence but was instead sent to a labour re-education camp, even though he refused to acknowledge his "error."[30] What these cases imply is that the CCP's approach to assessing and punishing an offence does not always follow a clear, logical line, thus making it difficult to speculate on the severity of someone's "political offence" merely based on whether he or she was put in a labour reform camp or a labour re-education camp.

It is also misleading to assume that *laojiao* inmates in Xingkaihu necessarily fared better than did *laogai* inmates. This issue is perplexing and intriguing. Certainly, *laojiao* inmates did enjoy some institutional advantages, such as nominal suffrage, limited wages, and greater free- dom pertaining to correspondence and reading than did *laogai* inmates, who were deprived of almost everything except for basic subsistence needs.[31] Corporal punishment, common for *laogai* inmates, was rare in *laojiao* camps.

These advantages, however, could be trumped in a number of ways. First, for political offenders, being placed in *laojiao* camps brought little improvement to their lot because their political stigma as class enemies worked to their disadvantage. By contrast, the situation a penal offender faced was fundamentally different. A penal offender in a *laogai* camp, whose offence was defined as criminal rather than as political in nature, very likely fared much better than would an ultra-rightist in a *laojiao* camp. This is an indication that political status carried significant weight. Second, while a *laojiao* inmate had to endure confinement of unknown duration, a *laogai* inmate's term was fixed. As no clear, fixed term was announced for *laojiao* inmates in the 1950s and early 1960s, such a per- son could be detained as long as, or even longer than, a *laogai* inmate.[32] Whereas Yin Jiliang, an active counter-revolutionary, served a five-year term in a *laogai* branch, Tan Tianrong and Peter Liu, both ultra-rightists, were incarcerated in *laojiao* camps for eleven years. Some *laojiao* inmates even served fourteen years.[33]

The hardship that *laojiao* inmates endured was also severe. Except during the Great Leap Forward, *laogai* inmates in Xingkaihu normally worked for eight or nine hours per day, not only because their work time was formally stipulated but also because their armed escorts served on fixed shifts. However, *laojiao* inmates, who were nominally entitled to more personal freedom, were often pressured to work as long as camp cadres believed it to be necessary. This was often presented to them as an opportunity to demonstrate their commitment to labour re-education.[34] Thus, political inmates in Xingkaihu *laojiao* camps thought their lot was worse than that of the *laogai* inmates. Some, such as Han Dajun, even pleaded to work in a *laogai* camp in order to avoid the heavier workload.[35]

IDEOLOGICAL REMOULDING AT XINGKAIHU

The ideological remoulding curriculum implemented at Xingkaihu was different from, and much more sophisticated than, what we have seen on the army farms. Descriptions gathered from available sources show that indoctrination, manipulation, and coercion were artfully combined in the ideological remoulding process.

The farm history *Xingkaihu nongchang shi* provides a general account of how camp cadres attempted to administer and "educate" inmates:

> Indoctrination and remoulding of prisoners were much more difficult than changing the harsh physical environment. In addition to taking care of their [i.e., inmates'] political study, labour, and work, the administrative cadres had to pay more attention to working on their thought, educating them, cultivating their consciousness of crime, guiding them to learn work techniques, and taking care of their dining and clothing. Through correctly carrying out the Party's labour reform policy, [the cadres] impelled them to mentally struggle to "repent and make a fresh start," aroused their yearning for a bright future, and remoulded them from individuals who loved idleness and hated working into new men who could support themselves through their own labour.[36]

Sweeping and general as it is, this paragraph is the most comprehensive description in the *nongchang shi* of ideological remoulding at Xingkaihu. Although the *nongchang shi* provides seemingly touching stories of how inmates undergoing remoulding made political progress (e.g., by raising work efficiency in irrigation programs or by engaging in emergency rescues at construction sites), just how they achieved their ideological transformation is not mentioned. For the authors of the *nongchang shi*, inmates of Xingkaihu happily accepted and internalized official teachings, and their praiseworthy behaviour was the outcome of the farm's thought-remoulding regimen and a manifestation of their ideological growth: "Under the leadership of the Party, many remoulded prisoners successfully opened a new spiritual world when pioneering the natural world."[37] Read in tandem with these politically loaded records, inmate narratives help reconstruct a more tangible and complicated picture.

An important method of thought remoulding involved political study sessions. As discussed in Chapter 2, political study sessions were kept to a minimum on the army farms. But Xingkaihu, as an institutionalized labour reform unit, held these sessions on a regular basis. In the *laogai* branches, political study sessions were surprisingly well organized. The *People's Daily* and the *Heilongjiang Daily,* official newspapers, were available – or, to be accurate, were compulsory reading, as was the *Study Report (Xuexi tongbao),* an internal publication specifically for inmates. After a day of strenuous labour, *laogai* inmates would return to their barracks for the mandatory one- to two-hour study session. With at least one camp cadre in charge, the main routine involved newspaper reading by the cadre or, alternatively, by a literate inmate. Afterwards, every inmate was required to speak: whether to rephrase or to parrot materials from the newspapers, to praise the Party's policies, or to eulogize economic achievements.[38] Inmates were also required to examine their daily thoughts and work, and to criticize their "erroneous" campmates. In the words of Chen Fengxiao, camp cadres made prisoners "bite each other like mad dogs."[39] In the *laojiao* camp in which Wu Ningkun stayed: "Every three months there was a two-day political campaign supposedly designed to speed up the reform of the inmates. We would be enjoined to inform against each other and confess old crimes we had concealed or new crimes we'd recently committed."[40] After such a political session, inmates who were found guilty or who said something politically inappropriate were ordered to write a "self-examination," or self-criticism, and to swear to make improvements.[41]

The political study session, despite being a well-regulated practice, was not the major technique used for thought remoulding at Xingkaihu. As a model labour camp run directly by Beijing police authorities, Xingkaihu developed a unique set of techniques to deal with inmates. One of these involved reminding inmates of their crimes and of the benevolence of the Party. Peter Liu recalls that, when he and his fellow campmates were sent to Xingkaihu, the first thing the farm chief did was to remind them "that we Bourgeois Rightists were guilty of [a] very grave offense against the Party, the state and the people, that we were here to receive a penalty far lighter than we deserved, and that we ought to be very grateful and do our very best to reform ourselves."[42] Chen Fengxiao recalls that his political instructor earnestly reminded him that it was the Party that had provided him with the opportunity to attend school after "liberation" but that he hadn't appreciated its kindness and had committed a serious crime.[43] The purpose of these lectures was, apparently, to arouse in the inmates a "crime consciousness," to inspire their gratitude towards the Party, and to render them content with their lot.

Camp authorities also used rewards and the option of early release to incentivize inmates. They encouraged inmates to perform good deeds – including working hard, reporting the faults of others, and rescuing public property at the risk of their own lives – in order to obtain a better chance of redeeming themselves. Lured by the prospect of early release, many inmates tried to work twice as hard or rushed to participate in emergency projects (e.g., fixing embankment breaches), some losing their lives in the process. In many cases camp authorities did keep their promises. From 1956 to 1959, 244 inmates deemed to "have turned over a new leaf" were released, and 330 labour activists were rewarded by having their sentences commuted; in 1962, the sentences of 265 convicts were reduced. For those who died working on important projects or saving public properties, memorial ceremonies were given, and their families received a certain amount of compensation.[44]

For prisoners in the Mao era, however, completing their term or being released early did not mean a return to normal life; rather, they had to continue working in the labour reform complex. For this reason, an important piece of thought work was to make all inmates resign themselves and prepare for a life-long stay in Xingkaihu. An intensive propaganda program concerning the future development of Xingkaihu was incorporated into the thought remoulding regimen. Camp cadres constantly gushed about the splendid prospects of Xingkaihu: collective efforts would turn the labour farm into "a land of plenty," majestic buildings would be erected on this rich land, and so on. Inmates were told that the Great Northern Wilderness, where Xingkaihu is located, "was to be transformed into a modern city with farms, industries, schools, cinemas, hospitals and even a university, and [that they] would be its first builders and first inhabitants." A Xingkaihu University was to be established in the future, and some inmates would have the opportunity to become professors.[45] In projecting a visionary future, and covering long-term internment in a blanket of rhetoric, the cadres attempted to portray forced labour in the harsh borderlands as a pleasant experience rather than as a punishment, and perhaps this helped inmates adapt to life in the labour camps.

Such indoctrination, however, by no means played itself out without manipulation and coercion. In the eyes of camp managers, commitment to thought reform had to be manifested through hard work. As Peter Liu recalls, inmates had to obtain better treatment by being sincere in "admit[ting] their faults," and camp cadres "identified desperate physical exertion with a proof of such sincerity." Thus, pressure to perform labour was strongly felt as outright coercion. In irrigation projects, for instance, camp cadres often used assessments posted on bulletin boards as well as compulsory labour contests to put pressure on inmate workers, and those who performed poorly were singled out for condemnation. "Worksite criticism meetings" were introduced to accelerate work. Such criticism meetings "served to keep everyone strained by alternating showers of honor and humiliation. As a result, work progressed more quickly," but some inmates died of physical exertion (see Chapter 4 for more about such deaths).[46] Those who survived were forced to carry on and were even made to sing improvised work songs. Peter Liu sarcastically expresses his "admiration" for the manipulation techniques of the camp cadres, which, he believed, "succeeded in making such exertion unanimous and virtually voluntary."[47]

Like those on Farm 853, the Xingkaihu authorities vigorously encouraged mutual surveillance and secret reporting as they believed that "mutual reporting and exposing [were] instrumental in giving a new push to convicts, and thus ensuring successful fulfillment of production targets."[48] Inmates were frequently reminded to deliver secret reports to camp cadres regarding the "hidden plans" or "likely riots" of their fellow prisoners. The results seemed rather encouraging. According to *Xingkaihu nongchang shi*, for instance, forty-one potential riots were exposed and preempted in 1962.[49] Whether these riots were truly conceived or merely imagined, the strategy of "reporting and exposing" helped create a tense atmosphere in the camps and to intimidate inmates into deference.

Inmates found that, in many cases, seemingly heart-felt educational efforts were bluntly accompanied by sheer force. When Peter Liu and his fellow prisoners were about to be sent from Beijing to Xingkaihu, a camp cadre who came to escort them gave a warm speech, of which the theme was "Welcome to Lake Xingkai!" "He spoke in a very friendly tone ... so that we almost forgot that he was also an agent of the dictatorship of the proletariat." He portrayed Xingkaihu as a paradise to live and work, and claimed that "many inmates did not want to leave after they had served their terms."[50] The goal of such a speech was to make inmates feel comfortable and so to facilitate their transportation. However, when they were loaded onto a special train, prisoners were surprised to find that the

railway station was lined with soldiers whose rifles were fixed with bayonets and that the train cars contained armed soldiers. When they arrived
at Xingkaihu, on the one hand, camp authorities warmly encouraged
them to devote themselves to building a brand new farm and to treat
Xingkaihu as their second homeland, and, on the other, surrounded them
with watchtowers from which armed sentries, who were on duty round
the clock, were ready to fire on anyone who strayed beyond the poorly
marked residential area.[51] Chen Fengxiao found that one of the camp cadres conducted his thought work amiably but always had a pair of shackles
nearby.[52] Camp authorities apparently did not feel awkward playing good
cop/bad cop – the warm re-education lecture on the one hand and the
bayonets, shackles, and watchtowers on the other. No doubt they believed
that thought work would be more effective if backed up by force.

Kate Saunders likens the CCP's ideological remoulding regimen to a
"wooden knife," considering it one of the most powerful methods of human manipulation ever utilized in that it is sophisticated enough to "kill
without having the victim's blood on [the killer's] hands," to "destroy all
personal relationships and feelings," and to make victims internalize the
state's criteria for appropriate conduct.[53] Her points are supported by the
stories of those who were rendered docile, sincerely admitted their guilt
for the crimes attributed to them, became the helpers of labour camp
cadres, and even voted for the execution of their campmates. To those
who were aware of the manipulative and coercive nature of the CCP's
remoulding strategy, however, the power of the wooden knife grew blunt.
According to Wu Ningkun: "I was slow in coming to realize that the
much-flaunted thought reform was nothing but a euphemism. In the
camps, where the thin veil of euphemism was cast aside, thought reform
became synonymous with brutal forced labor and naked coercion and in-
timidation."[54] Wu does not indicate when he arrived at such an awareness
– probably after he left Xingkaihu. However, when faced with student
inmates who were equipped with spiritual commitment and unyielding
personalities, the manipulative and coercive approaches of Xingkaihu
authorities did not work well and, as I show below, suffered an almost
immediate setback.

YOUNG INTELLECTUALS: DISOBEDIENT AND DISADVANTAGED

Of the various political inmates at Xingkaihu, the young intellectuals, especially ex-university students and young teachers, were most conspicuous.

These members of the group differed sharply from other political inmates in terms of their ideological commitment and behaviour. When they were purged in 1957, many, including Chen Fengxiao and Tan Tianrong, were pursuing or had completed their university/college education, which was instrumental in their thinking independently and forming dissenting ideas. It is not wrong to categorize them as "loyal opponents" since, as discussed in Chapter 1, they aimed to rectify rather than to displace the CCP government. However, their political statements –such as "the origins of bureaucratism and the problem of social hierarchy lie precisely in the current system," "new feudalism is more dangerous than old feudalism," and "the Party committees should withdraw from universities" – were among the sharpest critiques that appeared before the Anti-Rightist Campaign and were considered fatally subversive.[55]

Compared to many other victims of the Anti-Rightist Campaign, who wisely yielded to the political storm and acknowledged their crimes, these young intellectuals courageously asserted their defiance at the start of the campaign and even after they were arrested. Some of them, such as Liu Qidi, were initially treated as ordinary rightists, but their firm defence of their position and their obstinate denial of their guilt invited extra punishment. The available sources show that, at Xingkaihu, a considerable number of them resisted camp authorities in both word and deed – something that strikingly distinguished them from other inmates. Although these young offenders generally performed the physical labour assigned to them, their attitudes towards the ideological remoulding curriculum, including formulaic political study, were negative, cynical, and scornful. This irritated camp cadres, pushing them to maltreat these people.

Nevertheless, one should not assume that defiant young intellectuals existed only in Xingkaihu or, indeed, that all young intellectuals in Xingkaihu were defiant. Some audacious figures, such as Lin Zhao and Lin Xiling, were sent elsewhere. There may have been numerous defiant intellectuals in other camps (and not-so defiant ones in Xingkaihu) who did not write memoirs and whose stories were thus lost forever. We can only draw upon the sources (memoirs/recollections, archival material, etc.) that exist for a small number of people in order to analyze their experiences.

Chen Fengxiao (1936–)

Chen Fengxiao was born into a well-to-do family in Weifang, Shandong Province. Before his arrest in September 1957, Chen was a math student at Peking University and the chief leader of the Hundred Flowers Society, a well-known student dissident society in Beijing. Due to their vigorous condemnation of the Elimination of Counter-Revolutionary Campaign, of the emerging social inequality in the PRC, and of the Stalinist purge in the Soviet Union, Chen and his fellow students were accused of forming a "counter-revolutionary group," of "trying to stage a Hungarian-style incident," and of "attempting to change the political system of the PRC."[56] Realizing that punishment was unavoidable, Chen, in July 1957, burned the list of subscribers to their flagship journal *Public Square* (*Guangchang*) and other records, thus making it impossible to implicate many of their supporters.[57] He then made a wall poster that declared:

> "The conservatives ... will put all of their talents into play to look for a so-called reactionary or a counter-revolutionary. They are now interrogating some activists of this democracy movement, forcing them to admit their so-called anti-socialist crimes in order to locate the organizers of the movement for arrest ... I am an active participant and organizer of the movement: I initiated the foundation of the Forum of Freedom, participated in the Hundred Flowers Society, and later worked on the editorial board of *Public Square* ... I know the conservatives hate me to the bone. Then, please come and pursue me! I know you will trump up charges against me through fabrication and deduction; I can take all of this, but I want you to stop torturing innocent people."[58]

Such a provocative declaration stunned many of his school friends as well as his antagonists. During a time when betraying fellow dissidents in order to escape personal punishment had become the norm, Chen displayed extraordinary courage and character. Not only did he make public his political positions, he was also willing to sacrifice himself so that his fellow activists would not be incriminated. At first, such a bold and selfless act seemed to be more powerful than any government propaganda.

There was no immediate arrest at Peking University; however, in late summer, Chen decided to flee China. Without success, he sought refuge in the Indian embassy, the British Office of the Charge d'Affaires, and the Yugoslavian embassy. He then attempted to sneak onto a foreign cargo ship at the port of Tianjin in order to go abroad. He was arrested immediately and, in April 1958, was sentenced to a fifteen-year prison term for his counter-revolutionary treason. After months of imprisonment in Beijing, Chen was sent to a *laogai* camp in Xingkaihu.[59]

Like other convicts, Chen was assigned to a variety of tasks – digging trenches, building roads, planting rice, hoeing weeds, and so on. Due to the severe food shortages and crushing workload from 1959 to 1961,

Chen became so worn out that he was not sure that he could survive his term. Frequently witnessing the deaths of his fellow campmates added to his desperation and grievances.[60] Although he eventually survived, physical abuse was a lasting marker of his experience in Xingkaihu. With his untamable temperament, he spoke defiantly before camp cadres, openly satirized the concept of ideological remoulding, and refused to show appreciation for the Party's "benevolence." He talked with other political prisoners at will, seemingly without fear of punishment, and he even used a secret code to write down his reflections on sensitive political issues (such as the Sino-Soviet split, which was forbidden to discuss in Xingkaihu).[61] As the result of his obstinacy and unruly behaviour, he was often beaten and hung up, sometimes with twenty-four kilograms (forty-eight *jin*) of shackles on his feet, and sometimes he was badly burned with cigarettes or tied up and left outdoors in the cold wind. He was time and again handcuffed and placed alone in a small concrete cell. When camp guards executed condemned prisoners, he was often hauled out to the execution ground to witness this horror.[62] The aim of such abuse was to inflict both physical pain and psychological terror in an attempt to crush his spirit. It is likely that even the most tolerant camp cadres were annoyed to find that, in a camp in which most others behaved themselves, this skinny little student inmate was so irrepressible.

Ironically, Xingkaihu provided Chen with the ability to sharpen his theoretical teeth. During 1962–63, when his physical afflictions were gradually eased, Chen managed to read a fair number of newspaper articles and Marxist classics (the only reading allowed at the *laogai* camp). He re-examined some of Marx's premises, such as his theory of social change and his critique of capitalism; he also reflected upon the social reality of the PRC and the ideological confrontation between the Soviet Communist Party and the CCP in the early 1960s. He made careful note of his reflections in his diary – something that led to another bout of physical abuse when this was seized.[63] As a result of his political studies his dissent became even stronger (see below). Upon the completion of his term in 1972, Chen was transferred to a "forced job placement" camp as a resettled worker until 1979, when he was fully rehabilitated.

Tan Tianrong (1935-)

The story of Tan Tianrong shows how, in a labour camp, a student inmate could encounter discrimination for his/her intellectual independence and political critique of official ideology. He stood out in 1950s China as a talented physics student and as an ardent critic of Mao's deviation from orthodox Marxism, of the bureaucratization of the CCP, and of the flaws in the worldwide communist movement.[64] He firmly stood his ideological ground by declining and even mocking all condemnation, admonition, and other kinds of so-called help from university Party leaders, the Communist Youth League (of which he was then a member), his schoolmates, and so-called progressive professors. He borrowed lines from *The Internationale* – "This is the final struggle. Let us group together, and tomorrow the Internationale will be the human race" – to underline his stance, which was considered both arrogant and presumptuous.[65] Mao branded Tan as "the ringleader of rightist students," and thus he became a top student rightist in China and was subsequently demonized. Adding to Tan's enigmatic persona is the story that he, cognizant of his imminent arrest, chose to wait for the police in his dormitory, making good use of his time by conducting physics research. He was formally arrested in November 1958.[66]

In Xingkaihu, Tan was highly taciturn. Even though he treated the labour assigned to him with scholarly seriousness, he was so closely watched by camp cadres that it was difficult for him to communicate with others. His campmates preferred to stay away from him in order to avoid the constant surveillance. What distinguished Tan from other political inmates in the labour re-education camp was his unremitting pursuit of academic interests once he realized that his political endeavours had failed. He collected all the science texts he could find and quietly conducted research on quantum mechanics and mathematical logic whenever he had the chance – during hard-earned breaks or when blizzards made outdoor labour impossible.[67]

Tan also read Marxist classics such as *The Selected Works of Marx and Engels,* compiled by the CCP's Central Compilation and Translation Bureau. However, his careful reflection upon Marxism inspired him, giving him the tools to contest the political indoctrination of the labour camp and thus undermining the CCP's ideological remoulding agenda. In early 1963, official media claimed that the low prices of vegetables in the domestic markets was an indication of the people's good life under socialism. In a political study session, Tan argued that, on the contrary, this was the precise cause of the poverty suffered by the Chinese peasantry under a state-planned economy. Camp cadres considered his argument to be offensive, and his passionate self-defence incurred ruthless attacks not only by camp cadres but also by fellow campmates.[68] Deeply abhorred by the camp cadres, Tan was several times classified as an "anti-reform element" (*fangaizao fenzi*) and was subsequently punished with an extended period of confinement. In 1969, when he finally completed his eleven years of labour re-education, Tan was sent back to his home village in Hunan to perform "labour under mass surveillance" and was able to spend relatively peaceful years with his mother and his rustic fellow villagers.[69]

We find a striking similarity between Tan and Chen with regard to their ideological growth at Xingkaihu. If we consider their criticism of the CCP in 1957 as loyal opposition, their experiences in Xingkaihu, including their access to officially allowed materials, ironically facilitated their further alienation from the Party, from its doctrines, and from the myth of Chinese socialism. This put them on the path to becoming true dissidents. Tan's stories show how, as a young intellectual, he used Marxist concepts to critically analyze China under the CCP. Chen's ideological experience is even more revealing. He recalls: "Before I was sent to Xingkaihu as a counter-revolutionary, I had never suspected the socialist system itself but believed that socialism was superior to capitalism because it had eliminated exploitation ... But after contemplating newspapers and engaging in political studies in Xingkaihu, I grew to doubt Chinese socialism itself."[70] Chen specified that, between 1962 and 1965, he developed deep suspicions about the Marxist theory of social change, the Marxist analysis of social conflict under capitalism, and the alleged superiority of socialism: "I arrived at the conclusion that the propaganda in current newspapers was largely deceiving." He continued: "Although I was not entirely sure that Marxism was wrong in theory, I guessed it was unlikely to be a universal truth that could be applied to the whole world, or perhaps Lenin and Mao had twisted Marxist principles."[71] The ideological renewal he underwent in Xingkaihu made Chen an avowed critic of the CCP upon his rehabilitation. So, although ideological remoulding transformed many of these young intellectuals, it was often not in the direction desired by the Party.

Aside from Chen Fengxiao and Tan Tianrong, young inmates who defied camp authorities included Xuan Shouzhi, Gu Xiangqian, and Liu Qidi. Xuan, a graduate of Qinghua University, kept refusing to work regardless to which of Xingkaihu's branch farms he was sent, so he was put in solitary confinement – an experience that eventually crippled him. Gu, a former lecturer at the Beijing Film Academy, refused to admit the error of his ways and was thus repeatedly insulted. He maintained a hunger strike for a week and finally died in a camp cell.[72]

Liu Qidi was persecuted in both 1955 and 1957 for his ardent defence of literary critic Hu Feng and for his criticism of the repressive nature of the Elimination of Counter-Revolutionaries Campaign. His well-known saying "the world is on the verge of total darkness" and his speaking tours at various university campuses resulted in his being a renowned figure among students. In addition to his political criticisms, Liu, together with others, planned to penetrate the army and munitions factories in order to win supporters.[73] Eventually, Liu was sentenced to fifteen years. When sent to Xingkaihu in 1961, he was suffering from pneumonia and often coughed up blood. Due to his obstinate refusal to admit his crime, along with his defiance of the cadres, Liu was often hung up and beaten. After numerous bouts of torture, he collapsed and was finally driven insane. He was put in a solitary confinement cell, where he finally died after having been denied medical treatment.[74]

The stories recounted so far show that, unlike other labour camps in the 1950s and 1960s, Xingkaihu was distinct for the resistance, defiance, and protests of its political inmates.[75] Of course, not all political inmates at Xingkaihu spoke up and defied the cadres. Having suffered relentless attacks prior to being sent to Xingkaihu, many political inmates mentally collapsed. The accusations against them were frightening, the camp cadres powerful, and the physical labour daunting, all of which made them realize that direct confrontation with camp authorities would only result in further trouble – physical abuse, withholding of food, and extra workloads. Further, a labour camp was not the place to assert one's spiritual integrity, and, if they were to survive, inmates had to learn to come to get along with camp cadres. For these reasons, many political inmates tried to avoid coming into direct conflict with camp authorities, despite their profound grievances. Inmates such as Peter Liu, Wu Ningkun, and Yin Jiliang all adopted a strategy of "silence and endurance" so as to avoid trouble. When they argued for equal shares of food and shorter work hours, for instance, they tried to reason with camp cadres rather than to recklessly confront them.[76]

WORK AND LIFE IN XINGKAIHU

Xingkaihu inmates faced many types of strenuous manual work. Upon arrival, they cut the grass and weeds to clear a space to build accommodations, and they collected ice and snow for cooking and drinking.[77] During the winter, when temperatures dropped to minus thirty degrees Celsius or below, inmates on construction projects had to work very fast as it was too cold to stay idle. In early spring, with very little proper equipment, workers had to stand in icy mud to dig trenches or to level ground.[78] Work targets had to be fulfilled: those who failed to do so suffered not only at the hands of camp cadres but also from duty prisoners and other inmates. In Xingkaihu, as in other labour camps, work was assigned collectively according to the number of inmates in a given team. If an individual could not finish his share, this adversely affected the team. Camp cadres would blame duty prisoners, who, in turn, would personally or through other prisoners visit misfortune upon the individual who had displeased them.[79]

As previously indicated, the inmates in Xingkaihu were closely watched. The *laogai* inmates lived in guarded compounds encircled with electrical wire entanglements and watchtowers at each corner. The fields they worked were marked by string and little red flags. Anyone who ventured beyond the marked picket lines could be shot on the spot, and with the full authority of the law, by the People's Liberation Army guards who escorted them. Xiu Min, a campmate of Chen Fengxiao, was shot in the arm because he slightly crossed the marked line.[80] The living quarters of the *laojiao* inmates were marked by a large ring of sparsely placed wooden posts that were not connected with wire. A fellow inmate of Peter Liu was shot dead for accidentally crossing this unclear boundary at night.[81] Camp authorities refused to apologize or provide compensation as the victim was considered to have been a likely escapee.

Reading was allowed but restricted. The *laojiao* inmates enjoyed more freedom to read than did the *laogai* inmates: they could read science and technology texts as well as Chinese and foreign literature. Wu Ningkun recalls that he could read Shakespeare and the classical Chinese poet Du Fu, and recite them along with other literary campmates. Han Dajun could read texts on agricultural mechanics and even shared them with an inquisitive camp cadre. For the *laojiao* inmates, conducting research was also possible. Tan Tianrong could conduct physics research as long as he did well with his physical labour; Benjamin Lee, a camp doctor who graduated from a Rockefeller-funded medical college in Beijing, was able to research various concentration-camp diseases.[82] In comparison, *laogai* inmates could only read Marxist and Maoist texts along with official newspapers such as the *People's Daily* and the *Heilongjiang Daily*. Chen Fengxiao was initially allowed to bring a box of books, including math texts in Russian, a Bible, and several English literature masterpieces. When he arrived at Xingkaihu, however, all of these books were seized by the camp authorities and, several years later, were burned.[83]

At times, severe weather conditions in the borderland provided Xingkaihu inmates with time to relax. When blizzards raged and outdoor work was impossible, inmates were relegated to their barracks, and the camp head office "art and education troupe" would come over to provide entertainment (e.g., theatrical items or movies that eulogized the changes the Party had brought to the borderland) as a part of Xingkaihu's general education programs. In addition, right after busy seasons such as spring sowing, inmates might be given a short break, during which they played chess, walked within the compound, performed tai chi, or chatted among themselves.[84] So there were momentary lulls in the harshness of camp life.

Correspondence was allowed, with certain conditions. As a sign of the Party's benevolence, Xingkaihu inmates were permitted to write to their families once a month, but these letters were censored by camp cadres. As Peter Liu recounts:

> All our correspondence was under strict censorship. All incoming mails for us from our families were opened before they were distributed to the recipients, and all letters we wrote to our dear ones were submitted, stamped but unsealed, to the police officers who sent them out after examining their contents.[85]

Such censored mail had little to say about the real situation in the camp, but it did deliver comforting messages. Wu Ningkun recalls: "I told my wife I was getting along fine and there was nothing for her to worry about; she reassured me she and the two children were getting along fine and there was nothing for me to worry about." White lies brought seeming consolation to the couple but no true relief. For *laojiao* inmates, censorship was abolished for a time: "We ventured to give a few more details in our letters, but soon were told that censorship had been reinstated. No one bothered to explain why it was brought back."[86]

During the famine years, no one could describe hardship and hunger or request food in their correspondence. When Yin Jiliang wished to tell his mother in Beijing that he wanted some biscuits, he wrote: "Do you often visit Yili [the name of a food product factory]?" in order to get his request past the censors.[87]

ESCAPE AND PENALTY

Because of its harsh environment, offenders considered Xingkaihu to be a formidable place. Many convicts flinched at its name and likened being sent there to a death sentence. In the Beiyuan Detention Centre, Cong Weixi recounts, a rumour of possible banishment to Xingkaihu generated a gust of panic among detainees.[88] When their fates were sealed and they were destined for Xingkaihu, some tried to escape during the journey. When around five thousand convicts were on their way to Xingkaihu in April 1959, seven plotted a collective escape. The scheme failed, and four of the organizers were executed.[89]

Once having arrived at Xingkaihu, inmates found it difficult to escape due to the grim geographical and ecological environment. All of its branch camps were isolated from the interior and were surrounded by rivers, lakes, and hundreds of square kilometres of marshland, which would consume anyone who got lost in it during the wet season, even if he or she managed to escape the heavily guarded camp. Inmates fleeing to the wilderness during the winter could expect certain death during unpredictable blizzards. The only possible way out of Xingkaihu was through a human-made embankment guarded by PLA soldiers. Some tried, but none succeeded.[90] Some would-be escapees hoped to cross the border to the Soviet Union, which faced Xingkaihu across the shallow Songacha River. During the Sino-Soviet honeymoon, all escapees fleeing from Xingkaihu to the Soviet Union were sent back, and some were then executed.[91] The Sino-Soviet split brought a degree of hope to prisoners who desperately wanted to leave. A *laogai* inmate, Wang Xingbai, was one of those who successfully crossed the Songacha River. As a former Russian language instructor, Wang was at first treated with courtesy by the Russian border guards and sent to Moscow, but he was eventually extradited to China and paid for his adventure with a death sentence with a two-year reprieve. As far as Chen Fengxiao was aware, the majority of returned escapees were sentenced to execution or a death sentence with reprieve for committing the counter-revolutionary treason of attempting to escape.[92]

It would appear that escape from labour camps in inner Manchuria brought lighter punishment than was the case for escape from borderland labour camps: the former normally brought an extension of one's sentence and physical abuse rather than the death penalty. During his fifteen-year imprisonment in three prison camps (Tiebei Prison, Jinqianpu Labour Camp, and Zhennai Labour Farm) in Jilin Province, student inmate Hu Xianzhong tried to escape four times. Each attempt resulted in severe physical abuse, including being starved, being beaten, and being hung in the infamous position known as "Su Qin carries a sword on his back" (i.e., being handcuffed with one arm turned over the shoulder and the other twisted up from below). For his second escape, he had an extra three years added to his term. But he was never given the death penalty or death sentence with reprieve.[93] It seems that borderland labour camps received more attention than did interior camps and that the penalty for jail-breakers was more severe.

POLITICAL OFFENDERS VERSUS CRIMINAL OFFENDERS

One of the characteristics of Xingkaihu, and, indeed, of the entire prison system in Mao's China, was the practice of placing political offenders among criminal offenders in order to use the latter to monitor the former. As noted earlier, political offenders were those accused of political offences, while criminal offenders were those accused of such offences as murder, fraud, robbery, and rape.[94] Unlike in GMD prisons, where prisoners were locked up according to the nature of their offences, in CCP labour camps political prisoners were distributed to various units to prevent them from gathering and fomenting collective action. In Xingkaihu, political prisoners comprised no more than one-third of the entire inmate population. Peter Liu recalls that, in his labour team, non-political inmates included those who committed "larceny, hooliganism, corruption, murder and the like, the majority being thieves or pickpockets who had been enjailed before, and some were experienced jailbirds."[95] Yin Jiliang's team included, among others, those who were convicted of "sexual misconduct" such as sexual assault, rape, homosexuality, and/or adultery.[96] Although these offences were abhorred by the general public, the state saw them as less than threatening to the existing order. For instance, in a speech he delivered in February 1957, Mao identified "two different types of contradictions" within Chinese society: the one between the CCP (as the voice of the "working classes") and anti-socialist reactionaries, and the one between the ranks of the "people." For Mao, the former amounted to a fundamental political divergence and thus needed to be solved by dictatorship and suppression; the latter involved non-political problems and thus could be handled through "democratic centralism." Mao argued that offenders who committed larceny, fraud, murder, and hooliganism were certainly in need of punishment but that this should differ in nature from that meted out to reactionaries.[97]

With this political line having been drawn, the treatment of different categories of offenders differed significantly in both theory and practice. Political offenders were nicknamed "external contradictions," or "extercons," the class antagonists, while criminal offenders were nick-named "internal contradictions," or "intercons," the people among "ourselves." This was the biggest reason that criminal offenders received favourable treatment in labour camps. This official demarcation is echoed by the research of Aminda Smith: in the early 1950s, the CCP government initiated massive "consciousness-raising" programs for the Lumpenproletariat (petty thieves, beggars, and prostitutes), pushing them to reform themselves and to identify class enemies by whom they had been victimized. Although the result was mediocre at best – many persisted with their petty crimes and ended up being sent to labour camps – these as-yet-unreformed elements were spared being designated enemies of the state and, to this extent at least, were favoured.[98] With regard to Xingkaihu, Peter Liu got the strong impression that camp cadres had an "intrinsic hatred for Bourgeois Rightists while being more friendly to the intercons," and Chen Fengxiao recalls that some cadres explicitly emphasized the superiority of criminal offenders over political ones and encouraged the former to help watch the latter.[99] According to Liu, there was another reason the intercons received favour: "[They] were witty, deft in manual labor, thoroughly familiar with prison life, [and] never missed the chance of gaining benefit and pandering to the whims of the guards. They were vastly superior to us in working skill and experience and knew how to impress the work-point recorder."[100] Consequently, camp cadres were inclined towards using intercons as leaders of inmate squads or as cell bosses, whose responsibilities included watching, reporting on, and disciplining the extercons. The state and its agents intentionally facilitated the division between those who had committed political offences and those who had committed penal offences, using the latter to help with camp management.

Some political prisoners felt insulted to be placed alongside criminal convicts. As Yin Jiliang puts it: "We were irritated by being put among these criminals. As intellectuals, scientists, and writers punished for political errors, we felt deeply humiliated being forced to stay with those people."[101] This reveals Yin's sense of being morally superior to criminal inmates. Although some political offenders, such as Tan Tianrong, did not mind being placed among criminal offenders (probably because Tan was satisfied with being allowed to conduct research in the camp and was deeply absorbed in doing so), others held them in considerable contempt. Staying with them in the same cell, hearing their coarse language and street lingo, and daily witnessing their "unsanitary" habits were all unbearable for most political prisoners, many of whom considered themselves among the "civilized" social elite. Chen Fengxiao concealed his distaste for a penal convict who was locked with him in the same solitary confinement cell, but he struggled to physically avoid him.[102]

In the meantime, for their part, criminal offenders were not sympathetic towards the ultra-rightists or the active counter-revolutionaries not only because of their political stain (repeatedly mentioned by camp cadres) but also because of their aloofness, "mysophobia," and inability to carve out a better niche in the camps. Yin Jiliang remembers that only when less-schooled criminal inmates begged political inmates to help write confessions or letters home did they receive a degree of respect. Tan Tianrong recalls that a young hooligan was once trying to find fault with him and shouted: "You arch rightist; it will serve you right if you are beaten to death!"[103] Mühlhahn notes the splits, frictions, and prejudices that existed between criminal prisoners (to whom he refers as those "belonging to the people") and educated political prisoners (the so-called enemies of the people). He also notes that "criminal convicts enjoyed a higher prestige in prison because of their working-class background," while the enemies of the people, although well educated, were, within the *laogai* system, relegated "to the lowest status in the camp."[104] It is important, however, to be aware that the low status of the educated political convicts in Mao's China was not a result of their education but, rather, of the nature of their alleged offences. Uneducated criminals who had committed serious offences could also be charged as "counter-revolutionary murderers" or "counter-revolutionary arsonists," thus placing them within the ranks of enemies of the people. And, of course, educated elites could also be guilty of criminal acts or, if considered politically progressive, be incorporated into not only the rank of "the people" but even that of "revolutionary cadre."

Given the invisible wall erected between the political offender and the criminal offender, the ultra-rightists and active counter-revolutionaries often drew close to each other in Xingkaihu, especially when they shared similar experiences, education levels, and tastes. Wu Ningkun found that he had much to talk about with other ultra-rightists in his labour team. They talked about literature, their school years, their adversities, and so on. When delving into Chinese novels and classics, they sometimes forgot their fatigue and sorrow, and sometimes "forgot even where [they] were." According to Wu: "We poured out our heart to each other."[105] Such pleasant personal relationships were rarely found between the ultra-rightists and penal inmates. While there was a marked socio-psychological cleavage among Xingkaihu inmates, it is not surprising that ultra-rightists, as an in-group, had an affinity for one another.

This uneasy relationship not only prevented these two groups from forging any sense of collective identity but also provided camp authorities with the opportunity to strengthen their administrative control. In addition to appointing criminal inmates as cell bosses, camp cadres often incited criminal inmates to physically abuse political inmates. Yin Jiliang recalls that, if cadres found a political prisoner difficult to render docile, they would hint that the duty prisoner and his henchmen should find an excuse to beat him.[106] This practice went well beyond Xingkaihu. Hu Xianzhong, who was detained in several labour camps in Jilin Province, recalls that, when criminal offenders committed acts of violence against their political counterparts, the camp police intervened only if the victim was badly injured.[107] By encouraging the maltreatment of one group of prisoners by another, labour camp authorities were able to further their own ends: driving fear into the hearts of political prisoners who dared to be disobedient, giving criminal prisoners a sense of being people among "ourselves," and thus maintaining control over both groups.

However, not all political prisoners took the insults and bullying of the criminals: some fought back. One such prisoner was Chen Fengxiao, a native of Shandong Province, where the Water Margin tradition and the martial arts culture were strong.[108] One day, when a ruffian repeatedly troubled him at the worksite, Chen erupted and ferociously chopped him down to the ground with a spade. This resulted in Chen's being sent to a solitary confinement cell for three months. Since he had been regarded as a physically and mentally weak student, his attack to some extent readjusted the relationship between the political and criminal prisoners in his squad.[109] By and large, however, it was not easy to change the low status of intellectuals in Xingkaihu. In addition to their political blot, of which criminal prisoners could take advantage, hooliganism was rampant in Xingkaihu (as in other Chinese labour camps), and those who were less aggressive were particularly victimized by it. Intellectuals who were physically weak or who lacked the nerve to resort to violence were easy targets. It was commonplace for them to be robbed of food and physically bullied. Li, a leading horticulturist in 1950s China, frequently had his food stolen by the hooligans in his squad. Indignant, he tried to defend his food and even to rob others of theirs, but he always lost out.[110]

We need to be aware of the intricacy of the relationship between political and criminal prisoners. As mentioned, sometimes, when they needed help writing confessions or letters home, criminal prisoners had to curry favour with political prisoners. At times, political inmates felt that they could benefit from the life experience and skills of criminals inmates as they found that the latter were clever when it came to dealing with camp cadres and handling the hardships of daily camp life. Thus, when their interests were not in direct conflict, the persecuted intellectuals could learn and receive help from the criminals. Both Chen Fengxiao and Yin Jiliang recall that some warm-hearted criminal prisoners advised them on how to pretend to work hard in front of the camp cadres, how to save energy, and how to look for edible herbs during the famine years.[111]

In some cases, in terms of their behaviour, ethics, and philosophy, criminal prisoners exerted an unexpected influence upon political prisoners. One of the most revealing examples of this comes from Harry Wu, a Qinghe inmate in northern China. During his twenty years of internment, Wu considered criminal prisoner Xing to be the first real mentor in his life. A poverty-stricken peasant, Xing had roamed around the province and had done whatever he could to support himself before being sent to a labour re-education camp, where he befriended Wu. Xing advised Wu to take care of himself first and foremost. His motto, which deeply impressed Wu, was "in this place the strongest one is the best one." Xing also insisted that people were justified in doing whatever they could to survive and that stealing was "a small thing, not important, not a big deal at all."[112] At first, Wu could not accept Xing's indifference to principle and scruple. Gradually, however, his disapproval gave way to admiration: "I grew to admire him as the most capable and influential teacher of my life." He even came to believe that Xing was actually far more intelligent than he himself in that Xing knew more about how to survive in the camp: "To survive in the camps, I needed new skills and different attitudes."[113] Under the influence of a criminal prisoner, Wu began to embrace new values and to justify whatever means were necessary to ensure his survival. Wu confesses that he "had learned how to steal, how to protect [him]self, and finally how to fight." He even sometimes grabbed food from one of his fellow prisoners, beating him in order to do so. When a camp cadre asked him to serve as class record keeper, Wu jumped at the chance to write down everything his fellow prisoners said in order to earn an extra half cornbread at every meal. He felt comfortable in engaging in the type of behaviour that he would never have considered before. He admits, ironically, that this "new ethic of survival" was the most important result of his labour re-education.[114]

These stories paint a grim and ironic picture: inmates of different kinds were put together in Mao's labour camps to enable the labour reform regime to maintain effective control. Political inmates suffered not only from camp cadres but also from criminal inmates who assumed a superior political status and were more able to adapt to camp life. In the meantime, however, criminal inmates influenced their political counterparts in a unique way by teaching them how to handle their relations with camp cadres and how to maximize their material gains. They also shared their street ethics with them. Given the circumstances and the need to survive, some political inmates abandoned their former principles and scruples, and acted out of convenience and necessity. Their former ideas about integrity, dignity, and self-discipline gave way to the simple and basic need to survive.

CONCLUSION

In the 1950s and 1960s, Xingkaihu stood out as one of the most notorious labour reform regimes in the PRC, used to detain and to remould various offenders and social undesirables, including those victimized by the Anti-Rightist Campaign. In the name of offender rehabilitation and frontier reclamation, this labour reform complex became a testing ground for the state's ability to exert its ideological and physical control over people of various walks of life. Some of the most avowed critics of the government – university students, scientists, teachers, and so forth – spent years receiving labour reform or labour re-education in this desolate camp, where their lives were haplessly squandered. Placed under the close surveillance of camp cadres and discriminated against by criminals inmates, Xingkaihu's political inmates suffered experiences that typify those of persecuted intellectuals throughout the labour camps of the early PRC.

In this chapter, I examined the general experiences of Xingkaihu political inmates – their daily work and life; their frustration and resistance; the ideological remoulding techniques used by camp officials; the relations among camp officials, political inmates, and criminal inmates; as well as the structure and administrative features of the Xingkaihu labour reform complex. I argued that the inmates placed in labour re-education camps under administrative sanctions had not necessarily committed less serious offences than had those sentenced to labour reform camps and that the former did not necessarily fare better than did the latter. Student inmates received the worst treatment in Xingkaihu due to their defiance of camp authorities, their ideological commitment, and their courage in airing their opinions. Xingkaihu camp cadres skilfully employed a combination of indoctrination, manipulation, and coercion to carry out their ideological remoulding curriculum, in addition to using various rewards to incentivize inmates, make them work hard, and curb their behaviour. The transformative power of the remoulding regimen was generally effective, if occasionally compromised by the defiance of student inmates.

4
Life and Death in Beidahuang

"Hey, look yonder," Liu exclaimed, pointing to the east, "the shining Ussuri River, a vast expanse of whiteness. And further east ... that will probably be the dwelling place of the laomaozi *(Russians). Did you ever imagine that you, an old cadre, would end up here, in such primeval forests of Wanda Mountain, as a lumber worker?"*

"Yes, I did." I said ... "I was born in the Yangzi-Huaihe Plain, where there are no mountains or forests at all. So I liked to read about the mountains in the Northeast ... People portray the forests here like heaven – peaceful, quiet, bathed in sunlight, with birds singing and flowers blossoming. You could lie down on the soft grass anywhere you please and enjoy the warmth of the sun, with walnuts and mushrooms within arm's reach. In reality though, that is not the real world for us ... Just look at that hanging tree over there – with a gust of wind, it might fall down and crush you ... In lumber work, the very moment of felling a tree is exactly when one's life hangs in the balance."

—Huang Wu

Huang Wu, a writer and English literature translator who went through three years of "labour under supervision," reveals the sharp duality of Beidahuang – a lovely, vibrant world that nonetheless threatened death. As the natural beauty and vitality of this place wrapped the forsaken exiles in its seemingly serene embrace, many wished to immerse themselves in their fascinating new surroundings. Banishment to

Beidahuang did not spell the end of the world; rather, the exiles searched for something meaningful, positive, and consolatory. Their transient relief and consolation, however, were quickly dissolved due to the forced labour they had to perform and to the difficult working and living conditions they had to face. For the exiles, the various challenges to their survival were real and perceivable: death, grim and unpredictable, could descend at any time.

In this chapter, I examine some of the most bitter and unforgettable experiences of political inmates in both the Beidahuang army farms and the Xingkaihu labour reform complex, including heavy workloads, hunger, death, physical abuse, and suicide. These were the central themes of existence in Beidahuang between 1958 and 1962. While recognizing that there were some positive experiences, the bulk of this chapter focuses on what was carved into the memories of the political exiles (both army farm rightists and Xingkaihu inmates) – physical suffering and torment, death, dehumanization, and the subsequent distortion of human behaviour. I also suggest that, although the root cause of this misery was the Chinese Communist Party's labour reform policy, lower-level politics (i.e., the political and practical considerations of the camp/farm authorities) significantly contributed to it.

THE CALM BEFORE THE STORM

During the exiles' early stay in Beidahuang (approximately from the spring of 1958 to the spring of 1959), their lives did not seem unbearable. As they were offered relatively sufficient food, their basic needs for subsistence were ensured. Whereas the ultra-rightists and counter-revolutionaries in Xingkaihu were subjected to strict physical control, the situation of those sent to the army farms was more flexible, especially before the Anti-Rightist Campaign reached the army farms. Some exiles nursed grievances related to being sent from Beijing to Beidahuang, but they still saw a lovely world and, during the early stages, portrayed life in the Great Northern Wilderness in a positive light. Liu Meng recalls:

When I first arrived at Farm 850, I did not feel very badly, probably because I was young and energetic. I was surprised that the plain here in the northeast was really vast, and it took me an hour or so to reach the other end of the wheat field when I worked on an old-fashioned sowing machine. That's really fantastic. I had a feeling that I was being embraced by the vast sky and the earth.[1]

Although, in his memoir, Liu is sharply critical of the CCP policy of frontier banishment, he does not conceal his pleasure in the landscape of Beidahuang and his happiness when working there.

Dai Huang offers an even more positive description of his early experience on Farm 850.

What made us most excited was the spring there ... The blue sky, white clouds and wild flowers on the lush plains set each other off beautifully ... The plain itself was really an impressive sight back then. Almost every sunny morning, there would be a mirage in the eastern sky lasting for about half an hour – land, forest, houses, lakes, wagons ... everything was in it. One morning after a rain when we were allowed to take a day off, many of us walked along a trail all the way down to the edge of the forest. Listening to the twittering of birds, we collected various kinds of flowers and took them back.[2]

This kind of narrative reflects the exiles' passable lives and their satisfaction with the early stages of banishment and, indeed, stands in stark contrast to the miserable experiences of later years. During work breaks, as mentioned in Chapter 2, Beijing rightists were allowed many pastimes, such as painting, singing, playing musical instruments, practising Peking opera, or playing bridge. The rightists at the Yunshan Branch of Farm 850 even had time to build a flower nursery close to their residences.[3] Huang Wu, of Farm 853, at times enjoyed reading his favourite poet, Walt Whitman, and tried to imagine the linkage between his life as a lumber worker in Beidahuang and the imagery reflected in Whitman's poems.[4]

For some exiles, a passable life went hand in hand with a commitment to manual labour. Detailed analysis of this is provided in Chapter 5, but a couple of examples show that the inmates' devotion to manual labour mirrored their belief in the meaningful nature of that work. The early experiences of the rightists at Farm 853 are partly illustrated in Chen Ming's letter to his wife Ding Ling. As Ding Ling recalls:

[Chen] described floating snow in April as a picturesque scene, and he presented their work – lumbering in the snow, drilling wells, melting ice into cooking water, and building barracks – as being full of meaning. The

vast wilderness and the undulating mountains of Beidahuang were captivating to them. He and his friends were actually waging a war to transform
heaven and earth.[5]

Viewing his manual labour from a romantic perspective, Chen Ming
even suggested that Ding Ling come and join him, with little concern
about her physical fitness. Dai Huang, too, describes how the banished
rightists gained happiness through their back-breaking work and tried to
create some significance out of it. He writes: "In the field, people worked
cheerfully while in the sky cuckoos, larks, turtledoves, and quails sang
when flying, all of which constituted a wonderful scene of transforming
heaven and earth."[6] The inmates' positive attitudes towards, and even aes-
thetic perspective of, their labour reflect their satisfaction with their lives
and their ability to adapt to the conditions of their banishment. It seems
that, at least for some political exiles, distress, sadness, and a sense of loss
were temporarily forgotten and the nature of forced labour blurred.

From the recollections of political exiles, however, we find that their
pleasant memories of their time in Beidahuang – their appreciation of
the scenery, times of relaxation, belief in the meaningfulness of their
work, and so on – are related to specific factors: the early phase of banishment, sufficient food supplies, friendly farm cadres (for instance, Liu
Wen on Farm 850 and Li Fuchun on Farm 853), and so on. When these
factors changed – that is, when their banishment was prolonged, when
their sympathetic officers were replaced by unsympathetic ones, when
their workload became unbearable and food shortages frequent – their
memories of Beidahuang turn gloomy, and their descriptions of work
and life become narratives of resentment and suffering.

Death by Labour

Beginning in 1959, the intensive use of forced labour in Beidahuang
caused immense hardship for the exiles, and this was further compounded by food shortages. The escalation of this situation resulted in the un-
timely death of many exiles.

The banishment of political offenders coincided with the economic
adventure on the part of the People's Republic of China – the Great
Leap Forward of 1958–60. In Beidahuang, the GLF meant an ambitious
plan for land reclamation and high grain production targets,[7] which, in
turn, led to heavy workloads for exiles and a high number of deaths from

physical exhaustion both on army farms and in the Xingkaihu labour reform complex. One of the main reasons for this was the farm/camp cadres' belief that crop yield would rise proportionally with labour input. According to Peter Liu, in an irrigation project, all of the inmates were driven by camp cadres and were pressured by blackboard assessments of their achievements. Gan, a lean, pale inmate in his late forties, was so pressed and mocked for his slowness that he could barely take a breath without fear of being left behind. After several days of desperate physical exertion, Gan was found dead one night.[8]

Chen Fengxiao offers a bleak picture of death through hard labour at Xingkaihu's Branch 4:

> During more than forty days of spring sowing in 1960, the rain went on and on. In order not to miss the sowing season, all the convicts were herded to the field, raking and sowing in the rain with a mere patch of plastic to shield their bodies. We got up at three o'clock in the morning and went back after eight at night, terribly overwhelmed by the workload and cold. On a horrible day, several weak convicts fell down on the road back from work. They were taken back to the barrack, and died soon thereafter. Rather than dying of disease, they were actually worked to death.[9]

Mass death due to excessive forced labour occurred on army farms as well. On October 13, 1960, around one hundred hunger-stricken rightists at the Yunshan Branch of Farm 850 were herded out for a snowy day of intensive soybeans harvest, from which, after a whole day of ceaseless work, seven died on the road back. The absence of timely rescue also contributed to these deaths.[10]

Accidental death was not uncommon when exiles were ordered to perform unfamiliar work. During winter lumbering, inmates frequently suffered injury and death – being smashed by falling trees due to the difficulty of properly handling manual lumbering tools and being forced to work extra hours at night. In Huang Wu's lumber team, which consisted of fifty-six rightists, two were killed by falling trees and one was badly injured during the winter of 1958–59.[11] Dai Huang recalls that four of approximately one hundred campmates died of lumber-related accidents that winter.[12]

While the root cause of these casualties was the oppressive nature of state policy, which required inmates to perform manual labour with which they were unfamiliar, the indifference of camp/farm authorities towards human life was a contributing factor. When camp authorities set unrealistic work targets (e.g., the compulsory lumbering target on Farm 853 was eight cubic metres per person per day) and forced exiles to meet them regardless of their health or the time required, death was inevitable. Furthermore, camp authorities often failed to provide timely rescues. The tragic death of the seven rightists at the Yunshan Branch of Farm 850 on October 13, 1960, was, to a great extent, due to the farm cadres' refusal to send a rescue team at night on the grounds that the next day's work was "not to be affected." They did not even bother to call for a doctor to save those who were half-dead.[13] Rightists soon realized that their lives were less important than were those of draft animals.

Both in Xingkaihu and on the army farms, cases of death and injury were handled perfunctorily. The dead in Xingkaihu normally did not receive proper mourning, and bodies would be buried before families were notified. If maimed, inmates were to continue working in their barracks after having been treated, doing lighter work such as weaving baskets or straw ropes.[14] There is no indication that mourning ceremonies were performed on army farms. Wu Yongliang recalls that, when one of his friends died lumbering, his team leader (a cadre) refuted other rightists' request for a ceremony: "Chairman Mao told us that death for revolutionary work is perfectly normal; thus there is no need to make a fuss."[15] There were exceptions in Xingkaihu, however. If inmates died saving public property, they might be honoured with some ceremony and their families would receive consolation money.[16]

Deaths from overwork and the indifference of cadres, though astonishing, are less striking than are those from other forms of adversity. Starvation, disease, and/or lack of medical care were more fatal and more fundamental to the loss of human life in Beidahuang than anything else. During the years from 1959 to 1962, in particular, when the physically drained labourers were struck by prolonged food shortages, it was not only the old and the weak but also the able-bodied who fell.

HUNGER AND STARVATION

To many of the Beidahuang exiles, hunger was probably their most unforgettable experience, and mention of this topic unfailingly returns them to that time of fear. Since there was no uniform food rationing for either army farm rightists or prison camp rightists in the 1950s, the real food supply could vary depending on time and location and, thus, was subject to the manipulation of camp and farm authorities. Since their banishment coincided with the three successive years of famine caused by the GLF, their lot, as the outcasts of society, was particularly miserable.

During most of the 1950s, it seems, hunger was not the major problem for political offenders in certain detention centres and prisons if they obeyed the rules. Wu Yue and Chen Fengxiao remember that detainees received sufficient food in the Caolanzi detention centre in Beijing, and before October 1958 there was no limit on the staple food supply, although vegetables were meagre.[17] Certain "important prisoners," such as ex-high-ranking Party officials, were even served lavish amounts of food (by prison standards) – "four dishes and one soup." Pan Hannian, the ex-deputy mayor of Shanghai, for instance, even enjoyed milk, eggs, tea, and high-grade cigarettes when he served his sentence at Tuanhe Laogai Farm before the Cultural Revolution.[18]

During their early stay in Beidahuang, neither the rightists on army farms nor the inmates in Xingkaihu felt threatened by food shortages. This was due to the nationwide bumper harvest and to the fact that camp and farm authorities had to ensure that exiles were fit enough to carry out heavy workloads. "Upon arrival at the farm," recalls Liu Meng, "rightist labourers were allowed to eat as much as they could because the farm needed strong land reclamation workers," although some complained about having to eat coarse food such as corn gruel.[19] The situation was similar for inmates of Xingkaihu. Wu Ningkun recalls: "Food was much improved over that at the detention center in Beijing. The standard staple was still corn flour, but of edible quality. On a day of rest or a satellite-launching day, we would be fed rice or steamed bread made of wheat flour, along with vegetables that we had grown and fish we had caught. Later on, we raised pigs, and there was even a little pork."[20]

Beginning in the early summer of 1959, however, hunger quietly crept in. On Farm 850, Dai Huang recalls: "Grain rations began to be set and rapidly dropped, from 72 jin to 63 jin, and later, 54 jin, 48 jin, 40 jin monthly [1 jin is equal to 1.1023 pounds]. Our stomachs became increasingly empty." During the worst year, 1960, a rightist worker on Farm 853 had only an eight jin ration of grain per month.[21] Wu Yongliang recalls that the feeling of hunger became increasingly acute in the second half of 1959, although grain supplies were then at least somewhat replenished by vegetables.[22] As time passed, however, exiles had to rely solely on limited grains for nutrition and saw nary a trace of meat or dietary oil; their meagre daily rations, in the form of hardtack corn buns supplemented with watery vegetable soup, hardly alleviated their hunger pangs. Clearly, their diet was thus far from sufficient for subsistence.[23]

A noticeable phenomenon was that there seemed to be no uniform food rationing policy in the Xingkaihu labour reform complex, and inmates found that food rations varied considerably among the different branch farms. According to Han Dajun, who was transferred to three branches in 1960, grain rations per person were 60 *jin* corn flour monthly at Branch 2, 45 *jin* at Branch 8, but only 30 *jin* at Branch 7. Chen Fengxiao recalls that, at Branch 4, where he stayed, the grain ration was 30 *jin* on average.[24] The implication of this difference is that the heads of the various branch camps had considerable autonomy when it came to deciding upon grain rationing, and, consequently, the hunger inmates suffered varied noticeably.[25]

Philip Williams and Yenna Wu agree that the PRC's rationing of food to *laogai* inmates exerted more effective control over prisoners than did any other form of torture.[26] This argument may be tested both in general and in the context of Beidahuang. On the one hand, the CCP's food rationing policy may not have been consciously designed to inflict suffering upon class enemies as research does not reveal any evidence of official directives to this effect, besides which, the CCP leadership repeatedly spoke of displaying "revolutionary humanitarianism" towards prisoners. On the other hand, however, we see that lower-level CCP leaders – that is, camp/farm authorities – did manipulate food rationing for their own purposes. There are at least three manifestations of this. First, when an inmate behaved defiantly, camp cadres would punish her or him with food restrictions (e.g., as with Chen Fengxiao and Liu Qidi).[27] Second, food allocation was implemented according to the physical strength of an inmate and how much work he or she achieved. Both Chen Fengxiao and Peter Liu indicate that cereal rationing at their branches was decided by camp cadres who divided inmates into various grades: stronger inmates and duty prisoners got more food than others.[28]

Third, camp authorities reduced food rations for inmates and other farm workers (e.g., immigrant farmers recruited from the interior provinces) in order to be able to submit more grain to the granaries of higher authorities. In other words, low and decreasing food supplies were not necessarily the result of any grain shortage in this agricultural region. Farm barns were full of grain, according to Han Dajun and Yin Jiliang, who once worked to load them; Wu Ningkun also recalls that "the [Xingkaihu] farm reaped a bumper harvest of corn, rice, wheat and soybean in 1960, thanks to the good weather, the humus, and the slave labour."[29] A similar testimonial is offered by a *laogai* inmate in Hailun, another labour farm in Beidahuang. According to him, Hailun Farm did not see any crop failure from 1959 to 1961: "1961 [especially] was a year of pretty good harvest. Combine harvesters went back and forth in the golden fields of wheat, and hundreds of trucks raced to big national granaries with full loads of grain ... Later on, however, it was announced that the daily grain ration per worker would be reduced to 7 *liang* (350 grams)."[30]

Frank Dikötter's description of grain and rationing helps to provide a context within which to understand Beidahuang: while all of the cities in China were rationing grain during the famine, barns in many places where people were starving to death were full of grain and even plagued with insects and rats. The Chinese government increased its exports of grain in order to make a profit and to honour its foreign obligations; its allies, such as Albania, received large amounts of grain for free. Party officials, from the village all the way up to the province, tried to outdo each other in pledging greater and greater grain submissions.[31] When looking at Beidahuang labour camps, it makes perfect sense to draw a parallel between local Party secretaries and camp cadres as the reason the latter were so determined to submit more grain was their desire to show their devotion to the state and thus to earn political credit. Liu, the director of Xingkaihu's Branch 7, was notorious for cutting down on inmate food supply but was praised by the Party committee for his success in "economizing" grains.[32]

The recollections of individual inmates are echoed in official sources. First, when ordinary workers, including rightists, were rationed a starvation diet of eight *jin* per month, Farm 853 leaders voluntarily turned over significant amounts of grains to higher authorities, twice in 1960 (5 million *jin* the first time and 630,000 the second). For this, the Ministry of Land Reclamation commended farm leaders for their "853 revolutionary spirit."[33] Once its reputation was established, a farm would receive more demands for grain submission from higher levels. In May 1962, Minister Wang Zhen was still writing directly to the leaders of Farm 853, asking them to submit more grain and beans and to surpass the required target of eleven thousand tons.[34] Second, *Xingkaihu nongchang shi* clearly shows that the grain and soybeans harvested in 1959, 1961, and 1962 were far more than were used to feed farm workers, including inmates.[35] Supplying more grain to state granaries during a time of national famine was a particularly appreciated form of political activism on the part of camp leaders, but it exacerbated the food shortages for those under their charge.

The starvation suffered by Beidahuang inmates can also be seen through another lens. On the one hand, low food supply must be understood within the context of overall food shortages in China between

1959 and 1961, and the cut in food supply institutionally applied to almost everyone in Beidahuang, from farm leaders to ordinary labourers, from camp cadres to inmates. On the other hand, leaders and cadres always had ways to manipulate matters for their own benefit. The recollections of Chen Fengxiao, Yin Jiliang, and Peter Liu all indicate that the food shortage was less of a problem for Xingkaihu camp cadres than it was for inmates. This was not only because cadres did not have to perform heavy labour, as did inmates, but also because they were able to obtain extra-institutional supplies through, for instance, manipulating inmates' actual food supplies to increase their own and purchasing food through personal networks. On the army farms, cadres did not eat in the dining halls, as did ordinary workers, but in "small kitchens" reserved just for them.[36] How much extra benefit they enjoyed was not known to inmates, but the fact that none of the farm or camp cadres was reported to have died of starvation is telling. An official document of the Party committee of the Mudanjiang Land Reclamation Bureau shows that it was not uncommon for cadres to appropriate grain rationed to farm labours: "Some cadres abused their power to acquire extra rice and wheat flour, and those directly managing farm kitchens lived a pretty good life ... all of which resulted in serious consequences."[37] The self-serving behaviour of farm/camp cadres co-existed with, and exacerbated, the hunger suffered by inmates.

Overwhelmed by hunger, the inmates both on the army farms and in Xingkaihu made every effort to search for food. It seems that the vast fields of Beidahuang offered a variety of wild food. Whenever they had the chance, inmates would rummage through the fields for anything edible – wild herbs, grasses, plant roots, raw crops, and so on – and they even searched rat holes for caches of grain stored underground.[38] When nothing was found on the ground, famished people foraged through the trees. In the winter of 1960, at the Yunshan Branch of Farm 850, the bark of all the elm trees was peeled off and eaten.[39] Tree leaves were ground into flour, which was blended with powdered plant stalks and stems, chaff, nut cores, and seeds as food substitutes.

Small animals and wild species became targets of the hunt for food. Williams and Wu note that Mao-era prisoners often ate field mice, crickets, locusts, toads, grasshoppers, insect larvae, and so on.[40] In the case of Beidahuang, exiles focused on field rats and snakes, which were abundant in the wilderness. Many exiles regularly dug up the ground to catch field rats, which, for many, became a normal dietary fixture and an important source of nutrition. Yin Jiliang, Dai Huang, Liu Meng, and Yin Yi have many recollections of devouring field rats.[41] In their hunger, people also tried "to entice snakes out of their lairs" to add to their diet. Tang Zunwen, a former opera performer, was well known among his fellow rightists on Farm 853 for his technique of capturing snakes with which to treat his friends: "At times in that summer he went out to the riverside and came back with a couple of snakes. He took out their poison gland (in the case of venomous snakes), washed them, cut them into pieces, and cooked them in an iron barrel with a bit of salt to make tasty snake soup ... Even those who hated snake could not help but come and try."[42] During the years of famine, when meat and cooking oil were lacking, wild animals became precious foodstuff for this exile community.

After having been subjected to prolonged starvation, exiles, though alive, looked scarcely human. Dai Huang recalls that, due to the lack of nutrition, "people in [his] team became either badly emaciated or terribly swollen, depending on which stage of edema they were in."[43] When Peter Liu chanced to look at himself in a mirror, he was startled to see a literal skeleton that he simply could not identity as himself: "By early 1962, I was reduced to 90 pounds, about half of my former body weight, literally a bag of bones."[44] When Harry Wu, himself a *laojiao* inmate, first met the inmates transferred from Xingkaihu to Qinghe Labour Farm in 1962, he was astonished: "The brow bones above their eyes protruded under tightly stretched skin. Their mouths hung slightly open below hollowed cheeks. Their gaunt necks seemed unnaturally long."[45]

Obsessed with food, the exiles scarcely behaved as humans. In Beidahuang, political inmates learned to steal, rob, and fight for food. All too often, they were reduced to stealing raw grains – rice, wheat, beans, and tubers – from the fields. Chen Fengxiao's recollection is one of countless examples:

> During the fall harvest of this year (1960), it was very common that con-
> victs in Xingkaihu stole raw rice ... We pulled grains off rice ears, scrubbed
> them in our palms, blew away the shell, and chewed them slowly before
> swallowing to avoid appendicitis. I stole rice too. Many of us also snuck
> raw rice back to dormitories and ate [it] at night.[46]

Ralph Thaxton describes a practice known as *chiqing*, literally trans-
lated as "eating the green crops," which was popular throughout China's great famine years: countless rural people went to the collective fields and ate the green standing crops (wheat, corn, vegetables, etc.) before they were harvested. With *chiqing*, "they got 50 to 90 percent of their food

supply" during the throes of famine. Thaxton considers this to be "the most effective of all of the hidden forms of popular resistance to the run-away state procurement" as it allowed millions of half-starved villagers to survive the GLF famine. Given the large number of people who ate the green crops, it is clear that "this practice often had the tacit approval, and even support, of some of the local brigade leaders in villages."[47]

However, when engaging in *chiqing*, as well as in gorging on various wild plants and herbs, one ran the risk of being poisoned. In March 1961, Farm 853 reported to the Mudanjiang Land Reclamation Bureau that a famished farm worker had devoured raw corn and had died afterwards. Upon hearing this, the bureau issued a directive forbidding any farm workers under its jurisdiction from eating raw crops and wild plants.[48] This was understandably hard to enforce when dealing with half-crazed people who could think of nothing but their stomachs. *Xingkaihu nongchang shi* admits that accidental deaths due to the eating of poisonous wild herbs were frequent. According to Chen Fengxiao, thirteen convicts at Xingkaihu's Branch 4 died as a result of eating poisonous wild herbs in the spring of 1960.[49]

With their stomachs ruling their minds, rightists set aside any sense of shame. Some snuck into farm kitchens to steal corn bread, vegetables, or soup. At the Yunshan Branch of Farm 850, when food went missing from the kitchens it was not possible for farm cadres to discover the "thief" (assuming he or she was not caught on the spot) since there was no way anyone would confess.[50] Some, in extreme hunger, stole food from their campmates. Yin Yi himself had the experience of having the biscuits sent from his family stolen by his campmate.[51] "Of ten rightists, nine were thieves," according to Liu Meng: "If you are too shy to swipe something to eat in those circumstances, it would bring you sure death." Liu Meng confesses that he once stole a bottle of honey that his friends had entrusted him to deliver. On Farm 853, a certain Geng was found to have engaged in petty pilfering on seventy-three occasions over two years.[52] On army farms, the penalty for being caught thieving was merely a harsh scolding, but in Xingkaihu, it could be solitary confinement, as in the case of Ren Hongsuo.[53] Li Chao, a former university lecturer, snuck out at night to eat pigswill, for which he was publicly rebuked by a camp cadre as being "less than a pig."[54] It was difficult for exiles, including pro-fessors, scientists, and writers who had been accustomed to being regard-ed as role models, to retain moral integrity and self-esteem when driven by extreme hunger and instinct for survival. Their experiences, like those of people during the Holocaust, confirm the idea that those who suffer atrocious abuse will often be driven to previously unimaginable acts.

Williams and Wu note that, when they were desperately hungry, well-educated Chinese inmates fought for food.[55] As far as Beidahuang exiles were concerned, this phenomenon was certainly a result of long-term malnourishment, but it was also related to two other facts: (1) the social esteem of intellectuals, built in the imperial and the republic periods, had been badly shattered by political campaigns under the CCP, and (2) those who were physically weak had no choice but to fight for a means of subsistence. As Yin Jiliang recalls:

> My friend Mr. Li was one of the most prestigious horticulturists in China, but in Xingkaihu he did not display any self-respect at all. He often fought with other inmates just for a little bit of gruel left at the bottom of the barrel. He was always on the losing side in the end as he was very thin. One day, when he was in charge of distributing vegetable soup, he kept for himself a bit more. As a result, he was beaten black and blue.[56]

Obsessed with food, intellectuals put aside their sense of shame and feelings of prestige. Rightists on Farm 850 even physically fought to keep vigil over the dead in order to earn one extra corn bread.[57]

Rightists frequently wrote to their families and relatives for food. Dai Huang, Yin Yi, and Yin Jiliang all recall that they or their campmates secretly obtained food in this way and that those without families stole from others. A Farm 853 document notes: "Since the spring [of 1960] rightists in these three teams frequently obtained food from home ... Du Xianhao once received 5 or 6 jin of parched wheat flour. When asked by a cadre, he said this was medication for preventing edema. Even the poorest rightists wrote home for biscuits." The document deemed asking for food from one's relatives a sign of "seeking ease and comfort, and indulging in the decadent bourgeois lifestyle."[58] For this reason, such behaviour was condemnable.

It is worth noting that those who were not fully engaged in manual labour suffered less from hunger than did those who were so engaged. Ding Cong and Wu Zuguang, who were asked to work part-time at a local magazine and in an art troupe did not suffer as did Dai Huang and Yin Yi. Similarly, some Xingkaihu *laojiao* inmates do not remember being hungry. For example, being assigned to work in a "cultural and education troupe" (*wenjiao dui*) and thus being free from manual labour, ex-movie director Ba Hong admitted: "I did not suffer starvation or edema, nor did my friends in the *wenjiao dui*."[59] Hui Peilin, a female *laojiao* on Xingkaihu's "wild animal-raising team," recalls that around one hundred female inmates in her unit had no set food ration and that they even had fish, chicken, and fresh vegetables to eat. This was because her team director treated female inmates well.[60] It seems clear that the nature of one's work and the personality of one's cadres made a difference to one's life as an inmate.

It should also be noted that, while lowering the food supply, the authorities of both Beidahuang army farms and the Xingkaihu labour camp complex tried to keep starvation to a minimum. In some units, the workday was reduced to six hours in the winter of 1960, and the compulsory work quota was cancelled when farm/camp authorities found that inmates were being seriously weakened by hunger.[61] Authorities also promoted the consumption of various food substitutes (*daishipin*) to counteract the effects of food shortages. In September 1960, the Mudanjiang Land reclamation Bureau, the top army farm authority in Beidahuang, issued a directive requiring the use of corn stalks, sorghum stalks, bean stalks, wheat straw, oat straw, corncobs, acorns, grass seeds, and tree leaves as food substitutes.[62] In Xingkaihu, the camp kitchens provided inmates with food substitutes made of ground raw rice and raw corn mixed with powered corncobs and chaff. The camp and farm authorities also promoted "double steam baking," a cooking technique that involves steaming buns made of wheat, corn, or sorghum twice in order to add more bulk and to give one's stomach a fuller feeling.[63]

Exiles saw some relief methods, however, as opportunities for self-profiteering. Farm 850 kitchens, for instance, sometimes sold farm workers fried flour balls made of buckwheat as well as mixtures of soy flour with a bit of sugar for a much higher price than was normally charged.[64] This shows that, while regular rations were cut down, farm kitchens and (likely) farm authorities were making money from what was saved, thus confirming exiles' suspicion that the labour farms were not lacking in grain but, rather, that farm authorities were manipulating its use.

All of these measures, however, provided no more than temporary relief in the context of the massive human-made famine. With stringent food rations and a system of forced labour in place, hunger continued to overwhelm the inmates of Beidahuang. Death, the ultimate result of starvation and its related diseases, eventually overtook the exiles, including political exiles.

DEATH AND THE DEATH WATCH

Malnutrition, which was at the root of the mass deaths in the work farms/camps, manifested itself first in the form of disease, particularly edema (or dropsy). In Beidahuang, countless exiles died of edema, the typical symptoms of which are described by Yin Yi and Wu Yongliang:

> Starvation leads to emaciation. When it goes to the extreme, people will get swollen, starting from the feet and legs, and then slowly moving up. Finally one's face turns round and swollen. People at first merely take this as a symptom of a disease, rather than the prelude of death.[65]
>
> All the team members had edema without exception. A slight press would lead to a pit on the leg, and many had swollen faces that looked like they were growing fat. I belonged to the kind who got swollen in both the legs and face.[66]

This approximates the situation of many of the Beidahuang exiles as almost all their memoirs provide more or less similar accounts of edema. The first rightist to die of starvation-induced edema on Farm 850 was Tang Wenyi, who, in June 1960, perished on the road after a fruitless search for food. At the time, his legs were seriously swollen.[67] In his work *Jiusi yisheng* (A narrow escape from death), Dai Huang describes how six fellow rightists died of edema within a month in the fall of 1960. Some died on the road searching for food, and some died at night after work.[68] It was common that an edema-stricken inmate who had worked in the fields one day would be found dead in bed the next morning.

In Xingkaihu, aside from edema, inmates also died of diseases such as tuberculosis, fever, and dysentery, often the side effects of extended malnutrition compounded by a lack of medical care. In Xingkaihu, one or two camp doctors, who were often inmates themselves, were responsible for the medical care of approximately two thousand inmates in each branch camp. Although they were helpful and saved lives, as shown by Peter Liu and Wu Ningkun, in many cases they could not provide effective medical treatment simply because they lacked the personnel as well as such basic medicines as Aspirin. Mo Guixin, a patriotic singer who returned to his homeland from the United States in 1951 to serve the New China, died of dysentery.[69] Han Dajun recalls: "In the summer of 1959, our whole residence compound was infested with flies and serious enteritis spread. The only doctor in our branch did nothing to help us since there was no suitable medicine at all. Probably more than one-third died in that epidemic."[70] With malnourishment and a lack of adequate medical care, diseases like dysentery were fatal. And once seriously weakened by hunger, inmates' bodies grew increasingly susceptible to various diseases.

Yin Jiliang provides a gloomy account of his own experience at Xingkaihu's Branch 1:

> During the winter of 1961, agricultural work was rather light due to food shortages. We got up at 9:00 AM and went to bed at 3:00 PM to save energy. Two meals a day ... During that winter I fainted several times. Once was in December, when I fell down on the road back from the fields. I woke up to find myself in the mortuary. My mind was clear but I could not move or say anything. I heard later that, on that day, twelve of us fell unconscious, and only I came around.[71]

Wenche He'en, who was interned on Xiangride labour farm in Qinghai Province, recalls that, when in a state of unconsciousness, he was almost buried alive. His fall from the body transportation cart wakened him, at which point he let the corpse disposal men know that he was not dead.[72]

Paul Cohen, when discussing the experience of violent death during the Boxer Rebellion, argues that, "because of death's unique properties as the terminator and terminus of life, the fear and apprehension surrounding it are key to the formation of biographical consciousness."[73] So far, however, it seems that few inmates of Chinese labour camps (at Beidahuang or elsewhere) have discussed their near-death experiences. Perhaps those who survived the years of the great famine and then managed to live long enough to write their memoirs had not undergone the unusual experience of drawing close to death and then unexpectedly coming around. Or perhaps, once entering the phase of deep unconsciousness, few were fortunate enough to be awakened before being buried.

Watching their campmates perish was heartbreaking for many exiles. In October 1960, Luo Xiangcheng, a thin, sick rightist who was denied food by his team leader due to his inability to work, died on Farm 850. He was one of six of Dai Huang's campmates who died within one month.

> I fed Luo half of my lunch and carried him home on my back in the blizzard. But soon I found that I was so weak that my legs could not stop trembling ... It was impossible for the two of us to return to our barracks together. Luo said to me: "Leave me behind, Lao Dai, just go and save

yourself." Nobody was around, so I put Luo by a heap of soybean stalks, covered him with pods and stumbled to a barracks nearby for help … When we came back with lunch and a cart, Luo had lost consciousness, with his eyes closed and his lips blue … Three days afterward Luo died.[74]

Seeing the lives of many friends snuffed out so needlessly, one after the other, Dai Huang was for a long time deeply traumatized – such scenes haunted his dreams even after he was supposedly rehabilitated. Chen Fengxiao, until very recently, often had nightmares about how Liu Qidi was bloodily tortured and squeezed into a solitary confinement cell.[75]

To political exiles, corpse disposal – being asked to bury their campmates – was also a sad experience:

> The bodies of the seven dead were bound together with a single thick rope, put onto a cart, and then sent to the Yunshan foothill[s]. No body bags were available for them, let alone coffins … It was freezing cold and the blizzard was raging. Those sent to bury the dead had no strength to dig graves at all … Finally they found a place of natural depression, put in the bodies all together, and piled on them a hill of snow. That way a grave mound was made for the seven dead. No mourning ceremony, no wreaths … When leaving halfway and looking back to the grave mound, they found only the swirling snow and howling wind that swept the white hill.[76]

One can certainly understand the sadness that ex-inmates would feel over the deaths of their campmates – over watching them die and burying them. These heart-wrenching moments are clearly presented. However, it is not clear whether their sense of sadness was not stronger at the moment they composed these scenes in their memoirs than it was when the events depicted actually occurred. During the actual events, it is quite possible that the distress of the inmates was such that they became numb and so were unable to fully feel sadness. When death became a daily occurrence, inmates often became insensitive to the deaths of their campmates. According to Yin Jiliang: "In those years people died like flies, so I was used to death. When burying my campmates one after another that winter, I hardly had any feeling – no sadness."[77] Harry Wu recalls his mental state when his fellow campmate Chen, who was bedding next to him, was dying: "I felt nothing. My heart had grown cold, and my tears would not flow … No one in the room showed any interest in Chen's death."[78] On the army farms and in Xingkaihu, where inmates were tormented by an array of afflictions, where death had become normal, and where the boundary between life and death was so easily crossed, few inmates paused to contemplate the significance of such tragedies.

During the famine years, the dead were unlikely to be buried in a timely fashion. If inmates died in the winter, authorities of some branches of Xingkaihu did not bother to make arrangements for a prompt burial, partly because it was too difficult to dig graves in the frozen ground and partly because the Heilongjiang borderland functioned as an enormous freezer. In theses circumstances, camp directors would arrange to have corpses piled up outside to be naturally frozen.

> When the number of frozen, stick-like corpses reached the thirties or forties, they were to be sent by carts to the wilderness for disposal. The frozen ground was so hard that it could not be dug up with spades or picks, and so explosives were used. After a big pit had been blasted, the corpse carts would draw close. When the carts were tilted and the bars pulled out, all of the bodies would be summarily dumped into the pit.[79]

Some camp directors, who foresaw deaths in the upcoming winter, would prepare as many grave pits as possible in the warmer seasons. Ba Hong and his fellow campmates spent several weeks digging grave pits on the Sun Mound (*taiyang gang*).[80] A daily quota of three pits was set for each worker on his team.

Definitive death records regarding Xingkaihu inmates are lacking since neither police establishments in Beijing nor Xingkaihu authorities are willing to disclose such information. *Xingkaihu nongchang shi* documents in detail the natural calamities and difficulties that the camp confronted, including the amount of crops destroyed, financial deficits, and even the death toll of pigs and chickens. However, the death records of inmates are intentionally omitted.[81]

While official records are lacking, individual accounts – this is, inmate narratives – provide valuable information about the deaths incurred in a number of camp units. Chen Fengxiao recalls that, among the seventy-five convicts who were sent to Team 1 of Branch 4 in April 1959, only twenty-nine were still alive in January 1967, when they were evacuated from Xingkaihu. The majority of them had died in 1960 and 1961.[82] Han Dajun estimates that around one-third of the inmates in his labour brigade died in the famine years. Nevertheless, it is difficult to estimate the total death toll at Xingkaihu because the deaths in most of the camp units are neither represented in inmate narratives nor recorded in official sources.[83]

Regarding the death toll of rightists on the army farms, official statistics are inconsistent and highly dubious. While *Bawuling nongchangshi* (A history of Farm 850) states that, "during the serious famine period of 1959–60, eight rightists died of edema on the whole farm," the local history of its Yunshan Branch indicates ten deaths at this branch alone.[84] All these figures are contested by rightist survivors. According to Yang Congdao, who served as secretary for Farm 850 headquarters in 1960 and was involved in writing death reports, from May to November 1960, at the Yunshan Branch of Farm 850 alone, twenty-nine Beijing rightists died of starvation and illnesses such as pneumonia.[85] It seems that the official death figures are dramatically underestimated. In addition to this, the way farm authorities interpreted cause of death was highly problematic. Yang Congdao tells us that Farm 850 leaders advocated the use of such terms as "edema," "tuberculosis," "intestinal obstruction," and "diarrhea" to account for the cause of deaths. This, of course, creates the impression that inmates died of various diseases rather than of starvation.[86]

Nevertheless, certain labour farms did acknowledge mass deaths and asked lower-level Party branches to address this problem. The Farm 853 Party Committee, in its "Instructions on Addressing and Thoroughly Investigating the Issue of the Deaths" of March 25, 1961, stated: "Over the past winter and spring, our farm has been experiencing serious abnormal deaths. Bloody incidents occurred frequently, but some cadres did not learn their lessons. They paid no attention to human lives, but adopted a bureaucratic attitude, neither taking measures to address the issue nor finding out who was to blame for the deaths, nor properly handling the remaining problems ... We ask the Party committees of various branch farms to immediately investigate the issue and provide solutions." (Soon afterwards, Farm 853 provided a report to the Mudanjiang Land Reclamation Bureau regarding recent abnormal deaths on the farm – the deaths of workers and staff, *laogai* convicts, rightists, and children.)[87] Seemingly strong and earnest, such statements removed blame from the farm leadership itself, even though it had submitted an excessive amount of grain to the state and, in so doing, had failed to adequately feed its own farm workers, including rightist exiles.

The Mudanjiang Land Reclamation Bureau also submitted a self-criticism report to the Ministry of Land Reclamation. While the reliability of the statistics provided in the report is open to question, it reveals certain aspects about death in the land reclamation region of eastern Heilongjiang Province: "From October of last year (1960) to February of this year, 491 staff, workers and their families in our reclamation region died due to abnormal reasons ... 68 died of edema, 190 of edema combined with other chronic diseases, 133 of coldness, hunger, food poisoning and intestinal obstruction, and 70 of reasons unknown."[88] While the report reveals the seriousness of the number of deaths incurred, in using the phrases "died of edema" and "died of edema combined with other chronic diseases" as euphemisms for dying of starvation it appears to be trying to conceal the real reasons for such deaths. Medically speaking, dying from edema was undoubtedly the result of prolonged malnourishment and hunger, and dying from food poisoning and intestinal obstruction in the context of the great famine was largely due to devouring poisonous herbs, wild animals, and various "food substitutes." In other words, the official report obscures the real reasons for the massive death toll, thus making it less shocking.

The ambiguity of official records aside, most survivors found it difficult to pinpoint the precise number of those who died around them, never mind the number who died within a broader context. This, too, makes an accurate calculation of the number of deaths among political exiles during the Beidahuang banishment next to impossible. When interviewed, Tan Tianrong, Yin Jiliang, Liu Meng, and Zheng Xiaofeng all stated that they could not assess the death rates in their labour teams (although this, of course, does not make their narratives any less valuable). Placed in a specific location and overwhelmed by crushing woes, they were hardly cognizant of anything beyond their immediate world. In Xingkaihu and at the Yunshan Branch of Farm 850, when death became normal, an inmate, quite likely numbed by her/his physical and mental misery, would not necessarily be aware of who among his or her cellmates lived or died. When Shen Mojun was sent to a medical centre at Farm 850 for edema, he only knew that "the living and the dead flowed in and out like so many streams of water." He had no idea of how many dead were removed or how many new patients were brought in.[89] Harry Wu describes a similar situation at a branch of the Qinghe Labour Camp:

> Inside the 585 barracks it became more difficult to distinguish the dead from the living. At a glance there seemed no difference. Much of the day and night we lay in a state of near stupor. No longer did we pay attention when someone reached the end and went into last gasps or tremors. The only sign that a prisoner had died was that he failed to sit up at mealtime ... I don't know how many sick prisoners died that October. I don't even know how many died in my squad. The number in my room fluctuated

too much to keep track. Dead bodies went out and live bodies came in almost daily. I paid no attention. I never even learned their names.[90]

Death figures seemed irrelevant to the exiles, and an awareness of death most likely gave way to a concern for themselves – for those who remained alive and had further ordeals to suffer.

PHYSICAL ABUSE

Although countless *laogai* survivors have pointed to the alarming extent of physical abuse in the PRC labour camps in both the Mao and post-Mao periods, Chinese authorities keep claiming that, in China, physical abuse is prohibited by law,[91] and researchers' investigations into camp life have been restricted. For this reason, it is difficult to obtain police records relating to physical abuse in the PRC labour camps in general and in Beidahuang in particular. Further complicating this situation is the fact that, according to a police code enacted by the Ministry of Public Security, the use of *jieju* (disciplinary tools) was legally permitted. For instance, a document the ministry issued in 1956 stipulates that, in some situations, *jieju* may be applied in order to pre-empt an insurrection on the part of convicts.[92] According to this document, "certain disciplinary measures," such as the use of handcuffs, shackles, leg irons, and solitary confinement, can be applied to those inmates who disobey prison rules and who pose a threat to prison security. Thus, while the ministry keeps stating that it forbids physical abuse, thanks to the use of *jieju*, the door to doing so remains open. Furthermore, the way in which these disciplinary tools were to be used remained a grey area and, according to inmate narratives, was subject to manipulation, which led to atrocious forms of physical abuse.

Among the political exiles in Beidahuang, the rightists on the army farms probably suffered the least physical abuse. So far we know of no rightist recollections that indicate the use of physical torture, although many remember that those who could not complete their work targets were often denied food or rest, or were penalized with a heavier workload.[93] Some farm cadres perversely refused requests for medical leave. Certain Farm 853 cadres treated requests for such leaves as an excuse on the part of rightists to "refuse reform," as a sign of "passive resistance" or of "slacking at work." Ye Huazhan had to write to his parents for help,

and this severely angered farm cadres.[94] Ren Yaozhang repeatedly pleaded
for medical leave to get treatment for his acute tuberculosis, but the farm
supervisor declined his requests. He finally died in September 1960.[95]
The experience of Beidahuang rightists opens a small window onto the
issue of physical abuse. In 1961, an official report by the CCP's Central
United Front Department, Propaganda Department, and Organization
Department admitted that "some grassroots units badly treated the rightists ... insulting, beating and scolding them, and even visiting [upon them]
brutal corporal punishment."[96] It was certainly not rare or sporadic cases
of such abuse that caused concern among these top party establishments.

In Xingkaihu, there was a difference between the severity of physical
abuse suffered by labour re-education inmates and that suffered by labour
reform inmates. For labour re-education inmates, physical abuse was not
very common, probably because they had not been legally deprived of
their civil rights and were still under "administrative discipline" rather
than criminal sanction – something that would have made camp cadres
more scrupulous about visiting abuse upon them. For these people, physical abuse largely came from fellow inmates (sometimes instigated by
camp cadres), although, of course, it was a good idea not to irritate camp
cadres. Tan Tianrong recalls that, in his labour re-education branch, the
inmates who suffered corporal abuse were mainly those who did not get
along well with their campmates: "I did not have much enthusiasm for
drawing close to the cadres but I got along well with others in my team.
So I was never physically beaten."[97] Since camp cadres were not always
with the inmates after work, getting along well with one's fellow inmates,
especially duty prisoners, was very important for political inmates, who
were the minority in almost all camp cells. The recollections of other
labour re-education inmates, such as Peter Liu, Wu Ningkun, and Han
Dajun, mention their receiving oral abuse from camp cadres but not
physical abuse.

Corporal punishment, however, was common for labour reform inmates, as is clear from the experiences of Chen Fengxiao, Liu Qidi, and
Gu Xiangqian. It was mainly imposed upon those convicts who disobeyed camp cadres or camp guards. When a convict defied a cadre,
physical punishment was very likely to result, mostly in the form of being
handcuffed or put in leg irons. Sometimes physical punishment was imposed when camp cadres wanted to solve a disciplinary problem, extort a
confession, or, in the words of Williams and Wu, to "inflict physical pain
... [in order] to break one's spirit."[98] Punishment techniques also included using "tiger benching" (i.e., binding the offender onto a flat bench and

squeezing bricks between his/her legs and the bench in order to inflict physical pain) and placing victims in solitary confinement. The suffering of Chen Fengxiao and Liu Qidi, as shown in Chapter 3, reveals how the physical abuse inflicted upon intractable inmates far exceeded the official stipulations for what constituted "disciplinary measures."

A key issue concerns the use of handcuffs and leg irons for a much longer period, or at much heavier levels, than officially allowed. According to "The Instructions on the Use of Disciplinary Equipment on Convicts," enacted on January 29, 1957, the use of handcuffs and leg irons should not exceed two weeks.[99] However, Chen Fengxiao's experience indicates that the such equipment was used for over one month in Xingkaihu's *laogai* branches. Official rules dictate that the leg iron used is to be at most eighteen *jin*, but Xingkaihu camp cadres forged one of forty-eight *jin* to deal with Chen and other recalcitrant convicts (in this case, apparently an active counter-revolutionary challenged the camp cadres by claiming that he did not fear the twenty-four *jin* leg iron and wanted to try a forty-eight *jin* one).[100] Although camp authorities explained such excesses by arguing that the severity of the punishment varied according to the degree to which camp rules were violated and according to whether or not the offender was rendered sufficiently docile after having been sanctioned, it was apparent that Xingkaihu camp cadres overused these disciplinary tools.

Another device used to punish intractable prisoners involved being solitarily confined in a small concrete cell. The cell in Xingkaihu, according to Chen Fengxiao, was about one metre tall, one metre wide, and 1.5 metres long. According to Harry Wu, the cell he saw in a camp in northern China was about six feet long, three feet wide, and three feet high – slightly larger than a coffin. Locked in such a tiny cell, one was unable to sit, stand, or lie down in a comfortable position. If being handcuffed at the same time, then one had to eat without the use of one's hands and lie trapped in one's own excrement.[101] In Xingkaihu, those awaiting execution would be put in a solitary confinement cell. Non-condemned prisoners who were considered defiant or for some reason were hated by camp cadres were likely to be squeezed in with the condemned person so that they would have to endure the psychological torture of experiencing the deranged behaviour of the condemned (e.g., hysterical howls or laughter) prior to his execution.[102]

Exposure to mosquitoes was another source of physical abuse. Flying swiftly in swarms, the mosquitoes in Xingkaihu, like those on Farms 850 and 853, were a major source of distress for those who worked in the fields since "any area of exposed skin would soon be blackened with a layer of mosquitoes."[103] As mosquitoes in the Xingkaihu marshlands were considered more venomous than were those in other parts of Heilongjiang Province, camp cadres occasionally exposed inmates to them as a form of punishment – something that could lead to unexpected death. Wang Jinquan, a historical counter-revolutionary, was the victim of such brutality. One day, when he spoke back to a camp cadre, the cadre ordered his campmates to tie him up and throw him into a ditch full of grass. When he was released in the evening after work, Wang was found to have been fatally bitten by mosquitoes, his white prison shirt bloodstained and his face swollen. Three days later, Wang died.[104] At times, inmates abused each other in a similar manner. Peter Liu tells a story about how an unpopular *laojiao* inmate was stripped, tied up, and left outdoors overnight by his campmates: "The next morning they went out to release him, when he was already breathless, swollen all over beyond recognition."[105]

Physical abuse could be inflicted by camp cadres via inmates. Since abuse of prisoners was (and is) officially forbidden, camp cadres in Xingkaihu tended to deal with those they disliked in more insidious ways, such as by instigating a group of inmates to beat them up. When an inmate was thought to be insufficiently deferential, a cadre might order other inmates to "give him a lesson," or "give him help." Then these minions would jump on the victim, beating and punching.[106] Yin Jiliang said that, at his branch camp, camp cadres never beat inmates themselves but, rather, hinted that others should do so. After having instigated the abuse, camp cadres would normally leave so as not to be blamed if the inmate should be badly injured.[107] Even if an inmate were to be brutally abused in this manner, camp cadres could be assured that this would be attributed to internal strife among inmates, thus leaving them free from sanction. However, I should point out that former camp cadre Liu Junying, when interviewed, insisted that Xingkaihu cadres never inflicted physical abuse upon prisoners, either in person or via others, and that handcuffs, leg irons, and solitary confinement were used only to prevent riots and escapes.[108]

SUICIDE

Even before their banishment, intellectuals committed suicide: sometimes out of desperation, sometimes as a means of protesting their persecution, and sometimes to avoid future torment. In June 1957, when the

Anti-Rightist Campaign had just started, Qi Xueyi, a journalist for the *Beijing Daily*, publicly killed himself by suddenly jumping out of the fourth-floor window of the assembly hall in which a meeting to condemn his friend Liu Binyan was taking place. His suicide was interpreted by anti-rightist activists as his "sacrificing himself for the rightists" and "choosing to alienate himself from the people."[109] Qi was among the first people to commit suicide in order to protest the Anti-Rightist Campaign. The state considered such forms of suicide to be of a "reactionary nature."

When labelled as "bourgeois rightists" and thus treated as "enemies of the people" (or, more accurately "enemies of the state"), individuals had to decide whether "to live or to die" as they feared the sociopolitical consequences of being rightists and dreaded what might lie ahead of them. Those who were relatively optimistic chose to live, going to labour camps to redeem themselves; those who were pessimistic preferred to die (or at least contemplated committing suicide) in order to avoid further ordeals. On the Peking University campus, history professor Ding Zeliang drowned himself in Lake Weiming when he was informed that he had been designated a rightist. According to Zhang Jiqian (Ding's colleague), Ding had participated in the communist-led student movement in 1935; however, because he later quit the movement, he was repeatedly condemned in the political campaigns of the early 1950s. Startled by the fierceness of the Anti-Rightist Campaign, Ding greatly feared being "struggled against" once again, and this may explain his suicide.[110]

To many who were labelled rightists but did not commit suicide during the Anti-Rightist Campaign, life in the post-campaign years was unbearable: they lost their jobs, faced family crises, and were shunned by neighbours and friends. For these reasons, some attempted to end their lives at this time. "It is better to die than live," the ex-doctor Ye Songtao told his friend Wang Zhiliang, who had saved him from suicide. After Ye had been labelled a rightist and downgraded from doctor to sanitation worker, almost anyone in his work unit could abuse him by scolding, punching, and/or spitting on him at will. He was relocated to a cell right next to an X-ray room. He simply did not know how to survive the rest of his life. Although foiled in his suicide attempt, Ye eventually died of leukemia.[111] Once labelled a rightist, Bi Fangfang, an ex-junior researcher at the Chinese Academy of Science, tried to kill herself by overdosing on sleeping pills before she was sent to Beidahuang.[112]

When their sense of humiliation could not be overcome, when bad news arrived from their families, or when they felt insurmountable pressure from work targets or physical hardship, a considerable number of exiles in Beidahuang chose to commit suicide. A Farm 853 document mentions that the rightist Zhu Siyong committed suicide "due to his being knocked down by hardship and his fear of labouring in a difficult environment."[113] The death of Tong Aicheng was the result of his deep desperation and sadness. After he was sent to Farm 850, his wife divorced him, leaving their two children without proper care. Tong did not have enough money to support them, and he could not return to take care of them. He also faced an unbearable workload. In the end, after work one day, he hung himself from a tree.[114] Another rightist who committed suicide on Farm 850 was Cao Zuoren, who returned from Britain to serve the socialist motherland. Driven by hunger, he wrote to his father, who lived abroad, to ask for milk powder. For this, farm cadres repeatedly condemned him in public for "seeking ease and comfort" and for "bringing disgrace to the national prestige." Unable to bear this humiliation, one night Cao drowned himself.[115]

Some exiles committed suicide after being badly humiliated and physically abused in *laogai* camps. Yin Jiliang recalls:

> My campmate Qi was a well-read person on the farm ... There was once a famous saying, "The East Wind Prevails over the West Wind," which was considered as coming from Chairman Mao and thus had strong anti-imperialist undertones ... Qi happened to mention in a casual conversation that this saying originally came from a novel, *Dream of the Red Chamber*. For this, Qi was accused of viciously attacking the Great Leader and forced to make endless self-condemnations in struggle sessions for more than twenty days. One day, when he was ordered to stand on a discipline bench facing the audience to condemn himself, an activist dashed at him, slapping him on the face and kicking over the bench. He fell heavily and his glasses were cast off. Bleeding at the mouth, he crawled on the ground, fumbling for his glasses. He could not see anything, and nobody went up to help him. Several days later, he committed suicide by cutting his stomach open with a sickle, probably hoping to die as quickly as possible.[116]

At first glance, it might seem that Qi's suicide resulted from a minor issue – a disagreement over the origin of a literary phrase. However, the real problem was the perverse atmosphere in the labour camps: any word spoken by a political inmate could be twisted to make it politically offensive, at which point political denunciation could be escalated to the level of unbearable physical abuse. And this, in some cases, led to suicide.

Some far-thinking inmates contemplated a way to commit suicide that would enable their relatives and friends to avoid any negative ramifications. Realizing that outright suicide would transform his ultra-rightist status into that of counter-revolutionary, thus adversely affecting his family's social status, Peter Liu attempted a form of suicide that "would be taken for [a] natural death and would not raise suspicion." So he decided to allow his flu to develop into pneumonia by intentionally casting aside his quilt during a fall night and exposing himself to the cold.[117] Eventually, however, the camp doctor saved his life, and then his concern for his elderly mother brought his plans of suicide to an end.

One case of suicide in Xingkaihu was notably different from any other. Lin Cheng, a *laojiao* inmate with a medical degree, chose to die in defence of the dignity of fellow intellectuals rather than due to any physical or psychological abuse. As a labour camp doctor, Lin's work involved providing medical services to camp cadres, for which he was offered benefits of which other inmates could hardly dream – a single room, special meals, and an exemption from manual labour. Hunger and abuse as experienced by others did not occur to him either. Although his life in the camp was relatively easy, Lin was said to be deeply sickened by the humiliation and suffering that labour reform inflicted upon the educated elite. One day, on his medical tour to the field, he ended his mental affliction by cutting open an artery with a scalpel.[118] Suicide was Lin's final act of defiance against a regime he viewed as repressive and perverse.

CONCLUSION

Three points can be made about the suffering of Beidahuang's political inmates. First, the majority of them were banished to Beidahuang during the Great Leap Forward of 1958–59, and they stayed there throughout the great famine of the early 1960s. The intensive forced labour and food shortages that characterized these two stages of PRC history doubly threatened these ill-fated people, making their lives extremely difficult.

Second, the authorities of the labour reform regime (both in Xingkaihu and on the army farms) tended to show their commitment to the Party's GLF policies and strove to fulfill or even surpass the designated production targets. This resulted in manual labour in Beidahuang being extremely strenuous. Their dedication to the state, expressed in the slogan "saving grain to support the nation," meant a dramatic reduction of the food supply for all workers, including political exiles. Certainly, the fundamental cause of the starvation may be traced to demands from Party higher-ups. However, some sources show that Beidahuang labour farm/camp authorities were so excessive in their activism that they declined the leeway offered by higher authorities.[119] The local activism of the labour reform authorities exacerbated human suffering, thus entailing a heavy loss of life.

Third, the governing party and the existing political system deemed the political inmates in Beidahuang, as well as those in other parts of China, to be antagonists; consequently, they were considerably demonized. Any mistreatment, including physical abuse, undernourishment, and dehumanization, was normally not considered excessive, and any leniency that may have been conferred upon other farm workers was unlikely to be extended to them. In times of economic hardship, they were the last group to receive humane care.

We also find that the suffering of Beidahuang inmates varied significantly depending on location and on the farm/camp cadres who were responsible for supervising them. The administrative policies of different labour regimes (and even of different units within the same regime) were not uniform. The Beijing rightists who were bearing lighter political punishments suffered lighter abuse than did Xingkaihu inmates in general; however, at specific branch farms, such as Yunshan, the physical torment was daunting and the death rate – including suicides – striking due to the harshness of branch cadres. Repressive labour reform policies were carried out in a hard or a soft manner at local levels, depending on who was in charge.

5

Inner Turmoil and Internecine Strife among Political Exiles

The need for absolute goodies and absolute baddies runs deep in us, but it drags history into propaganda and denies the humanity of the dead: their sins, their virtues, their efforts, their failures. To preserve complexity, and not flatten it under the weight of anachronistic moralizing, is part of the historian's task.

—Robert Hughes

Political exiles in Beidahuang were plagued by harsh physical conditions, heavy workloads, prolonged starvation, and maltreatment. Sources show that, at the same time, they were no less plagued by psychological torment, victimized by the desire for, and the inability to achieve, self-redemption and ideological renewal. In this chapter, I attempt to reveal their psychological world, showing how political exiles, especially rightists on the army farms, accepted the official viewpoint of themselves and submitted to the labour reform arrangements. While feeling wronged and distressed, many still expressed allegiance to the governing party in general and, in particular, showed their commitment to remoulding through labour in the hope of redeeming themselves.

I also examine the internecine strife among the persecuted and banished. In order to survive, to display their activism, to curry favour with camp/farm authorities, and to achieve early release, some political exiles reported and denounced their fellows, betrayed their friends, and even joined in the physical abuse of their campmates. Erosion of conscience and moral integrity was all too common, as was post-traumatic stress disorder in later years. In the face of a repressive regime, political exiles were often unable to develop either a collective consciousness or any form of group solidarity.

COMMITMENT TO LABOUR REFORM

When the Anti-Rightist Campaign came to an end and the fate of rightists was sealed, the mentalities of those labelled were complex and varied. While some committed Party members and Party followers felt acute mental agony – deep sadness and depression for having been brutally wronged – a considerable number of others who had had experience with the CCP's campaign culture (such as Zhang Bojun and Ding Ling), and those less politically assertive (such as Yin Yi), quickly bowed to the pressure and engaged in self-condemnation, not necessarily due to sincerely recognizing their crimes but simply in order to avoid further trouble.[1] It is impossible to know how many rightists debased themselves for such reasons, but it is not presumptuous to say that some made what appeared to be earnest confessions after weighing "losses and gains" rather than determining what was "right or wrong." Hu Ping provides rich accounts of how some famous rightists used extreme language to condemn their own "anti-Party, anti-people" and their "treacherous" crimes in order to be forgiven and thus be allowed to "make a new start."[2]

It seems, however, that many did, in fact, sincerely acknowledge what they believed to be their crimes. Their indoctrination convinced them that it must be they rather than the Party who were in the wrong and that, for this reason, they must search the depths of their souls to atone for their wrongdoing. Lu Gang, who was sent to Hulan Farm in Heilongjiang Province, recalls:

> I was trying to see the campaign in a positive light even if I was given a hard time. An editorial in the *People's Daily* stated that rightists were the henchmen of Western imperialists ... Through a painful "thought struggle," I eventually realized that the comment was correct and that, during the Hundred Flowers Campaign, my criticism of Party cadres did speak for the interest of the imperialists. In the same way as I did, many of my fellow rightists admitted that we were wrong and that the Anti-Rightist Campaign was right.[3]

The heated political environment of the campaign, the mass criticism, the denunciations from colleagues and friends, and the forced recognition of the correctness of the charges – all of this created such psychological pressure that an individual often succumbed to the logic of her or his critics and persecutors. Many rightists acknowledged that they had been poisoned by bourgeois ideologies, that their criticisms during the Hundred Flowers Campaign were anti-Party and anti-socialist in nature, and that they had committed political crimes and so deserved to be punished. Some, such as Wang Zheng and Huang Miaozi, clearly reveal these points in their memoirs or recollections.[4] Others, such as Yin Yi's colleagues, felt grieved at being so labelled but still recognized the need to change their worldview in the New China. Many Beijing rightists wrote lengthy self-criticisms, swearing to cleanse themselves of bourgeois ideologies and attain redemption.[5]

Many rightists, especially the young idealists and those who had revolutionary backgrounds, continued to endorse the Chinese Communist Party and the "revolutionary cause," and they tried to see their misfortune in a positive light. Ding Ling, for instance, recalls that, when they first arrived in Beidahuang, she and her husband agreed: "We should stick to our beliefs and ethics as communists, ignore what we have suffered, share weal and woe, and break a new path in the cold northern frontier of our motherland." Dai Huang convinced himself that, "even while insulted and humiliated, we should still rouse our revolutionary spirit, enrich ourselves with a new life, and look for light in darkness." On the labour team in which Dai was placed: "Although many of us had been expelled from the Party, we still saw the Party as our mother."[6] These statements should perhaps be treated more as an indication of earnest feelings than as hyperbole or affectation. In the 1950s, adherence to the Party line was the ideological choice of many intellectuals: their spiritual and even their personal lives could not be detached from the Party and its values. Xiao Fan, a young rightist and ex-Communist Youth League member, even tried to organize a Marxist study group among army farm rightists, only to be stopped by a seasoned Yin Yi, who warned that the local Party cell would consider any non-officially sponsored "small group activity" among rightists to be illegal and offensive.[7]

As discussed in Chapter 2, some Beijing rightists (such as Li Kegang and Wang Qingbin) demonstrated considerable defiance on the army farms. However, there are also different stories. For many rightists, their acknowledgment of their faults and their continuing endorsement of the

CCP led to their positive attitudes towards labour reform. Some rightists destined for Beidahuang army farms believed that they needed to undergo remoulding in order to rid themselves of erroneous thoughts, achieve political and ideological perfection, attain spiritual growth, and steel their mental strength "through trial and tribulation." Thus, some, such as Huang Miaozi and Ding Cong, happily accepted labour reform.[8] This attitude is perhaps related to Mao's claim that rightists would be treated benevolently. In a speech he made on October 13, 1957, for instance, Mao stated: "Rightists are an antagonistic force. But we do not treat them as landlords or counter-revolutionaries ... let them remould themselves through labour ... Once they have rectified themselves, they will be allowed to return to the ranks of the people."[9] This announcement was instrumental in cheering frustrated rightists and convincing at least some of them that they had a "bright future." In the spring of 1958, whereas many considered labouring in the wilderness to be an unwarranted sanction and felt dismal about it, others treated it as a positive phenomenon. Some rightists even sang "Hymn of the Communist Youth League" en route to Beidahuang, as though they were embarking on a holy mission in the Great Northern Wilderness.[10]

Whereas Xingkaihu inmates were under immense managerial pressure to perform heavy physical labour (see Chapter 3), on the army farms the pressure came from both farm cadres and rightists themselves, who evinced a certain degree of enthusiasm and volunteerism. Indeed, when arriving at Beidahuang, a considerable number of Beijing rightists were enthusiastic about engaging in manual work. Sources published thus far positively point to this, even though some counter-proof exists. Huang Miaozi recalls that, in order to construct the July First Reservoir that was to be dedicated to the thirty-seventh anniversary of the CCP, in response to the call of farm cadres he and his fellow rightists happily worked for a week with hardly any rest.[11] For the rightists in Dai Huang's team, work on a hydraulic project and grass-cutting were daunting, and living conditions were appalling, "but none of [them] complained and all of [them] laboured hard and cheerfully." Ni Genshan, too, recalls: "We all wanted to remould ourselves and atone for our sin through labour, so people were full of drive and enthusiasm." In the first summer, some activists even demanded more work than was originally assigned and cheerfully sang work songs while labouring.[12] The pressure to labour hard was there, but many rightists responded positively to it in the early stages, when they were not abused.

Some political exiles not only actively engaged in manual labour but also verbally extolled the virtues of doing so. Chen Ming's praise of his work led Ding Ling to make the final decision to join him in Beidahuang. Huang Miaozi, in his letters home, positively portrayed his sent-down life, the work in which he engaged, and the job satisfaction that physical labour brought him. He also said that, through the significant changes brought about by physical work, he realized: "Labour creates the world, and only under the leadership of the Party could the wilderness be turned into a metropolis and poverty into wealth."[13] Some rightists composed songs such as "Jointly Build Our Beidahuang" and "The Song of Lumbering" to express their joyfulness and their commitment to the "transformation of heaven and earth" in the borderlands.[14] Although people were evidently trying to find a way to cheer themselves up and boost their morale, or even to impress farm cadres, it cannot be denied that there was a surprising degree of genuine volunteerism.

From these sources, it seems that the rightists' involvement in labour reform was not only state-imposed but also self-imposed, and some of them actually viewed their banishment in a somewhat positive light. How do we make sense of this phenomenon? Certainly rightists were forcibly sent to Beidahuang and the manual labour there was unquestionably mandatory. However, the Great Northern Wilderness seemed to provide a unique chance for some of them to contribute to socialism: they grew crops to fill the national granary, they felled wood for urban reconstruction, and they reclaimed the virgin land for the generations to come, all of which, at least for some of them, made this phase of their life meaningful and worthwhile, part of a grandiose plan for the transformation of both the physical world and their inner spiritual world. They translated the external demand for labour reform into an internal drive. Within the overblown atmosphere of building "a brand new Beidahuang" and a wealthy homeland, those subjected to labour reform and those enforcing it seemed to have a common goal, language, and ideological grounding. Trying to see things positively, rightists saw themselves more as the builders of socialism than as exiles, at least in the early stages. It is reasonable to assume, therefore, that, in the case of Beidahuang, the labour reform imposed by the authorities and the rightists' commitment functioned as two props to support the forced labour regime. The high morale of these rightists collapsed mostly because they were worn down by the prolonged, daunting work, severe food shortages in the famine years, and, in the case of Farm 850, personnel change in farm administration (from relatively benevolent cadres to harsh ones) and, in the case of Farm 853, the belated local-level arrival of the Anti-Rightist Movement.

It is to be noted, however, that the degree to which rightists committed themselves to self-remoulding and their labour assignments varied significantly. The memoirs of Liu Meng and Wu Yongliang reveal little about their enthusiasm regarding these things. Some recognized the existence of this behaviour among other rightists but rarely analyzed their own attitudes. It is possible that they simply did not develop such a mindset. It is also possible that they did not bother to recount their "foolishness" during those years and/or are unwilling to commit it to paper decades after the fact. The case of Huang Miaozi may help us to understand the complexity of this. He acknowledges that, in his letters home, he truly revealed his mind at the time – his sincere commitment to ideological remoulding, his inner struggle for political progress, his effort to "dig deep to [his] very soul," his criticism of the "bourgeois thoughts" of other rightists, and his gratitude to the Party for "saving" him (see Chapter 2). When reviewing these letters in 1997, Huang told his biographer Li Hui that, in retrospect, they reveal a "self-cheating mentality" over which he felt sadness and bitterness.[15] For many others, it was unlikely that they realized in 1957–58 that they were being mentally manipulated, as their desire to be remoulded was indeed genuine. In the 1990s and 2000s, however, it must be heartbreaking for them to reflect upon their naiveté and the process by which they were psychologically exploited. With previous written records (i.e., the nine letters he wrote to his wife) as an aid, Huang is able to reveal his mindset in those years, and he demonstrates courage in analyzing his naiveté. For those who do not have written records upon which to draw, reflecting upon one's past mental states is not only painful but also bothersome.

When analyzing rightists' apparent dedication to ideological remoulding, we need to be aware of their probable hidden agendas. Rightists wished to impress farm authorities with their dedication to "building socialism" and their commitment to, and progress in, remoulding themselves through labour. They wanted to do this in order to get rid of their rightist label. With the harsh physical environment, daunting work, and loneliness, most rightists were undoubtedly longing to be allowed to return to Beijing, despite their rhetoric about building a brand new Beidahuang. As indicated in Chapter 2, when the rightists left Beijing, many were told by the heads of their work units that, if their labour reform went well, their stay in Beidahuang would likely be short. In Beidahuang, the edifying speeches given by farm cadres, though few, encouraged rightists to "try [their] best to get [their] rightist hats removed." They were told: "Removal of your hats and your return to Beijing depend on your work performance."[16] All of this led rightists to believe that self-redemption was possible and that their release depended on their hard work.

With this in mind, many rightists spared no effort to demonstrate their willingness to put in good work performance as a sign of their re-pentance, self-renewal, devotion, and political progressiveness. Doing this, they hoped, would reduce their term of banishment. Liang Nan recalls: "The vast majority of the labelled laboured with all their might, even risking their lives, in order to get their 'hats' removed and improve their situation ... nor was I an exception."[17] Farm 853 leaders, too, specu-lated that many rightists worked hard just to have their hats removed and to be able to return to their work in Beijing: "They are labouring now for the purpose of not labouring later."[18] Their well-proclaimed dedication to reform through labour reflected their desire to end such a life and to have their political stigmata removed.

The mentality of the *laojiao* (labour re-education) rightists in Xing-kaihu seems to be similar, though not exactly the same, as that of rightists on the army farms. When they were rounded up by the police and sent away for labour re-education, none of them were told the length of their internment; however, an official document, "The Resolutions on Re-Education through Labour," provided a degree of hope. According to this document: "Labour re-education personnel could be released and reas-signed to other jobs with the approval of the labour re-education organi-zations, provided that they behave well during the period of re-education ... when situations permit."[19] When the *laojiao* inmates first arrived at Xingkaihu, camp authorities announced that their detention periods de-pended on their individual performances and that whoever worked and behaved well could be released. This enabled inmates to speculate about their futures. Thus, ultra-rightists, including Wu Ningkun, spared no ef-fort in their work: "[I] hop[ed] like everybody else that my exertion at physical labor would put me in the good graces of the officers and bring closer the day of release."[20]

The key issue here is "admitting crime" (*renzui*), which may be traced to an ancient Chinese tradition. Confucian doctrine emphasizes "self-examination," or "introspection" (*zixing*). According to the Analects, willingness to perform "self-examination thrice a day" (*sanxing wu shen*) enabled an individual to search and cleanse faults, cultivate virtues, and maintain moral perfection. This moral code, however, was predominant-ly for "gentlemen" (*junzi*) rather than for "little men" (*xiaoren*). In the labour camps of the People's Republic of China, crime-consciousness was a major criterion of virtue, and it was used to judge an inmate's conduct. Oral recognition of crime was necessary but far from sufficient. One had to convince camp authorities of one's crime-consciousness by one's good work performance as camp cadres linked satisfactory physical labour with one's sincerity in "admitting crimes." Those whose work performance was poor were considered to be lacking such consciousness and were thus singled out for condemnation.[21] To avoid being deemed unwilling to atone for their crimes, many political inmates in *laojiao* camps did everything they could to put in a good work performance.[22]

Despite their sincere efforts, however, political exiles found that it was not easy to stand out among so many people who were also trying to put their best foot forward. For some, work performance might not be sufficient to show their political commitment and progress. More active gestures, such as "drawing close to the government" (*kaolong zhengfu*) or "drawing close to the organization" (*kaolong zuzhi*), seemed to provide a shortcut. This entailed actively responding to the authorities' calls for thought reports, and, for some exiles, this meant putting down others in order to elevate oneself. This being the case, internecine strife, betrayal, and the reporting and denouncing of fellow inmates constituted a conspicuous part of Beidahuang banishment.

Internecine Strife in the Pre-Banishment Context

Anne Thurston presents the Cultural Revolution as a failure of morality, a rupture of conscience in Mao's China. She also provides insight into the causes of this rupture of conscience. Under the CCP, she argues, when Confucian norms were destroyed, people forgot the values of loyalty, honesty, and respect for other people. They attacked others in order to get ahead, to climb higher on the ladder of political success, and to avoid being attacked by others. People acted out of expediency rather than out of morality.[23] Although such observations are mainly based on Thurston's interviews with students and intellectuals who went through the Cultural Revolution, they provide a useful framework within which to approach the experiences of those persecuted in the 1950s. It is valid to say that the failure of morality and the rupture of conscience identified by Thurston and other observers began in the 1950s, earlier than many would think. They originated in Mao's mass campaigns, which encouraged internecine strife and backstabbing.

It was not surprising to see internecine strife among intellectual elites during Mao's political campaigns of the early 1950s. At this time, the CCP explicitly encouraged mutual surveillance, mutual denunciation, and secret reporting, and it suggested that redemption would be the reward for this behaviour.[24] This strategy worked well before 1957. When Ding Ling and her former *Literary Gazette* colleague Chen Qixia were attacked as members of an "Anti-Party clique" in 1955, Chen mentally collapsed. In confessing to various anti-Party crimes, he handed over to a Party cell all the correspondence he and Ding had exchanged in the previous years and accused Ding of attempting to "seize the leadership of literary circles." Ding Ling was also denounced by many of her other colleagues. Renowned writers Lao She and Mao Dun, for instance, actively joined in the scathing attack directed her way.[25]

In the early summer of 1957, when the political winds shifted in favour of the Anti-Rightist Campaign and persecution loomed large, a considerable number of intellectuals chose to expose their colleagues and friends in order to demonstrate their political allegiance and save themselves. False accusations, denunciations, and betrayals were widespread and sudden changes of face surprising. Almost all the rightists featured in this book were denounced or betrayed by their colleagues and friends.[26] While some attacks came from people who lacked clear judgment and were merely following the political trend, or from those who believed the Party line and followed it to the letter, many denounced their colleagues and friends out of various degrees of political calculation. Well-known playwright Tian Han managed to label his colleague Wu Zuguang in order to save himself, and writer Lao She actively joined him in this.[27] In keeping with the political winds, Wu Han, historian and head of the Beijing committee of the China Democratic League, fired the first shot at his superiors Zhang Bojun and Luo Longji.[28] During the Anti-Rightist Campaign, many revered intellectuals were active in incriminating their colleagues and friends, and they used the blood of their victims to maintain their own rank.

The reasons for denigrating others, even betraying friends, mostly had to do with self-protection and self-redemption. When the Anti-Rightist Campaign began, the CCP called upon "all the supporters of the Party and Socialism" to endorse the campaign and to disclose the reactionary ideas of others; if they did not, then they themselves would risk being condemned. For the purpose of self-protection, silence was less useful than was finding someone to attack. Artist Sun Chengwu (a Party member) kindly warned his colleague of the risk of being labelled. To his surprise, his colleague sold him out to the Party: while Sun was labelled for "disclosing Party secrecy" and sent to Beidahuang, his colleague was lauded as an "anti-rightist activist."[29] The goal of "atoning for one's crime by doing good deeds" had been achieved.

For those who were trying to find scapegoats, friends, colleagues, and comrades turned out to be the most suitable targets as the accusers knew them and were aware of their weak spots. When political pressure was high and labelling quotas were set, many were frightened, and their survival instinct overshadowed their sense of ethics, conscience, and friendship. Targeting one's close colleagues and friends, exposing their confidential information, and raising trivial issues to the level of political principle were among the best ways of showing one's fidelity to the Party and thus giving one a better chance of surviving the campaign, although in private he/she might be considered unethical. For Luo Longji, the most vicious attack came from his girlfriend of seventeen years. She used her knowledge of his personal life to frame and slander him, accusing him of being a "wolf in sheep's clothing."[30] Presumably, she hoped that throwing Luo into water might secure her place in the boat.

The story of writer Liu Shaotang is also illuminating. According to Liu, the most dismaying attack on him came from a female colleague – a woman whom he had treated like a sister: "We almost had nothing secret between each other." When Liu was designated as a rightist, she, too, was on the verge of being so labelled. In her desperation, she falsely attacked Liu over a trivial issue – his reluctance to pay sufficient Party membership dues. In all likelihood, Liu would have been labelled even without her accusation as the main charge against him was "taking a stance against Chairman Mao's thought on literature." However, her betrayal was a bitter blow for him: "It broke my heart," Liu recalls.[31] When in peril, seemingly caring people could become more vicious than anyone, even they themselves, had expected.

Nevertheless, one did not always secure self-protection by treacherously attacking others. Once an individual was internally selected as a target, his or her fate was, in most cases, sealed. As labelling quotas were set and required a large amount of work, Party cells seldom freed potential targets. The revolutionary woman who incriminated Liu Shaotang, for instance, was not exempt from being labelled, and she died in distress several years later.[32] Another example is Deng Youmei, a novelist in Beijing. When the Writers Union of Beijing convened a mass condemnation meeting against Liu Shaotang on October 11, 1957, Deng had not yet been publicly referred to a rightist. And so, in order to demonstrate his activism, he sharply accused Liu. Ironically, just as Deng concluded his speech and was enjoying the warm applause of the audience, the chair denounced him as a rightist.[33] Peter Liu shed more light on this situation:

> It happened that people who had criticized the Party more sharply (during the Hundred Flowers period), or those whose history was "complicated," were eager to vindicate themselves by coming out with vigorous attacks on Rightists, and ironically these were apt to become Rightists themselves. As a result, there were cases in which a very eloquent defender of the Party and the cause of socialism stood crest-fallen a few days later on the stage a few meters aside of the rostrum he had just taken. Ironically, again, critics of these ill-fated warriors could find themselves in their shoes in no time.[34]

A desire for self-protection, for catching the political tide, made people opportunists. Nevertheless, these people often found that the strategy of incriminating others did not always ensure that they themselves were not persecuted.

Falsely accusing their friends left many anti-rightist activists mentally distraught. Some felt guilty and expressed a degree of repentance. In his memoir, novelist Ba Jin painfully admits that his harsh condemnation of Ding Ling and Ai Qing was nothing more than "throwing stones at those in dire straits."[35] When Wu Zuguang returned from Beidahuang in 1961, Cao Yu, a friend who had attacked him during the campaign, came to see him, expressed his deep remorse, and asked for his forgiveness.[36] Before his death, famous translator Feng Yidai published his diary, in which he spoke of regretting how he had willingly became a "secret worker" of a Party cell, watching and reporting on his rightist friends, including Zhang Bojun, Luo Longji, and Ding Cong.[37] Such remorse may reveal a guilty conscience. Nevertheless, it seems that, in the post-campaign – and even the post-Mao – period, few people publicly repented their less than exemplary behaviour. So far, a considerable number of memoirists have told us that backstabbing was prevalent in the Anti-Rightist Campaign and in the labour camps, and they have told how they themselves were victimized. However, with few exceptions (such as Dai Huang), they omit the names of the attackers. Furthermore, few memoirists admit to having ever attacked or betrayed others, which is probably one of the most salient weaknesses of their memoirs. Although it is embarrassing to publicly admit faults of this kind, and although it is difficult to speculate about which memoirists condemned their colleagues/campmates but failed to chronicle having done so, one may reasonably assume that this lack of self-exposing narratives also reflects the reluctance of people to dig deep into their own souls and to conduct the appropriate self-interrogation.

With regard to post-Anti-Rightist Campaign stories, since a considerable number of the perpetrators in 1957 were themselves victimized shortly afterwards without examining their moral issues, it is not surprising that they continued this behaviour on the labour farms.

INTERNECINE STRIFE IN BEIDAHUANG

Several Beidahuang rightists still remember the warmth that they first encountered in the exile communities: friends on the same labour team helped each other with work, collected donations for the needy families of fellow exiles, and, in some cases, shared hard-to-come-by food.[38] When farm authorities were slow to provide help for those endangered in the "Yunshan incident" (see Chapter 4), some rightists volunteered to search for their lost friends, even though they themselves were also physically spent.[39] Rehabilitated rightists take care to keep these moving stories alive through their memoirs; however, they also note that, in their exile communities, there was no lack of people who tried to show their ultra-activism by reporting, defaming, and attacking their fellow inmates.

Some activists pointed to issues that seemed rather political. On Farm 850, Chinese poetry specialist Hou Delin gave a low rating to a verse of one of Mao's poems, and this was instantly reported by a rightist squad leader. Hou was scolded as a "stubborn reactionary," repeatedly denounced in public, and forced to do extra work.[40] Similar stories also occurred on Farm 853. A report of the Ministry of Culture's inspection panel shows that quite a few rightists came to the panel to inform on other rightists. For instance, Sun reported on Liu Yousheng. Apparently Liu had seen birds in the sky and had said "Birds are enjoying freedom." Sun interpreted this to mean that Liu believed that he himself did not have freedom, and this is what he reported to the panel.[41] The exposure of the rightist kingdom incident (see Chapter 2), of which Huang Wu was guilty, was also due to the report of his campmate Pan. Some rightists who were unable to get their labels removed in the first round of a "label removal" session resorted to informing on others in the hope of having them removed in the second round.[42]

Many of the issues for which people were reported to the authorities were trivial. Practising drawing, reading history books, and singing foreign songs were all subject to being twisted and reported as distractions from labour or signs of bourgeois taste. This would happen even though these pastimes were not explicitly banned.[43] In some branch farms, incidents such as catching field rats to eat or complaining about the lack of sufficient food were presented as "disgracing socialism." When old friends Ding Cong, Huang Miaozi, and Gao Fen happened to be assigned to the same labour team on Farm 850, some rightists came to remind farm cadres that they had once formed a small clique in Beijing and suggested that they be split apart.[44] Informers did not necessarily bear personal grudges against their targets. When one wanted to win favour from authorities by informing on someone else, and it was difficult to discover anything politically suspect with which to do so, one turned to trivial issues to fabricate an indictable case.

On the army farms, direct contact between farm cadres and rightists was mainly limited to work time; as well, despite the rhetoric employed by official media, many cadres did not have any real interest in ideologically intervening with the rightists, except for reprimanding them in order to get them to work hard. It was the informers among the banished, including those appointed by farm authorities as squad or platoon leaders, who made the situation fester. Some of these rightist heads willingly "drew close to the organization (the Party)" and/or were interested in building good relations with camp cadres.[45] In daily life, they were very similar to other rightists except for assisting cadres with organizing workers. During work, meals, and rest time, they would stay with the others, chatting and joking with them as normal. Some of them, however, in an attempt to help their personal situation, would remember what their fellow rightists said and secretly report to the cadres anything they believed to be problematic. The reports of platoon leaders Zhang and Jiao at the Yunshan Branch of Farm 850, for example, led to farm cadres repeatedly verbally abusing Dai Huang and others.[46]

Based on these secret reports, many of which were far-fetched, frightening charges would be laid and, in struggle sessions, other rightists would be mobilized against their fellow campmates. After the farm cadres had given a keynote speech, all other rightists involved in the session would be asked to participate in the mass denunciation of those considered guilty. People in such sessions were hardly able to remain silent. Some participated with a degree of enthusiasm, and many followed this trend. In the struggle sessions over the rightist kingdom incident on Farm 853, some rightists analyzed the reactionary nature of the incident, and charged these people [i.e., the targets] for trying to establish a rightist kingdom of millions to confront the Party and the state. Some exposed the daily behaviours of these people, raising every small issue to the political level; some even strongly suggested severe punishment. The condemnation sessions lasted for several nights; the atmosphere was tense, and everybody was scared.[47]

In these situations, even those who were reluctant to join in the attack were required to say something against those accused. Dai Huang and Wu Yongliang acknowledged that many joined in the condemnation just for the sake of appearance. Their criticisms, less harsh than those of others, often took the form of offering admonition and advice, combined with self-criticism, in the hope of not only satisfying camp cadres but also minimizing the damage done to the targets – their campmates.[48] It was very unusual for anyone to keep silent.

As I have shown in Chapter 2, labour farm authorities encouraged internal strife, mutual surveillance, and secret reports as part of their strategy to "isolate a small number of arch-reactionaries and split up the target group."[49] Farm cadres at the ground level were certainly aware of this strategy and its effect upon banished intellectuals. Li Fuchun, a cadre on Farm 853, recalls: "There were so many feuds among those literati (wenren). Everybody wanted to get ahead of others; some liked to drop 'small reports' (secret reports) to us and blew even the tiniest thing to huge political proportions."[50] Although true, this comment obscures the fact that this behaviour was, to a great extent, the result of official policy. At times, however, farm cadres did not bother to make a fuss over these far-fetched "small reports" or accusations. For example, bored with the over-the-top rhetoric inspired by the rightist kingdom incident, the chief director of Farm 853 finally put an end to the escalating condemnation session, treating it as an inappropriate joke on the part of the rightists, and did not punish those implicated.[51] It should be mentioned that having this particular political show stopped by farm authorities was an unexpected outcome.

Nevertheless, it was sad for rightists to hear the ferocious denunciations uttered by their campmates, some of whom they may well have chatted with the day before. Dai Huang recalls that several campmates originally supported him in his suspicions regarding the high crop yields myth. However, when camp cadre Zhu decided to condemn Dai for his suspicions and ordered other rightists to join in, most of them changed their opinions into condemning Dai or declared that they were drawing a line between themselves and Dai.[52] Being betrayed by friends was a brutal blow and caused enormous mental trauma. Dai Huang recalls that rightist Yang Taiquan even refused to talk with others on the army farm: "During work, meals and rest time, he always expressed himself with eye contact, gestures, nods, or shakes of his head, rather than saying anything. When we chatted and joked, he sometimes could not help but smile; but the smile was transient, and he quickly turned his back to conceal his feelings."[53] This determination to remain silent seems to indicate psychological trauma, a kind of self-punishment for one's previous naiveté and outspokenness, and a sign of one's determination to no longer trust one's companions.

Ultra-activism also existed in Xingkaihu labour reform complex. As an institutionalized labour reform regime, Xingkaihu formally promoted political activism. As mentioned in Chapter 3, camp cadres, in the name of mutual help, openly encouraged secret reporting and mutual surveillance, and inmates were enjoined to criticize each other during political study sessions. All this created an atmosphere favourable to informers who were eager to show their political progressiveness. Chen Fengxiao recalls that almost every aspect of his daily life, including his chats with other political prisoners and his silence during study sessions, was subject to being reported by his campmates. Chen's campmate Ding Tong, an ex-newspaper editor and sentenced counter-revolutionary, not only fingered Chen for his satirical comment on Lin Biao's eulogizing of Mao but also physically abused him. Dismayed and confused as to why his gentlemanly campmate had suddenly turned so vicious, Chen eventually concluded that, even while being persecuted, individuals such as Ding Tong retained their personality of political opportunist.[54]

Internecine strife among persecuted intellectuals would sometimes lead to feuding and physical abuse, reflecting their increasing personal animosity towards each other. In the Qinghe labour camp, where Harry Wu stayed, those who were unhappy with their campmates would act out their grudges and resentments in a political setting – lodging false accusations against the people they hated and joining in prearranged struggles against them. When two rightists, Guo and Wang, were denounced as anti-Maoist elements, they were brutally attacked by four other rightists.

To my horror, the four activists, themselves fellow rightists, began viciously to strike and kick their captives, shouting for them to confess ... Then before our eyes two activists stripped off the helpless men's clothing. One of the men being struggled against slumped to the floor ... Soon the two victims were strung by their wrists from the crossbeam in the roof. I saw someone come in with a belt dipped in water and begin beating one of the men, against whom I knew he held a grudge.[55]

Although the extreme violence described in the above quotation might not occur frequently, it is indicative of a profound moral rift in the minds of some rightists or, at the very least, of a corruption of human conscience. Williams and Wu contend that intellectual prisoners were more likely than were ordinary criminals to attack other prisoners' ideology and/or report their misdeeds; and sometimes they would actively help cadres beat other prisoners.[56] With his personal experience, Cong Weixi comments: "The Anti-Rightist Campaign made me understand that the attacks on intellectuals by their like were extremely vicious, and the struggle sessions I went through revealed again that, when unconscientious rightists attacked their fellow rightists, they could be ten times [more cruel] than other individuals."[57]

In their memoirs, political exiles acknowledge the "human weakness" displayed in such internecine strife. Some (such as Wang Shuyao) attribute this phenomenon to the fallibility of human nature combined with instinct, from which the persecuted intellectuals were not immune; others (such as Yin Yi) believe that this moral degeneration was caused by frequent Maoist campaigns that severely eroded traditional values and contaminated the souls of individuals.[58] Still others frankly admit their inability to avoid displaying such weakness but insist that they did not go beyond a certain point. Wu Yue, for example, says: "I am not denying the fact that I was an activist in the labour camp; I always worked hard to show I was striving for political progress, and to curry favour from cadres, but I never framed others."[59] Cong Weixi's introspection seems convincing but is skilfully defensive. When Artist Li Binsheng, Cong's friend, was groundlessly accused of using cartoons and traditional Chinese painting to defame socialism, he was subjected to a condemnation session, in which all the rightists in his labour group, including his friends and former colleagues, applied all their skill to condemn him and thus display their own piousness. Cong confides, interestingly, that he did not say anything against poor Li; however, this was not so much because he was reluctant to do as simply because so many were attacking Li that he did not get a chance to do so himself.[60]

There were a number of rewards for such activists. They could be promoted to platoon or squad leaders on the army farms, or they could be promoted to inmate group chiefs or cell bosses in the labour camps. They could also expect to be provided with a little more food and a lighter workload than other inmates and could wield considerable power over them, even enforcing physical punishment. In Xingkaihu, when ordinary convicts received monthly food rations of thirty *jin* on average, cell bosses could receive forty-two *jin*. On Farm 850, Dai Huang and Ni Genshan witnessed some rightist platoon leaders orally or physically abuse other rightists and deny them food. Wang Shuyao acknowledges the benefits he enjoyed as a *laojiao* group chief at Qinghe camp and regrets his improper behaviour: he was allowed to do half the work of others per day; reported, condemned, and scolded other inmates; and, after work, he rested while asking other inmates to serve him food.[61] For those on the army farms, their ultra-activism played a role in their early release. With their fellow rightists denounced and disgraced, the opportunity for them to have their labels removed and to acquire early release increased. According to Dai Huang, those appointed as platoon or squad leaders had a relatively easier time than did others in getting their rightist hats removed: "Some got their rightist hats removed in the first wave of 'label-removal' in 1959 precisely because they were active in reporting others and drew close to farm cadres."[62] Although we lack hard evidence to prove the connection between ultra-activism and hat removal (see Chapter 6), it is reasonable to assume that labour farm leaders were, in general, pleased with such people and that it was tempting for these activists to suppress others in order to elevate their own status.

In fact, however, political activism played little role in the early release of *laogai* or *laojiao* inmates in Xingkaihu. First, for *laogai* inmates, sentences were "legally" fixed and decisions to mitigate them were rare and, if they did occur, were overwhelmingly based on work performance rather than on political play-acting. In November 1959, only fourteen convicts had their sentences reduced in all of Xingkaihu. They all achieved this due to their "remarkable performance" in agricultural work or for saving "public properties," but, as Peter Liu puts it, "no political shows would bring any benefit."[63] Camp authorities surely encouraged political activism, but such activism rarely carried much weight when it came to sentence mitigation. Second, for *laojiao* inmates, any sign of resisting labour re-education would likely get their internment extended, but "good deeds" such as attacking others or becoming zealously involved in struggle sessions did not necessarily guarantee early discharge (despite official propaganda to this effect). Tan Tianrong, Han Dajun, Peter Liu, and Wu Ningkun (all *laojiao* inmates) provide no cases of early release for whatever reason during their internment in Xingkaihu. For *laojiao* inmates in the 1950s and early 1960s, whether or not they were granted release was something that was largely decided by national politics rather than by individual performance. When Xingkaihu's *laojiao* inmates were transferred to Qinghe, some ultra-rightists were told that they would have to serve another three-year term at most beginning on May 24, 1961. Yet when May 24, 1964, arrived, many inmates were kept interned due to the tightening of administrative control over "undesirable elements" within the context of the Socialist Education Movement.[64] Unlike on army farms, in institutionalized labour camps political activism, including incrimination of fellow inmates, could rarely improve the lot of activists. These people were essentially misled by camp cadres.

Nevertheless, activism continued to prevail. As long as camp cadres kept encouraging the effort at self-redemption, there were always inmates who were willing to try. Even those with little hope of redeeming themselves strove to show their political piousness by attacking other inmates. Ding Tong, as mentioned earlier, was sent to a Xingkaihu *laogai* branch after having been charged, however innocent, with being a "historical counter-revolutionary plus [an] active counter-revolutionary," making it almost impossible for him to have his sentence mitigated. Yet he still vehemently participated in the denunciation, and physical abuse, of Chen Fengxiao.[65] As Williams and Wu argue, such political activism probably amounted no more than a "bizarre public performance,"[66] a floor show that likely served no practical purpose. Another possibility is that inmates whose activism was encouraged by camp cadres were simply not aware of the internal line of official policies and the fruitless nature of their endeavours, and so hoped that their performance might bring them redemption.

Psychological Distress and Low Morale

Despite their efforts to extricate themselves from their misfortunes, many political exiles came to realize that, their labels ("rightist" or "counter-revolutionary") functioning as a sword of Damocles, the duration of their banishment could be indefinite, that they had no control over their lives, and that it was not certain they would ever see their families again. With their early enthusiasm for work having faded and their internment having been prolonged, frustration, distress, desperation, and fear of dying in the great wilderness overwhelmed many. When Huang Wu and his fellow rightists talked about when their banishment could possibly be terminated, they sadly agreed that they would likely end up as "the first generation of land pioneers," stay forever, and have their "bones buried in the black soil." In early 1960, rightist Zhu Qiping, realizing that he would probably die of starvation, sent his only belonging, a watch, back to his wife in Beijing as a sign of farewell.[67]

Psychological suffering was profound and often unbearable. When political exiles felt repeatedly insulted, when they tried to redeem themselves but their efforts were not appreciated, and when they saw no hope of freeing themselves from a life of daunting labour and starvation, their mental pain was no less bitter than their physical pain. Some used the Chinese idiom "a boundless sea of bitterness" (*kuhai wubian*) to express their distress;[68] others took refuge in their imagination or in literature. Sometimes they used metaphors or similes from classical literature – such as "the Heavens and Earth are not benevolent, so human beings are treated as beasts" or "life is like the morning dew" – to communicate with their more literary campmates. When they found reality wretched, the world of fantasy, imagination or literature perhaps provided temporary relief.[69] Still, some contemplated suicide. When Peter Liu attempted to end his life by turning his self-inflicted cold into pneumonia, his thought went: "I was going to leave this world of bustling labor, struggles, suspicions, condemnations, humiliation, prejudice, hunger and poverty. To cope with these took courage, but to leave them was easy."[70] Others, such as Ni Genshan and Chen Fengxiao, turned to suicide under similar mind conditions; the only difference was that Ni wanted simply to hang himself, while Chen wanted to take a camp cadre with him.[71]

In some cases, mental agony resulted in a state of numbness – a state in which one no longer felt anger or sorrow. When Wu Yongliang was asked to take a night watch for his four fellow rightists who had died of hard labour, he found himself in this state of "non-feeling":

At that moment, I felt my mind was empty – no fear, no sorrow, not even resentment. During the last three years, what could be called freedom, dignity, personality, and taste – those a human being once owned or was supposed to own – seemed to be entirely missing. This is probably the ideal state of "thorough reconfiguration of oneself" (*tuotai huangu*).[72]

Lack of feeling is a manifestation of extreme frustration, bitterness, and desperation, the result of long-lasting psychological ravaging and distress.

In profound mental pain, some political exiles became increasingly depressed and withdrawn. Huang Wu's story about his friend Wang Dahua is revealing: Wang's banishment to Beidahuang and the death of his wife left his little daughter without proper care, and she was accidentally killed by a passing truck. The reticent Wang thus became even less talkative, and the only time his roommates heard his voice was when he softly called for his daughter during the night. One day, Wang found a little monkey in the forest. He brought the monkey back to the team barracks, fed it with his limited food, and talked to it gently. When he went out to walk, he let the monkey sit on his shoulder. The monkey, which he essentially treated as his daughter, became his only spiritual support. Before long, however, the monkey was hung by someone on Wang's labour team. Wang buried the monkey and resumed his silence.[73]

Mental trauma, physical suffering, prolonged hunger, and uncertainty about the future resulted in political exiles growing increasingly eccentric, intolerant, and self-absorbed. Dai Huang recalls that, in 1960, at the Yunshan Branch of Farm 850: "People only cared about their own personal gain or loss; any sense of understanding, friendship, consideration, and help began to wane." Quarrels and fights arose over trivial issues. When someone failed to do his equal share of work, or if someone took someone else's food, he would likely be hurled out, beaten, and even tied to a tree and exposed to the cold.[74] In Xingkaihu, exile communities were also full of tension. Chen Fengxiao's violent eruption against his trouble-making campmate (see Chapter 3) was a result of accumulated grievances.[75]

The tensions among political exiles and their far from exemplary behaviour may be seen as the result of state policies and how they were manipulated at the local level. When camp officers encouraged small reports, when internments were prolonged, when the chances of release became dim and terms of banishment seemingly endless, people became volatile and often turned on each other. This mood was also apparent in the period after the Beidahuang banishment. When *laojiao* inmates were first transferred to Tuanhe Farm in June 1962, they lived relatively harmoniously for a short period of time as the cadres there hinted that they might soon be released due to China's easing political climate. They were deeply hopeful that they would soon be able to see their families. However:

> This good will faded as the weeks of summer passed and we received no word about release. The personal tensions, the continuing fights over food, and the disputes over labor assignments reflected our mounting frustrations and our dwindling hopes.[76]

Still, the reprehensible behaviour of some exiles and their mistreatment of their campmates cannot be entirely attributed to state policies and their implementation. The mistreatment of fellow rightists by certain platoon chiefs, as described by Dai Huang and Ni Genshan, undoubtedly reflects the moral corruption that will fester in any suitable environment. In some cases, interestingly, the employment of violence might have been intended to counteract selfishness (and moral weakness), and this complicates the issue. Harry Wu tells the story of how he used violence when dealing with a self-centred campmate. As a squad leader, Wu was responsible for making a fire to warm the dormitory on winter nights. One day, when he was busy with something else, he asked his fellow inmate Lu to help build the fire. Lu blatantly refused on the grounds that this was not supposed to be part of his work. Outraged that Lu dared to challenge his authority, Wu decided to carry out his order by force:

> "Follow my order," I shouted, "or you'll regret it." Lu shook his head. I stood up and grabbed his foot. "Do it!" I said, and twisted his foot hard. "Let go of me, I'll go," Lu cried, and the tension passed. He went outside to fetch the cornstalks from the ox cart and load them into the stove.[77]

A number of themes may be identified in this story: the selfishness of Lu, Wu's use of force, and Lu's eventual surrender. It is difficult to know how prevalent such instances might have been. From the sources available on Beidahuang, however, one may determine that internecine strife and moral rupture were quite common and that those victimized by a repressive regime did not have much of a sense of collective identity. Indeed, they actively participated in attacking, abusing, and dehumanizing each other.

CONCLUSION

The Anti-Rightist Campaign and the banishment consequent upon it comprised a significant phase in the psychological journey of Chinese intellectuals. Affected by CCP ideology and hoping to continue serving the nation under the Party, many persecuted intellectuals willingly adhered to the Party line, reasserted their allegiance to the Party, and repented their "faults" and "crimes." This self-abasing attitude led to their deference to the labour reform regime. During their banishment, many made strenuous efforts to work hard enough to please labour reform authorities and, thus, eventually be allowed to leave the labour camps.

A considerable number of political inmates were caught up in internecine strife during their time in exile. False accusations, betrayals, and informing existed in all exile settlements, indicating that political inmates, especially intellectuals, had been morally damaged not only by CCP ideology but also by their own desires and weaknesses. Having suffered long-term persecution and internment, intellectual rightists dealt with their fear and anxiety by seeking self-redemption through victimizing others. As a result, these people, who had long been seen (and had seen themselves) as role models in Chinese society, experienced the erosion of their moral integrity, dignity, self-esteem, and sense of identity. Some returned from Beidahuang having lost their faith and even their consciences. They rejected friendships and questioned all that used to give meaning to their lives. The persecution and banishment produced by Mao's Anti-Rightist Campaign not only left countless Chinese physically damaged but also defiled the sanctity of the human spirit.

6

End without End

We were living in two different worlds, across an unbridgeable gap. Staying behind in America, he was able to reap successes and honors and live a happy life in security and affluence. Returning to China, I struggled through trials and tribulations and barely made it to this day of rehabilitation.

—Wu Ningkun reflects upon his life and that of
his school friend, Nobel Laureate Tsung-Dao Lee

The years 1960 and 1961 brought a number of significant changes to the political exiles in Beidahuang. Due to the state's desire to show its benevolence, and its apprehension regarding the mass deaths in the border regions, many rightists had their labels removed and were relocated to the interior. Some were allowed to return to their previous work units. The ultra-rightists were transferred from Xingkaihu *laojiao* camps to Qinghe and Tuanhe Farms in northern China to continue their labour re-education. The number of political exiles in Beidahuang drastically declined.

While the rightists sent from central civilian organizations and the ultra-rightists in the Xingkaihu *laojiao* camps benefited from the policy change in the early 1960s, the *laogai* inmates and the rightists sent from military organizations were left behind to continue their labour reform in the borderlands of Heilongjiang Province. For many who were set free, however, the conclusion of their banishment ended neither their status as political pariahs nor their suffering due to this status. They frequently had to engage in agricultural labour on local farms, were required to go through various ideological remoulding sessions, and were subject to continuous harassment in ensuing political campaigns (not least of which was the Cultural Revolution).

In this chapter, I examine the process of "label removal" (otherwise known as "hat removal," or *zhaimao*) as it was applied to Beijing rightists and the withdrawal of political exiles from Beidahuang. I also look at how these people fared in later years and their rehabilitation in the post-Mao era.

MAO'S PROPOSAL, "HAT REMOVAL," AND RIGHTISTS

The remission of rightists originated in a proposal from Mao Zedong, the chief architect of the Anti-Rightist Campaign and the person who promulgated the practice of remoulding through labour. On August 24, 1959, Mao wrote a letter to his deputy, Liu Shaoqi, regarding the adjustment of the policy on rightists:

> I am convinced that we can convert at least 70% of the rightists within a certain period of time. Within the next seven years or more, say, it is possible to convert 10% of them per year and remove their "hats" ... At the tenth anniversary of the country, remove the "hats" of 10% of the rightists, i.e., forty-five thousand, based on how they have remoulded themselves. This would be instrumental in teaching lessons to the rightists, general bourgeoisies, intellectuals, and the members of "democratic parties."[1]

So far no source has been found to indicate that Mao had a clear idea of what percentage of rightists had truly "turned over a new leaf" at this point. His decision to remove the hats of 10 percent of rightists each year, like his previous one of putting hats on these same people, seems subjective and arbitrary, although it was welcome. In the same letter, Mao indicated that the newly hatless rightists needed to be continuously watched: "if they have a relapse, just put the rightist hats on them again."

The reasons for this initiative may be deduced from an analysis of national politics. Due to the emerging problems associated with the Great Leap Forward and dissatisfaction among the general public and the CCP members, it was necessary for the CCP Central Committee to grant some sort of sociopolitical respite in order to ensure a relaxed atmosphere.[2] Together with the celebration of the upcoming tenth anniversary of the People's Republic of China (October 1, 1959), conditional pardoning of a certain number of rightists was instrumental in showing the benevolence of the Party and building up a warm political environment.[3] The hat removal initiative was one of the strategic considerations of the CCP's high leadership.

Ironically, this initiative was bound up, as an integrated package, with another program – the amnesty of sentenced convicts (prisoners of war or POWs from pre-communist regimes and penal criminals) currently detained in PRC prison camps. In the same letter, Mao suggested the remission of the sentences of a certain number of "POWs and ordinary convicts who had truly turned over a new leaf" to enhance National Day celebrations.[4] This suggestion reveals that, in Mao's perspective, those who aired political dissent were little different from those who fought communist troops on the battlefield or endangered society through committing various criminal offences.

Mao's directive set in motion the hat removal of rightists as well as their withdrawal from rural areas and borderlands. On September 17, 1959, the CCP Central Committee issued "Instruction on the Hat Removal of Rightists Who Have Shown Real Repentance," which required that the hat removal initiative be carried out "during the celebration of National Day." The preconditions that rightists had to meet in order to qualify for hat removal included: (1) truly realizing their faults, professing to be completely convinced, and showing real repentance; (2) verbally and behaviourally endorsing the leadership of the Party and the socialist road; (3) upholding the general Party line, the GLF, and the people's commune; and (4) performing well in their work.[5] Despite the urgency to create the desired atmosphere, however, it was too close to October 1, 1959, to carefully scrutinize individual rightists in order to determine who could safely have their hats removed and who could not. In early December, the names of the first group of famous rightists to have their hats removed (142 people, all from central government organizations, institutions of higher learning, and democratic parties) were publicly announced.[6] In terms of the entire country, the process was rather cautious. When the first round of the program was completed in early 1960, 37,506 people in total had their rightist labels removed, which accounts for 8.5 percent of all rightists.[7]

The work of hat removal for Beijing rightists in Beidahuang started in October 1959. It seems that army farm authorities took this issue seriously. A working plan of Farm 853 requested each branch farm to treat the issue of hat removal seriously and to carefully assess the personal records and labour performance of rightists before drafting a removal list: "any irresponsible attitude towards this matter is absolutely forbidden."[8] When farm authorities found it difficult to clearly grasp the essence of the Party document, they tried to evaluate rightists according to: their attitudes towards the farm leadership and Party branches, their attitudes towards farm work and their contributions to production, and their attitudes towards bad elements and erroneous thoughts.[9] Several "central inspection teams" (*zhongyang kaochatuan*) were sent to the farms to help evaluate the records of Beijing rightists and the success of their ideological remoulding. They verified the files, made direct contact with individual rightists on Farm 853 (but not on Farm 850), and consulted farm heads regarding the number and names of those who were to be pardoned.[10] The final result, to the dismay of many, was that only a small portion of rightists passed the scrutiny. On Farm 850, forty-six Beijing rightists had their hats removed (accounting for 5 percent of all Beijing rightists in this location), and on Farm 853 the number was forty-four (13 percent). They were allowed to leave the farms for their new posts in Beijing, Shanxi, Inner Mongolia, and so on or in other less harsh locations in Heilongjiang Province. Those left behind were enjoined to try their best to remould themselves.[11]

Understandably, rightists' reactions to the removal program differed. Whereas many were disappointed at not being able to shake their hats off, and some were disgruntled by the lack of transparency of the removal processes, those who had their hats removed expressed gratitude and further repentance. Sun Zhanke said: "I committed serious offences before; I appreciate the chance for education and reform the Party granted me. Delabellization has provided me with a new start for my thought reform."[12] Some unsuccessful candidates engaged in self-debasement in order to make a good impression and not jeopardize any future chances. Shi Zhiting stated: "It is correct to keep the rightist hat on me, and this shows the Party's care for me. I will not be disheartened and will try to get the hat removed next time."[13]

The reports of starvation and death turned out to be a decisive reason for the central government's eventual removal of rightists from the borderlands. During their short stay on the army farms in 1959, the inspection teams had heard of the food shortages and edema, but they did not take them seriously and there is no record indicating that they reported these problems to the high leadership. In 1960, however, various reports of rightist deaths arrived in Beijing, caused concern to the central government, and, to a great extent, prompted it to accelerate the label removal process and the relocation of rightists (including those who still bore hats) from the borderlands to the interior.

So far, no official sources regarding how the central authorities made the decision to evacuate the rightists have been disclosed. Individual recollections and biographies do provide various theories, although all these are yet to be verified. Some biographies indicate that certain well-connected rightists and their families wrote to the State Council reporting the conditions in Beidahuang and that this prompted the evacuations. For instance, the well-known figure Xie Hegeng and his wife wrote to Premier Zhou Enlai and the vice-chairman of the state, Dong Biwu, regarding the hardship Xie was suffering in Beidahuang. Zhou and Dong quickly arranged for Xie's return.[14]

Journalists Dai Huang and Yin Yi offer another explanation, although it is unsubstantiated by official sources. They claim that, in the fall of 1960, when Premier Zhou Enlai discovered the discrepancy between the number of Beijing rightists who had been sent to Beidahuang army farms and those who were still alive, he demanded an explanation from the heads of the Mudanjiang Land Reclamation Bureau. When he found out that the majority of deaths were due to edema, malnutrition, and disease, Zhou fully realized the deteriorating situation of these rightists and demanded their complete withdrawal.[15] This version of events is common among the rightists whom I interviewed. They are convinced that it was Premier Zhou who saved them. Although some find it incredulous that Zhou actively saved those reactionaries whom he had helped send away, in the post-Mao context many people were ready to see Zhou as a benevolent leader, a fatherly figure.

On September 17, 1960, CCP central authorities issued another document that signalled a degree of urgency in solving the rightist problem. It demanded a continuation of the effort to remove the labels of rightists and suggested that the removal quota for 1960 should be around 15 to 20 percent of the total. It continued: "Those who do not meet the standard for hat removal, but have laboured for a long term (more than two years) and behaved properly, could also be recalled and assigned suitable jobs."[16] With these instructions, the central inspection teams were sent to Beidahuang once again, this time in November 1960, to implement a second, much larger, round of hat removal. Of approximately 870 rightists on Farm 850, 127 were able to get their hats removed.[17]

While the inspection teams were doing their paper work and going through bureaucratic procedures, the death rate on the army farms escalated. Within less than a month in the winter of 1960, six of Dai Huang's fellow rightists died of starvation and related diseases.[18] The long-awaited hat removal gave rise to an unexpected result – the sudden deaths of rightists due to the combined effects of surprise, jubilation, and extreme physical weakness. After the inspection team announced his hat removal and gave him permission to return to Beijing, Guo Guanjun, a young linguist and translator, bid farewell and sent presents to those still "under hats." The next morning, he was found dead in his bed. Dai Huang and Yang Congdao also recorded other joy-induced deaths during and immediately following hat removal days, just after rightists had rejoiced, shouting: "We are saved!"[19] The deaths of rightists at this juncture reveals a grim picture: the rightists in Beidahuang were being destroyed by hunger, malnutrition, and lack of medical care even as their salvation was approaching. The fact that many were too ill to attend *zhaimao* meetings and that some died right after receiving the news of their release indicates the severity of the conditions in which they succumbed to starvation and how it outpaced their political salvation.

Under these circumstances, the central authorities made a quick decision. In December 1960, the inspection team on Farm 850 announced that, except for those who had previously worked in the military, all Beijing rightists could leave the army farms. The chief of the inspection team proclaimed: "Those who have had their 'hats' removed are to be reassigned jobs; those still wearing 'hats' but having behaved well are also to be given new jobs." In conjunction with this, farm authorities offered political appraisals and provided suggestions for job reassignment.[20] From December 1960 to January 1961, the majority of Beijing rightists left the Beidahuang army farms after having experienced monstrous afflictions.[21]

EVACUATION OF THE *LAOJIAO* INMATES

While rightists on the army farms were evacuated mostly due to starvation and the rising death toll, *laojiao* inmates left the Xingkaihu labour reform complex mainly because of the government's concern over border stability. As discussed in Chapter 3, Xingkaihu was located right next to the Soviet border in the east. Being "backed up by the Soviet elder brother" had been one of the main reasons that Xingkaihu had been chosen as the camp location as the Chinese police figured that escape would be difficult and that, should it occur, the Soviets would ensure the smooth extradition of escapees. However, this advantage was rapidly transformed into a disadvantage in the early 1960s with the emergence of the Sino-Soviet rift and ensuing tension on the borderlands.[22]

The Xingkaihu labour camp complex was also plagued with its own problem – understaffing and the consequent difficulty of efficiently managing inmates. In 1960, for instance, Xingkaihu had 13,318 inmates and only four hundred camp cadres and staff. Branch 5 held approximately 450 inmates who were overseen by fewer than twenty camp cadres.[23] The camp authorities' apprehension was manifested in their frequent requests for more camp cadres and their construction of a new picket line (an earth dyke) in October 1960 to prevent inmates from escaping.[24] Although the shortage of camp cadres and managerial personnel in Xingkaihu was not the major reason for the mass withdrawal of *laojiao* inmates, the camp authorities' concern about handling so many inmates no doubt played a role in this action.

In December 1960, the majority of ultra-rightists were evacuated from Xingkaihu *laojiao* camps to Qinghe Farm in northern China; and, in the following year, around six hundred *laogai* convicts were sent to interior provinces.[25] Camp authorities explained the transfer as a manifestation of the Party's kindness and leniency towards the detainees. Peter Liu and his campmates were told by a branch camp director, Zhang, that this relocation "was the result of a lenient policy towards us criminals, which was meant to better help us in our reform." *Xingkaihu nongchang shi*, too, stresses the government's care of "the weak and the sick," who would receive better food and medical treatment in new locations.[26] However, those transferred insist that this action merely reflected the government's concern over border security. Peter Liu recalls: "We later learned that the purpose of the relocation was to prevent secret collaboration between bourgeois rightists and the Soviet revisionists across the border. Zhang's version of leniency was therefore irrelevant." Camp cadre Liu Junying also admits that those who were sent to the interior from his branch "were actually dangerous elements" and that: "Our chiefs wanted to keep the inmates here at a minimal level."[27] Although in 1960, the inmates, half-dead from hunger, showed no sign of wanting to riot or to disobey, the government still seemed to be wary and sought to pre-empt any trouble that might arise in labour camps due to a possible frontier conflict with the Soviets.

THOSE LEFT BEHIND – MILITARY RIGHTISTS AND *LAOGAI* CONVICTS

While a host of rightists from central civilian organizations were withdrawn from Beidahuang, almost all of those from military units (such as the People's Liberation Army's General Political Department, the National Defence Industry Commission, and navy headquarters) were left behind, unable to return to their original posts. According to a Party directive of November 2, 1959, none of these ex-rightists was allowed to resume his or her former post. Wang Keqin, an ex-navy lieutenant, recalls that his relocation was based on a document issued by the Central Military Commission at the end of 1959, which stipulated that all ex-military rightists were to be assigned to jobs in the regions close to where they had been undergoing labour reform rather than be returned to their original work units or major cities.[28] Apparently, ex-rightists were still considered politically untrustworthy, and it is not surprising that the Party was particularly guarded against those who had once served in the military.

In Beidahuang, the Mudanjiang Land Reclamation Bureau issued a document that contained two important regulations: (1) for rightists who would continue to labour in the land reclamation region, suitable work needed to be offered, based on necessity and possibility; and (2) for rightists who had already been allocated new jobs, efforts needed to be made to appraise and decide the scale of their salaries, to explain the Party's care for them, and to encourage them to better reform themselves.[29] With this document, ex-military rightists were mostly relocated to nearby farms, local enterprises, and/or schools, with their status changed to agricultural worker, industrial worker, office employee, or school staff member, respectively. Their salaries increased and they were granted a degree of mobility. Many worked in the province for more than ten years. After having his label removed in 1961, Wang Keqin found his life and lot improved, though not significantly. He continued to labour on Farm 850 as a lumber worker and then as a coal miner, and his salary increased to sixty-two *yuan* (which was still lower than his military pay in Beijing). What he found significant, however, was that, through a personal connection, a couple of years later he managed to find better employment in a nearby lumber centre, where he became a truck dispatcher. It was not until 1976 that he was allowed to return to Beijing, where he was finally reunited with his wife.[30]

The most desirable work for the ex-military rightists left behind was in local schools, which was in keeping with the policy established by the Party: "Provide them with appropriate jobs, but not important posts."[31] Chen Erzhen, a former engineer at the PLA's Bayi Movie Studio, was relocated to a middle school in a nearby county seat, where he at first worked at odd jobs: cleaning things, boiling water, and ringing the school bell. When the school head happened to learn that Chen was an American-trained graduate of the University of California, and that he had travelled and worked in over ten countries, Chen was allowed to substitute teach math, physics, history, drawing, English, and Japanese whenever the regular teachers were on leave. While he was still considered politically unreliable, he gradually came to be recognized as an indispensable teacher.[32] Being a schoolteacher was among the best jobs an ex-military rightist could obtain in post-1957 Heilongjiang Province.

Like ex-military rightists, *laogai* convicts (including sentenced political prisoners) were retained in the borderlands after the majority of *laojiao* inmates had left, although their status and the treatment they received differed from that extended to relocated military rightists. Confined separately in Xingkaihu, *laogai* inmates were unaware of the mass evacuation of the *laojiao* ultra-rightists in 1960; that six hundred of their fellow convicts had been transferred to the interior also escaped their notice.[33] Life kept on, bitter and hopeless. The only good thing, and something that ex-*laogai* convicts love to recall when interviewed, was that their food supplies increased in the summer of 1962. Improved harvests brought an end to the three years of famine, and this had positive implications for Xingkaihu inmates. While grain continued to be transported to the national granaries, branch camps acquired greater autonomy with regard to growing vegetables; consequently, vegetable supplies for the inmates increased dramatically.[34] Hunger was mitigated, and the most difficult years had passed.

At times, many *laogai* inmates felt pressured by the intensification of China's external relations. In the spring of 1962, Chiang Kai-shek, the president of the Republic of China, who kept claiming sovereignty over the Mainland, initiated a plan to attack China's southeastern coast, and he anticipated a popular rising in response to it.[35] Though it was never carried out, this scheme put the CCP government on alert. While the ramifications of this situation varied according to locality, political inmates in Xingkaihu were adversely affected: all the historical counter-revolutionaries were relocated to Branch 2, and all the active counter-revolutionaries were put into a special brigade and continuously watched by well-armed soldiers. Working hours were reduced, and convicts were herded back to their closely guarded quarters before dark in order to prevent possible riots.[36] As well, due to the continuing deterioration of the Sino-Soviet relationship, the labour reform complex of Xingkaihu began to contract. Branch 1, located right next to the border river, was abandoned and its inmates distributed to other branches. Beijing police authorities began to build a new labour camp complex at Yinhe, far away from border areas, and no new inmates were sent to Xingkaihu after 1963.[37]

Nevertheless, it was domestic rather than external politics that eventually terminated the Xingkaihu labour reform regime and changed the life course of its remaining inmates. With the outbreak of the Cultural Revolution in 1966, the CCP's Beijing municipal authorities were heavily pounded by the Red Guard movement, making it difficult for the Beijing Public Security Bureau to run Xingkaihu from long distance. In September 1966, Xingkaihu was handed over to the Heilongjiang provincial police organ; in February 1967, it was put under military control. Further change occurred in April 1969, when all the remaining inmates – the *laogai*, *laojiao*, and *jiuye* inmates – were transferred to other labour camps in Heilongjiang Province.[38] Chen Fengxiao was at first transferred to Changshuihe Farm in Bei'an County and then to Wulan Farm in Zhalaite County, where he completed his term in 1972. Yin Jiliang, as a *jiuye* inmate, was transferred to Suiling Farm. Hui Peilin, also a *jiuye* worker, was sent to a weaving mill on Yinhe Farm and then to a nearby commune.[39] Xingkaihu ceased to be a labour reform complex and became, instead, a destination for thousands of urban youths seeking a rustic experience during the Up to the Mountains and Down to the Countryside Movement.[40]

With most political exiles resettled in Beijing or other localities, the post-1957 frontier banishment to Beidahuang came to an end. For the victims of the Anti-Rightist Campaign, however, the withdrawal from the Great Northern Wilderness did not necessarily mean an end to their social ostracism. Relocated rightists still had to periodically perform their remoulding-through-labour sessions on local farms; the inmates evacuated from Xingkaihu were still trapped in China's extended penal regime, and continued their forced labour in dozens of other labour reform centres in Heilongjiang Province or northern China until they were finally rehabilitated at the end of the 1970s, with the start of the post-Mao era.

QINGHE AND TUANHE: *LAOJIAO* INMATES IN THE NEW SETTLEMENTS

In the winter of 1960, the vast majority of *laojiao* inmates were transferred from Xingkaihu to Qinghe Farm in northern China, where Tan Tianrong, Peter Liu, Wu Ningkun, and Han Dajun experienced the next phase of their camp lives.

Qinghe Farm, located in Ninghe County, Greater Tianjin, was another labour reform complex established by the Beijing Public Security Bureau outside Beijing. Starting from the early 1950s, various political outcasts, including former landlords, officials and soldiers of the ex-Guomindang regime, and criminal offenders, were sent there to build a state farm from this three-hundred-square-kilometre water-logged area. Just as it did with Xingkaihu inmates, the Anti-Rightist Campaign swelled the ranks of Qinghe inmates: thousands of rightists were sent to fourteen branches of Qinghe Farm, and these were followed by petty criminals who had been arrested in Beijing.[41] Starting in the winter of 1960, when Xingkaihu *laojiao* rightists were transferred to Qinghe Farm, their life trajectories criss-crossed those of Qinghe inmates such as Harry Wu and Cong Weixi.[42]

Upon arrival at Qinghe, Xingkaihu transferees found themselves thrown into another horrifying world that featured "high walls that were topped by [electric] wire." As Wu Ningkun notes: "We were taken into the monstrosity by sour-faced officers, through an entrance guarded by several soldiers holding rifles with fixed bayonets. Above them in the turrets were other soldiers holding submachine guns."[43] The gloomy scene and the treatment they received shattered the hopes of these *laojiao* rightists, who had expected their lot to improve in the interior.[44]

The first thing they encountered on Qinghe Farm was the continuing deterioration of food supplies. As noted in Chapter 4, inmates in Xingkaihu were officially rationed at least thirty *jin* of grain when they performed heavy labour. Soon after they arrived at Qinghe, however, their grain rations dropped to eighteen *jin* of sweet potato flour, and even this was at times replaced by food substitutes made of powdered corncobs, bean stalks, elm bark, rice grass, and so on.[45] Hunger drove inmates to search everywhere they could be for anything edible, such as frogs, vegetable roots, and grass, and even these were often quickly exhausted. Qinghe was haunted by hungry ghosts during 1961 and early 1962. The death rate was probably higher here than it was in Xingkaihu. According to Wu Ningkun, the grave pit of an inmate he buried bore the number 61,301.[46] Those still alive felt their lives slowly withering away.[47] To those relocated from Xingkaihu, the years on Qinghe Farm comprised another horrible period of tribulation: their previous experiences in the borderlands were merely a part and parcel of their entire ordeal within the PRC's labour reform system.

During their confinement on Qinghe Farm, *laojiao* rightists were heavily dismayed by how officials interpreted their labour re-education period. According to the *laojiao* regulations promulgated on August 3, 1957, *laojiao* inmates who displayed real repentance and who behaved well in labour camp could be released (see Chapter 5). Although many ultra-rightists fell into police custody and began their internment shortly after the Anti-Rightist Campaign, and many worked hard for redemption, none were released until May 24, 1961, when Qinghe camp authorities suddenly announced that this date constituted the beginning of their labour re-education.[48] This meant that their previous years of internment and suffering had been spent in vain. Many *laojiao* ultra-rightists, such as Cong Weixi, Wu Yue, and Peter Liu, felt the deep injustice of this, but none dared to question the rationale behind it: those in Liu's labour team "all appreciated the favor of the socialist legal system [and] were grateful for the leniency shown [them] by Chairman Mao and the Party."[49]

Camp authorities did not provide any explanation for this decision, and no official record has been found regarding whether it was applicable only to the inmates of the camps close to Beijing or to those of the camps throughout China. Nevertheless, two official documents enacted in November 1961 and May 1962, respectively, might help us to understand the ambiguity of state policy and practice regarding *laojiao* rightists. The first document, "Circular on Cleaning up Labour Re-Education Rightists," put out by the Ministry of Public Security, revealed that the central police authorities had no intention of any longer keeping *laojiao* rightists in labour camps: "Except for those who behaved exceptionally badly, all of those having engaged in labour re-education for three years should be released. Some of those who have laboured in such institutions fewer than three years but performed relatively well can also be released as you see fit ... They should be free from physical work this winter and given a chance to rest and study." The second document, "Report on the Conference of National United Front Work," put out by the Central United Front Department, reads: "With regard to the rightists and the hat-removed elements who have completed their labour re-education and thus need to be sent back to cities, it is necessary to hold them for a period of time and to make efforts to support them on the spot."[50] According to the memoirs of Xingkaihu and Qinghe inmates, the first document was not seriously followed. In practice, various labour camps, in collaboration with local governments, tended to keep *laojiao* rightists within the labour reform regime or, alternatively, to send them to rural villages. This reflects the state's intention of keeping these dubious elements away from urban areas.[51]

For Qinghe rightists, the newly established *laojiao* terms ranged from half a year to three years, depending on individual cases. Many ultra-rightists coming from Xingkaihu were given severer verdicts than others. Han Dajun was given a two-year term, Peter Liu three years, and Tan

Tianrong at first two and a half years and then an extra year due to his "anti-ideological remoulding" attitude. Those given shorter terms were almost all criminal offenders.[52] For political offenders, however, even these discriminatory terms of internment were not actually observed: some, such as Peter Liu and Han Dajun, were kept in *laojiao* camps until 1969, when they were nominally released and sent to *jiuye* camps.

In the summer of 1962, approximately four hundred survivors of *laojiao* internment were transferred from Qinghe to Tuanhe Labour Farm in the southern suburb of Beijing.[53] The Tuanhe period was probably the best these *laojiao* rightists had experienced since 1957. The three lean years had passed, and food rations gradually increased from eighteen *jin* of grain supplements to forty-five *jin* of real grain per month. Finding these *laojiao* inmates extremely weak, the camp cadres in Tuanhe treated them mercifully. Workloads were light, management flexible, and political pressure slight. They were allowed to read literature and academic works, and some even began writing novels or doing translations.[54] During the Cultural Revolution, the camp cadres of Tuanhe made a considerable effort to protect the inmates under their charge from unauthorized assaults by the Red Guards.[55]

In 1969, *laojiao* rightists eventually saw their labour re-education brought to an end. Some of those who were native to rural areas, such as Tan Tianrong, were allowed to return to their native villages; others, such as Peter Liu, were transferred to forced job placement camps; still others were used as manual labourers in iron and coal mines.[56] Whereas they were still trapped in China's extended penal system and subjected to continuous discipline, post-1957 *laojiao* rightists, as a special political group, eventually vanished.

BEIJING RIGHTISTS AFTER THEIR RELEASE

After their release, Beijing rightists in the interior provinces fared reasonably better between 1961 and 1964 than they had in Beidahuang. A Party document issued in November 1959 claims to grant ex-rightists who had not been dismissed from public positions "suitable jobs based upon work needs, their work capacities, and their expertise"; and a document issued in September 1961 requires that rightists who had been placed in state farms, people's communes, and industrial enterprises be withdrawn from manual labour for a period of rest and political study. This was to "enable them to recover their physical strength. The sick should be provided medical treatment and the needy given some sort of financial assistance."[57] Although the actual implementation of these policies was open to question, at least Beijing rightists no longer had to perform strenuous manual labour, and they were sufficiently fed. For those whose marriages were still intact, family reunions were possible: the old and weak were given a degree of special care, and some professionals and artists were given posts close to their areas of expertise, although at lower ranks and with lower pay than they had enjoyed in the pre-1957 period.

The changes were modest, though by no means insignificant to the languishing rightists. They remained the political and social underclass, and thus continued to be institutionally obsolete and marginalized. According to three Party documents enacted on September 17, 1959; November 2, 1959; and August 17, 1962, respectively, removal of the rightist label did not mean rehabilitation, and the removal policy was not universal. For ex-rightists, newly assigned jobs were to be of lower rank than their original ones; they were not to be placed in important organizations or key positions, nor could they be promoted without long-term trial and scrutiny. Even if their labels were removed, "student ultra-rightists" were not allowed to resume their student status, and rightists who had previously been Party members could not have their membership restored. They could be relabelled, if necessary. Their children were not permitted to study in important fields (such as aeronautics) at university or to be employed in important work units.[58]

With these directives in place, it was difficult for returning political exiles to re-establish themselves in society or to resume their normal life. Even though some were assigned jobs in their areas of expertise, ex-rightists had little chance to employ the full range of their talents. Their basic subsistence needs were met, but they were economically insecure and were denied many job options. A Party document issued in May 1962 shows that some of the returning rightists and ex-rightists were unable to find any employment as their previous work units simply refused to take them back. Some were relocated but could not register as residents and thus lost their livelihoods.[59] In later years, while a small number of high-ranking rightists led relatively peaceful lives, political winds constantly swirled around most. Furthermore, all rightists, with or without hats, were classified under the *heiwulei* (five black elements), together with landlords, rich peasants, counter-revolutionaries, and criminals.[60] They were constantly watched, distrusted, and spurned. What follows are examples of the various fates that befell different individuals.

DIFFERENT LIFE TRAJECTORIES

The rightists who settled down to work in their old areas of expertise were few: most were assigned irrelevant jobs. Released from Beidahuang, artist Ding Cong returned home in the fall of 1960 and re-registered as a Beijing resident. Unable to resume his original position as executive editor of the *People's Pictorial*, he was reassigned to a job at the International Bookstore of China (*Zhongguo guoji shudian*), his main work being to design promotional calendars. It was not until two years later that he was assigned a new job at the Art Gallery of China, thus being able to continue his career as an artist. Alert to the ever-changing political climate and fearing ungrounded accusations, Ding avoided engaging in the satirical style of cartoon drawing at which he excelled; instead, he strove to portray things "positively" and to sing the praises of socialist construction. Among his motifs were the Vietnamese War and Beidahuang landscapes. His cautiousness was rewarded in that he lived a relatively peaceful and cozy life between 1961 and 1966. Although he was still seen as a "hatless rightist" (*zhaimao youpai*), ineligible to hear Party directives or to be appointed to important positions, he nevertheless retained his membership in the Chinese People's Political Consultative Conference and was thus provided with special food supplies, including eggs, meat, and even a decent grade of cigarettes. His happy-go-lucky temperament and his distance from politics enabled him to lead a much better life than was available to many other rightists.[61]

The experience of Huang Miaozi was slightly different from that of Ding Cong. Huang, luckily enough, returned to his previous work unit, the People's Fine Arts Press, as an editor. Before 1966, when the Cultural Revolution broke out, his most significant work was a project known as the Chinese Art History Monograph Collection. His biographer, Li Hui, believes that Huang carefully avoided becoming involved in political issues, choosing, instead, to fully immerse himself in research on Chinese literature and art history. His house became a salon for famous artists in China.[62]

Not many returning rightists were able to live on their expertise and lead such an easy life as did Huang Miaozi. Even though they were allowed to return to their former work units, most could not resume their former jobs. When, for example, Dai Huang returned to the New China News Agency he was not given a chance to resume being a journalist. This was not only because he was deemed to have performed poorly in

Beidahuang but also because the position of journalist was considered to be too politically important to be occupied by a rightist.[63] At first he was sent to tend an orchard and to carry water and deliver vegetables for his fellow workers. Once his work performance was deemed satisfactory, he was reassigned to his former work unit as a copyist, collecting and pasting newspaper clippings into scrapbooks.[64]

The story of Dai Huang indicates the CCP's suspicion of ex-rightists, especially those whose previous occupations were of political and ideological significance (e.g., journalists and government employees). Compared to Ding Cong and Huang Miaozi, who were valued for their artistic talents and thus allowed to work in Beijing, ex-rightists whose expertise was in the media, humanities, and social sciences were neither trusted nor appreciated and were placed in irrelevant posts in the provinces. Wu Yongliang is an example. After returning to the *Dagong Daily*, it was arranged that Wu would work in the reference room for half a year. In the summer of 1961, because of his "unclear" history, it was not considered appropriate for him to live in Beijing, so he was sent, with his family, to a county secondary school in Guizhou Province, where his work consisted of ringing the school bell, mimeographing, and block-printing. This is how many returning rightists fared in the early 1960s:[65] major cities and palatable posts were out of the question for the majority of them.

Continuing Commitment to the Wilderness

Many rightists, during political study sessions or in their thought reports, used rhetoric that indicated their determination to "make up [their] minds to work in the borderlands for the long term,"[66] to display their commitment to labour reform. Needless to say, few of them opted not to return to Beijing when they finally got the chance to do so. Once a release order was given, the most common scenario involved Beijing rightists quickly packing their luggage, bidding farewell to their campmates, and boarding the first passenger (or even cargo) train that passed through the nearest railway station.

In the 1960s, Ding Ling was probably the only rightist who was somewhat unwilling to leave Beidahuang. Despite her earnestness in performing manual work and her personal connection with high official Wang Zhen, Ding was unable to have her rightist label removed either in 1959 or in 1960; consequently, she and her husband Chen Ming were left behind when most rightists were withdrawn from the army farms.[67] Interestingly, although her husband's rightist label was removed in 1961 and the political pressure on Ding eased, the couple were reluctant to return to Beijing. In 1963, the CCP Central Propaganda Department and the Writers Association of China sent a message asking for the return of Ding and Chen, but Ding politely declined this "kindness" on the grounds that she needed more time to engage in self-remoulding at the grassroots level. The explanation seems plausible if we consider her 1960 pledge: "I will engage in physical labour for a long term, and stay with workers, peasants, and soldiers all my life." However, according to Chen, the real reason for her reluctance was that Ding felt uneasy about returning to work with colleagues who had labelled her a rightist.[68]

Thus, the couple stayed put, continuing to make Beidahuang their refuge from political harassment and to demonstrate their commitment to the CCP. While her basic needs were ensured, Ding showed substantial enthusiasm for local affairs – helping in the literacy program, sponsoring community hygiene and road-repairing projects, mediating neighbourhood feuds, writing wall newspapers, and promoting local plays. She also helped farm workers with their family histories (*jiashi*), which were meant to condemn the "old China" and eulogize the new one that had emerged after the "liberation." Although she continued to wear a rightist hat, it seems that she and her husband were content because they saw their lives, which were closely integrated with the masses, as meaningful.[69] In her prose work *Du Wanxiang*, drafted in this period, Ding Ling portrays Beidahuang as a romantic area, the army farm as a lovely place, and the woman protagonist as suffused with socialist consciousness. All the messages she delivered indicate that she fully identified with Party history and Party values; that she had fully integrated into, and deeply loved, the life she was living; and that she was working as a revolutionary writer at the grassroots level.

This view of things is closely linked to Ding's perception of her relationship with the CCP. She believed that her persecution and that of other intellectuals was an aberration of the Party leadership and that it did not stain the Party's ideology or greatness. She thought of her misfortune as a trial, as a part of the course of her life. "A Communist should withstand all kinds of trials," she said. Consequently, she never held a personal grudge against the Party and refused to hold it responsible for her years of suffering: "I would not have had the nerve to go through those years without the indoctrination the Party has given me for so many years." After her case was reversed, Ding Ling expressed an even more favourable attitude towards the Party. She wrote a letter to the CCP Central Committee, articulating her deep appreciation of the Party's rectification of her case, and asked to rejoin it: "The Party! Mother! You are truly great! ... I will be a loyal soldier of the Party forever."[70] Ding Ling's attitude during her exile and her revolutionary oratory upon being released are not popular among those intellectuals who experienced years of persecution and ostracism. In the post-Mao period, especially during the 1980s, a considerable number of writers criticized Ding as a "Party stick," as a "Red clothes priest," or as "old shameful" for her refusal to recognize the social suffering that occurred under the CCP and her intolerance of writings that exposed the darkness of Mao's China.[71]

RENEWED ATTACKS IN POLITICAL CAMPAIGNS

Despite the relatively peaceful period before 1966, returning rightists were politically vulnerable. A significant number of them suffered renewed persecutions during the various campaigns, especially the Socialist Education Movement and the Cultural Revolution, although they were not made the main targets of these campaigns. Starting in September 1962, when Mao re-emphasized the theory of class struggle and the need to identify who comprised the class enemies and who comprised the people, many rightists once again found themselves facing various charges.[72] Some, including Dai Huang, Nie Gannu, and Ni Genshan, were sent to labour camps or simply put in jail.

Dai Huang's story fully illustrates the unpredictability of Party politics and the naiveté of some intellectuals: he repeated what he had done during the Hundred Flowers Campaign. In a transient political thaw initiated by the CCP Central Committee in 1962, and under the warm encouragement of his work unit heads, Dai composed a lengthy report, "Reviewing My Journey of Those Years," in which he reiterated his point of "taking a stand against the privilege mentality of the Party," recollected his three years of experience in Beidahuang, and discussed the causes of the setbacks China had suffered since 1957.[73] A couple of months later, however, Dai found himself once again in a political trap: his report was deemed a "poisonous weed" and a "new sign of class struggle." Thus, just as in 1957, he was again scathingly accused and, in April 1964, was again arrested. For the next fourteen years, he spent most of his time in various labour re-education camps and, when released, he went to forced job placement camps in Qinghe, Tuanhe, and several others in Shanxi Province.[74] Dai's experience sharply contrasts with that of Ding Cong and Huang Miaozi in that he failed to learn a lesson from 1957 and yet again tried to follow the Party's advice to "make a clean breast to the Party" and, thus, again ended up being persecuted. This case of "continuing naiveté" resonates with what Cao Shuji presents in his research. In the Open Your Heart to the Party Campaign of May 1958, many rural schoolteachers in Henan Province who had somehow escaped being labelled as rightists just a few months earlier could not refrain from speaking up on behalf of peasants. In the end, a total of 1,914 teachers were newly classified as rightists in Nanyang District.[75]

The Cultural Revolution (1966–76) saw another bout of attacks on the victims of previous campaigns. Most rightists went through various forms of tribulation – labour re-education camps, "cowsheds" (i.e., makeshift accommodations used to intern class enemies and other political undesirables), and jails. Indeed, the chief targets of the Cultural Revolution were bourgeois academics and capitalist roaders (i.e., Party bosses who were thought to have implemented capitalist policies or followed a revisionist line). While thousands of Party functionaries who persecuted rightists in 1957 now stepped into the shoes of their former victims and bore the brunt of the attacks, powerless and ostracized rightists as well as ex-rightists were, for the most part, seen as "dead tigers." However, since they had been categorized as one of the five black elements, they were still seen as an antagonist force, or as "ox-ghosts and snake spirits" (*niu gui she shen*), and thus were at risk of being attacked. In many cases, after the capitalist roaders had suffered through a number of premeditated attacks, it was the turn of rightists and others in disfavour to be condemned in public struggle sessions. Ritualized humiliation involved "hatting," face painting, and mass condemnation, which might be followed by physical abuse, house searches, internment in cowsheds, or expulsion to rural areas or labour camps.[76]

The degree to which individual rightists suffered varied, depending on local politics. While Wu Yongliang and Liu Meng were not subjected to physical abuse, they were scared into burning all their diaries, photographs, and correspondence. Ding Ling and Ni Genshan suffered increasing denunciation and physical abuse from local Red Guards. Ding's spine and one leg were injured, her home searched, and her manuscripts seized. Ni became almost deaf as the result of a brutal beating.[77]

Some ex-rightists were imprisoned during the Cultural Revolution. After returning to Beijing and acquiring an acceptable job in the People's Literature Press, Nie Gannu spent a great deal of time writing poems, some critiquing the Anti-Rightist Campaign and the "socialist reality," which he showed to his friends. *Penal Files on Nie Gannu* indicates that some of the friends with whom he often had dinner reported these reactionary poems, as well as Nie's other writings, to Beijing police authorities. This led to Nie's arrest and a life sentence. Another version of Nie's arrest is that, in 1966, fearing that the Red Guards might find his poems, Nie had them delivered to his friend Hu Feng, whom he mistakenly thought to have been released. The result was his immediate arrest.[78] After two years of being confined in a cowshed and performing menial labour, Ding Ling and Chen Ming were both arrested and put in the notorious Qincheng Prison in the northern suburb of Beijing. They were released in 1975, but it was not until 1979 that Ding's status was reclassified and her sentence revoked.[79] Huang Miaozi and his wife were also put in Qincheng Prison due to their relationship with GMD officials during the pre-1949 period. This was considered a serious "historical problem." The stories of Nie, Ding, and Huang show that, in subsequent political upheavals, rightists were repeatedly assaulted for past offences.

Ironically, imprisonment during the Cultural Revolution – a time when political turmoil engulfed the nation – was an unexpectedly good experience for some rightists. Being formal penal regimes with armed soldiers on guard, prisons were not easily assaulted by the Red Guards – something that differed significantly from the situation outside "the wall of confinement."[80] For political prisoners exempt from the death sentence, imprisonment was perhaps the best way to avoid the baffling horror of the Cultural Revolution. During the first two years of his term, Nie Gannu was detained in Banbuqiao Prison in Beijing, where his personal safety was ensured, medical care and food supplies were fairly good (eggs and meat were available), there was not much physical work to do, and reading newspapers and reciting Mao's Little Red Book constituted the major part of a prisoner's daily life. All of this made Nie somewhat nostalgic for this phase of his post-1957 experience.[81] When Ding Ling suffered terrible abuse from the local Red Guards on Baoquanling Farm, she saw the military cadres sent to arrest her as life savers, and her husband Chen Ming also acknowledged that their experience in Qincheng Prison was much better than what they had anticipated.[82] Although Chinese prisons during the Cultural Revolution were by no means oases, as they held and often maltreated a considerable number of intellectuals and artists purged by Mao's leftist cohorts, it is generally known that these prisons did provide many political outcasts with a refuge from the Red Guards. While Ding Ling, Nie Gannu, and Huang Miaozi were relatively safe in prisons, countless rightists and ex-rightists, such as Huang Shaoxiong and Fu Lei, were brutally abused by the Red Guards and eventually committed suicide.[83]

Despite being in a predicament, many young rightists stood up to condemn the evil forces unleashed by the regime responsible for the Cultural Revolution; for this reason, they were maltreated in prison or even executed. Student rightist Lin Zhao was executed in 1968 due to her condemnation of the CCP leadership. Dismissed from Peking University in 1958, Lin Zhao was sent to a labour re-education camp in Beijing for two years. Granted a sick leave in 1960, Lin left for Shanghai, where she participated in the compilation of an underground journal, *Xinghuo* (*Spark*), in order to air her dissent. She also wrote to the CCP Central Committee asserting her opinions on an array of political issues, such as the Great Leap Forward and China's foreign policy, for which she was sentenced to a twenty-year prison term. In jail, Lin continued her protest through engaging in hunger strikes, chanting poems, and shouting slogans. She cut her fingers so she could use her blood to write. She also kept condemning Mao's personality cult and totalitarian tyranny. She was shot in Shanghai on April 29, 1968. Afterwards, a policeman visited her family to collect five cents for the expense of the bullet.[84]

Like Lin Zhao, other rightists were executed during the Cultural Revolution after facing such new charges as "anti-Mao Zedong thought" or "attacking the proletarian dictatorship." In 1970, when the Striking Counter-Revolutionaries Campaign was under way, four rightists were labelled active counter-revolutionaries and executed in Nanjing, as was rightist Zhang Chunyuan, a co-editor of *Spark*, in Lanzhou. In 1976, ex-student rightist Zhang Xikun was executed in a labour camp in Sichuan upon being charged with "trying to organize a group riot."[85] In these cases, young rightists were punished for political offences that, although sporadic, challenged the post-1966 CCP regime. At this point, previous rightist offences were relegated to the backstage.

REHABILITATION

With the advent of political change after Mao's death, victims of the Anti-Rightist Campaign were rehabilitated. Due to the effort of post-Mao leaders, especially Hu Yaobang, the director of the Central Organization Department, the CCP Central Committee issued two documents in April (No. 11, 1978) and September 1978 (No. 55, 1978), respectively, which demanded complete hat removal for all rightists and careful rectification for those who had been wronged in the Anti-Rightist Campaign.[86] These central decrees opened the floodgate for massive rectification during the post-Mao political thaw. As a result, almost all rightists (including those who had died) had their labels removed. By 1980, the verdicts on more than 540,000 rightists, out of the officially recognized figure of 552,877, had been reversed.[87] Survivors were informed by the work units that had labelled them twenty years earlier that the charges against them had been revoked and that their incorrect classification would be corrected.

Compared to the treatment of the Party officials who were purged during the Cultural Revolution, however, rightists' rehabilitation was politically incomplete. The Party formally asserted that the Anti-Rightist Campaign per se had been necessary because there were genuine rightists who had been trying to overthrow the Party's rule; however, it admitted that the campaign had committed excesses and thus had hurt the innocent.[88] The authorities carefully chose the term *gaizheng* (to correct) rather than *pingfan* (to rehabilitate) to define the mass redressing of the cases of wronged individuals. In addition, the government refused to provide non-Party rightists monetary compensation for the salary they lost as a result of having been incorrectly classified. Many rightists received no apology when the authorities announced the correction of verdicts that had devastated their lives for more than twenty years. For some, the political appraisal or resolution handed to them was worded in quite a reserved fashion, although they were cleared of major charges.[89]

With grievances mixed with sighs of relief, a resigned lament for their lost years, and, for some, a desire to serve a revitalized nation, rehabilitated rightists entered the era of post-Mao reform – an era characterized by fewer political campaigns and more individual freedom. As the survivors of decades of persecution, many were in their fifties or sixties; for them, social stability and personal security assumed the utmost importance. In the new sociopolitical environment, many of them settled into jobs – either in their previous professions or in related work – where their expertise, though rusty, was valued as the country marched towards the Four Modernizations (i.e., the modernizations of agriculture, industry, national defence, and science and technology). Chen Fengxiao, Tan Tianrong, Peter Liu, and Wu Ningkun all found employment as teachers in universities, colleges, or high schools; Dai Huang, Yin Yi, Zheng Xiaofeng, and Wu Yongliang returned to their previous occupations as journalists or newspaper editors; Ding Ling returned to her career as a renowned writer, travelled around the country, collected sources for her literary creations, and restated her faith in the bright future of socialist China.[90] Many of those dismissed from the Party (Fang Lizhi, Liu Binyan, Wu Zuguang, Dai Huang, etc.) were invited to return to help rebuild its tarnished reputation. The CCP promoted the concepts of "correctly handling historical issues" and "looking forward" in order to encourage people to forget the unhappy past and instead focus on China's reconstruction. In that rehabilitated rightists largely came to terms with the life pattern the Party set for them (at least in the late 1970s and early 1980s), and in that they were willing to serve the more promising country that was emerging under the Party, the CCP seems to have succeeded in fixing its relationship with them.

But for ex-rightists, their post-1957 experiences – twenty more years of persecution, banishment, and maltreatment – had a devastating impact on the rests of their lives. In addition to their psychological wounds (see Chapters 4 and 5) and their disappointment with the Party's refusal to apologize for the Anti-Rightist Campaign, they felt a strong sense of loss. They felt they had lost their best years, the chance to display their talent, and the chance to realize their dreams. Nothing could make up for this, although they still tried to find meaning in their lives. One day in 1979, Wu Ningkun had the opportunity to meet Dr. Tsung-Dao Lee (Li Zhengdao, the 1957 winner of the Nobel Prize for physics), his University of Chicago school friend, who, in 1951, had seen Wu off in San Francisco on his journey back to their homeland. During their fifteen-minute talk, Wu sensed the enormous gap, social and intellectual, that separated them.

> I quickly sensed we were living in two different worlds, across an unbridgeable gap. Staying behind in America, he was able to reap successes and honors and live a happy life in security and affluence. Returning to China, I struggled through trials and tribulations and barely made it to this day of rehabilitation. Secure in the "imperialist fortress of America," he was hailed as a patriot in Communist China, feted by every top leader of the Party and the government, and whisked about in a chauffeur-driven Red Flag limousine as an honored guest of the state. Recalled to serve the motherland, I was denounced as an enemy of the people and had survived labor camps, starvation, and proletarian dictatorship.[91]

Although deeply frustrated by this comparison, an amusing thought flashed through Wu's mind: "What would have happened if I had been the one to see him off back to China on that July afternoon in San Francisco? Would I perhaps be sitting in his armchair and he in mine?" When contemplating his answer, he paradoxically cherished some of his bitter experience over the past twenty years, but he concluded: "God forbid he [Lee] should ever have been in my accursed shoes."[92]

Conclusion

In the 1950s and 1960s, the Chinese Communist Party used China's borderlands to facilitate its agenda of state consolidation and economic growth. By sending various offenders to the borderlands, the state aimed to crush forces of opposition (real or imagined), remove undesirable elements from the interior, facilitate land reclamation, and further the ideological remoulding of offenders. In this book, I investigate the political banishment of rightists to Beidahuang on the northeastern frontier, the implementation of the CCP's remoulding through labour regimen at the local level, and the struggle of political inmates – those purged in the Anti-Rightist Campaign – against the torments of the exile settlements. While summarizing my major themes, I now attempt to address some of the broader issues related to persecution, China's intellectual community, CCP politics, and the ramifications of banishment.

I treat the Anti-Rightist Campaign and the punitive exile consequent upon it as ill-conceived and self-destructive acts carried out by the CCP during its attempt to consolidate power. The CCP purged not only political dissidents, who turned out to be few in number, but also those who were suspected of having the potential to pose a threat, in order to build up momentum for a thorough political cleansing. As it turned out, even the loyal opponents and supporters of the CCP were purged by the heads of work units and/or local party bosses either to meet labelling targets or to serve their personal needs. During these purgings, a phenomenon euphemistically referred to as the "revolution consuming its sons" became manifest. When the Party leadership was unable to clearly identify the sources of a threat, it tended to expand the scope of its target, thus enabling local Party bosses to take advantage of political campaigns to eliminate their rivals. In these circumstances, a considerable number of Party loyalists and Party followers were rendered victims—demoted, imprisoned, or banished, their revolutionary credentials bearing little weight. By punishing those who criticized, but who actually supported and/or sympathized with, the regime, the CCP damaged at least a part of its ruling base.

The suffering endured by political exiles did not come only from the state and its agents: it was also self-imposed. Indoctrinated with Party ideology, many political exiles acknowledged their offence, wished to cleanse their minds of "erroneous thoughts," and worked hard to show their repentance and to achieve self-redemption through manual labour. This struggle for redemption was a self-imposed affliction. When they discovered that their fate was decided more by Party policies than by their individual efforts at labour reform, many exiles found themselves in psychological agony. Internecine strife exacerbated their misery and led to moral corruption.

The fortune of political exiles was determined by a combination of high politics and local politics. The CCP high leadership wanted an integrated agenda of land reclamation, ideological remoulding, and controlled rehabilitation. This was to be brought about through both formal and informal labour reform regimes. The labour camp or farm authorities, as the local agents of the state, did make efforts to accommodate the agendas of the higher echelon. Overwhelmingly, however, they used political exiles as slave labour to achieve economic growth, especially agricultural production. Their local activism, including their seeming commitment to Great Leap Forward politics, "saving grain for the national granaries," and reducing food supplies for farm workers, greatly exacerbated the misfortune of the rightist exiles.

I also consider border banishment to be one of the CCP's most important strategies for enforcing its rule. The CCP banished not only politically subversive elements but also other groups. In addition to rightists, convicted criminals were sent to the borders to engage in land reclamation and other projects, and demobilized soldiers were sent to develop army farms. The mass sending-down of urban youth (including the Red Guards) in the 1960s and early-mid 1970s served to clear up the mess created by the Cultural Revolution and to de-urbanize overcrowded urban centres.[1] Whenever the political or economic need arose, China's borderlands functioned as a dumping ground.

Nowadays, both the Xingkaihu complex and the Beidahuang army farms have ceased to function either as labour reform camps or as a destination for exiles. Both have become civilian production units and thus appear no different from the dozens of other prospering state farms in the Heilongjiang borderlands. Proud hosts will show farm visitors the vast expanses of thriving wheat fields and rice paddies stretching as far as the eye can see (demonstrating the accomplishments of the older generations in the area of frontier reclamation) and the flourishing fisheries, dairies, and wild-animal raising enterprises (demonstrating the blessings of the "transformed" natural world). The life of the residents in the borderlands, they say, is approaching that of those in towns and cities under the Party's liberal economic policies, which were implemented after the Third Plenum of 1978.

Just as local leaders and the official media glorify these admirable achievements, and as the institutional structure of the labour reform regime disappears, so Beidahuang's past as a destination of internal exile fades from public sight, its former function forgotten. In the meantime, the state tries to erase this part of history from national memory by suppressing public concern and scholarly interest in the Beidahuang of the 1950s and 1960s. Army farm files are restricted, early documents on Xingkaihu are kept in the archives of the Beijing Public Security Bureau, and any unofficial investigation into the history of banishment is prohibited.

An important way of neutralizing Beidahuang's troubled past involves monopolizing and reinterpreting its history. Except for government-sanctioned local histories and gazetteers, no official sources have been formally released showing Beidahuang's history of receiving thousands of involuntary migrants in the late 1950s. We find, interestingly, that the rightist banishment has not been entirely erased from the local histories of Farm 850, the Yunshan Branch of Farm 850, or Farm 853; rather, it has been reinterpreted to show the rightists' involvement in frontier pioneering, the idea being that they were warmly treated on the army farms and contributed to the development of the borderlands. Xingkaihu's labour camp history focuses on cadres' efforts to facilitate the ideological renewal of inmates and to help them develop useful work skills. As the stories of the labour camps are embellished, much of their history evaporates: "killing history by rewriting history."

In Xingkaihu, the local administration did not simply demolish the vestigial camp buildings, prison cells, or other reminders of the existence of a large labour reform complex; rather, it left them standing, made use of them, or allowed them to become obsolete, slowly eroded by the everyday life of local people. The camp headquarters is now the administration building for the Xingkaihu State Farm; the discarded red-brick camp cells have been transformed into storage spaces used by local residents; a camp yard has become a chicken run; and old offices are being used by a weaving group. When the former campsite becomes a part of the everyday life of local communities, a dark page of local history is diluted. Historical remnants are consumed by contemporary acts that aim to either deliberately or unconsciously forget the past. There is certainly no place to construct any form of memorial for those who suffered and died in this part of the borderland. There is nothing to compare to the memorials that have been dedicated to the Holocaust victims or to those who died in Security Prison 21 under the Khmer Rouge.

The stories of the banishment and labour camps will not be easily forgotten, however. Survivors keep the public memory alive through memoirs, historians continue to delve into the subject, and filmmakers occasionally craft critical, rightist-themed gems so carefully camouflaged that they pass CCP censorship with flying colours (the most recent of these is Zhang Yimou's *Coming Home*). However, the most important reason that the rightist persecution and the labour camps will not be forgotten is their devastating effect on both individuals and the nation as a whole. This makes any attempt to erase their memory impossible.

The physical and psychological sufferings of the political exiles are becoming increasingly well known. The general picture we have thus far shows that hundreds of thousands of victims of the Anti-Rightist Campaign struggled in various labour reform settlements – such as Jiabiangou in Gansu, Bailanggou in Qinghai, Qinghe near Tianjin, and Shaping in Sichuan, to name but a few – and were subjected to maltreatment not only by camp officials but also by their campmates. Daunting labour, hunger, and physical and psychological abuse were daily experiences. Numerous exiles languished and perished. Interpersonal contamination was also common as suffering was inflicted not only on victims but also on their families. Spouses were either implicated or pressured to condemn their partners and/or renounce their relationship with them. Those who refused to do so lived under the shadow of having been categorized as "problematic" families, with their children adrift and suffering such discrimination as being barred from university education and decent employment. Even after returning from banishment, rightists (and their families) lived under suspicion and ostracism for years.

One can only imagine the waste of human talent. Of about 5 million educated elites, more than half a million were purged in 1957–58 and forced to leave their professional posts, many for more than twenty years. Of those who survived the harsh years, many suffered intellectual death. This terrible waste of human intelligence was the direct result of CCP policies that scapegoated the country's most needed minds during the years of national economic reconstruction: this squandering of human talent is both tragic and almost impossible to comprehend. However, we have to remember how the CCP viewed human talent. On the one hand, the Party wanted to enlist the expertise of bourgeois intellectuals to modernize China while its own "Red experts" were not fully fledged, and Mao often talked about granting rightists the chance to work for the nation; on the other hand, the Party did not hesitate to remove many rightists from their professional posts and place them in labour camps. The key reason for this seeming contradiction is that, as Joel Andreas puts it, Mao did not accept the conviction of intellectuals that their expertise made them more fit than the communists to run the country.[2] Thus, once such convictions turned intellectuals into regime enemies, and priority was given to eliminating any such threats to the state, their expertise was no longer appreciated. Or, as the CCP would put it, one's talent must be employed in the service of the people; otherwise, it is worthless.

Another social ramification of the Anti-Rightist Campaign and the labour farms was that they drove the politics of fear into people's hearts. The CCP used the "kill-the-chicken-to-scare-the-monkey" strategy in this campaign and the banishment. Once an individual had been purged and sent far away, his/her family, friends, and colleagues were likely to be frightened into compliance. The victims themselves often readily accepted their penalty in order to avoid further trouble or implicating their families. Similarly, in labour camps or banishment settlements such as Xingkaihu and the Beidahuang army farms, officials used the threat of prolonging one's internment as an effective psychological tool, successfully scaring most inmates into subservience. By driving fear into the hearts of individuals, the CCP succeeded in intimidating a large population.

Consequently, China's political development was negatively affected. The 1957 rightist persecution occurred during the period when the CCP was consolidating its power and prior to its adventurous socioeconomic program, the Great Leap Forward. By punishing assertive intellectuals and other dubious elements, the state successfully muffled dissent and cleared the way for its programs. In particular, the Party leadership launched the GLF and the People's Commune without any significant resistance from the educated elites. The 1957 purge and consequent banishment paved the way for further Party blunders. Because its treatment of rightists did not encounter any resistance, the state continued to use purging and banishing as proven means of removing unfavourable elements – for example, relocating ex-landlords and returning rightists to rural areas in the early 1960s,[3] rusticating the Red Guards during the Cultural Revolution, and sending university graduates to villages and factories for short-term "tempering through labour" after the 1989 crackdown. The post-1957 banishment provided a precedent for later banishments in the Mao era and, to lesser extent, in the Deng era.

With regard to the purged individuals, certain broader issues merit discussion. I show that the victims of the Anti-Rightist Campaign became perpetrators in the labour reform settlements in that some of them actively engaged in reporting and incriminating their fellow campmates in an effort to show their fidelity and to earn early release. Related to this phenomenon is the so-called "dog-eat-dog" syndrome, or what I prefer to call the "chain-of-prey" syndrome. In the context of the People's Republic of China, this refers particularly to the following phenomenon: an individual or a group of people, after showing their political allegiance by engaging in the persecution of others in one campaign, could not avoid being themselves purged in subsequent campaigns. It was the CCP's "campaign culture" that forced people to prey on others – their friends, their colleagues, and so on. The victims of the Anti-Rightist Campaign were undoubtedly wrongly labelled in that they suffered from the CCP's perverse and ill-conceived method of eliminating political opponents. A careful investigation of the experiences of some, however, indicates that they were not as benign as they are often thought to be. Ding Ling suffered unfair treatment for more than twenty years and is thus considered to have been one of the best known literary victims of unjust treatment. That being said, the records since the 1940s are not always to her credit. As Tani Barlow puts it: "Ding Ling had been heavily implicated in the Communist Party's efforts to control all literary expression for many years, and she was equally involved in struggles for power inside the state bureaucracy."[4] Prior to her purge in the mid-1950s, Ding had been actively involved in the wrongful treatment of other intellectuals, such as liberal writers Wang Shiwei and Xiao Jun in the 1940s and Shen Congwen in the early 1950s. The campaign against *The Story of Wu Xun*, the movie that was condemned as advocating education and reform rather than revolution, was led by Ding Ling.[5] Her radical stance was clear before she herself became a target of vicious attacks, and, ironically, it did not save her from such attacks. As for other victims in 1957, sources show that some, including leading student rightists Tan Tianrong and Lin

Xiling, had been activists in the Elimination of Counter-Revolutionaries Campaign of 1955.[6] A glimpse into their past reveal their original revolutionary aggressiveness.

As mentioned in Chapter 1, some intellectuals took advantage of the Anti-Rightist Campaign to persecute their rivals and thus help consolidate their own positions. It turned out, however, that they themselves became targets of the next wave of persecution during the Cultural Revolution. Zhou Yang, the chief persecutor of Ding Ling, was sent to prison and barely survived. Lao She, a vigorous denouncer of Wu Zuguang, Cong Weixi, and others in 1957, committed suicide after being brutally abused by the Red Guards and coldly treated by his family. Wu Han, the person who had a hand in labelling dozens of the members of the China Democratic League, died in prison, with all his family members implicated. Numerous stories indicate that, in the late 1960s, the fate of these anti-rightist warriors was even worse than was that of their prey of the 1950s. As for the upper echelons of the Party leadership, many of the hardliners who advocated harsh punishment for rightists, such as Liu Shaoqi, Peng Zhen, and Luo Ruiqing, themselves fell into disgrace during the Cultural Revolution and were badly treated by Mao's cohorts.[7] They were not even given the chance to be re-educated but were simply put in jail, where they were tortured, and some died. Those treated leniently were cooped up in cattle pens and, when released, were sent to the countryside to perform physical labour, just as had their victims in 1957. Although, on the surface, their participating in the purging of others does not seem to be logically connected to their being purged in turn, the fact is that their revolutionary aggressiveness and harshness towards the regime's enemies helped construct a Party culture steeped in ruthlessness and a desire to cleanse and suppress. Their revolutionary roots and their professed commitment to Party ideology did not exempt them from being purged when Mao felt it necessary and expedient. The same observation applies to the Red Guards, who, after completing their mission of sweeping away Mao's targets, were seen by Mao as troublemakers, suppressed by the military, and sent to the countryside.

The lot of these Party followers, Party loyalists, and revolutionary seniors – from the leftist writers of the 1940s to the top leaders purged in the 1960s – has both sociological and political implications. In a sociological sense, these people clearly formed a chain of prey. Predators in one circumstance could be easily turned into prey in another, when the social ecology changed or when new predators appeared. In a political sense, the stories of the political outcasts in Mao's China repeatedly demonstrate that those who closely followed Party teachings would likely be deserted, that those who were deeply involved in communist politics would eventually become its victims, and that those who actively attacked others were eventually attacked themselves. All this was due to the Party's need to constantly cleanse itself, the ever-changing agenda of the top leader(s), the lack of legal and institutional guarantees, and, not least, the volatile mood swings of Mao Zedong. All of these people were victims of communist politics. Those purged in 1957 and banished afterwards constituted a mere link in a series of persecutions, and the stories of the Beidahuang rightist exiles account for only a few out of the millions of miserable experiences that passed unnoticed.

The effectiveness of border banishment needs to be reassessed. To what extent was the state's agenda achieved through purging and banishing? In terms of crushing forces of opposition and intimidating the masses, the CCP seems to have achieved its goal. Large numbers of critics were silenced, driven out of cities, and reduced to becoming manual labourers, and this often happened with next to no resistance from either the victims or the general public. It would seem that the CCP had reason to convince itself of the success of its coercive strategies.

But what about the alleged transformative power of political campaigns and banishment? The state boasted that it had succeeded in changing the behaviour of offenders and in rejuvenating the spirits of the Chinese people. It is plausible that, through various thought remoulding regimens, the Party's ideology influenced the thoughts of many Chinese, including those originally in disfavour. When a campaign was imposed from above, intellectuals shut their mouths, adhered to political guidelines, and obeyed the Party establishment. Many rightist exiles reasserted their allegiance to the regime and endorsed the Party's labour reform policy. Some, upon returning from Beidahuang, expressed their continuing devotion to the nation and the CCP in wording prescribed by the Party; and many others became less vocal than they had been before their banishment. Persecution and banishment seemed to have a crushing impact on the minds and behaviour of many exiles, especially the intellectuals.

The real transformative effects, however, were probably mediocre at best and counter-productive at worst. In the first place, banishment generated a strong sense of disillusionment and resentment among many intellectuals and increased their alienation from the state, as was found in the case of Beidahuang exiles. When the sending-down was implemented in 1958, Party propaganda stressed educational goals (i.e., making exiles truly repent their faults, achieving spiritual growth, and becoming

dedicated workers for socialism). In the labour reform settlements, however, political education often led to psychological abuse, and remoulding through labour was reduced to sheer slave labour. Experiencing an
array of human woes and afflictions, rightist exiles realized the nature of
punishment through labour. Some were physically and verbally submissive, while others rose to condemn the labour reform practices and thus
invited further penalty. Except for forcing people to conceal their hatred
and resentment, so far from transforming the ideological perspectives of
political exiles, the Party merely eroded the sympathy these people had
for it in the early PRC years. Thus, the Party's desire to ideologically reconfigure political offenders was far from realized, even though ideological conformity was forced upon both rightists and the larger population.

    Furthermore, to the majority of political exiles, the combination of
indoctrination, coercion, and manipulation deployed during their banishment served as a means of transforming how they managed daily
politics and helped them to improve their strategies for dealing with the
Party and its local agents, the camp cadres. Going through the tribulations of being purged and banished, political outcasts realized the importance of properly managing their interpersonal relations with their
bosses, with those who had any say over their lots, and with those with
whom they dealt in daily life. People returned from banishment having
developed more sophisticated strategies for expressing their voices; their
skill in handling interpersonal relations (including subtle signals from
their superiors) had greatly improved; and they had a better sense of how
to protect themselves, survive, and advance. This is what their "thought
progress" amounted to. This is how their minds were reprogrammed.

    Most important, being purged and banished helped to destroy some
intellectuals' belief in Marxist ideology and fostered political dissent in
late- and post-Mao China. Having experienced persecution and years of
banishment, those who had initially argued for the revitalization of the
Party began to show their alienation from it. Some persecuted intellectuals thought that Marxism was fundamentally flawed and that, under the
CCP, China's political system was erring. The student exiles I examine in
this book, such as Chen Fengxiao and Tan Tianrong, developed dissenting views that were stronger than those they had held before banishment.
The Party's treatment of its followers and loyal opponents deepened their
comprehension of communist politics. After the Cultural Revolution,
the strongest criticisms of Chinese Marxism and the CCP regime came
from those who had been purged in 1957, and these are the people who
comprised the genuine dissidents and liberal intelligentsia in the Deng

era. Vocal critics of the CCP and human rights campaigners, such as Liu Binyan, Wang Ruowang, and Fang Lizhi, drew wisdom for their criticism of the CCP's ideological extremism and political autocracy from their experiences of being purged and banished in the post-1957 years. For instance, Liu Binyan defined the essence of the CCP's political leftism as a case of "mutual destruction and mutual cruelty": "It makes human being inhuman. It makes a free man unfree. It turns a person of independent personality into a submissive tool. It turns man into beast."[8] In the 1980s, despite some exceptions, ex-rightists were conspicuously critical of China's political framework and the Party's ideologies. Thus, persecution and banishment were detrimental not only to China's educated elite but also to the Chinese Communist Party itself.

Appendix A: Interview List*

Ba Hong, movie director (Beijing: July 17, 2004)
Chen Dongbai, middle school teacher (Panjin, Liaoning: August 17, 2002)
Chen Erzhen, engineer (Beijing: July 18, 2004)
Chen Fengxiao, university student (Weifang, Shandong: July 3, 2004)
Chen Ming, editor (Beijing: August 19, 2002; July 5, 2004)
Dai Huang, senior journalist (Beijing: July 17, 2004)
Ding Cong, artist (Beijing: August 20, 2002)
Gu, government official (Changchun: September 22, 2002. Gu prefers that his given name not be released.)
Guo Daohui, retired official (Beijing: May 26, 2006)
Han Dajun, scientist (Beijing: July 5, 2004)
He Fengming, journalist (Beijing: June 7, 2008)
He Shanzhou, university department head (Vancouver: October 22, 2003)
He Ying, literature journal editor (Changchun: September 21, 2002)
Hu Xianzhong, university student (Changchun: September 23, 2002)
Hui Peilin, journalist (Beijing: July 19, 2004)
Li Xin, Party cadre (Beijing: October 6, 2002)
Liu Junying, retired labour camp cadre (Beijing: July 16, 2004)

*Except for those of Guo Daohui, Liu Junying, Wang Shusen, Wang Zhiliang, and Zhang Jiqian (who are informants in the stories of their colleagues or friends), all the positions and jobs listed are those the interviewees held before the Anti-Rightist Campaign.

Liu Meng, journalist and government employee (Beijing: October 4, 2002)

Peter Liu, translator (Beijing: July 7, 2004)

Lu Gang, Party official, college head (Dalian: August 6, 2002)

Lu Wencai, college teacher (Dalian: August 5, 2002)

Ma Shifu, college student (Dalian: September 27, 2002)

Tan Tianrong, university student (Qingdao: June 29, 2004)

Wang Hongren, junior police officer (Changchun: September 22, 2002)

Wang Keqin, military officer (Beijing: July 18, 2004)

Wang Li, junior clerk (Dalian: September 29, 2002)

Wang Meng, writer (Beijing: October 5, 2002)

Wang Shusen, professor emeritus (Dalian: August 2, 2002)

Wang Zhiliang, retired doctor (Dandong, Liaoning: August, 12, 2002)

Wen Zicheng, college student (Dalian: September 18, 2002)

Wu Yue, journal editor (Beijing: October 5, 2002)

Xu Ying, journalist (Beijing: July 19, 2004)

Yan Tunfu, university student (Beijing: July 8, 2004)

Yan Xueli, middle school teacher (Dandong, Liaoning: August 12, 2002)

Yang Congdao, military technician (Beijing: July 11, 2004)

Yin Jie, college student (Dalian: September 19, 2002)

Yin Jiliang, journalist (Beijing: October 3, 2002)

Zhang Jiqian, professor emeritus (Beijing: August 20, 2002)

Zheng Xiaofeng, journalist (Beijing: July 6, 2004)

Appendix B: Note on the Sources and Methodology

Banished to the Great Northern Wilderness is based on a variety of sources, including primary sources (such as Party documents, camp archives, personal interviews, memoirs of surviving exiles, and other autobiographical materials) and secondary sources (such as biographies, reports, and journals). I also use local histories and gazetteers, which were reworked and compiled under official auspices, as they do have testimonial and historical value; however, I treat them with caution.

Biographies

Since the late 1980s, due to public concern for the victims of Maoist purges and the relaxation of the political atmosphere, biographical works on rightists sent to Beidahuang have appeared in increasing numbers. Writers and artists such as Ding Ling, Ai Qing, Ding Cong, Huang Miaozi, and Nie Gannu, among others, have seen their biographies composed by junior writers and journalists. These sources are of great value in that they provide general descriptions of these intellectuals in the Mao era as well as sketches of their lives in exile. They were indispensable to my reconstruction of people's experiences. The weakness of some of these works, however, is that they do not provide an intimate portrayal of the protagonists during their banishment, something that could reveal their individual character. In the case of *A Biography of Ding Cong*, for instance, while Ding's experience is situated within the larger context of the exile community, there is little specific narrative relating to his personal stories: his real life and activities are only vaguely described, except for a mention of his part-time employment at an army farm magazine.[1] In addition, some of these biographies pay little attention to how the protagonists were integrated with their fellow exiles and/or how they dealt with labour farm/camp officials. Perhaps even more telling is the fact that some protagonists dispute the accuracy of their stories as told in these writings.[2]

MEMOIRS

The publication of the memoirs of banished intellectuals has, to a degree, addressed the problems presented by the biographies. Since the late 1980s, literati rightists such as Ding Ling, Liu Binyan, Huang Wu, Dai Huang, Yin Yi, and Wu Yongliang have all published memoirs or autobiographical works. (Most memoirs deal not only with their experiences in exile but also with their lives afterwards.) Short recollections of specific events during their banishment also appeared in magazines and newspapers. From these writings, we can discover not only their routine lives in exile but also their inner world – their grievances, their complex feelings towards ideological remoulding, their self-abnegation, and their reflections upon the camps/farms after rehabilitation.

These memoirs vary considerably in terms of providing information about the lives of the authors and what happened in the labour camps/farms of the 1950s and 1960s. In general, the works published in the 1980s are cautious in their descriptions of the grimness of labour camps and exile settlements.[3] Sensitive topics such as the maltreatment of inmates by camp officials or the massive death tolls were either omitted by the authors or removed by the censors (or publishers) before publication. Some authors, when interviewed, expressed their pain at being forced to delete some crucial parts of their experiences. In comparison, memoirs published in the 1990s and afterwards, such as *Jiusi yisheng* (A narrow escape from death) by Dai Huang, *Huishou canyang yi han shan* (The setting of the sun over the mountain) by Yin Yi, and *Yuxue feifei* (Floating rain and snow) by Wu Yongliang, were more straightforward. However, memoir literature that discloses the atrocities and bitterness individuals suffered in the labour reform settlements are not easy to publish within the People's Republic of China, not only due to state censorship but also to publishers' reluctance to accept manuscripts that might bring them trouble. Some authors had their works published by chance, taking advantage of a momentary relaxation in censorship but suffering afterwards by being forbidden to reprint (or receiving a warning).[4]

In this climate, some memoirs and autobiographical pieces were secretly printed and circulated underground among close friends, such as *Cuowei* [Disjunction] by Niu Weina, and "Meiyou qingjie de gushi" [Stories without plot] by Tan Tianrong. Some were published in Hong Kong or North America, either in Chinese or in English. Among these are *Chensi ji* [On contemplation] by Ni Genshan, *Mirror* by Peter Liu (Liu Naiyuan), and *A Single Tear* by Wu Ningkun. Free from Chinese censorship, these publications expose the countless injustices and atrocities of the laogai system (which the PRC government has been at pains to conceal), and they provide poignant and insightful narratives concerning the authors' lives in exile settlements.[5]

PERSONAL INTERVIEWS

The sensitive nature of the topic at hand necessitated personal contact with the survivors of the CCP's banishment policy. In thirty-nine personal remembrances collected through oral interviews in Beijing, Shandong, northeastern China, and North America, I have been able to find information that does not appear in published sources and to correct errors contained in existing memoirs and biographies.[6] However, a number of my interview requests were declined: some survivors were unwilling to open the floodgate of bitter memories; others, including ex-labour camp cadres and those who administered the banishment, shunned interviews in order to avoid unexpected trouble.[7] Many interviewees provided vivid, forceful descriptions of their camp life – descriptions that they were reluctant to convey in written records. Through these interviews I was also able to discover stories of those who could not write their recollections and those who lost their lives during the banishment.

The method I used in conducting the interviews was as follows: I made arrangements through personal contacts; I gave interviewees a general idea of what my interests were; I met them one on one (both due to the sensitivity of the issues raised and for their own protection); and I began each interview with a semi-structured conversation containing simple questions. I encouraged interviewees to talk without restraint, to allow the free flow of their thoughts, to give more details on specific events, and to recall their mental state at the time of exile. If clarifications were needed, I contacted interviewees more than once. For those who were from the same work unit or labour camp, questions were repeated and testimonies cross-checked.

OTHER ORAL TESTIMONIES

Another type of interviewee – colleagues or friends of the persecuted whom I met by chance while making primary interview arrangements – offered supplementary yet eye-opening information. Some told stories that differed somewhat from those recounted by the designated interviewees or provided different perspectives on them. Some of them recalled sad stories of friends who had died in Beidahuang or elsewhere before they were rehabilitated: in this way, the dead were able to speak through the living to recount their tales of woe one last time. The narratives of these "accidental interviewees" enriched my understanding of the designated interviewees and, at the same time, forced me to more closely scrutinize the information offered by the latter.

All of these source materials – biographies, memoirs, interviews, and oral testimonies of accidental others – are cross-checked, confirmed, mutually supplemented, and mutually reinforced, thus allowing for the possibility of piecing together significant parts of the life experiences of political exiles in the northeastern borderlands. Not only did these sources provide insight into the Anti-Rightist Campaign and the post-campaign banishment, but they also permitted in-depth investigation of the distinctions among the victims in terms of why they were purged, their behaviour in exile, their physical and mental suffering, their self-perception, the ways in which they interacted with their fellow inmates, and so on. These materials remind me of the uniqueness of the individual experience and of the need to avoid simplistic generalization.

OFFICIAL SOURCES

Official sources used in this research range from the speeches of Mao Zedong (both those compiled in published collections and those smuggled out of China separately) to state statutes and the reports of CCP organizations (*The Chinese Anti-Rightist Campaign Database [1957–]* is a valuable reservoir of official sources), from personal collections of indictments to papers associated with their being readdressed, from labour farm archives to officially sponsored local histories and gazetteers.

Chinese archives have been more open in recent decades. Whereas internal documents generated by prison camp administrations and public security authorities still remain classified and thus beyond the reach of ordinary researchers, some archives with information on rightists were accessible in roundabout ways, particularly via personal connections (successful in some cases but not in others). This is how I gained access to the Farm 853 Archives. Due to the CCP's refusal to admit the repressive nature of the Anti-Rightist Campaign, and its desire to minimize public discussion and scholarly discourse related to this topic, however, the vast majority of official sources on the treatment of rightists remains restricted.[8] Still, officials and establishment historians above a certain rank usually have access to it. The materials in public security archives, such as those dealing with demographics, theft, murder, adultery, and street gangs, are easy to acquire, but the records on rightist offenders in labour camps are still sensitive. At times, I was thrilled to find relevant titles in some archive catalogue only to be told that the items were still classified.

Over decades, many Party documents (such as the directives of the CCP Central Committee and Mao's speeches at Party conferences) have been disclosed, shipped overseas, and incorporated into *The Chinese Anti-Rightist Campaign Database (1957–)*. This book, *Banished to the Great Northern Wilderness,* greatly benefits from documents that deal with the disposal of rightists and their post-banishment relocation and resettlement. Publication of select Party documents and state statutes, such as *Jianguo yilai zhongyao wenxian xuanbian* (Selected collections of important documents since the establishment of the People's Republic of China) and *Zhonghua renmin gongheguo gongan falu quanshu* (Comprehensive collection of laws on public security in the People's Republic of China) also mitigate the shortage of available archives. These official documents were useful in enabling me to understand the criteria used to identify rightists, the general guidelines for their treatment, basic labour reform policies, regulations on labour re-education as applied to ultra-rightists, the criteria used to define counter-revolutionaries, and so on. However, they were less useful in enabling me to understand how decisions were made regarding the different treatment of different rightists, how state agencies administered banishment, and how exiles were actually managed in labour camps and exile settlements.

The histories and gazetteers of labour farms compiled under official auspices, such as *Xingkaihu nongchang shi* (A history of Xingkaihu Farm) and *Bawusan nongchangzhi* (Gazetteer of Farm 853) are of great value for knowing the general operation of the farms, but they are flawed by obvious errors and the deliberate omission of crucial statistics and events. (See Chapter 4 for the errors in *Xingkaihu nongchang shi* and *Bawuling nongchangshi* regarding the death records of inmates.) I use provincial gazetteers and county gazetteers such as *Heilongjiang shengzhi: guoying nongchang zhi* (Gazetteer of Heilongjiang Province: The state farms volume) and *Mishan xianzhi* (Gazetteer of Mishan County) to contextualize the banishment and labour camps established in specific locations as well as to provide supplementary material.

Among the most important official sources for this book are the untapped farm archives that I collected from Farm 853. They include: the farm authorities' (in the name of either the farm Party committee, its political department, or its organization section) reports on the rightist work submitted to higher authorities, the Inspection Panel of the Ministry of Culture's records of briefing sessions with the farm's Party committee, the farm's work plans and reports on delabelling rightists, and so on. These archives reveal the labour farm's perspective on the rightists, its intended plans and strategies for controlling and remoulding them, as well as the voices, activities, and mental states (for or against ideological remoulding) of the rightists themselves. In many cases, the authors of the archives tended to emphasize the stubbornness of the rightists, the difficulties in remoulding them, the efforts made by the farm, and its successes (providing examples of rightists who showed their gratitude for being saved by the Party). In addition, the archives display the farm's ambitious program for land reclamation and its high submission target for the production of grain, which resulted in severe food shortages. The archives also include the documents of interaction (work reports, instructions, etc.) among Farm 853, its higher authorities, the Mudanjiang Land Reclamation Bureau, and the Ministry of Land Reclamation regarding grain submission, famine, deaths, famine relief, and so on.

Questions remain regarding how to most effectively use existing sources to reconstruct the post-1957 Beidahuang banishment. Given the specific structure of the sources that substantiate the research – that is, sources mostly drawn from the memoirs and recollections of the persecuted individuals, labour farm archives, official documents, and local histories and gazetteers – questions arise: How do we assess the existing memoir literature and official sources? How do we analyze the experiences of the exiles without being misled by the limitations or biases of these sources?

Before moving to official sources, I first look at memoir literature and interviews. It is recognized that memoir literature (including that written by those disadvantaged by state power) occupies an important place in historical study as it provides unparalleled accounts of the experiences of a specific group or individual.[9] Memoirs are important not only because they often revolve around major political and social events, such as the Anti-Rightist Campaign in Mao's China or the summary executions of the urban bourgeoisie in Pol Pot's Cambodia, but also because each of the memoirists undergoes an event differently based on his/her life experiences and personal beliefs. The disparities in memoirists' experiences and differing descriptions are what make each memoir independently valuable and prevent historians from drawing any uniform conclusions about any specific historical event.

When dealing with the memoir literature, however, we have to be aware of potential issues, one of which is human memory. Memoirs, as well as interviews, are produced many years after the main events took place and thus suffer a certain loss of accuracy. Human memory is selective: the events recorded in memoirs are often considered by the memoirist to be unusual or traumatic – something she/he considers to be important. When these aspects of life experience are accentuated, "normal" life may be almost completely omitted. More important, memoirs, though chiefly used as a means for people to look back on their lives, are often self-serving. Peter Zarrow, when analyzing the memoirs produced by former Red Guards, comments that each memoirist creates his or her own Cultural Revolution, and, taken together, they display a variety of motivations: to make something useful out of their suffering, to bring meaning to their apparently wasted lives, and to construct an acceptable version of themselves.[10] Paul Cohen, when analyzing the narratives of the Boxer Rebellion, maintains that individual participants in historical events embrace "the entire range of human emotions and goals" in reconstructing the past.[11]

Although not intending to be bound by either Zarrow's or Cohen's frameworks, I feel it beneficial to keep their viewpoints in mind when assessing the sources produced by banishment survivors. So far, all the autobiographies, memoirs, and interviews used in *Banished to the Great Northern Wilderness* were produced after the mid-1980s – twenty years or more after their banishment. Since very few diaries, letters, notes, or other written records of banishment have survived the political turbulence of the Cultural Revolution (some rightists simply did not make any written records of their life in exile),[12] survivors had to reconstruct their past based overwhelmingly on their memory, which is not free from "emotional attachment," accentuating certain aspects of their experiences (such as traumatic events), and unconsciously omitting mention of others. Furthermore, I find that, in both memoirs and interviews, stories provided by individuals from the same labour reform unit often differ considerably.[13] This reinforces my suspicion that certain parts of people's memories are less than reliable.

There is yet another challenging area to consider. Political exiles in the People's Republic of China differ sharply from, for example, those in China of the Boxer Rebellion in terms of their education, their social status, and the social context in which they lived. They are not only the "direct experiencers" of past events but also writers of history. They are not dissimilar from the post-Mao Red Guard memoirists who try to make use of their experience to forge their identity. Highly literate, they were capable of comprehending the history of the Anti-Rightist Campaign, the general idea of the banishment, and its implications. When they told their individual stories, it seems, they aimed not only to recollect their experiences but also to suggest how they would be perceived by readers and remembered in history.[14] Some of them tried to highlight their identity as one of a million of Mao's victims and carefully crafted their narratives so that they might be perceived as such, thus gathering public empathy for shared painful experiences.[15] Furthermore, their narratives were not immune to the influence of the post-Mao political climate and contemporary literature – that is, when they described the severity of the banishment and their personal experience, their tone, their narrative structure, and the message they conveyed were interwoven with their cognizance of post-Mao social currents. For instance, when recalling their mindsets at the time of banishment, certain concepts common to later years inserted themselves into their narratives. This is seen in their use of a grammatical style and terms common in the 1990s to depict their inner world of the 1950s.

I would argue that, despite their rational purposes and emotional states, memoirists are unlikely to override their commitment to faithfully present their stories. However, problems remain regarding what they stress, what they omit, and what is simply ambiguous. Some told how they were maltreated by labour camp or farm cadres but avoided mentioning their actual interaction with them; some elaborated on the harshness of camp life but said little about their survival strategies; some painted themselves as courageous fighters for social justice or intellectual freedom, for which they were persecuted, without mentioning how their strong personalities had partially contributed to their troubles; still others strove to show their unremitting commitment to the Party even though they had been wrongly purged. In several cases, an individual's self-portrayal differed from the impressions her/his fellow exiles had of her/him.

It is also necessary to identify the problems associated with official sources. First of all, official reports and Party edicts are often more normative than descriptive: they may reflect official policies, regulations, and plans, but they provide little information on how organizations, government agencies, and labour camps actually function. The Farm 853 Archives claim that the farm made an effort to investigate the lives and thoughts of rightists and to offer suitable plans to remould them; however, they say little about how these plans were actually carried out or how farm cadres actually administered the rightists and conducted their thought work. Second, information contained in official documents or labour farm archives could be fictitious. For instance, a considerable amount of information included in the Farm 853 Archives regarding rightists' words and deeds came from the secret reports of rightists who wished to earn political credit by incriminating others. Obviously, such sources might twist the facts and obscure the actual situation. Therefore, when one compares issues presented in farm archives with how these same issues are recollected by rightists, he/she should not be surprised that they often differ dramatically. As I have shown in Chapter 2, the rightist kingdom incident is portrayed in farm reports as a serious political hazard, whereas in rightists' memories it is portrayed as a joke. We can only imagine the extent of the discrepancies between farm archives and rightist narratives, and how many other issues could be misrepresented.

Another important issue is the degree to which the ideological remoulding of rightists was accomplished – something that is boasted of in both post-1957 Party documents in general and labour farm archives (e.g., the Farm 853 Archives) in particular. (In later years, the assumption that most rightists could eventually be remoulded formed the basis for the CCP's label removal program.) This boast is not confirmed in rightist narratives. In their memoirs, Farm 853 rightists talked about being moderately treated by farm cadres, and, although they mentioned demanding labour requirements and even stormy struggle sessions, none of them indicated any serious ideological remolding efforts or any meaningful effect that such efforts had on their minds. The recollection of the rightists may be selective, but they still challenge the credibility of certain farm documents. Another possibility is that the authors of the farm reports might have taken rightists' thought summaries at face value and considered them as evidence of real repentance and ideological renewal.

I realize that the sources collected for this book do not simply mirror or reproduce the reality of banishment and camp life, and that a great deal of caution needs to be taken when approaching them. With regard to the memoir literature and interviews, I pay special attention to cross-checking survivors' narratives with other sources (including official documents) in order to identify the extent to which their recollections might differ from what is contained in other primary sources or might contradict historical records. In doing this I attempt to filter out inconsistencies and inaccuracies in these narratives. I have carefully identified mutually conflicting narratives or have simply left them out. I also exclude any overtly emotional descriptions. I only use those narratives that I consider to be plausible and, in so doing, hope to have established a firm basis for analysis.

I treat official documents, including farm archives, as merely one source of information rather than anything "authoritative." I bear in mind the authorship of these documents: Party cadres, who invariably attempted to make readers see rightists and labour camps through the official prism. I am aware of how the use of derogatory terms/phrases such as "deliberate sabotage," "spreading rumours," or "spreading poisonous ideas" complicate and distort reality. I also know that the intended readers of these documents were chiefly Party officials of different ranks rather than the general public or researchers, for the purposes of propagation of Party policies or demonstration of the labour farm's work achievements. For all these reasons, I realize that the official documents may considerably obscure what actually happened in the labour camps and exile settlements and, thus, need to be treated with caution and scruple.

I am fully aware that, among the thousands of persecuted individuals who were banished to Beidahuang, only a small number have made their stories known to the public and accessible to academics. What I have touched upon is merely a small portion of the experience of a large population. *Banished to the Great Northern Wilderness*, then, does not offer a comprehensive treatment of Beidahuang exile; rather, it investigates a very specific set of conditions and experiences, leaving a more general investigation to future scholarship.

Glossary

Beidahuang 北大荒	the Great Northern Wilderness
Beidahuang wenyi 北大荒文艺	Literature and art in Beidahuang
buyaolian 不要脸	shameful
chiqing 吃青	eat the green crops
chunzhu 蠢猪	stupid pig
daishipin 代食品	food substitutes
duizhang 队长	brigade leader
fan'an feng 翻案风	trend of reversing verdicts
fangaizao fenzi 反改造分子	anti–reform element
fangeming 反革命	counter-revolutionary
fenchang zhang 分场长	director of branch farm
fulu 俘虏	captive
guanjiao ganbu 管教干部	managerial/camp cadre
guomindang youyi 国民党右翼	nationalist right wing
gu wei jin yong 古为今用	make the past serve the present
heiwulei 黑五类	five black elements
huai hen zai xin 怀恨在心	nurse a grievance in the heart
hukou 户口	household registration
jiandu laodong 监督劳动	labour under supervision
jieju 戒具	disciplinary tools
jiuye 就业	forced job placement
jiyou pai 极右	ultra-rightist
junliu 军流	military exile
kaolong zhengfu 靠拢政府	draw close to the government

kaolong zuzhi 靠拢组织   draw close to the
                                   organization

kuhai wubian 苦海无边   a boundless sea of bitterness
laodong ganhua yuan 劳动感化院   redemption-through-labour
                                   reformatory

laogai 劳改 (laodong gaizao 劳动改造)   labour reform
laojiao 劳教 (laodong jiaoyang 劳动教养)   labour re-education
laomaozi 老毛子   Russians
laotou 牢头   cell boss
lishi fangeming 历史反革命   historical counter-
                                   revolutionary

liufang 流放   banishment
louwang youpai 漏网右派   escaped rightist
mao dong 猫冬   hide from the winter
ming zhe bao shen 明哲保身   act wisely by playing it safe
niu gui she shen 牛鬼蛇神   ox-ghosts and snake spirits
nonggong 农工   agricultural worker
nongchang 农场   farm
– Bawuling nongchang 八五零农场   Farm 850
– Bawuer nongchang 八五二农场   Farm 852
– Bawusan nongchang 八五三农场   Farm 853
– Tangyuan nongchang 汤原农场   Tangyuan Farm
– Xingkaihu nongchang 兴凯湖农场 Xingkaihu Farm
renzui 认罪   admit crime
Sanjiang pingyuan 三江平原   Three River Plain
sanxing wu shen 三省吾身   self-examination thrice
                                   a day

sixiang huibao 思想汇报   thought report
tufei 土匪   bandit
tuotai huangu 脱胎换骨   thorough reconfiguration
                                   of oneself

wenjiao dui 文教队   culture and education
                                   troupe

wenren 文人   literati
xiafang ganbu 下放干部   sent-down cadre
xianxing fangeming 现行反革命   active counter-revolutionary
xiaozao 小灶   small kitchen
xinghuo 星火   spark
Xingkaihu 兴凯湖   Lakes of Xingkai
xingshi fan 刑事犯   criminal convict

xunhua 训话	rebuke
yaomo guiguai 妖魔鬼怪	demons and ghosts
youpai 右派	rightist
youpai zhuanlie 右派专列	rightist express
you du bu fang 有毒不放	have poison but not release it
zhaimao 摘帽	hat removal
zhaimao youpai 摘帽右派	hatless rightist
zhidaoyuan 指导员	political instructor
zhongxingfan 重刑犯	heavily sentenced convict
zhongyang kaochatuan 中央考察团	central inspection team
zhuajiu youpai 抓阄右派	lot-drawing rightist
zichan jieji youpai 资产阶级右派	bourgeois rightist
zichanjieji youyi shili 资产阶级右翼势力	bourgeois rightist force
zixing 自省	self-examination

Notes

Epigraph: Tang Qi, "Dawn in the Great Northern Wilderness." Geremie Barmé and John Minford, eds., *Seeds of Fire: Chinese Voices of Conscience* (New York: The Noonday Press, 1989), 69.

1 Scholars such as Philip Williams and Yenna Wu agree that the twentieth century was a "century of concentration camps," that the phenomenon of massive government control over "undesirable" but legally innocent citizens had spanned the globe (including British camps to intern Boer women and children, Japanese camps to imprison enemy civilians during the Second World War, and deadly camps throughout the Eurasians land mass under the regimes of Stalin, Hitler, and Pol Pot), and that the PRC prison camps formed a part of the global century of concentration camps. See Philip F. Williams and Yenna Wu, *The Great Wall of Confinement: the Chinese Prison Camp through Contemporary Fiction and Reportage* (Berkeley: University of California Press, 2004), 1, 2, 6.

2 Western scholarship on the Anti-Rightist Campaign and the PRC's political persecution is briefly surveyed in the "Historiographic Considerations" section of this chapter.

3 Note that not all those persecuted in Beijing were subject to banishment, nor were all those banished sent to the northeastern borderlands (some were sent to labour farms in interior provinces or to industrial enterprises close to Beijing). See Chapter 2 for details.

4 Dai Juying (from the Ministry of Culture) was seventeen when sent to Farm 850. Dai Huang, *Jiusi yisheng: Wo de youpai licheng* [A narrow escape from death: My experience as a rightist] (Beijing: Zhongyang bianyi chubanshe, 1998), 103. Fifty-four years old, Nie Gannu was probably the oldest of the exiled rightists.

5 According to an official document issued by the CCP Central Committee on March 10, 1956, "counter-revolutionaries" referred to spies, those who formed the backbone of reactionary parties, ringleaders of secret societies, bullies, bandits, the leaders of Hu Feng's counter-revolutionary group, traitors, Guomindang, or Nationalist Party military officers and government officials above a certain level as well as those who had landlord, rich

peasant, and/or bourgeoisie backgrounds and were actively engaged in sabotaging the new government. See "Zhongyang shi ren xiaozu guanyu fangeming fenzi he qita huaifenzi de jieshi ji chuli de zhengce jiexian de zhanxing guiding" [An interim provision by the central ten-member panel regarding policy demarcations over the definition and treatment of the counter-revolutionaries and other bad elements], printed by the five–member panel of the Chinese Communist Party's Tianjin Committee. As Julia Strauss points out, however, given the absence of objective standards, determining exactly who counted as a full-fledged counter-revolutionary was far from straightforward in the 1950s, and identifying who were the bullies, the hardened bandits, and the traitors was a subjective process. The regime's own guidelines on how to classify and handle counter-revolutionaries was a far-reaching hodgepodge – sometimes even including local hoodlums and gangsters as well as those who, in most environments, would be considered merely criminal. See Julia Strauss, "Paternalist Terror: The Campaign to Suppress Counterrevolutionaries and Regime Consolidation in the People's Republic of China, 1950–1953," *Comparative Studies in Society and History* 44, 1 (2002): 90–91. In other words, seemingly distinctive counter-revolutionary categories could blend into criminal ones. For instance, criminal offenders whose offences were deemed serious might be classified as counter-revolutionaries, with such labels as "counter-revolutionary murderers" or "counter-revolutionary arsonists." In order not to expand further an already unwieldy subject, I use the term "counter-revolutionaries" to refer to those who were singled out during the Anti-Rightist Campaign.

6 *Banished to the Great Northern Wilderness* focuses primarily on what happened in the Beidahuang borderlands. To contextualize this research, I also analyze some of the experiences of persecuted individuals in other parts of northeast China. I occasionally discuss labour camps in north China, such as the Qinghe Farm, to which the inmates from the northeast frontiers were transferred in the early 1960s.

7 Zhongguo jianyu shi bianxie zu, *Zhongguo jianyu shi* [A history of prisons in China] (Beijing: Qunzong chubanshe, 1986), 327; Williams and Wu, *Great Wall of Confinement*, 39–41.

8 Frank Dikötter, "The Emergence of Labour Camps in Shandong Province, 1942–1950," *China Quarterly* 175 (September 2003): 803–17.

9 Cao Shuji, *Zhongguo yiminshi* [A history of Chinese migration] (Fuzhou: Fujian renmin chubanshe, 1997), vol. 5: 275–80. For more about the general pattern of banishment in imperial China, see Joanna Waley-Cohen, *Exile in Mid-Qing China: Banishment to Xinjiang, 1758–1820* (New Haven: Yale University Press, 1991), chap. 3, "Exile and Expansion prior to the Qing." Cao Shuji also estimates that approximate twenty thousand military exiles (*junliu*) were sent to Liaodoing during the Hongwu reign (1368–80) of the Ming Dynasty. See Cao, *Zhongguo yiminshi*, vol. 5: 280.

10 Waley-Cohen, *Exile in Mid-Qing China*, 57.

11 Ibid., 57–59; Cao, *Zhongguo yiminshi*, vol. 6: 499.

12 Sun Xiaoli, *Zhongguo laodong gaizao zhidu de lilun yu shijian* [Theories and practices of China's labour reform system] (Beijing: Zhongguo zhengfa daxue chubanshe, 1994), 41. Waley-Cohen believes that the widespread use of frontier banishment reflected the Qing's reluctance to execute any but the most serious offenders, a concern for benevolent rule, and a "pragmatic recognition that China's people were a highly valuable resource." See Waley-Cohen, *Exile in Mid-Qing China*, 51.

13 See Waley-Cohen, *Exile in Mid-Qing China*, 58–59, 178, 224.

14 Frank Dikötter, *Crime, Punishment and the Prison in Modern China* (New York: Columbia University Press, 2002), 350–52.

15 Ibid., 352.
16 Aleksandr Solzhenitsyn, *The Gulag Archipelago, 1918–1956: An Experiment in Literary Investigation* (London: Collins and Harvill Press, 1974–78), part 6: 340.
17 Ibid., 343.
18 See Sun, *Zhongguo laodong gaizao zhidu de lilun yu shijian*, 15–17. In an April 1951 document, Mao Zedong instructed "to punish [a] considerable number of offenders with life sentences, and remove them from their native places for state projects such as road construction, river conservation, and land reclamation ... The Soviet Union used to handle serious offenders in this way" (ibid., 15). See also Zhu De, "The Talk on the First National Conference for Public Security Work," October 7, 1949, in Harry Wu, *Laodong jiaoyang yu liuchang jiuye* [Re-education through labour and forced job placement] (Washington: The Laogai Research Foundation, 2004), 11. In terms of prison construction, the notorious Qincheng Prison was designed by Soviet experts in the late 1950s. See Yao Lun, "The Origin of Qincheng Prison," webpage of the Ministry of Public Security of the PRC, 2007-01-01.
19 J. Otto Pohl, *The Stalinist Penal System: A Statistical History of Soviet Repression and Terror, 1930–1953* (Jefferson, NC: McFarland, 1997), 10.
20 Ibid., 13–15; Sun, *Zhongguo laodong gaizao zhidu de lilun yu shijian*, 182–83.
21 Harry Wu, *Laogai: The Chinese Gulag* (Boulder, CO: Westview Press, 1992), 3.
22 Harry Wu, for instance, argues for this position based on his first-person experience. See Wu, *Laogai*, 3–5.
23 Tani Barlow and Gary Bjorge, eds., *I Myself Am a Woman: Selected Writings of Ding Ling* (Boston: Beacon Press, 1989); Yi-tsi Mei-Feuerwerker, *Ding Ling's Fiction: Ideology and Narrative in Modern Chinese Literature* (Cambridge: Harvard University Press, 1982); James P. McGough, *Fei Hsiao-tung: The Dilemma of a Chinese Intellectual* (White Plains, NY: M.E. Sharpe, 1979); and R. David Arkush, *Fei Xiaotong and Sociology in Revolutionary China* (Cambridge: Council on East Asian Studies, Harvard University, 1981) are among the important works of scholarship on Ding Ling and Fei Xiaotong. For Fang Lizhi, see James H. Williams, "Fang Lizhi's Expanding Universe," *China Quarterly* 123 (September 1990): 459–84; and James H. Williams, "Fang Lizhi's Big Bang: A Physicist and the State in China," *HSPS* 30, 1 (1999): 49–87. For Liu Binyan, see Perry Link, ed., *Two Kinds of Truth: Stories and Reportage from China* (Bloomington: Indiana University Press, 2006). Sebastian Veg believes that the Chinese publications on the Anti-Rightist Campaign are overwhelmingly focused on the intellectual elites in Beijing and the intellectual debates in 1957 rather than the everyday lives of those labelled as rightists and banished to faraway provinces. See Sebastian Veg, "Testimony, History, and Ethics: From the Memory of Jiabiangou Prison Camp to a Reappraisal of the Anti-Rightist Movement in Present-Day China." *The China Quarterly* 218 (2014): 516–17.
24 Jean-Luc Domenach, *Chine: L'archipel oublié* (Paris, Fayard, 1992); Wu, *Laogai*.
25 For instance, Williams and Wu, *Great Wall of Confinement*, make use of fiction and non-fiction sources to present complex pictures of prison life in Mao and post-Mao periods. They do this by examining the cycle of incarceration in the PRC prison camps, from arrest and detention to death or release. James D. Seymour and Richard Anderson, *New Ghosts, Old Ghosts: Prisons and Labor Reform Camps in China* (Armonk: M.E. Sharpe, 1998) primarily describe the prison camps of northwestern China as they existed in the post-Mao period. They focus on the functions and management of the *laogai* system and de-emphasize its economic role.

26 Research works published in Hong Kong, beyond the reach of PRC censorship, such
as Hua Min, *Zhongguo da nizhuan: Fanyou yundong shi* [China's great reversal: A history
of the anti-rightist campaign] (New York: Ming-ching chubanshe, 1996); and Shen
Zhihua, *Sikao yu xuanze: Cong zhishifenzi huiyi dao fanyoupai yundong* (1956–1957)
[Reflections and choices: From the conference on intellectuals to the anti-rightist
movement (1956–1957)] (Hong Kong: Xianggang zhongwen daxue dangdai zhongguo
wenhua yanjiu zhongxin, 2008) are chiefly about persecution during the Anti-Rightist
Campaign rather than the post-campaign experiences of the purged.

CHAPTER ONE: THE ANTI-RIGHTIST CAMPAIGN AND POLITICAL LABELLING

Epigraph: Xunzhao Lin Zhao de Linghun (Searching for the spirit of Lin Zhao),
documentary movie by independent filmmaker Hu Jie, 2004.

1   Julia Strauss explores the Campaign to Suppress Counter-Revolutionaries in the early
PRC. She argues that, by unleashing terror upon political competitors and displaying
paternalist care for its followers, the CCP successfully consolidated the regime. See Julia
Strauss, "Paternalist Terror: The Campaign to Suppress Counterrevolutionaries and
Regime Consolidation in the People's Republic of China, 1950–1953," *Comparative
Studies in Society and History* 44, 1 (2002): 80–105. The frontier banishment I discuss
differs from that which occurred in the campaign of 1950–53 in a number of ways.
However, it bears striking similarities to it in terms of the state agenda achieved, such
as eliminating political opponents, controlling social groups, and, ironically, consuming
much of the revolutionary elite itself.

2   See Jonathan Spence, *The Search for Modern China* (New York: W.W. Norton, 2013),
511–12; Merle Goldman, "The Party and the Intellectuals," in *The Cambridge History
of China*, ed. Denis Twitchett and John K. Fairbank, vol. 14: 251–53 (Cambridge:
Cambridge University Press, 1987); R. David Arkush, "Introduction" and Hualing
Nieh, "Preface," in *Literature of the Hundred Flowers*, ed. Hualing Nieh, vol. 1: 3–18
(New York: Columbia University Press, 1981).

3   See Fang Lizhi, *Fang Lizhi zizhuan* [Autobiography: Fang Li-zhi] (Taibei: Tianxia
yuanjian chuban gufen youxian gongsi, 2013), 160; Goldman, "The Anti-Rightist
Campaign," in *Cambridge History of China*, ed. Twitchett and Fairbank, vol. 14: 253–58.

4   For Lin Xiling's criticism of the Party, see Niu Han and Deng Jiuping, eds., *Yuan shang
cao: Jiyi zhang de fan youpai yundong* [Grass on the plains: The Anti-Rightist Campaign
in memory] (Beijing: Jingji ribao chubanshe, 1998), 151–58; Merle Goldman, *Literary
Dissent in Communist China* (Cambridge: Harvard University Press, 1967), 201, 237. For
Zhang Bojun's criticism, see Niu Han and Deng Jiuping, eds., *Liuyue xue: Jiyi zhang de fan
youpai yundong* [Snow in June: The Anti-Rightist Campaign in memory] (Beijing: Jingji
ribao chubanshe, 1998), 255–58; and Ye Yonglie, *Fan youpai shimo* [The whole story of
the Anti-Rightist Movement] (Xining: Qinghai renmin chubanshe, 1995), 125–27.

5   Frederick C. Teiwes, *Politics and Purges in China: Rectification and the Decline of Party
Norms, 1950–1965* (Armonk: M.E. Sharpe, 1993), 26.

6   Cao Shuji, "An Overt Conspiracy: Creating Rightists in Rural Henan, 1957–1958," in
Maoism at the Grassroots: Everyday Life in China's Era of High Socialism, ed. Jeremy Brown
and Matthew D. Johnson, 77–101 (Cambridge: Harvard University Press, 2015).

7   Teiwes, *Politics and Purges in China*, 217. Goldman's argument can be found in
Twitchett and Fairbank, eds., *Cambridge History of China*, vol. 14: 256; Roderick

MacFarquhar's thesis is presented in his *The Origins of the Cultural Revolution: Contradictions among the People, 1956–1957* (London: Oxford University Press, 1974).

8 See Twitchett and Fairbank, eds., *Cambridge History of China*, vol. 14: 242–44. For other leaders' positive echo of Mao, see Zhou Enlai, "The Report on Question of Intellectuals," January 14, 1956, in Song Yongyi, ed., *The Chinese Anti-Rightist Campaign Database (1957–)* (Hong Kong: The University Services Centre for China Studies at the Chinese University of Hong Kong, 2010).

9 Mao's motives, though hard to fathom, have been interpreted by scholars, his associates, and his servants as including a wide range of considerations, from preventing the emergence of a "privileged" class to avoiding the loss of the revolutionary spirit, from pre-empting anti-communist insurrection (as had happened in Poland and Hungary) to using non-party intellectuals to criticize such party leaders as Liu Shaoqi and Deng Xiaoping. See Roderick MacFarquhar, Timothy Cheek, and Eugene Wu, eds., *The Secret Speeches of Chairman Mao: From the Hundred Flowers to the Great Leap Forward* (Cambridge: Harvard University Press, 1989), 6–10; Bo Yibo, *Ruogan zhongda juece yu shijian de huigu* [Recollections of several important policies and events] (Beijing: Zhonggong zhongyang dangxiao chubanshe, 1993), 605–7; Li Zhisui, *The Private Life of Chairman Mao: The Memoirs of Mao's Personal Physician* (New York: Random House, 1994), 198–99.

10 Niu Han and Deng Jiuping, eds., *Jingju lu: Jiyi zhong de fan youpai yundong* [The thorny road: The Anti-Rightist Campaign in memory] (Beijing: Jingji ribao chubanshe, 1998), 9; Teiwes, *Politics and Purges in China*, 202–3; Roderick MacFarquhar, *The Hundred Flowers Campaiagn and the Chinese Intellectuals* (New York: Octagon Books, 1974), 24. Another element that accounted for their hesitation concerned the conflicting signals that emerged within the Party leadership in the spring of 1957. Whereas Mao Zedong and Zhou Enlai advocated rectification of the Party and enlistment of different opinions, other top leaders, such as Liu Shaoqi and Peng Zhen, did not. See Teiwes, *Politics and Purges in China*, 166.

11 See MacFarquhar, Cheek, and Wu, *Secret Speeches of Chairman Mao*, 358; Mao Zedong, *Mao Zedong xuanji* [Selected Works of Mao Zedong] (Beijing: Renmin chubanshe, 1977), vol. 5: 414.

12 See Niu and Deng, *Liuyue xue*, 331–43; Niu and Deng, *Jingji lu*, 154–58, 195–98; Twitchett and Fairbank, *Cambridge History of China*, vol. 14: 251–53. Roderick MacFarquhar, too, documents these various criticisms. See MacFarquhar, *The Hundred Flowers Campaign and the Chinese Intellectuals*.

13 Chu Anping, the newly appointed chief editor of *Guangming Daily*, criticized Mao and Zhou with regard to the CCP's monopoly of state leadership. See Dai Qing, *Liang Shuming, Wang Shiwei, Chu Anping* (Nanjing: Jiangsu wenyi chubanshe, 1989), 236–38.

14 MacFarquhar believes that the Anti-Rightist Campaign reflected Mao's personal anger and embarrassment over his major defeat in the Hundred Flowers Campaign. Facing sharp external criticism, MacFarquhar argues, Mao was compelled to agree with other leading figures who advocated that critics be severely sanctioned, and he had to defend himself by asserting that his initial plan was "to let the demons and hobgoblins come out of their lairs then we will be better able to wipe them out." See MacFarquhar, *Origins of the Cultural Revolution*, chap. 18. See also Roderick MacFarquhar, "The Secret Speeches of Chairman Mao," in MacFarquhar, Cheek, and Wu, *Secret Speeches of Chairman Mao*.

15 The *People's Daily* editorial of June 8, 1957, "Zheshi weishenmo?" [What is this for?] suddenly called for an attack on those who "wanted to use the rectification campaign

to wage class struggle." This editorial, together with Mao's inner-CCP instruction "Organizing Forces to Counterattack Rightists," indicates the Party's decision to engage in a formal counter-action against its critics. See MacFarquhar, *Origins of the Cultural Revolution*, 262; Mao, *Mao Zedong xuanji*, vol. 5: 431–33.

16 "Zhonggong zhongyang zuzhibu guanyu jixu zhixing zhongyang [1978] 55 hao wenjian jige wenti de qingshi" [Request of the Chinese Communist Party Central Organization Department over several issues with regard to the implementation of the centre's no. 55 document of 1978), August 29, 1979, in Song, *Chinese Anti-Rightist Campaign Database*. However, considering that official figures are strikingly inconsistent from 1958 to 1979; that the official calculation does not include rightists among high school students, former capitalists, and those singled out after 1959; and that a significant number of individuals who were at first labelled "rightists" and later "counter-revolutionaries" or "criminals" were not counted as rightists; some scholars estimate that there were around 650,000 direct victims of the Anti-Rightist Campaign and that these did not include over 2 million "anti-socialist elements" or the "middle-rightists" (*zhongyou fenzi*). See Hua Min, *Zhongguo da nizhuan: Fanyou yundong shi* [China's great reversal: A history of the Anti-Rightist Campaign] (New York: Ming-ching chubanshe, 1996), 147–55.

17 See Mao, *Mao Zedong xuanji*, vol. 1: 3–9; vol. 2: 660–61; vol. 4: 1182–85. Particularly in the pre-1949 period, Mao talked about the existence of rightists among Chinese intellectuals. According to Mao, intellectuals who did not entirely trust the CCP but, rather, favoured the imperialists were "the rightists in People's China." However, he also stated that "they were not GMD reactionaries, although there were a great deal of reactionary and anti-people thoughts in their minds." See Mao, *Mao Zedong xuanji*, vol. 4: 1374.

18 Mao Zedong, "Things Are Changing," in Mao, *Mao Zedong xuanji*, vol. 5: 423–29. Mao composed this inner-Party memo as a warning about the "anti-Party attack by the rightists"; however, at the same time, he insisted that the Party continue encouraging "the blooming and contending."

19 See Niu and Deng, *Liuyue xue*, 255–58; Liu Meng, *Chuntian de yu qiutian qing* [The whisking of rain in spring, the clearing of skies in autumn] (Beijing: Zhongguo gongren chubanshe, 2003),139.

20 Deng Xiaoping, *Guanyu zhengfeng yundong de baogao* [Report on the rectification campaign] (Beijing: Quanguo zhengxie xuexi weiyuanhui yin, 1957), 16. The citation here summarizes Deng's points rather than providing the full text.

21 The title of the Party document is "Criteria for the Labelling of Rightists," October 15, 1957, in Zhongyang wenxian yanjiushi, ed., *Jianguo yilai zhongyao wenxian xuanbian* [Selected collections of important documents since the establishment of the People's Republic of China], vol. 10: 613–17.

22 On October 15, 1957, the CCP Central Committee acknowledged that, from the beginning of the campaign, it was the local Party committees that had determined the criteria for labelling rightists. See Zhongyang wenxian yanjiushi, *Jianguo yilai zhongyao wenxian xuanbian*, vol. 10: 613–14. Party senior Bo Yibo also admitted that the major anti-rightist struggles had almost concluded in provincial capitals and universities/colleges before the CCP Central Committee had issued the criteria for labelling rightists. See Bo, *Ruogan zhongda juece yu shijian de huigu*, 621.

23 See, for instance, Hu Ke, *Huaishu zhuang* [Scholar Tree Village] (Shanghai: Shanghai wenyi chubanshe, 1963), 7–10, 54, 66.

24 For the five black elements, see Liu Shaoqi's speech on May 5, 1958, in Fang Jungui, ed., *Liu Shaoqi wenti ziliao zhuanji* [A special collection of materials on Liu Shaoqi] (Taibei:

Zhonggong yanjiu zazhishe, 1970), 297. The insults and humiliation experienced by rightists are cited in numerous sources. For instance, Chen Dengke recalls that, after the campaign, a rightist couldn't help but lower his or her head in deep shame whenever encountering a friend or neighbour. See Zheng Xiaofeng, *Ding Ling zai Beidahuang* [Ding Ling in the Great Northern Wilderness] (Wuhan: Hubei renmin chubanshe, 1989), 78. When rightist Li Guowen was sent to a construction site in Shanxi, he was isolated from all other workers (except during work), and he had to have lunch by himself at a designated table, where a placard read: "Reserved for Rightist Li Guowen." See Hu Ping, *Chan ji: kunan de jitan* [Allegorical words: The bitter sacrificial altar] (Guangzhou: Guangdong luyou chubanshe, 2004), 499. Yin Yi recalls that, even after he had completed his term in Beidahuang, his colleagues and neighbours still avoided saying hello when seeing him on the street. See Yin Yi, *Huishou canyang yi han shan* [The setting of the sun over the mountain] (Beijing: Shiyue wenyi chubanshe), 104– 5.

25 Whereas movies such as *The Legend of Tianyun Mountain* and *Herdsman* were celebrated at the end of the 1970s because of their patriotism, *Unrequited Love* was officially condemned in China because of its "anti-Party" undertones. For other positive portrayals of rightists, see Dai Qing, "Chu Anping yu Dang Tianxia," in her *Liang Shuming, Wang Shiwei, Chu Anping* (Nanjing: Jiangsu wenyi chubanshe, 1989), 113–231.

26 Hua, *Zhongguo da nizuan*, 148–53.

27 Dai Huang, *Jiusi yisheng: Wo de youpai licheng* [A narrow escape from death: My experience as a rightist] (Beijing: Zhongyang bianyi chubanshe, 1998), 419.

28 Lu Gang, Party official, college head, interview, Dalian, August 6, 2002.

29 Yue Daiyun, a student and then teacher at Peking University in the early years of the PRC, recounts why she, as well as many youths, became a sincere supporter of the CCP. Unhappy with the GMD's corruption and malfunctioning, Yue enthusiastically joined the communist-led student movements and became a Party member at the age of eighteen. She optimistically envisioned "a new society based on complete equality, free of corruption" under the Party leadership. This conviction was the basis for her political activism and identification with the Party during the first decade of the PRC. See Yue Daiyun and Carolyn Wakeman, *To the Storm: The Odyssey of a Revolutionary Chinese Woman* (Berkeley: University of California Press, 1985), 16–22.

30 Fang Lizhi, *Fang Lizhi zizhuan* [Autobiography: Fang Li-zhi] (Taibei: Tianxia yuanjian chuban gufen youxian gongsi, 2013), 162.

31 Dai, *Jiusi yisheng*, 45–52.

32 See Wang Meng, "Young Newcomer in the Organization Department," in *Literature of the Hundred Flowers*, ed. Nieh Hualing, vol. 2: 473-511 (New York: Columbia University Press, 1981); Goldman, *Literary Dissent in Communist China*, 179–80.

33 Niu and Deng, *Liuyue xue*, 257; Ye, *Fan youpai shimo*, 125–27.

34 MacFarquhar, *Hundred Flowers Campaign*, 85, 101– 2.

35 Niu and Deng, *Yuan shang cao*, 4–5, 9, 28.

36 Ibid., 153, 156.

37 *Dongbei renda xiaokan* (Northeastern People's University newsletter), October 21, 1957; Wang Shusen, professor emeritus, interview, Dalian, August 2, 2002. Students in Tianjin also made use of the existing structure of political parties (e.g., the Peasants and Workers Democratic Party) and the Christian Church to attack the CCP's local branches and Party members. See MacFarquhar, *Hundred Flowers Campaign*, 142–43.

38 Eddy U, "Intellectuals and Alternative Socialist Paths in the Early Mao Years." *China Journal* 70 (2013): 8, 10.

39 Niu and Deng, *Yuan shang cao,* 57.

40 Ibid., 164.

41 Wang Meng, writer, interview, Beijing, October 5, 2002.

42 Dai, *Liang Shuming, Wang Shiwei, Chu Anping,* 179–80.

43 U, "Intellectuals and Alternative Socialist Paths," 10, 13, 14.

44 James D. Seymour, *China's Satellite Parties* (Armonk: M.E. Sharpe, 1987), 52–53; Dai, *Liang Shuming, Wang Shiwei, Chu Anping,* 179–80; Niu and Deng, *Liuyue xue,* 255–57, 281–83.

45 Bo, *Ruogan zongda juece yu shijian de huigu,* 619.

46 Hu, *Chan ji,* 371. Mao Zedong, "Speech on Wuhan Conference," April 6, 1958, in Song, *Chinese Anti-Rightist Campaign Database*; CCP Central Committee, "Instructions Regarding Removal of the 'Hats' of Rightists Who Have Shown Real Repentance," September 17, 1959, in Song, *Chinese Anti-Rightist Campaign Database.*

47 CCP Central Committee, "Criteria for the Labelling of Rightists," October 15, 1957, in Zhongyang wenxian yanjiushi, *Jianguo yilai zhongyao wenxian xuanbian,* vol. 10: 613–17.

48 Forster explores such abuse in Zhejiang local politics, although in a different time period. He suggests that, for competing political forces during the Cultural Revolution, pragmatic considerations trumped the political line: "The claim that callow youth and hard-boiled workers beat, tortured and killed each other over an issue as seemingly remote from their daily terms of reference as the loyalty of political leaders to an ill-defined 'revolutionary line' of Chairman Mao may detach political action from its social basis." See Keith Forster, *Rebellion and Factionalism in a Chinese Province: Zhejiang, 1966–1976* (Armonk: M.E. Sharpe, 1990), 6–7.

49 Teiwes, *Politics and Purges in China,* 22.

50 See Teiwes, *Politics and Purges in China,* chap. 5. In *Rebellion and Factionalism in a Chinese Province,* Keith Forster discusses how, during the Cultural Revolution, the pervasive factional divisions within both Party bureaucracy and Red Guard organizations featured the provincial politics of Zhejiang and gave rise to ceaseless chaos.

51 A PLA document admits that there was a "small circle in the General Political Department headed by Chen Yi" that relentlessly disparaged other vice-directors of the department. See "Zhongguo renmin jiefangjun zong zhengzhibu guanyu Chen Yi wenti de jueding" [The decisions of the General Political Department of the People's Liberation Army on the problems of Chen Yi], January 4, 1958, in Song, *Chinese Anti-Rightist Campaign Database*; Ou Jiajin, *Chen Yi pingzhuan* [A critical biography of Chen Yi] (Beijing: Zhongguo wenlian chubanshe, 2000), 196–97; Guo Daohui, interview, Beijing, May 26, 2006.

52 See Goldman, *Literary Dissent in Communist China,* 11–17, for the factional split between Lu Xun's group and Zhou Yang's group.

53 Although Ding Ling and her husband Chen Ming insisted that literary differences constituted the main cause of the conflict between Ding and Zhou Yang, many believe that it was personal animosity between Ding and Zhou. This animosity dated back to the 1940s, the period of the Yan'an Rectification and the Yan'an Literary Anti-Japanese Association. In the early 1950s, Ding increasingly disapproved of Zhou's being the boss of China's literary world (Zhou was then the president of the Writers Association of China and the deputy director of the Central Propaganda Department of the CCP), and she did not even try to conceal her personal distaste towards him in public. Ding's

criticism of the "paternal authority" of Party cadres over writers was believed to be directed at Zhou, while Zhou, for his part, accused Ding's *Literary Gazette* of being an "independent kingdom" outside the influence of Party leadership. Ding's increasing hostility towards Zhou and her unwillingness to come to terms with him prompted his decision to bring her down. In January 1958, Ding Ling was labelled an "anti-Party element" and a "rightist." See Zhou Liangpei, *Ding Ling Zhuan* [A biography of Ding Ling] (Beijing: Shiyue wenyi chubanshe, 1993), 72–8; Ding Ling, *Fengxue renjian* [The blizzard world] (Xiamen: Xiamen daxue chubanshe, 1987), 121.

54 Twitchett and Fairbank, *Cambridge History of China*, vol. 14: 255–56; Li Xin, Party cadre, interview, Beijing, October 6, 2002.

55 Zhou, *Ding Ling Zhuan*, 46. For information on Sha Wenhan, see Hu, *Chan ji*, 357.

56 Hu, *Chan ji*, 308–10; MacFarquhar, *Hundred Flowers Campaign*, 263–64.

57 Teiwes, *Politics and Purges in China*, 26.

58 Ge Peiqi, *Ge Peiqi huiyilu* [The memoir of Ge Peiqi] (Beijing: Zhongguo renmin daxue chubanshe, 1994), 138–39. Other than official reports, there is no evidence that Ge ever said such harsh things, nor are there any third-party sources that explain the gap between Ge's own narrative and the official version of his talks. Based on his analysis of different sources, Hu Ping believes that Ge's position included the following: Party leaders do not show sufficient respect to intellectuals; the relationship between the CCP and the masses deteriorated after the liberation; Party cadres badly alienated themselves from the masses; the masses will no longer support the CCP's military struggles if war happens, and, for this reason, we will all be killed by our enemies. See Hu, *Chan ji*, 226–27.

59 Ge, *Ge Peiqi huiyilu*, 139; Niu and Deng, *Liuyue xue*, 305.

60 "Beijing shi zhongji renmin fayuan dui Ge Peiqi de panjueshu (1959-06-29) he Ge Peiqi zhai fating shang de ziwo bianhu (1959-03-04)" [The verdict of Beijing Intermediate People's Court on Ge Peiqi, 29 June 1959, and Ge Peiqi's self-defence at court, 4 March 1959], in Song, *Chinese Anti-Rightist Campaign Database*; Ge, *Ge Peiqi huiyilu*, 151–62.

61 Li Hui, *Ren zai xuanwo: Huang Miaozi yu Yu Feng* [People in the eddy: Huang Miaozi and Yu Feng] (Jinan: Shandong huabao chubanshe, 1998), 270.

62 For instance, both Yin Yi and Xu Ying were accused of being rightists because they, as journalists of *Guangming Daily*, wrote reports on "blooming-and-contending" meetings on certain university campuses. See Yin, *Huishou canyang yi han shan*, 18–20; Xu Ying, journalist, interview, Beijing, July 19, 2004; Dai, *Jiusi yisheng*, 102.

63 CCP Central Committee, "Criteria for the Labelling of Rightists," October 15, 1957.

64 Lu Gang, interview.

65 Teiwes, *Politics and Purges in China*, 9–10.

66 Twitchett and Fairbank, *Cambridge History of China*, vol. 14: 240–41; Dai, *Hu Feng zhuan*, 94–107; Li, *Lishi Beige*, 15–19. Shu Wu, Hu Feng's friend, submitted to a Party organization a number of letters he had received from Hu in the 1940s. This convinced Mao that Hu was "a disguised counter-revolutionary" and "a loyal running dog of Chiang Kai-shek" and, thus, helped seal his fate. See *People's Daily*, May 13, 1955, for the materials that Shu Wu revealed.

67 Lin Xiling, "The First Speech at Peking University," May 23, 1957, in Niu and Deng, *Yuan shang cao*, 151–52; Goldman, *Literary Dissident in Communist China*, 197.

68 Niu and Deng, *Yuan shang cao*, 113–14.

69 Zhang Xiaofeng, "Hu Feng anjian yu youpai xuesheng" [Hu Feng's case and student rightists], unpublished essay; Chen Fengxiao, "Unforgettable Memory," unpublished

essay. Zhang Xiaofeng (Hu Feng's daughter) tells the stories and lists the names of more than ten students that she knows who were persecuted in the Anti-Rightist Campaign for their defence of Hu Feng.

70 See Zhongyang wenxian yanjiushi, *Jianguo yilai zhongyao wenxian xuanbian*, vol. 7: 134–48; *People's Daily*, July 18, 1957. False accusations were so rampant that even Luo Ruiqing, the minister of public security, acknowledged that, during the campaign, "mistakes and maltreatment occurred when innocent people were arrested; in some organizations and work units, some of those who should not have been attacked were attacked." See Zhu Zheng, *1957 nian de xiaji: Cong baijia zhengming dao liangjia zhengming* 1957 [The summer of 1957: From hundred schools of thought contending to two schools of thought contending] (Zhengzhou: Henan renmin chubanshe, 1998), 258.

71 Luo Longji, "The Speech Regarding Establishing 'Rehabilitation Committee,'" in Niu and Deng, *Liuyue xue*, 276–78; MacFarquhar, *Origins of the Cultural Revolution*, 271–73.

72 Li Xin, interview.

73 Gao Hua, *Hongtaiyang shi zhenyang shengqi de: Yan'an zhengfeng yundong de lailong qumai* [How did the red sun rise: A history of the Yan'an rectification movement] (Hong Kong: Xianggang zhongwen daxue chubanshe, 2003), 411–73. In both cases, the CCP elite leaders, Mao included, required that cases of false accusations be re-opened and that the wronged be rehabilitated.

74 Harry Wu, *Bitter Wind: A Memoir of My Years in China's Gulag* (New York: John Wiley and Sons, 1994), 22–23; Liu, *Chuntian de yu qiutian qing*, 58. Wang Shusen, interview.

75 Zhang Xikun, "Weidaozhe luoji dagang" [Outline of the apologists' logic], in Niu and Deng, *Yuan shang cao*, 125; Liu, *Chuntian de yu qiutian qing*, 59–60.

76 Yin Jiliang, interview.

77 At first, CCP elite leaders vacillated in their response to the Hungary incident, but after the Soviet suppression of the revolt, they decided to support the Soviet stance and interpreted the revolt as a counter-revolutionary rebellion instigated by imperialist and anti-communist forces. See MacFarquhar, Cheek, and Wu, *Secret Speeches of Chairman Mao*, 8–9; Liu Shaoqi, "The Report on the Second Plenum of the Eighth Congress of the CCP," in Fang, *Liu Shaoqi wenti ziliao zhuanji*, 295.

78 Yan Xueli, middle school teacher, interview, Dandong, Liaoning, August 12, 2002.

79 He Shanzhou, university department head, interview, Vancouver, October 22, 2003.

80 Tani Barlow and Gary Bjorge, eds., *I Myself Am a Woman: Selected Writings of Ding Ling* (Boston: Beacon Press, 1989), 43.

81 He Ying, literature journal editor, interview, Changchun, September 21, 2002.

82 Yin Jie, college student, interview, Dalian, September 19, 2002. Note that, in China, one's school grades were often revealed to other students.

83 *My Father and Mother* was produced by Guangxi Movie Studio, 1999. *Blue Kite* was produced by Beijing Movie Studio, 1992.

84 Yang Kuisong, "Baifenbi yu kuodahua: jiejidouzheng zhili moshi de jingyan he jiaoxun" [Percentage and magnification: Experiences and lessons from the class struggle-based administration model], unpublished essay, obtained in 2015.

85 Bo, *Ruogan zhongda juece yu shijian de huigu*, 619–20.

86 Mao Zedong, "Things Are Changing," May 15, 1957, in Mao, *Mao Zedong xuanji*, vol. 5: 424.

87 CCP Central Committee, "Instructions on the Steps and Strategies for the Anti-Rightist Struggle," June 10, 1957, in Song, *Chinese Anti-Rightist Campaign Database*; Mao

Zedong, "The Speech on the Supreme State Conference," October 13, 1957, in Red Guard Materials, *Mao Zedong sixiang wansui* [Long live Mao Zedong thought], n.p., vol. 12: 69.

88　Fang Lizhi recalled that his fiancée Li Shuxian, a young faculty member at Peking University, was left alone until September 1957, when the CCP Beijing Municipal Committee decided that labelling quota for Peking University had to exceed 5 percent of the entire population of its faculty and students, which resulted in her being rounded up in the rightist group. See Fang, *Fang Lizhi zizhuan*, 169–70.

89　Hua, *Zhongguo da nizhuan*, 149–50. A great variety existed. In Changchun, identified rightists in all the secondary specialized schools took 4.65 percent of their teachers, but those singled out within the Central Committee of the China Democratic League reached 59 percent, accounting for about 33 percent of its entire membership. See Shen Zhihua, *Sikao yu xuanze: Cong zhishifenzi huiyi dao fanyoupai yundong* [Reflections and choices: From the conference on intellectuals to the Anti-Rightist Movement] (Hong Kong: Xianggang zhongwen daxue dangdai zhongguo wenhua yanjiu zhongxin, 2008), 656; Gao Congmin, Zhongguo minzhu tongmeng fanyoupai douzheng de jiben qingkuang [The basic situation of the anti-rightist struggle in the China Democratic League]. (Printed by Minmeng zhongyang bangongting, January 1958), 4.

90　Teiwes, *Politics and Purges in China*, 7.

91　Both Liu Meng and Yin Yi provide cases in which work unit heads or individual Party members disagreed with labelling their colleagues as rightists, only to find themselves being accused of being rightists and/or being expelled from the party in the end. Liu, *Chuntian de yu qiutian qing*, 138, Yin, *Huishou canyang yi han shan*, 21.

92　Wang Zhiliang, retired doctor, interview, Dandong, Liaoning, August 12, 2002.

93　Lu Gang, interview; Hu, *Chan ji*, 377.

94　Hu, *Chan ji*, 374.

95　Lu Gang, interview.

96　Dai, *Jiusi yisheng*, 112.

97　Cai Wenhui, *Class Struggle and Deviant Labelling in Mao's China: Becoming Enemies of the People* (Lewiston, NY: Edwin Mellen Press, 2001), 155.

98　Lu Gang, interview.

99　Lu Wencai, college teacher, interview, Dalian, August 5, 2002. Hu, a campmate of Liu Meng, was labelled precisely because he remained silent during the "Blooming and Contending" mass gathering. See Liu, *Chuntian de yu qiutian qing*, 136.

100　Hu, *Chan ji*, 395.

101　Ibid., 395.

102　Niu and Deng, *Jingji lu*, 86–87.

103　Ibid., 402–4.

104　Wang Li, junior clerk, interview, Dalian, September 20, 2002.

105　Cong Weixi, *Zouxiang hundun* [Going towards chaos] (Beijing: Zhongguo shehui kexue chubanshe, 1998), 254.

106　Dai, *Jiusi yisheng*, 103; Yin, *Huishou canyang yi han shan*, 72.

107　Cong, *Zouxiang hundun*, 28–29.

108　Beijing dianying zhipian chang, "Guanyu Ba Hong tongzhi zhengzhi lishi wenti de fucha" [On reinvestigation of Comrade Ba Hong's political history), June 12, 1986.

109　Zhang Zhicai, *Yongyuan zai chulian* [In love forever] (Beijing: Jiefangjun wenyi chuban-she, 1992), 313.

110 Chen Dongbai, middle school teacher, interview, Panjin, Liaoning, August 17, 2002.
111 Ding Cong, artist, interview, Beijing, August 20, 2002.
112 Wang Hongren, junior police officer, interview, Changchun, September 22, 2002.
113 Wang Shusen, interview; *Dongbei renda xiaokan*, December 6, 1957, and April 3, 1958.
114 Zhonggong zhongyang tongzhanbu, "Guanyu quanguo tongzhan gongzuo huiyi de baogao" [The report on the national conference for united front work], May 28, 1962. Song, *Chinese Anti-Rightist Campaign Database*.
115 Liu, *Chuntian de yu qiutian qing*, 137.
116 Starting from the *People's Daily* editorial "The Working Class Is Speaking Out" on June 10, there was extensive press coverage of the stormy condemnation of "vicious and vile" rightists voiced by peasants and workers in various provinces. See Hu, *Chan ji*, 417–21, for particular stories.
117 See Mao's speeches, on October 9, October 13, and December 8, 1957, respectively, in Red Guard Materials, *Mao Zedong sixiang wansui*, vol. 13: 55–75.
118 See Teiwes, *Politics and Purges in China*, 222.
119 So far, no official documents specifying the sending down of rightists have been found either at the central level or the local level. Rightists such as Lu Gang, Wang Hongren, and Ding Cong recall that, when being forcibly sent down, none of them was presented with an official warrant. The heads of their work units all said that the arrangement for labour reform was carried out according to "instructions from above," yet they were shown no specific document to this effect. Song's *Chinese Anti-Rightist Campaign Database* contains copious Party documents regarding the verdicts of individual rightists: they were deprived of Party membership, dismissed from public office, or expelled from school and sent to labour under supervision or labour re-education. However, none of these documents specified how the rightists were to be sent down or how their banishment was to be conducted.
120 See CCP Central Committee, "Instructions on Sending down Cadres into Manual Labour," in Zhongyang wenxian yanjiushi, *Jianguo yilai zhongyao wenxian xuanbian*, vol. 11: 196.
121 Mao had long considered manual labour to be an important means of remoulding various offenders and dealing with politically problematic elements. For instance, in his statement "On People's Democratic Dictatorship," made in June 1949, Mao claimed that the people's government should force the reactionaries "to remould themselves through labour into new men" and that this forced labour should be combined with "propaganda and educational work." See Mao, *Mao Zedong xuanji*, vol. 4: 1366.
122 The memoirs of Dai Huang and Cong Weixi, among others, mention this process. Fang Lizhi, due to his involvement in the Hundred Flowers Campaign at Peking University, was expelled from the CCP and sent to the countryside in Hebei to perform manual labour. See Fang, *Fang Lizhi zizhuan*, 170–75.
123 Hu, *Chan ji*, 376–77; Yan Tunfu, university student, interview, Beijing, July 8, 2004. Yan believes that, although Mao suggested in his Hangzhou Conference Speech, January 4, 1958, that 80 percent of student rightists should be allowed to continue their schooling (see Song, *Chinese Anti-Rightist Campaign Database*), Beijing municipal authorities forestalled him by quickly sending student rightists to various industrial and agricultural units before his speech was officially announced.
124 Wu, *Bitter Winds*, 34–35.
125 Dai, *Jiusi yisheng*, 76–77; Cong, *Zouxiang hundun*, 28–36.

CHAPTER TWO: BEIJING RIGHTISTS ON THE ARMY FARMS OF BEIDAHUANG

Acknowledgment: This chapter features some material published in "Border Banishment: Rightists in the Army Farms of Beidahuang" in *The Chinese State at the Borders*, ed. Diana Lary (Vancouver: UBC Press, 2007), 198–220.

Epigraph: Yin Yi, *Huishou canyang yi han shan* [The setting of the sun over the mountain] (Beijing: Shiyue wenyi chubanshe, 2003), 25–26.

1 Central Committee of the CCP and State Council, "The Stipulations on Disposal of the Rightists among State Employees and University Students," January 13, 1958, in Song Yongyi, ed., *The Chinese Anti-Rightist Campaign Database (1957–)* (Hong Kong: The University Services Centre for China Studies at the Chinese University of Hong Kong, 2010).

2 Bawusan nongchang dangwei [Farm 853 Party committee], "Dui youpai fenzi yinian ling liugeyue gaizao de gongzuo zongjie" [The work summary of the ideological remoulding of rightists over the past one year and six months], October 1959, Farm 853 Archives.

3 See Wang Zhen zhuan bianxiezu, *Wang Zhen zhuan* [A biography of Wang Zhen] (Beijing: Dangdai zhongguo chubanshe, 2001), 68–70; Heilongjiang shengzhi difangzhi bianweihui, *Heilongjiang shengzhi guoying nongchang zhi* [Gazetteer of Heilongjiang: The state farms volume) (Harbin: Heilongjiang renmin chubanshe, 1992), 6.

4 Wang Zhen zhuan bianxiezu, *Wang Zhen zhuan*, 70, 74–78; Heilongjiang shengzhi difangzhi bianweihui, *Heilongjiang shengzhi guoying nongchang zhi*, 92–94. Li Hui, *Ren zai xuanwo: Huang Miaozi Yu Yu Eeng* [People in the eddy: *Huang Miaozi Yu Yu Eeng*] (Jinan: Shandong huabao chubanshe, 1998), 297. The CCP Central Committee's intention to expand the army farms is also clear in a Party document entitled "Suggestions on the Development of the Army Farms," March 20, 1958. It states that the development of army farms could not only provide employment for demobilized soldiers but could also facilitate agricultural growth and, in some regions, strengthen national defence and maintain public order. It held that army farms should be encouraged in areas where large amounts of uncultivated land were available and local labourers lacking.

5 Ding Ling, *Fengxue renjian* [The blizzard world] (Xiamen: Xiamen daxue chubanshe, 1987), 3.

6 Yin Yi, for instance, recalls that he took a "rightist express" to Beidahuang. See Yin Yi, *Huishou canyang yi han shan* [The setting of the sun over the mountain] (Beijing: Shiyue wenyi chubanshe, 2003), 26. However, Dai Huang indicates that he and his five fellow rightists went to Beidahuang in a small, uncoordinated group. See Dai Huang, *Jiusi yisheng: Wo de yapai licheng* [A narrow escape from death: My experience as a rightist] (Beijing: Zhongyang bianyi chubanshe, 1998), 95.

7 Cong Weixi, *Zouxiang hundun* [Going towards chaos] (Beijing: Zhongguo shehui kexue chubanshe, 1998), 48–49.

8 Although sending the rightists for manual labour was a state policy and there was great pressure to do so, some flexibility was allowed regarding choosing exile destination. Liu Meng, originally to be relocated to Qinghai Province, was allowed to go to Beidahuang instead due to his strong resistance to going to the northwest. See Liu Meng, *Chuntian de yu qiutian qing* [The whisking of rain in spring, the clearing of skies in autumn] (Beijing: Zhongguo gongren chubanshe, 2004), 63–64.

9 Wu Yongliang, *Yuxue feifei: Beidahuang shenghuo jishi* [Floating rain and snow: True stories of life in the Great Northern Wilderness] (Beijing: Zhongguo xiju chubanshe,

2002), 30–31, 43. Yin, *Huishou canyang yi han shan*, 74–75; Dai, *Jiusi yisheng*, 103–5. Xie Hegeng had an advantageous political background in pre-1949 China. As an underground CCP intelligence operative, he once worked as a secretary for high Guomindang officials Li Zongren and Bai Congxi. In 1948, the GMD sent him to study in the United States, but he still maintained close contact with the CCP. For this reason, he was arrested by the US Immigration and Naturalization Service. After being released and returning to China in 1955, he was appointed an official in China's Ministry of Foreign Affairs. See Yao Lan and Deng Qun, *Bai Congxi shenbian de zhonggong mimi dangyuan* [The underground CCP member working with Bai Chongxi] (Beijing: Zhonggong dangshi chubanshe, 1998).

10 Hu Ping, *Chan ji: 1957 kunan de jitan* [Allegorical words: The bitter sacrificial altar] (Guangzhou: Guangdong luyou chubanshe, 2004), 378.

11 See Zhang Yihe, *Wangshi bingbu ruyan* [Do not let bygones be bygones] (Beijing: Renmin wenxue chubanshe, 2004), 57.

12 Ding, *Fengxue renjian*, 14.

13 For instance, in a talk with the leaders of democratic parties in December 1957, Mao said: "For well known figures such as Zhang and Luo, we will still give them status and suitable work to do." The first reason Mao gave for this was to win over the "middle elements." ("If we treat these rightists too harshly, those in the middle will feel hurt.") The second reason was that lenient treatment would help convert them. See Mao Zedong, "Talk with the Leaders of Democratic Parties," December 8, 1957, in Song, *Chinese Anti-Rightist Campaign Database*.

14 Yang Bin, *Liubian jilue* [Notes from the willow palisades] (Taibei: Guangwen shuju, 1968), 4, 12; Thomas R. Gottschang and Diana Lary, *Swallows and Settlers: The Great Migration from North China to Manchuria* (Ann Arbor: University of Michigan Press, 2000), 46.

15 See Mei Jimin, *Beidahuang* [The Great Northern Wilderness] (Taibei: Shuifurong chubanshe, 1975) 5–6. Mei believes that, as the vast territory of eastern Siberia was legally under Qing jurisdiction due to the Treaty of Nerchinsk signed by the Qing and Russia in 1689, the term "Beidahuang" had broader implications, including the territories north of Amur River.

16 Ibid., 6.

17 Zhang Linchi et al., eds., *Dangdai Zhongguo de nongken shiye* [Land reclamation in contemporary China] (Beijing: Zhongguo shehui kexue chubanshe, 1986), 24–26.

18 For a general account of Shandong migration to Manchuria, see Gottschang and Lary, *Swallows and Settlers*.

19 Jiang Dongping, "Weiman riben kaituotuan de zuie lishi" [The evil history of Japanese pioneer group], *Zongheng*, 4 (1999): 47–49; Heilongjiang shengzhi difangzhi bianweihui, *Heilongjiang shengzhi guoying nongchang zhi*, 4.

20 Regarding banishment to northern Manchuria, see Joanna Waley-Cohen, *Exile in Mid-Qing China: Banishment to Xinjiang, 1758–1820* (New Haven: Yale University Press, 1991), 56–57.

21 Yin, *Huishou canyang yi han shan*, 31; Wu, *Yuxue feifei*, 10–11; Ni Genshan, *Chensi ji* [On contemplation] (Hong Kong: Tianma chuban youxian gongsi, 2005), 65.

22 Wu, *Yuxue feifei*, 8. According to Wu, the journalist You Zai of *Dagong Daily* pleaded to remain in Beijing on the grounds of health problems, only to be declined immediately by his work unit and scolded by anti-rightist activists.

23 Ding, *Fengxue renjian*, 16–18; Zhou Jianqiang, *Nie Gannu Zhuan* [A biography of Nie Gannu] (Chengdu: Sichuan renmin chubanshe, 1987), 219–20.
24 Ding, *Fengxue renjian*, 16–17. One of Ding's pastimes after being purged was to browse through copies of *People's Pictorial* looking at photos of the Xing'an Mountains in Heilongjiang Province.
25 Cong, *Zouxiang hundun*, 7, 121.
26 In May 1942, Mao gave his famous "Talks at the Yan'an Forum of Literature and Art," in which he required writers and artists to adhere to the Party line – to go to the grassroots and write about them in order to properly serve the masses and to qualify as progressive writers. The Yan'an Talks served as a guideline for the production of literature and art in Mao's China. See Mao Zedong, *Mao Zedong xuanji* [Selected works of Mao Zedong]. (Beijing: Renmin chubanshe, 1967) vol. 3: 807– 8.
27 Ding, *Fengxue renjian*, 17.
28 Zhou, *Nie Gannu Zhuan*, 220.
29 Xin Suwei, *Ding Cong zhuan* [A biography of Ding Cong] (Beijing: Zhongguo gongren chubanshe, 1993), 182–84.
30 See Zheng Xiaofeng, *Ding Ling zai Beidahuang* [Ding Ling in the Great Northern Wilderness] (Wuhan: Hubei renmin chubanshe, 1989), 78; Wu, *Yuxue feifei*, 14. Many others indicate that they went through similar experiences after the campaign. Ding Ling as well as leading rightists Zhang Bojun and Chu Anping were all renounced by their children. See Ding, *Fengxue renjian*, 64; Hu, *Chan ji*, 423–24. Opera performer Xin Fengxia was pushed by her boss to divorce her husband Wu Zuguang, but she firmly declined. See Niu and Deng, *Jingji lu*, 87.
31 Ding, *Fengxue renjian*, 17–18; Xu Chengbei, "Nie Gannu zhai Beidahuang" [Nie Gannu in Beidahuang], in Niu and Deng, *Yuan shang cao*, 308.
32 When Ding Cong was about to leave for Beidahuang, the director of his work unit encouraged him to give his best performance during labour reform and promised to get him back in one year. Xin, *Ding Cong zhuan*, 186. Qian Tonggang's boss estimated that half to one year would likely be the length of their send-down. See Wu, *Yuxue feifei*, 96.
33 Dai, *Jiusi yisheng*, 97.
34 Ibid. Yin, *Huishou canyang yi han shan*, 28.
35 According to the farm history and gazetteer, 925 rightists were sent to different branches of Farm 850 and 486 rightists were sent to Farm 853, totalling 1,411. See *Bawuling nongchangshi* [History of Farm 850], 30; and *Bawusan nongchangzhi* [Gazetteer of Farm 853], 2. However, the figures for Beijing rightists provided in these sources are not consistent with those provided in other sources. For instance, Wang Zhen zhuan bianxiezu, *Wang Zhen zhuan*, 78, indicates 1,039, but Zheng Jiazhen's *Zhongguo dongbeijiao* [The northeast corner of China] (Harbin: Heilongjiang renmin chubanshe, 1998), 66, indicates 1,327. A possible reason for such difference is that the farm history and gazetteer include the rightists sent from military units in Beijing while others do not. Another possible reason is that the spouses of the Beijing rightists who came along might be incorporated into rightist lists in some sources but not in others.
36 Significant information about these political exiles can be obtained from their memoirs and biographies. Zheng Jiazhen, in his lengthy *Zhongguo dongbeijiao*, also describes the life of Ding Ling, Ai Qing, Nie Gannu, and Wu Zuguang in Beidahuang.
37 *Bawuling nongchangshi*, 30; Bawusan nongchang dangwei, "Dui youpai fenzi yinian ling liugeyue gaizao de gongzuo zongjie," October, 1959.

38 *Bawuling nongchangshi*, 30–31; Wang Zhen zhuan bianxiezu, *Wang Zhen zhuan*, 68, 81;
   Heilongjiang shengzhi difangzhi bianweihui, *Heilongjiang shengzhi guoying nongchang
   zhi*, 76.
39 *Bawuling nongchangshi*, 30.
40 Dai, *Jiusi yisheng*, 117–18; Yin, *Huishou canyang yi han shan*, 35–37.
41 Zheng Xiaofeng, journalist, interview, Beijing, July 6, 2004. Huang Wu, *Mahuatang
   waiji* [Additional collection of Mahua Hall] (Guangzhou: Guangdong wenhua chubanshe, 1989), 45.
42 *Bawuling nongchangshi*, 31; Dai, *Jiusi yisheng*, 113–15; Liu, *Chuntian de yu qiutian qing*,
   94–96; Wang Zhen zhuan bianxiezu, *Wang Zhen zhuan*, 78–79; and Ding, *Fengxue
   renjian*, 14–15. All of these sources acknowledge Wang Zhen's visit and his paternal
   care for the rightists.
43 *Bawuling nongchangshi*, 31; Dai, *Jiusi yisheng*, 115. Regarding rightists' comments
   on "civilized banishment," see Dai, *Jiusi yisheng*, 119–20.
44 Dai, *Jiusi yisheng*, 103.
45 Xu, "Nie Gannu zhai Beidahuang," in Niu and Deng, *Yuan shang cao*, 309.
46 Dai, *Jiusi yisheng*, 86–87; Liu, *Chuntian de yu qiutian qing*, 108–10; Wu, *Yuxue feifei*,
   87–89; Yin, *Huishou canyang yi han shan*, 41. All of these sources document various
   family crises, most of which ended in divorces. After Dai Huang had been labelled a
   rightist, for example, his wife quickly divorced him. One of their children was given to
   an acquaintance, and another was consigned to the care of a relative.
47 "Zhongyang wenhuabu kaochazu xiang 853 changdangwei huibao qingkuang" [The
   inspection panel of the Ministry of Culture: Records of briefing session with Farm 853
   Party committee], May 1959.
48 Huang, *Mahuatang waiji*, 5, 16, 26.
49 Zhang, *Dangdai Zhongguo de nongken shiye*, 18–19.
50 Ni, *Chensi ji*, 69; Dai, *Jiusi yisheng*, 115–16.
51 Dai, *Jiusi yisheng*, 125–26.
52 Ibid., 120; Wu, *Yuxue feifei*, 7, 64. Dai Huang recalls that, when constructing an irrigation canal, he and his friends were once asked to work for fifty-six hours with hardly
   any sleep. See Dai, *Jiusi yisheng*, 127.
53 *Bawusan nongchangzhi*, 3.
54 Huang, *Mahuatang waiji*, 189.
55 Ibid., 44–45; Dai, *Jiusi yisheng*, 178; Yin, *Huishou canyang yi han shan*, 59. Yunshan nongchangshi admits that, because of the lack of usable roads, tens of thousands cubic metres
   of lumber were simply left in the mountains. See Yunshan nongchang shizhi bangongshi,
   Yunshan nongchangshi [A history of the Yunshan Farm] (Jiamusi: n.p., 1995), 3.
56 Hu, *Chan ji*, 502; Dai, *Jiusi yisheng*, 175. Dai Huang was himself a survivor of charcoal
   making; he once fainted in a charcoal kiln and was rescued by his friends, who performed artificial respiration.
57 Niu and Deng, *Yuan shang cao*, 309–10.
58 Yin, *Huishou canyang yi han shan*, 48–49; Ni, *Chensi ji*, 77. On a wheat-harvesting day
   in summer 1959, Dai Huang's labour team was denied food for nine hours due to their
   having been slowed by the rain. Dai, *Jiusi yisheng*, 158–59.
59 Bawusan nongchang zhengzhibu [Political department of Farm 853], "1960 nian yinian lai youpai fenzi sixiang qingkuang huibao" [Report on the thoughts of the rightists in the year 1960], August 30, 1960. Yin, *Huishou canyang yi han shan*, 49; Zheng
   Xiaofeng, journalist, interview, Beijing, July 6, 2004; Ni, *Chensi ji*, 72.

60 Yin, *Huishou canyang yi han shan*, 53; Wu, *Yuxue feifei*, 66: Dai, *Jiusi yisheng*, 201.
Farm 853's "Yanjiu youpaidui wenti de jilu" [Records on discussion of the problems in
the rightist teams, March 29, 1959] shows that rightists could be scapegoated in certain
circumstances. In the spring of 1959, some farm workers, especially the demobilized soldiers, requested a transfer from Farm 853. Whereas farm leaders considered such requests
as a serious problem, they believed that these people were instigated by the rightists.
61 Wu, *Yuxue feifei*, 79–80. Wu also recalls that, during the period when his labour team
was working in the mountains, it was so cold inside their makeshift straw huts that
"neither pen nor ball-pen could be used since ink would simply freeze."
62 Mudanjiang nongkenju dangwei [The Party committee of the Mudanjiang Land
Reclamation Bureau], "Guanyu fandui teshuhua de jueyi" [The decision on anti-
privileges], February 25, 1961.
63 Dai, *Jiusi yisheng*, 127–28; Yin, *Huishou canyang yi han shan*, 64.
64 Wang Zheng, "Meng hui huangyuan" [Dreaming back to the wilderness], in *Lishi zai
shenpan* [Retrial by history], ed. Liu Meng (Chengdu: Sichuan renmin chubanshe,
1996), 338.
65 Many survivors of Beidahuang say that mosquitoes were among their worst experiences
there. See, Yin, *Huishou canyang yi han shan*, 33; Wu, *Yuxue feifei*, 60; Zheng, *Zhongguo
dongbeijiao*, 67.
66 Williams and Wu believe that, in comparison to the practice of the Soviet Gulag, which
"almost never compelled its inmates to preach, listen to propaganda, or write self-criticisms and confessions," indoctrination sessions in Mao's labour camps were usually taken
extremely seriously and struggle sessions were intense as they sought "to reprogram prisoners' thinking while forcing them to become adept at play-acting and rhetorical jousts." See
Philip Williams and Yenna Wu, *The Great Wall of Confinement: The Chinese Prison Camp
through Contemporary Fiction and Reportage* (Berkeley: University of California Press,
2004), 8, 112–13. Saunders speaks of the psychological impact of remoulding efforts on
camp inmates, arguing that the remoulding regimen was not unlike applying a "wooden
knife" to human conscience. See Kate Saunders, *Eighteen Layers of Hell: Stories from the
Chinese Gulag* (London: Cassell Wellington House, 1996), chap. 6. Such observations are
somewhat challenged by recent scholarship. Smith, for instance, indicates that the alleged
successful transformation of the Lumpenproletariat (beggars, prostitutes, and petty criminals) in the 1950s was no more than official exaggeration. Many of these people were re-
educated numerous times but failed to reform, which prompted the state to consider them
irredeemable and transfer them to forced labour camps, together with the "enemies of the
people." See Aminda Smith, *Thought Reform and China's Dangerous Classes: Re-Education,
Resistance, and the People* (Lanham, MD: Rowman and Littlefield, 2013), 10–11.
67 Bawusan nongchang zhengzhibu [Political department of Farm 853], "Dui jinhou
youpai gaizao gongzuo de yijian" [Opinions on the work of remoulding rightists in the
future], July 5, 1960. Here, Farm 853 leaders were incorrect: many of the Beijing rightists had been dismissed from their posts before being sent down by their work units.
68 Nie Gannu, *Nie Gannu zixu* [Nie Gannu's own account] (Beijing: Tuanjie chubanshe,
1998), 450, 452.
69 The happiness derived from, and the dedication to, physical work on the part of Dai
Huang and his fellow team members are recorded in Dai, *Jiusi yisheng*, 122–23.
70 Wu Yongliang painfully indicates that, at the beginning of the Cultural Revolution, he
burned all the notes he made in 1961–62 regarding his Beidahuang experience because
he feared his house might be searched by the Red Guards. See Wu, *Yuxue feifei*, 11–12.

71 Li, *Ren zai xuanwo*, 307–21.

72 Ibid., 324. In 1997, Huang also told his biographer that, in retrospect, such "self-cheating" expression was merely "a cure for psychological wounds [that occurred] when human nature and feelings were deformed."

73 Wu Yongliang recalls that almost all of his campmates brought with them the works of Marx, Engels, and Lenin and that they tried to "wash their souls by reading these works." See Wu, *Yuxue feifei*, 11. Nie Gannu brought many of Mao's works with him. See Niu and Deng, *Yuan shang cao*, 309. Yin Yi says that many of the books that he brought to Beidahuang were not read and were discarded afterwards. See Yin, *Huishou canyang yi han shan*, 28.

74 Dai, *Jiusi yisheng*, 119.

75 Bawusan nongchang dangwei, "Dui youpai fenzi yinian ling liugeyue gaizao de gongzuo zongjie," October, 1959.

76 Bawusan nongchang zhengzhibu, "1960 nian yinian lai youpai fenzi sixiang qingkuang huibao," August 30, 1960.

77 Ibid.

78 Bawusan nongchang dangwei, "Dui youpai fenzi yinian ling liugeyue gaizao de gongzuo zongjie," October, 1959.

79 Bawusan nongchang zhengzhibu, "1960 nian yinian lai youpai fenzi sixiang qingkuang huibao," August 30, 1960.

80 Bawusan nongchang dangwei, "Dui youpai fenzi yinian ling liugeyue gaizao de gongzuo zongjie," October, 1959. Yin Yi of Farm 850 also mentions that one of his friends complained about how rightists were maltreated, saying: "We have already got into such a plight. What else do we need to be afraid of?" See Yin, *Huishou canyang yi han shan*, 44.

81 Bawusan nongchang dangwei, "Dui youpai fenzi yinian ling liugeyue gaizao de gongzuo zongjie," October, 1959.

82 Cao Shuji, "An Overt Conspiracy: Creating Rightists in Rural Henan, 1957–1958," in *Maoism at the Grassroots: Everyday Life in China's Era of High Socialism*, ed. Jeremy Brown and Matthew D. Johnson, 77–101 (Cambridge: Harvard University Press, 2015).

83 Huang, *Mahuatang waiji*, 47–48; Zheng, *Zhongguo dongbeijiao*, 95; Liu, *Lishi zai shenpan*, 345.

84 "Bawusan nongchang guanyu dui youpai fenzi de zhengzhi sixiang he laodong qingkuang de zongjie" [Final report of Farm 853 regarding the political thoughts and labour performance of rightists], November 1, 1958. Even two years later, farm authorities still believed that many rightists lacked the confidence to reform themselves and that they were always trying to get their political status changed "at the mere rustle of leaves in the wind." See Bawusan nongchang zhengzhibu, "1960 nian yinian lai youpai fenzi sixiang qingkuang huibao," August 30, 1960.

85 *Bawusan nongchangzhi*, 3.

86 Bawusan nongchang dangwei, "Dui youpai fenzi yinian ling liugeyue gaizao de gongzuo zongjie," October, 1959.

87 Ibid.

88 Bawusan nongchang zhengzhibu, "1960 nian yinian lai youpai fenzi sixiang qingkuang huibao," August 30, 1960.

89 Ibid.

90 Bawusan nongchang dangwei, "Dui youpai fenzi yinian ling liugeyue gaizao de gongzuo zongjie," October, 1959.

91 Ibid.

92 Ibid.

93 "Menglian kugan, zhengqu quanmian dayuejin: Bawusan nongchang daibiao tuan de baogao" [Drilling and working hard to achieve the all-round Great Leap Forward: The report of the Farm 853 delegation], 1958.

94 Bawusan nongchang zhengzhibu, "1960 nian yinian lai youpai fenzi sixiang qingkuang huibao," August 30, 1960.

95 Ibid.

96 Bawusan nongchang dangwei, "Dui youpai fenzi yinian ling liugeyue gaizao de gongzuo zongjie," October, 1959.

97 Bawusan nongchang zhengzhibu, "1960 nian yinian lai youpai fenzi sixiang qingkuang huibao," August 30, 1960.

98 Ibid.

99 *Bawuling nongchangshi*, 400.

100 Yin, *Huishou canyang yi han shan*, 63.

101 Wu, *Yuxue feifei*, 97–98.

102 Ibid., 70–71.

103 In the case of the Yunshan Branch, cadres Lu and Zhu often used this sort of coarse language during *xunhua* to scold workers for their failure to fulfill work quotas. See Dai, *Jiusi yisheng*, 131; Yin, *Huishou canyang yi han shan*, 51; Wu, *Yuxue feifei*, 66.

104 Li, *Ren zai xuanwo*, 305; Wu, *Yuxue feifei*, 66–67.

105 Yin, *Huishou canyang yi han shan*, 63.

106 Comparative analysis of the memoirs (Liu Meng, Nie Gannu, Huang Wu, Dai Huang, Wang Zheng, Yin Yi, and Wu Yongliang were all sent to different farms or branch farms) shows that the rightists at the Yunshan Branch of Farm 850 suffered more than did other rightists who had been banished to Beidahuang. They endured longer work hours, poorer accommodations, more stringent food supplies during the great famine, and a higher death rate.

107 Niu and Deng, *Yuan shang cao*, 311–12; Yin, *Huishou canyang yi han shan*, 34–36, 81–83; Dai, *Jiusi yisheng*, 128–29; Wu, *Yuxue feifei*, 37–38; Wang, "Meng hui huangyuan," 347–48.

108 See Anne Applebaum, *Gulag: A History* (New York: Doubleday, 2003), 184.

109 Dai, *Jiusi yisheng*, 131–33; Wu, *Yuxue feifei*, 54–55; Yin, *Huishou canyang yi han shan*, 51–60.

110 Yin, *Huishou canyang yi han shan*, 51; Wu, *Yuxue feifei*, 65.

111 Yin, *Huishou canyang yi han shan*, 97.

112 Jonathan D. Spence, *The Gate of Heavenly Peace: The Chinese and Their Revolution, 1895–1980* (New York: Viking, 1981), 339.

113 Ding, *Fengxue renjian*, 48–56; Tani Barlow and Gary Bjorge, eds., *I Myself Am a Woman: Selected Writings of Ding Ling* (Boston: Beacon Press, 1989), 44; Zheng, *Ding Ling zai Beidahuang*, 19–23.

114 Ibid., 2, 73, 84. A similar mentality was also expressed by other rightists. For instance, Ding Cong changed his pen name to Xuepu ("learning from commoners") during his Beidahuang exile and then, more than ten years afterwards, to A'nong ("a farmer").

115 Ding Ling, "Jianjue chedi gaizao, zhengqu zaori huidao geming de wenyi dajiating lai" [Conduct determined and thorough reformation, in order to return to the big family for revolutionary art and literature], August 10, 1960, in Song, *Chinese Anti-Rightist Campaign Database*.

116 Chen Ming, editor, interviews, Beijing, August 19, 2002; July 5, 2004.
117 Ding, *Fengxue renjian*, 6.
118 Zhou Hongxing, *Ai Qing zhuan* [A biography of Ai Qing] (Beijing: Zuojia chubanshe, 1993), 441–44; Zheng, *Zhongguo dongbeijiao*, 76–77.
119 Xin, *Ding Cong zhuan*, 188–89, 192; Zhang Jie, *Wu Zuguang beihuan qu* [Wu Zuguang: Vicissitudes of life] (Chengdu: Sichuan wenyi chubanshe, 1986), 343–44. A policy of Farm 853 that involved "using talents in appropriate posts" seemed instrumental with regard to reassigning those such as Wu. See Bawusan nongchang zhengzhibu, "Dui jinhou youpai gaizao gongzuo de yijian," July 5, 1960.
120 Ding Cong, artist, interview, Beijing, August 20, 2002; and Yang Congdao, military technician, interview, Beijing, July 11, 2004.
121 See Zhongyang wenxian yanjiushi, ed., *Jianguo yilai zhongyao wenxian xuanbian* [Selected collections of important documents since the establishment of the People's Republic of China] (Beijing: Zhongyang wenxian chubanshe, 1996), vol. 12: 528–29.
122 Yin, *Huishou canyang yi han shan*, 70–71; Wu, *Yuxue feifei*, 108–9. Yu Shanpu and Yang Congdao, "Beidahuang liuren mingdan" [The list of names of Beidahuang exiles], unpublished note; Yang Congdao, interview. The "label removal" project is examined in detail in Chapter 6.

CHAPTER THREE: POLITICAL OFFENDERS IN XINGKAIHU LABOUR CAMP

Acknowledgment: With kind permission from Springer Science + Business Media: "Discovering Xingkaihu: Political Inmates in a PRC Camp," *East Asia: An International Quarterly* 25 (2008): 267–92.
1 Zhonghua renmin gongheguo gongan falu quanshu bianweihui, ed., *Zhonghua renmin gongheguo gongan falu quanshu* [Comprehensive collection of laws on public security in the People's Republic of China] (Changchun: Jilin renmin chubanshe, 1995), 331–32.
2 "Qingkuang yu jingyan" [Information and experience], in *Renmin gongan* [People's public security] 1 (1958): 31; Chen Fengxiao, *Mengduan Weiminghu: Ershier nian laogai shengya jishi* [Broken dreams at Weiming Lake: True stories of my twenty-two years of *laogai* experience] (Washington: The Laogai Research Foundation, 2005), 48; Harry Wu, *Bitter Winds: A Memoir of My Years in China's Gulag* (New York: John Wiley and Sons, 1994), 53.
3 General information regarding how various offenders were placed in detention centres and prisons is drawn from Wu Ningkun, *A Single Tear: A Family's Persecution, Love and Endurance in Communist China* (New York: Atlantic Monthly Press, 1993), 73–75; Peter Liu, *Mirror: A Loss of Innocence in Mao's China* (Philadelphia: Xlibris, 2001), 189–92; Wu, *Bitter Winds*, 47–58; as well as Chen, *Mengduan Weiminghu*, 48–49. Interviews with Yin Jiliang, Han Dajun, and Wu Yue also confirm the massive intake of offenders.
4 Chen, *Mengduan Weiminghu*, 48.
5 Wu, *Bitter Winds*, 65–66. Another inmate, Wu Ningkun, mentions that the Qinghe labour farm "was packed to bursting." See Wu, *Single Tear*, 102.
6 Xingkaihu changshiban, *Xingkaihu nongchang shi* [A history of Xingkaihu Farm] (Mishan: n.p., 1988), 399.
7 For various offenders and even the general public in the Mao era, Xingkaihu was synonymous with severe punishment and death. Literature and movies in the post-Mao period also dramatize the harshness of Xingkaihu. In the movie *Blue Kite*, for example, one of the protagonists, Lin Shaolong, was among those who died in Xingkaihu.

8 Xingkaihu changshiban, *Xingkaihu nongchang shi*, 4, 387; Mishan xianzi bianweihui, *Mishan xianzhi* [Gazetteer of Mishan County] (Beijing: Zhongguo biaozun chubanshe, 1993), 188–89.

9 Xingkaihu changshiban, *Xingkaihu nongchang shi*, 387–88. This initiative was in accordance with a speech made in 1952 by Minister of Public Security Luo Ruiqing at the First National Conference for Labour Reform Work: "Large-scale production projects using convict labourers should be avoided at national defence points, in major cities, in important industrial zones, and in heavily populated regions; instead, we should steadily move convict labourers, step by step and group by group, to the Northwest, Northeast, and the Sichuan-Xikang border region of the Southwest where the land is vast and population sparse." See Luo Ruiqing, "Speech at the First National Conference for Labour Reform Work," June 28, 1952.

10 Heilongjiang shengzhi difangzhi bianweihui, *Heilongjiang shengzhi: guoying nongchang zhi* [Gazetteer of Heilongjiang Province: The state farms volume) (Harbin: Heilongjiang renmin chubanshe, 1992), 77.

11 Xingkaihu changshiban, *Xingkaihu nongchang shi*, 3, 9, 45, 46; Yin Jiliang, journalist, interview, Beijing, October 3, 2002.

12 Xingkaihu changshiban, *Xingkaihu nongchang shi*, 36, 394; Chen, *Mengduan Weiminghu*, 88–89.

13 Chen, *Mengduan Weiminghu*, 88–89. *Xingkaihu nongchang shi* acknowledges that convicted labourers contributed to the establishment of the Xingkaihu farm and that some of them lost their lives. See the Prelude in *Xingkaihu nongchang shi*.

14 In Xingkaihu as well as in other PRC prison camps, police officers in charge of inmates were generally referred to as camp cadres, or *guanjiao ganbu*, and they ranged from political instructors to team leaders to managerial secretaries. Appointed by the Beijing Public Security Bureau, the camp cadres in Xingkaihu were responsible for disciplining inmates, administering their lives, supervising their work, and providing them with political tutelage. See Xingkaihu changshiban, *Xingkaihu nongchang shi*, 396–97; Yin Jiliang, interview.

15 Xingkaihu changshiban, *Xingkaihu nongchang shi*, 10. *Xingkaihu nongchang shi* does not specify the extent of the influx of inmates during these two years. However, statistics for a longer period are available. Between 1955 and 1967, the number of police officers and camp cadres totalled 1,783; convicts, *laojiao* inmates, and other urban undesirables totalled 21,364; and supporting workers totalled around 2,200. Xingkaihu changshiban, *Xingkaihu nongchang shi*, 9. It is estimated, therefore, that various offenders comprised over 84 percent of the Xinkaihu population.

16 Xingkaihu changshiban, *Xingkaihu nongchang shi*, 35, 44; Chen Fengxiao, university student, interview, Weifang, Shandong, July 3, 2004; Yin Jiliang, interview.

17 Harry Wu, *Laogai: The Chinese Gulag* (Boulder, CO: Westview Press, 1992), 1, 6; Sun Xiaoli, *Zhongguo laogai gaizao zhidu de lilun yu shijian* [Theories and practices of China's labour reform system] (Beijing: Zhongguo zhengfa daxue chubanshe, 1994), 119. Pre-trial detention centres, prisons, and juvenile re-education camps are integral parts of the PRC's prison camp system but are not the focus of this research.

18 Mühlhahn's source for the incarceration of juvenile delinquents in Xingkaihu is Amnesty International. See Klaus Mühlhahn, *Criminal Justice in China: A History* (Cambridge: Harvard University Press, 2009), 246. However, neither official sources nor memoir material provide any record of this type of detainee in Xingkaihu.

19 Xingkaihu changshiban, *Xingkaihu nongchang shi*, 396.

20 Yin Jiliang, interview.

21 Tan Tianrong, university student, interview, Qingdao, June 29, 2004.

22 Compared with other labour camps, the percentage of political inmates in Xingkaihu was not high. According to Fu Hualing, for instance, political offenders incarcerated in Shandong First Laojiao Institution accounted for 59 percent of all Laojiao people between 1957 and 1960. See Fu Hualing, "Re-Education through Labour in Historical Perspective," *China Quarterly* 184 (2005): 815. However, considering the fact that all the political offenders sentenced in Shandong for labour re-education during this period were sent to this institution, as Fu indicates, and that some of the political offenders arrested in Beijing were sent elsewhere, this distinction seems less surprising.

23 PRC State Council, "The Resolution on Re-Education through Labour," August 3, 1957, in *Zhonghua renmin gongheguo xianxing falu xingzheng fagui huibian* [The comprehensive collection of current laws and administrative regulations of the People's Republic of China], ed. Guowuyuan fazhiju (Beijing: Zhongguo falu chubanshe, 1995), 104. This regulation also applied to other individuals, such as those who refused to accept designated jobs or those who allegedly engaged in "sexual misconduct."

24 Liu, *Mirror*, 189; Niu Weina, *Cuowei: Wo he wojia jidai zhishifenzi de gushi* [Disjunction: The stories of intellectuals in my clan) (n.p., printed in Los Angeles, 2003), 135; Wang Shuyao, *Yanyuan fengyu zhu rensheng* [My turbulent life and times at Beijing University] (Washington: The Laogai Research Foundation, 2007), 225–26. Wang recalls that, right after signing his labour re-education application at the Peking University Physics Department's main office, he was led to the campus security office to receive his *laojiao* notification.

25 Liu Junying, a camp cadre at Branch 5 of Xingkaihu, recalls that the historical counter-revolutionaries under him were generally docile and obeyed camp rules, so he did not give them a hard time. Liu Junying, retired labour camp cadre, interview, Beijing, July 16, 2004.

26 Chen Fengxiao and Liu Qidi (student dissidents at Peking University) were both sentenced to fifteen years for their sharp criticisms during the Hundred Flowers Campaign. See Chen, *Mengduan Weiminghu,* 59.

27 "Political" means something relating to politics. In the PRC context, this relates to one's stance towards the CCP government, Maoist socialism, the "people's democratic dictatorship," and the Party's significant policies. However, as we see from following the cases of Han Chuntai and others, many of those persecuted for political reasons were actually persecuted for something far different.

28 Chen, *Mengduan Weiminghu,* 85.

29 Mühlhahn, *Criminal Justice in China,* 213.

30 Tan Tianrong, "Meiyou qingjie de gushi" [Stories without plots], unpublished essay, 2. Tan received a light sanction, possibly because he did not try to flee or resist but, rather, stayed in his dormitory doing research while waiting for the arrival of police.

31 Wu, *Single Tear,* 65, 107. According to Han Dajun, *laojiao* inmates in Xingkaihu received a monthly stipend of seventeen *yuan* Chinese RMB. See Han Dajun, scientist, interview, Beijing, July 5, 2004.

32 In his article "Re-Education through Labour in Historical Perspective," Fu Hualing defines *laojiao* as an administrative punishment, according to which the police bypass the criminal process and summarily subject a person guilty of minor offences "to a maximum of three years' incarceration." See Fu, "Re-Education through Labour in

Historical Perspective," 811. Actually, the 1957 "Resolution on Re-education through Labour" did not specify the length of a *laojiao* term, and the "three-years" rule was not formally established until 1979, although it was once implemented in the early 1960s. See "Guowuyuan guanyu laodong jiaoyang de buchong guiding" [State Council supplementary provisions concerning re-education through labour], November 29, 1979, in Gonganbu zhengcefalu yanjiushi, *Gongan fagui xuanbian* [Selected collection of laws and regulations on the public security] (Beijing: Qunzhong chubanshe, 1981), 296.

33 Tan, "Meiyou qingjie de gushi," 2; Liu, *Mirror,* 259, 314. Both were detained from 1958 to 1969. See also Meng Bo, "Laogai jishi" [Stories in Laogai], in Xiao Ke et al., *Wo qinli guo de zhengzhi yundong* [Political campaigns that I have experienced] (Beijing: Zhongyang bianyi chubanshe, 1998), 73–74.

34 Wu, *Single Tear,* 89; Tan, interview. Tan said that the several months that he worked in a *laogai* camp constituted the best period of time he spent in Xingkaihu.

35 Han Dajun, interview. Harry Wu documents a case in which a female *laojiao* inmate asked a journalist to help her be transferred to a *laogai* camp. See Harry Wu, *Laodong jiaoyang yu liuchang jiuye* [Re-education through labour and forced job placement] (Washington: The Laogai Research Foundation, 2004), 10.

36 Xingkaihu changshiban, *Xingkaihu nongchang shi,* 397.

37 Ibid., 390, 397.

38 Chen, *Mengduan Weiminghu,* 110, 118, 125.

39 Ibid., 110.

40 Wu, *Single Tear,* 97.

41 Yin Jiliang, interview.

42 Liu, *Mirror,* 213. Camp cadres also told rightists that, for the crimes they had committed against the government, "each and every one of [them] would be executed in a capitalist country." See ibid., 254.

43 Chen, *Mengduan Weiminghu,* 95.

44 Xingkaihu changshiban, *Xingkaihu nongchang shi,* 42–44, 396–97, 406.

45 Chen, *Mengduan Weiminghu,* 87; Wu, *Single Tear,* 93.

46 Wu, *Single Tear,* 89; for "worksite criticism meetings," see Liu, *Mirror,* 244.

47 Liu, *Mirror,* 224.

48 Xingkaihu changshiban, *Xingkaihu nongchang shi,* 406.

49 Ibid. However, the source did not provide any further information regarding what these riots really were and how many inmates were involved in them.

50 Liu, *Mirror,* 203–4.

51 Ibid., 205, 209.

52 Chen, *Mengduan Weiminghu,* 101.

53 Kate Saunders, *Eighteen Layers of Hell: Stories from the Chinese Gulag* (London: Cassell Wellington House, 1996), 77, 80.

54 Wu, *Single Tear,* 99.

55 Niu and Deng, *Yuan shang cao,* 42, 108.

56 Beijing shi renmin jianchayuan qisushu – Jingjian (58) fen fanqizi di 454 hao [Indictment of the People's Procuratorate of Beijing, 1958, procurator file no. 454]. For the statements of Chen and his friends in the Hundred Flowers Society, see Roderick MacFarquhar, *The Hundred Flowers Campaign and the Chinese Intellectuals* (New York: Octagon Books, 1974), 135–38; Niu and Deng, *Yuan shang cao,* 215–23.

57 Yan Tunfu, university student, interview, Beijing, July 8, 2004.

58 Chen Fengxiao, wall poster "Ruci jiliang" [Such manoeuvres], July 5, 1957, in Song Yongyi, ed., *The Chinese Anti-Rightist Campaign Database (1957–)* (Hong Kong: The University Services Centre for China Studies at the Chinese University of Hong Kong, 2010).

59 Chen, *Mengduan Weiminghu*, 29–30, 59–60. Chen was provided with (and still keeps) the indictment but not the letter of verdict.

60 Ibid., 106–7.

61 Ibid., 93–94, 130–32. From Caolanzi Detention Centre to Tongzhou Prison to Xingkaihu, Chen rarely kept silent when the police scolded him, speaking back at every opportunity.

62 Chen, *Mengduan Weiminghu*, 132–33, 153–55.

63 Ibid., 118–23. Because the notes he made in his dairy were intentionally opaque so that camp cadres would not be able to fully understand them, Chen was subjected to a form of torture known as "tiger benching" to force him to confess his reactionary ideas. See Chen, *Mengduan Weiminghu*, 132–33.

64 For the political statements of Tan Tianrong, see MacFarquhar, *Hundred Flowers Campaign*, 135–37; Niu and Deng, *Yuan shang cao*, 28–67.

65 Zhongguo qingnian chubanshe, ed., *Zai fan youpai douzheng zhong xiqu jiaoxun: Ji dang de hanwei zhe he qingnian de bailei* [Drawing lessons from the Anti-Rightist Campaign: On the defenders of the Party and the degenerates among the youth] (Beijing: Zhongguo qingnian chubanshe, 1957), 95, 98.

66 Tan, interview. Mao's criticism of Tan can be found in his "Speech on the Shanghai Conference," July 8, 1957, in Red Guard Materials, *Mao Zedong sixiang wansui* [Long live Mao Zedong thought] (n.p., 1967), 182.

67 Tan, "Meiyou qingjie de gushi," 3. This same "science and resistance" pattern also appears in the work of Fang Lizhi. See James H. Williams, "Fang Lizhi's Expanding Universe," *China Quarterly* 123 (September, 1990): 459–84.

68 Meng, "*Laogai* jishi," In Xiao Ke et al., eds., *Woqinli guode zhengzhi yundong*, 80–82.

69 Ibid., 82–83; Tan, interview. Tan claims that his stay in his home village in Hunan was the best time he had after having been labelled an ultra-rightist. Although drawing a political line between him and themselves, his fellow villagers rarely troubled him or disrupted his research.

70 Chen, *Mengduan Weiminghu*, 119.

71 Ibid., 119, 122–24.

72 Han, interview.

73 MacFarquhar, *Hundred Flowers Campaign*, 135–36; Zhang Yunpeng, "Zhuangzai wuqi, beizai wuqi" [Glories and tragedies of 1957], in *Mobuqu de lishi jiyi: Nankai wuqi huiyi* [Inerasable memories of history: Recollections of Nakai University, 1957], ed. Chen Shengxi and Zhang Zhenqiang (n.p., 2015), 25; Beijing shi renmin jianchayuan qisu-shu – Jingjian (58).

74 Chen Fengxiao, "Wufa wangque de jiyi" [Unforgettable memories], unpublished essay, 3; Zhang Xiaofeng, "Hu Feng anjian yu youpai xuesheng" [Hu Feng's case and student rightists], unpublished essay, 4.

75 Recollections of political inmates in other Chinese labour camps have increasingly appeared in recent decades. These include: Wu, *Bitter Winds*; Li Caiyi, *Feng xiaoxiao lu manman* [Soughing wind and endless road] (Guangzhou: Haizhu chubanshe, 2001); Wenche He'en, *Kunan de licheng* [Difficult journeys] (Washington: The Laogai Research

Foundation, 2003); Yang Xianhui, *Gaobie Jiabianguo* [Farewell Jiabiangou] (Shanghai: Shanghai wenyi chubanshe, 2003); Huang Zhan, *Yongyuan de Beidahuang* [The everlasting Beidahuang] (Washington: The Laogai Research Foundation, 2004), He Fengming, *Jingli Wode 1957 nian* [Experience: My 1957] (Lanzhou: Dunhuang wenyi chubanshe, 2006). These recollections contain very little information about how persecuted intellectuals continued to be ideologically assertive and/or behaviourally defiant.

76 At times Peter Liu spoke politely to his camp cadre Zhang regarding his receiving a smaller ration of cereal than other inmates due to his poor performance at work. Although Zhang firmly declined his request for more food, Liu chose not to irritate him by pursuing the issue. See Liu, *Mirror*, 229–30.

77 *Xingkaihu changshiban, Xingkaihu nongchang shi*, 391, 397.

78 Wu, *Single Tear*, 92; Liu, *Mirror*, 224; Han, interview. Chen, *Mengduan Weiminghu*, 93.

79 Chen, *Mengduan Weiminghu*, 92. Cell bosses, or *laotou*, were prisoners who were designated to head other prisoners. They were physically strong, became close with camp authorities, and, thus, were entrusted with assisting camp cadres to administer inmates at the squad or team levels. In addition to wielding considerable power over fellow inmates, they were also responsible for completing the work assigned to their squads or teams.

80 Chen, *Mengduan Weiminghu*, 110, 112, 186.

81 Liu, *Mirror*, 211–12.

82 Wu, *Single Tear*, 100–1; Han, interview; Tan, "Meiyou qingjie de gushi," 3.

83 Chen, *Mengduan Weiminghu*, 118.

84 Tan, interview; Chen, *Mengduan Weiminghu*, 93–94. However, if political inmates gathered and chatted frequently, camp cadres would intervene. Chen was once relegated to solitary confinement for his frequent chats with other counter-revolutionaries and his refusal to admit such an error.

85 Liu, *Mirror*, 241.

86 Wu, *Single Tear*, 108.

87 Yin, interview.

88 Cong, *Zouxiang hundun*, 118–21. However, Wu Ningkun presents a contrary example. In the Banbuqiao Detention Centre, many detainees did not fear being sent to any labour camp, including Xingkaihu, as long as they could get enough food to eat and leave their crowded and filthy prison cells: "After two months of incarceration on a starvation diet, we all jumped at the prospect of working in the sun on a full stomach." See Wu, *Single Tear*, 77.

89 Chen, *Mengduan Weiminghu*, 90–91. Chen's narrative here challenges Mühlhahn's argument that "insurgent behavior was to be punished, the most severe punishment being the extension of the inmate's prison term." See Mühlhahn, *Criminal Justice in China*, 225.

90 Peter Liu recalls that, after careful preparation, an inmate at Branch 8 got away from the encampment. Armed with a map, a compass, and food he had stolen from the kitchen, he marched deep into ripe wula grass just before an autumn dawn, gradually entering ankle-deep water. Assuming he was going in the right direction, he walked for the whole day; however, he ended up in neck-deep water and silt. In a panic he shouted for help. A peasant, who was rowing by collecting wild duck eggs, saved him and returned him to the camp. See Liu, *Mirror*, 240.

91 Chen, *Mengduan Weiminghu*, 88, 124; Yin Jiliang, interview.

92 Chen, *Mengduan Weiminghu*, 124–25.

93   Hu Xianzhong, *Yangmou xia de rensheng* [My life as a pawn in Mao's political game] (Washington: The Laogai Research Foundation, 2008), 70, 77.
94   Although political offenders sent to Xingkaihu were the victims of Maoist campaigns and a considerable number of them were intellectuals, I do not claim that all political inmates were ethically different from, or superior to, criminal offenders. And, needless to say, not all the intellectuals interned in Xingkaihu were classified as political offenders.
95   Liu, *Mirror*, 230.
96   Yin Jiliang, interview.
97   Mao, *Mao Zedong xuanji*, vol. 5: 364–66.
98   Aminda Smith, *Thought Reform and China's Dangerous Classes: Re-Education, Resistance, and the People* (Lanham, MD: Rowman and Littlefield, 2013), chap. 3.
99   Chen, *Mengduan Weiminghu*, 73–74; Liu, *Mirror*, 231.
100   Liu, *Mirror*, 231.
101   Yin Jiliang, interview.
102   Chen, *Mengduan Weiminghu*, 101–2.
103   Yin Jiliang and Tan, interviews. Harry Wu's campmate, Xing, thought that Wu's school education was useless. See Wu, *Bitter Winds*, 66.
104   Mühlhahn, *Criminal Justice in China*, 260.
105   Wu, *Single Tear*, 102–4.
106   Yin Jiliang, interview.
107   Hu Xianzhong, university student, interview, Changchun, September 21, 2002.
108   The Water Margin tradition involves fighting oppression by corrupt officials.
109   Chen, *Mengduan Weiminghu*, 106–7.
110   Yin Jiliang, interview.
111   Chen, *Mengduan Weiminghu*, 99–100; Yin Jiliang, interview. Chen Fengxiao also recalls learning from a sentenced larcenist about how to avoid theft and from elderly convicts about how to effectively engage in rice planting. Chen Fengxiao, university student, interview, Weifang, Shandong, July 3, 2004.
112   Wu, *Bitter Winds*, 63, 66–67.
113   Ibid., 64, 80.
114   Ibid., 68, 81, 107.

CHAPTER FOUR: LIFE AND DEATH IN BEIDAHUANG

Epigraph: Huang Wu, *Mahuatang waiji* [Additional collection of Mahua Hall] (Guangzhou: Guangdong wenhua chubanshe, 1989), 34.
1   Liu Meng, journalist and government employee, interview, Beijing, October 4, 2002.
2   Dai Huang, *Jiusi yisheng: Wo de youpai licheng* [A narrow escape from death: My experience as a rightist] (Beijing: Zhongyang bianyi chubanshe, 1998), 117. A rightist who had lived in Switzerland even claimed that Beidahuang rivalled Geneva in terms of its natural beauty. See Wu Yongliang, *Yuxue feifei: Beidahuang shenghuo jishi* [Floating rain and snow: True stories of life in the Great Northern Wilderness] (Beijing: Zhongguo xiju chubanshe, 2002), 43.
3   Wu, *Yuxue feifei*, 36–37; Dai, *Jiusi yisheng*, 117.
4   Huang Wu, *Mahuatang waiji* [Additional collection of Mahua Hall] (Guangzhou: Guangdong wenhua chubanshe, 1989), 36. Huang Wu particularly enjoyed "Song of the Broad-Axe" by Walt Whitman, who spoke of the lives of American lumbermen in the nineteenth century.

5 See Ding Ling, *Fengxue renjian* [The blizzard world] (Xiamen: Xiamen daxue chuban-she, 1987), 17. Chen Ming was first deported to Beidahuang in March 1958 and then sent back a letter that encouraged Ding Ling to come and join him.

6 Dai, *Jiusi yisheng,* 122.

7 For instance, in 1959, the land reclamation target of Farm 850 was 51,000 hectares, doubling that of 1958, and the grain production target that year was 36,000 tons, triple that of 1958. Bawuling nongchangshi bianxie bangongshi, *Bawuling nongchangshi* [A history of Farm 850] (Hulin, Heilongjiang: n.p., 1986), 35.

8 Peter Liu, *Mirror: A Loss of Innocence in Mao's China* (Philadelphia: Xlibris, 2001), 224–25.

9 Chen Fengxiao, *Mengduan Weiminghu: Ershier nian laogai shengya jishi* [Broken dreams at Weiming Lake: True stories of my twenty-two years of laogai experience] (Washington: The Laogai Research Foundation, 2005), 105. What Chen describes here happened in 1960, just after the high point of the Great Leap Forward; however, the intensive and excessive use of weak labourers was the crucial reason for their deaths.

10 Dai, *Jiusi yisheng,* 225–32. This mass death in Yunshan is also recounted by Yin Yi, *Huishou canyang yi han shan* [The setting of the sun over the mountain] (Beijing: Shiyue wenyi chubanshe, 2003), 87–89; and Wu, *Yuxue feifei,* 133–34. Dai Huang believes that more than one year of prolonged hunger rendered the rightists at this branch farm extremely weak and frail, which, compounded with intensive labour in vile weather, caused this mass death.

11 Huang, *Mahuatang waiji,* 37, 59.

12 Dai, *Jiusi yisheng,* 141–43. Casualties also occurred in daily farm work when convicts were unable to properly handle electric farm machines. See Chen, *Mengduan Weiminghu,* 100. Some exiles died trying to save their tools. Since camp leaders promoted the notion that "one must give priority to public property over one's own life," inmates would be harshly condemned for losing their tools. In this circumstance, some were crushed by falling trees or landslides when trying to save "public property." See Wu, *Yuxue feifei,* 90; Dai, *Jiusi yisheng,* 141; Xingkaihu changshiban, *Xingkaihu nongchang shi* [A history of Xingkaihu Farm] (Mishan: N.p. 1988), 359.

13 Dai, *Jiusi yisheng,* 231, 233. According to Dai, when the October thirteenth tragedy happened, the head of the Yunshan Branch did not even bother to send for doctors to rescue those in danger, with the result that rightists had to perform first aid for their campmates.

14 Chen, *Mengduan Weiminghu,* 100.

15 Wu, *Yuxue feifei,* 91.

16 After three convicts had died saving tools in a construction accident, they were hon-oured at a public gathering and limited compensation was offered to their families. See *Xingkaihu changshiban, Xingkaihu nongchang shi,* 397.

17 Wu Yue, journal editor, interview, Beijing, October 5, 2002; Chen, *Mengduan Weiminghu,* 47.

18 Yan Peng, "Pan Hannian zai Tuanhe nongchang," [Pan Hannian in Tuanhe Farm] *Zongheng* 10 (1998): 24-30. Contrary evidence exists, however. Peter Liu, who was put in Banbuqiao detention centre in Beijing, recalls that, during the first couple of months, he was in "a desperate fight with a gnawing hunger." "For all the consummate skill of the cooks, the food was far from enough, so that at the end of each meal I felt I was barely half full. My guts used to rumble at bedtime; so did those of my cellmates." See Liu, *Mirror,* 192–93.

19 Liu Meng, journalist and government employee, interview, Beijing, October 4, 2002. Sources from other rightists, such as Wu Yongliang, also indicate that they had enough food during their early stay on the army farms. See Wu, *Yuxue feifei*, 33.

20 Wu Ningkun, *A Single Tear: A Family's Persecution, Love and Endurance in Communist China* (New York: Atlantic Monthly Press, 1993), 96.

21 Dai, *Jiusi yisheng*, 157; Bawusan nongchangzhi bianshen weiyuanhu, *Bawusan nongchangzhi* [Gazetteer of Farm 853] (Beijing: n.p., 1986), 388. Whether the exiles could receive designated rations is highly dubious. Some exiles complained that their limited rations were subject to frequent appropriation by farm leaders and managerial staff. Yang Congdao and Wang Keqin recall that, while ordinary workers, including rightists, fed on food substitutes and thin porridge in the farm dining halls, farm leaders ate in a "small kitchen" (*xiaozao*) and enjoyed special food. Dai Huang recalls that, when grain rations per person dropped to thirty *jin* per month in December 1959, a rightist at Yunshan Branch could only receive two small *wuotous* (bread-like Chinese food buns, mainly consisting of corn flour, corn chaff, or, in some rural areas of northeast China, sorghum flour) for breakfast and lunch, and very little porridge for dinner. This was far less than what should have been provided. Dai, *Jiusi yisheng*, 174.

22 Wu, *Yuxue feifei*, 114.

23 Chen, *Mengduan Weiminghu*, 104; Liu, *Mirror*, 228. As Huang Miaozi wrote in a letter home in June 1959, rightists on his team normally had three meals a day: "two porridge and one solid food or, alternatively, two solid food and one porridge when work is heavy; the meals are mostly corn gruel, corn breads and cabbage leaves with no or little dietary oil." See Li Hui, *Ren zai xuanwo: Huang Miaozi yu Yu Feng* [People in the eddy: Huang Miaozi and Yu Feng] (Jinan: Shandong huabao chubanshe, 1998), 322.

24 Han Dajun, scientist, interview, Beijing, July 5, 2004; Chen Fengxiao, *Mengduan Weiminghu*, 104.

25 It seems that food supplies for camp cadres were institutionally less than those for inmates. Liu Junying, a former camp cadre at Branch 5, states: "When the convicts in my farm were rationed more than thirty *jin*, I was only given twenty-eight *jin*." So Liu argues that inmates' complaints about their hunger were no more than a "psychological effect." See Liu Junying, retired labour camp cadre, interview, Beijing, July 16, 2004.

26 Philip F. Williams and Yenna Wu, *The Great Wall of Confinement: The Chinese Prison Camp through Contemporary Fiction and Reportage* (Berkeley: University of California Press, 2004), 89.

27 When Chen and Liu were both put into solitary confinement cells, their daily food ration was 0.38 *jin* (0.4 pounds) as the Xingkaihu authorities were convinced that one could survive on this ration if one remained motionless in one's cell. See Chen, *Mengduan Weiminghu*, 67.

28 Liu, *Mirror*, 227, 229; Chen, *Mengduan Weiminghu*, 104–5.

29 Wu, *Single Tear*, 108; Han, interview; Yin Jiliang, journalist, interview, Beijing, October 3, 2002.

30 Huang, *Yongyuan de Beidahuang*, 87.

31 See Frank Dikötter, *Mao's Great Famine: The History of China's Most Devastating Catastrophe, 1958–1962* (New York: Walker, 2010), chaps. 10, 15, and 17.

32 Han, interview.

33 *Bawusan nongchangzhi*, 387; Zheng Jiazhen, *Zhongguo dongbeijiao* [The northeast corner of China] (Harbin: Heilongjiang renmin chubanshe, 1998), 163.

34 "Wang Zhen tongzhi gei chang lingdao de xin" [The letter of comrade Wang Zhen to the farm leadership], May 29, 1962, collected from Farm 853 Archives.

35 According to *Xingkaihu nongchang shi*, grain and soybean output at Xingkaihu from 1959 to 1962 was, respectively, 26,074,300 *jin*; 17,354,100 *jin*; 26,808,000 *jin*; and 30,469,000 *jin*; divided by the population in the relevant year, grain/bean ration per capita should have been, respectively, 1,276 *jin*; 675 jin; 1,091 *jin*; and 1,201 *jin* on average. See Xingkaihu changshiban, *Xingkaihu nongchang shi*, 10, 61. Obviously, the grain/bean rations inmates actually received was far less than the average.

36 Dai, *Jiusi yisheng*, 261; Wang Keqin, military officer, interview, Beijing, July 18, 2004.

37 Mudanjiang nongkenju dangwei [The Party committee of the Mudanjiang Land Reclamation Bureau], "Guanyu fandui teshuhua de jueyi" [The decision on anti-privileges], February 25, 1961, Farm 853 Archives. The rightists complained about grain shortages. For instance, Zhuang Ronghua of Farm 853 said: "In the old society it was the minority of people who did not have enough to eat, but now in the new society it is the majority." See Bawusan nongchang dangwei [Farm 853 Party Committee], "Dui youpai fenzi yinian ling liugeyue gaizao de gongzuo zongjie" [The work summary of the ideological remoulding of rightists in the past one year and six months], October 1959, Farm 853 Archives.

38 Dai, *Jiusi yisheng*, 213; Ni Genshan, *Chensi ji* [On contemplation] (Hong Kong: Tianma chuban youxian gongsi, 2005), 83; Liang Nan, "Chaosheng zhe" [pilgrims], in *Huishou rensheng* [Reflections on our life], ed. Liu Meng (Beijing: Shidai wenyi chubanshe, 1992), 9. Wu Yongliang also recalls that he and three of his fellow rightists were once sent for soybeans stored in holes by field rats and that their six days' work produced more than ten bags of soy beans as important additions to food supplies. See Wu, *Yuxue feifei*, 112–13.

39 Liang Nan, "Chaosheng zhe," in Lui, *Huishou rensheng*, 16. Some rightists on Farm 850 found that the garbage dumps close to farm cadres' living compounds might contain leftover chicken and fish bones or rotten vegetables. Dai Huang and some of his friends at times visited these garbage dumps. See Dai, *Jiusi yisheng*, 248, 259.

40 Williams and Wu, *Great Wall of Confinement*, 94.

41 Liu Meng, *Chuntian de yu qiutian qing* [The whisking of rain in spring, the clearing of skies in autumn] (Beijing: Zhongguo gongren chubanshe, 2003), 141; Yin, *Huishou canyang yi han shan*, 75–76; Yin Jiliang, interview; Dai, *Jiusi yisheng*, 242. Dai Huang describes how, in their hunger, they devoured captured voles: "After work that day, we began to prepare these voles ... We put water in a washing basin, mixed these voles with salt and chili powder, and boiled them. When they were cooked, we ate them all very fast ...When we could not find voles, we started to pick up raw corn to eat." However, camp cadres sometimes disapproved of searching for rats to eat. Yin Yi recalls that one of his fellow exiles caught rats to cook but was condemned by farm cadres for "trying to discredit socialism." See Yin, *Huishou canyang yi han shan*, 76.

42 Huang, *Mahuangtang waiji*, 25. Wang Zheng, in his "Menghui huangyuan" [Dreaming back to the wilderness], in *Lishi zai shenpan* [Retrial by history], ed. Liu Meng (Chengdu: Sichuan renmin chubanshe, 1996), 340, also recalls Tang's excellent ability to catch snakes to make soup for his fellow rightists. Harry Wu, an inmate in Qinghe Farm in north China, also describes how he caught hibernating snakes in the winter of 1961. See Wu, *Bitter Winds*, 134–35.

43 Dai, *Jiusi yisheng*, 173.

44 Liu, *Mirror*, 261–62.
45 Wu, *Bitter Winds*, 114–15.
46 Chen, *Mengduan Weiminghu*, 109. Harry Wu, in *Bitter Winds*, also describes his personal experience. In a north China labour camp he was assigned work delivering chemical powder within the camp area, which provided him with an opportunity to pass a vegetable garden run by the camp police. He recounts: "Several times a day I would stare at the cabbages and cucumbers, warning myself not to take risk, but one night when I was hungrier than I had ever felt, the smell of cucumbers overwhelmed my caution. For the first time in my life, I stole ... Four or five more times in the next two weeks I visited the police garden." See Wu, *Bitter Winds*, 58–59.
47 Ralph Thaxton, "How the Great Leap Forward Famine Ended in Rural China," in *Eating Bitterness: New Perspectives on China's Great Leap Forward and Famine*, ed. Kimberley Manning and Felix Wemheuer (Vancouver: UBC Press, 2011), 260–62.
48 Mudanjiang nongkenju [Mudanjiang Land Reclamation Bureau], "Guanyu 853 nongchang zhigong luanchi sheng baomi zaocheng siwang de tongbao" [Circular on the death of a worker at Farm 853 due to eating raw corn], April 4, 1961, Farm 853 Archives.
49 Xingkaihu changshiban, *Xingkaihu nongchang shi*, 404; Chen, *Mengduan Weiminghu*, 105.
50 Yin, *Huishou canyang yi han shan*, 76.
51 Ibid., 66–67.
52 Liu Meng, interview, and his *Chuntian de yu qiutian qing*, 134; Bawusan nongchang zhengzhibu [The political department of Farm 853], "1960 nian yinian lai youpai fenzi sixiang qingkuang huibao" [Report on the thoughts of rightists in the year 1960], August 30, 1960, Farm 853 Archives.
53 Yin, *Huishou canyang yi han shan*, 76; Han Dajun recalled, when interviewed, that his campmate Ren Hongsuo crept into a camp kitchen at night trying to lift *wuotous* but was caught and sent to a solitary confinement cell.
54 Chen, *Mengduan Weiminghu*, 108–9.
55 Williams and Wu, *Great Wall of Confinement*, 91: "Even well-educated PRC inmates would often jostle and fight with other prisoners over the little bit of gruel left at the bottom of the vat and rummage through rubbish heaps in search of something edible."
56 Yin Jiliang, interview.
57 Dai, *Jiusi yisheng*, 260.
58 Bawusan nongchang zhengzhibu, "1960 nian yinian lai youpai fenzi sixiang qingkuang huibao."
59 Ba Hong, movie director, interview, Beijing, July 17, 2004.
60 Hui Peilin, journalist, interview, Beijing, July 19, 2004.
61 Wu Yongliang remembers that, in the fall of 1960, when he was transferred to Branch 1 of Farm 850, he and his rightist friends were allowed to work from 8:00 AM until only 2:00 PM to save energy. After a meal of thin gruel at 5:00 PM, they went to sleep. See Wu, *Yuxue feifei*, 139–40. Xingkaihu changshiban, *Xingkaihu nongchang shi*, 404, also indicates half-day labour in the winter of 1960.
62 Zheng, *Zhongguo dongbeijiao*, 159. Dai Huang, Yin Yi, and Wang Keqin all describe the poor quality and terrible taste of the food substitutes. Such substitutes, which were low in starch, provide little nutrition and can adversely affect the human digestive system. Du Xunfan, Wang's friend, died of intestinal obstruction due to the roughness of these food substitutes. Wang, interview.

63 Chen, *Mengduan Weiminghu*, 105. Some sympathetic farm cadres, through their personal connections, helped rightists purchase food from outside the army farms. Sometimes they even allowed them to use their own networks to purchase foodstuffs. Dai Huang recalls that one of his political instructors collected money from rightists and managed to purchase biscuits and bean powder for them from elsewhere. See Dai, *Jiusi yisheng*, 181.

64 Ni, *Chensi ji*, 77.

65 Yin, *Huishou canyang yi han shan*, 74.

66 Wu, *Yuxue feifei*, 140. Harry Wu provides a more detailed description: "For the first time I saw a person with one leg swollen and the other as thin as a stick. I began to recognize the symptoms of edema. First someone's foot would swell so that he could not wear his shoe. Slowly, the swelling would move up through the ankle, the calf, the knee, the thigh. When it reached the stomach and made breathing difficult, a person died quickly." "I had watched the swelling travel up Ma's body. His skin stretched so tight it became bright and smooth like glass. During his last days he seemed to experience increased energy and cheerfulness. His thin, pale face regained some rosy color. I later recognized those changes as typical of the last days of edema." See Wu, *Bitter Winds*, 102, 106.

67 Wu, *Yuxue feifei*, 123; Dai, *Jiusi yisheng*, 244–45.

68 Dai, *Jiusi yisheng*, 244–47. Dai recounts that some rightists tragically died while carrying food for chickens – millet, for instance – while they themselves were denied this food.

69 Peter Liu recalls: "Soon after the new prisoners settled down, No. 7 Branch Farm became epidemic of acute enteritis, also said to be dysentery ... practically all of the 200 plus inmates were affected and some died. Mo Guixin's case was not so bad at the beginning. He was one of the few who were hospitalized as a special favor. Before long he complained of belly ache which quickly worsened into acute agony. The doctor diagnosed gastric perforation and could do nothing." See Liu, *Mirror*, 226.

70 Han, interview. Comments regarding camp doctors vary significantly. Whereas Han Dajun complains about the poor performance and the irresponsibility of his camp doctor at Branch 7, Peter Liu is grateful for his camp doctor at Branch 8 (Dr. Li saved Liu's life when he tried to commit suicide). See Liu, *Mirror*, 246–47. In Qinghe Farm, according to Harry Wu, inmates who had reached an advanced stage of starvation would be sent to the Prison Patient Recovery Centre, where four medical workers were employed. However, "their primary job was not to treat our illness, as they had no medicine to dispense, but to report which prisoner drew close to death and then to record the cause of death in the person's file." See Wu, *Bitter Winds*, 116.

71 Yin, interview.

72 Wenche He'en, *Kunan de licheng* [Difficult journeys] (Washington: The Laogai Research Foundation, 2003), 90–91.

73 Paul A. Cohen, *History in Three Keys: The Boxers as Event, Experience, and Myth* (New York: Columbia University Press, 1997), 176.

74 Dai, *Jiusi yisheng*, 239–40. A similar experience tortured Ba Hong when he saw his friend Mo Guixin for the last time at the medical centre in Xingkaihu: "I called him again and again but he still could not recognize me even though his eyes were open ... I had to leave for work. I knew that was probably the last time I could see him." See Ba, interview.

75 Chen, "Wufa wangque de jiyi," 3.

76 Dai, *Jiusi yisheng*, 233–34.

77 Yin Jiliang, interview.

78 Wu, *Bitter Winds*, 125–26.

79 Hu Ping, *Chan ji: 1957 kunan de jitan* [Allegorical words: The bitter sacrificial altar, 1957] (Guangzhou: Guangdong luyou chubanshe, 2004), 553.

80 The Sun Mound (*taiyang gang*), notorious for being the main graveyard for the countless dead of Xingkaihu and bearing an ironic name, is a water-made ridge at the north end of Great Xingkai Lake. Ever since the establishment of the Xingkaihu labour complex, numerous inmates have been buried there. The side of the mound that faces the lake was thickly dotted with graves, upon some of which were placed small stones or wooden tablets with the words "the grave of XXX." When deaths increased rapidly, camp authorities did not even bother to make tablets anymore; instead, they simply used red bricks upon which the names of the dead were written in chalk. After a rain shower, the words were washed away, and the names of the dead became unknown. See Cong, *Zouxiang hundun*, 157–58.

81 Regarding the impact of the famine upon Xingkaihu, the most comprehensive description in *Xingkaihu nongchang shi* reads: "With the decrease of grain and bean output brought about by natural calamities, hunger severely threatened people's health. Edema, night blindness, and malnutrition happened frequently. Grain rations had to be reduced and non-staple foods decreased as well. People tried all means to fill their stomachs ... Ten people died of eating poisonous wild herbs. In particular, the death rate of the elderly and weak convicts increased." See *Xingkaihu nongchang shi*, 403–4. The obvious omission of important statistics makes this narrative less than useful for determining the death toll.

82 Chen, *Mengduan Weiminghu*, 111. In his unpublished essay "Xingkaihu jishi" [Stories of Xingkaihu], Chen estimates that, of the approximately 200 to 250 convicts on the same team, no fewer than 50 died during the three famine years.

83 Compared with other cases in China's labour camps, the death rate at Xingkaihu was not the worst. According to Wu Ningkun, the death rate at Qinghe camp in north China was higher than that in Xingkaihu: the grave pit for an inmate he buried bore the number 61,301. See Wu, *Single Tear*, 136. In Jiabiangou *laojiao* camp of Gansu, by early 1961 there were only around five hundred survivors among close to three thousand rightists. See Yang Xianhui, *Woman from Shanghai: Tales of Survival from a Chinese Labor Camp* (New York: Pantheon Books, 2009), viii. According to journalist Dai Huang, by the end of 1960, 1,001 of more than twelve hundred inmate labourers died of starvation in Jinxi *laogai* coal mine of Liaoning Province, and those left fed on frogs, grasshoppers, and butterflies. See Dai, *Jiusi yisheng*, 266. Domenach estimates that about 40 percent of all inmates in China died in the famine years of 1959 to 1962, totalling 4 million deaths in the camps. See Jean-Luc Domenach, *Chine: L'archipel oublié* (Paris: Fayard, 1992), 242.

84 Bawuling nongchangshi bianxie bangongshi, *Bawuling nongchangshi*, 31; Yunshan nongchang shizhi bangongshi, *Yunshan nongchangshi* [A history of the Yunshan Farm] (Jiamusi: n.p., 1995), 5.

85 Yang Congdao, "Bawuling Yunshan xumuchang liuren feizhengchang siwang mingdan" [The list of abnormal deaths at Yunshan Branch, Farm 850]. Unpublished note, author's collection. Ni Genshan lists the names of thirty-three rightists who died at Yunshan Branch from 1958 to 1960. See Ni, *Chensi ji*, 88–90.

86 Yang Congdao, military technician, interview, Beijing, July 11, 2004.

87   Bawusan nongchang dangwei [Farm 853 Party committee], "Zhonggong 853 nongchang weiyuanhui guanyu chuli yu chedi qingcha siren wenti de zhishi" [The instructions of Farm 853 Party committee on addressing and thoroughly investigating the issue of deaths], March 25, 1961, Farm 853 Archives; and Bawusan nongchang dangwei, "Guanyu 6 ming zhigong, 1 ming laogaifan, 3 ming youpai, 6 ming xiaohai feizhengchang siwang de baogao" [The report regarding the abnormal deaths of 6 workers and staff, 1 *laogai* convict, 3 rightists, and 6 children], April 7, 1961, Farm 853 Archives.

88   Mudanjiang nongkenju dangwei [The Party committee of the Mudanjiang Land Reclamation Bureau], "Guanyu dangqian kenqu gongzuo de jiancha baogao" [The examination report on the current work of the land reclamation region], April 6, 1961, Farm 853 Archives.

89   Dai, *Jiusi yisheng*, 250.

90   Wu, *Bitter Winds*, 122–23.

91   For instance, Ma Yuzhen, Chinese ambassador to the United Kingdom, in a letter to Kate Saunders, claimed: "Torture is forbidden in Chinese prison[s]. The authorities look after prisoners in accordance with laws and treat them with humanitarianism." See Kate Saunders, *Eighteen Layers of Hell: Stories from the Chinese Gulag* (London: Cassell Wellington House, 1996), 40.

92   Ministry of Public Security of the People's Republic of China, "The Regulations on Prohibition of Physical Abuse," March 11, 1956, in Zhonghua renmin gongheguo gongan falu quanshu bianweihui, ed., *Zhonghua renmin gongheguo gongan falu quanshu* [Comprehensive collection of laws on public security in the People's Republic of China] (Changchun: Jilin renmin chubanshe, 1995), 679.

93   Dai, *Jiusi yisheng*, 197–98. Wu Yongliang recalls that cadre Zhu, at the Yunshan Branch farm, designated certain heavy but meaningless work, such as transporting wooden planks on one's back for long distances, as a punishment for rightists whom he believed to be not sufficiently dedicated to labour. See Wu, *Yuxue feifei*, 56–57.

94   Bawusan nongchang zhengzhibu, "1960 nian yinian lai youpai fenzi sixiang qingkuang huibao."

95   Yang, interview.

96   Zhongyang tongzhanbu, zhongyang zuzhibu, zhongyang xuanchuanbu, "Guanyu quanguo gaizao youpai fenzi gongzuo huiyi de baogao" [The report of the national conference on the work of reforming rightists], September 27, 1961, in Song Yongyi, ed., *The Chinese Anti-Rightist Campaign Database (1957)* (Hong Kong: The University Services Centre for China Studies at the Chinese University of Hong Kong, 2010).

97   Tan Tianrong, university student, interview, Qingdao, June 29, 2004.

98   Williams and Wu, *Great Wall of Confinement*, 70.

99   See Zhonghua renmin gongheguo gongan falu quanshu bianweihui, *Zhonghua renmin gongheguo gongan falu quanshu*, 341–42.

100 Chen, *Mengduan Weiminghu*, 70, 94, 132–33, 154–55.

101 Ibid., 107; Wu, *Bitter Winds*, 180. Kate Saunders describes the experience of a juvenile offender who was put into a "cage." This cage, which measured 2.5 metres by 1 metre and held twenty people, was certainly more horrible than the solitary confinement cell used at Xingkaihu and Qinghe in terms of its smallness. See Saunders, *Eighteen Layers of Hell*, 20.

102 Chen, *Mengduan Weiminghu*, 102–3.

103 Liu, *Mirror*, 238.
104 Chen, *Mengduan Weiminghu*, 98.
105 Liu, *Mirror*, 239.
106 Chen, *Mengduan Weiminghu*, 36–37.
107 Yin, interview.
108 Liu Junying, interview.
109 Liu Binyan, *Liu Binyan zizhuan* [Autobiography of Liu Binyan] (Taibei: Shibao wenhua chuban qiye youxian gongsi, 1989), 16. Cong Weixi, who was also present at the meeting, recalls: "When the high pitch of condemnation echoed around the hall, a man a couple of rows in front of me suddenly stood up. Before I realized what would happen, he quickly dashed onto the balcony of the fourth floor and jumped down like a diver ... Blood! I saw blood when I looked out. I covered my eyes and had no guts to see anymore ... Then I heard someone shouting downstairs: 'This guy sacrificed himself for rightist Liu Binyan.'" See Cong, *Zouxiang hundun*, 5–6.
110 Zhang Jiqian, professor emeritus, interview, Beijing, August 20, 2002.
111 Wang Zhiliang, retired doctor, interview, Dandong, Liaoning, August 12, 2002.
112 Huang, *Mahuatang waiji*, 5.
113 Bawusan nongchang dangwei, "Dui youpai fenzi yinian ling liugeyue gaizao de gongzuo zongjie."
114 Dai, *Jiusi yisheng*, 192–93.
115 Ibid., 247; Ni, *Chensi ji*, 77–78.
116 Yin Jiliang, interview.
117 Liu, *Mirror*, 243–45.
118 Cong, *Zuoxiang hundun*, 164; Ba, interview.
119 For instance, Farm 853 leaders originally submitted 6 million *jin* of grain to the Mudanjiang Land Reclamation Bureau in 1960, but the bureau returned 1 million *jin* in consideration of the severe grain shortages on the farm. This case shows that higher-ups sometimes softened grain requisition quotas. However, a number of months later, Farm 853 authorities again submitted 630,000 *jin* to the bureau, trying to show their commitment and ignoring the fact that their own farm workers were subsisting on a starvation diet of eight *jin* of grain (around nine pounds) per month. See *Bawusan nongchangzhi*, 387. In this case, local activism surpassed the demands of higher authorities.

CHAPTER FIVE: INNER TURMOIL AND INTERNECINE STRIFE
AMONG POLITICAL EXILES

Epigraph: Robert Hughes, *Culture of Complaint: The Fraying of America* (New York: Oxford University Press, 1993), 120.
1 As a "top rightist," Zhang Bojun later explained his submitting to the accusation against him as his attempt to quickly end the campaign and save many others from being implicated. See Zhang Yihe, *Wangshi bingbu ruyan* [Do not let bygones be bygones] (Beijing: Renmin wenxue chubanshe, 2004), 291. Yin Yi signed his agreement with the verdict on his rightist status as he believed that, if he refused to sign, his punishment would become more severe and that his already reduced salary would be reduced even further. Yin's colleague Han accepted all the charges against him because he feared being laid off immediately if he did not. See Yin Yi, *Huishou canyang yi han shan* [The setting of the sun over the mountain] (Beijing: Shiyue wenyi chubanshe, 2003), 23.

2 Hu Ping, *Chan ji: 1957 kunan de jitan* [Allegorical words: The bitter sacrificial altar, 1957] (Guangzhou: Guangdong luyou chubanshe, 2004), 435–36.

3 Lu Gang, Party official, college head, interview, Dalian, August 6, 2002. Lu recalls: "At that time I was really convinced that I had fallen short of the expectations of the Party that had given me an ideological education for so many years; it was right for the Party to brand me a rightist because I truly wrote something harmful to it ... Stripping me of my Party membership was a way of purifying the Party. I was willing to accept it. So I did not hold a grudge against either the Party or the persons who designated me as a rightist."

4 See Huang Miaozi's self-criticism in Li Hui, *Ren zai xuanwo: Huang Miaozi yu Yu Feng* [People in the eddy: Huang Miaozi and Yu Feng] (Jinan: Shandong huabao chubanshe, 1998), 287–88. Wang Zheng says that he and his fellow exiles on Farm 853 continually tried hard to cultivate the "correct understanding" of the Anti-Rightist Campaign. See Liu Meng, ed., *Lishi zai shenpan* [Retrial by history] (Chengdu: Sichuan renmin chubanshe, 1996), 342.

5 Yin, *Huishou canyang yi han shan*, 27.

6 Ding Ling, *Fengxue renjian* [The blizzard world] (Xiamen: Xiamen daxue chubanshe, 1987), 4; Dai Huang, *Jiusi yisheng: Wo de youpai licheng* [A narrow escape from death: My experience as a rightist] (Beijing: Zhongyang bianyi chubanshe, 1998), 96, 122.

7 Yin, *Huishou canyang yi han shan*, 30.

8 Huang Miaozi, *Huang Miaozi sanwen* [The prose of Huang Miaozi] (Guangzhou: Huacheng chubanshe, 1998), 200.

9 Mao Zedong, *Mao Zedong xuanji* [Selected works of Mao Zedong] (Beijing: Renmin chubanshe, 1977), vol. 5: 491.

10 Dai, *Jiusi yisheng*, 95.

11 Li, *Ren zai xuanwo*, 298–99.

12 Dai, *Jiusi yisheng*, 121; Ni Genshan, *Chensi ji* [On contemplation] (Hong Kong: Tianma chuban youxian gongsi, 2005), 67; Yin, *Huishou canyang yi han shan*, 36. Work enthusiasm was also manifested in labour re-education camps elsewhere. On Cong Weixi's labour team, some rightists even refused to take a rest when they were injured or fell ill. See Cong Weixi, *Zouxiang hundun* [Going towards chaos] (Beijing: Zhongguo shehui kexue chubanshe, 1998), 139.

13 Li, *Ren zai xuanwo*, 310–11.

14 Dai, *Jiusi yisheng*, 119, 122.

15 Li, *Ren zai xuanwo*, 324.

16 Dai, *Jiusi yisheng*, 158; Yin, *Huishou canyang yi han shan*, 53. Sometimes, educators gave conflicting signals. In May 1959, an inspection panel of the Ministry of Culture issued a slogan on Farm 853 – "Take agriculture as your occupation and the army farm as your home" – that caused panic among rightists. See "Zhongyang wenhuabu kaochazu xiang 853 changdangwei huibao qingkuang" [The inspection panel of the Ministry of Culture: Records of briefing session with Farm 853 Party committee], May 1959, Farm 853 Archives.

17 See Liu Meng, ed. *Huishou rensheng* [Reflections on our life] (Beijing: Shidai wenyi chubanshe, 1992), 2. Liu Meng also recalls: "No sooner had we arrived than we hoped to keep contact with, and to return to, our original work units." See Liu Meng, *Chuntian de yu qiutian qing* [The whisking of rain in spring, the clearing of skies in autumn] (Beijing: Zhongguo gongren chubanshe, 2003), 96.

18 Bawusan nongchang dangwei [Farm 853 Party committee], "Dui youpai fenzi yinian ling liugeyue gaizao de gongzuo zongjie" [The work summary of the ideological re-moulding of rightists over the past one year and six months], October, 1959, Farm 853 Archives.

19 Guowuyuan fazhiju, ed., *Zhonghua renmin gongheguo xianxing falu xingzheng fagui huibian* [Comprehensive collection of current laws and administrative regulations of the People's Republic of China] (Beijing: Zhongguo falu chubanshe, 1995), 104.

20 Wu Ningkun, *A Single Tear: A Family's Persecution, Love and Endurance in Communist China* (New York: Atlantic Monthly Press, 1993), 89.

21 Peter Liu, *Mirror: A Loss of Innocence in Mao's China* (Philadelphia: Xlibris, 2001), 223–24. However, the situation of political convicts at *laogai* branches differed from that of those at *laojiao* branches. As sentenced culprits, their term was fixed, whether it be for a year or for life. Their adequate performance merely secured their punctual release and freed them from additional penalty. Only those who made "eminent contributions" could have their terms reduced. See Chen Fengxiao, *Mengduan Weiminghu: Ershier nian laogai shengya jishi* [Broken dreams at Weiming Lake: True stories of my twenty-two years of *laogai* experience] (Washington: The Laogai Research Foundation, 2005), 104; Xingkaihu changshiban, *Xingkaihu nongchang shi* [History of Xingkaihu Farm] (Mishan: n.p., 1988), 397. Neither the recollections of Chen Fengxiao nor those of Yin Jiliang (both were sentenced as counter-revolutionaries) provided any record relating to the dedication of *laogai* inmates to manual work.

22 Exception did exist, however. As is shown in Chapter 3, *laojiao* inmate Xuan Shouzhi stubbornly refused to work and was thus placed in a solitary confinement cell, where he was crippled.

23 See Anne F. Thurston, *Enemies of the People* (New York: Alfred A. Knopf, 1987), 278–79.

24 In June 1957, Mao Zedong stated: "We are skilfully pushing those in the left and the middle elements to attack the rightists, which turns out to be very effective." See Mao Zedong, *Mao Zedong xuanji*, vol. 5: 432. Chen Fengxiao recalls that one of his Hundred Flowers Society comrades was not sentenced due to his exposure of the crimes of Chen and others. See Chen, *Mengduan Weiminghu*, 59–61.

25 Jonathan D. Spence, *The Gate of Heavenly Peace: The Chinese and Their Revolution, 1895–1980* (New York: Viking, 1981), 336.

26 For instance, some of those who joined in framing Dai Huang were his "comrades in arms," who had once fought with him on the battlefields and worked closely with him. See Dai, *Jiusi yisheng*, 77.

27 Li Wenhui, *Shiji laoren de hua: Wu Zuguang juan* [Words of seniors of the century: Wu Zuguang volume] (Shenyang: Liaoning jiaoyu chubanshe, 2000), 130; Niu Han and Deng Jiuping, eds., *Jingji lu: Jiyi zhong de fan youpai yundong* [The thorny road: The Anti-Rightist Campaign in memory] (Beijing: Jingji ribao chubanshe, 1998), 90–91. Ye Yonglie, *Fan youpai shimo* [The whole story of the Anti-Rightist Movement] (Xining: Qinghai renmin chubanshe, 1995), 513. Lao She denounced Wu's spiritual world as a "manure pit, full of maggots, monsters and demons." His condemnation of Cong Weixi was also extreme. Because in his novel *An Unpleasant Story* Cong revealed the dark side of rural 1950s China, Lao She accused him of "trying to instigate peasant rebellion against the Communist Party." See Cong, *Zouxiang hundun*, 25.

28 Ye, *Fan youpai shimo*, 326.

29 Yin, *Huishou canyang yi han shan*, 40.

30 Zhang, *Wangshi bingbu ruyan,* 282–83. What was even more heart-breaking was the betrayal of family members. When Dai Huang was denounced by his colleagues and comrades, his wife joined them and put out a wall poster accusing Dai of plotting to organize an anti-Party clique within the CCP. See Dai, *Jiusi yisheng,* 61.

31 See Niu and Deng, *Jingji lu,* 334.

32 Ibid., 334.

33 Cong, *Zouxiang hundun,* 32.

34 Liu, *Mirror,* 173–74.

35 Ba Jin, *Suixiang lu* [Random thoughts] (Hong Kong: Sanlian shudian, 1979), 2.

36 Li, *Shiji laoren de hua,* 101. In some cases, repentance was expressed even during the highly charged labelling period. Yin Jie recalls: "Yu Engui, my roommate and good friend, was forced to expose me. One night when she returned from a political session, she cried and cried over my shoulder, and begged my pardon. She said that she was not allowed to go home for food or sleep unless she came up with something against me." Yin Jie, college student, interview, Dalian, September 19, 2002.

37 See Feng Yidai, *Hui yu ri lu* [A diary of regrets] (Zhengzhou: Henan renmin chubanshe, 2006), 44.

38 Dai, *Jiusi yisheng,* 151; Ni, *Chensi ji,* 79; Huang, *Mahuatang waiji,* 19, 58; Zhang Jie, *Wu Zuguang beihuan qu* [Wu Zuguang: Vicissitudes of life] (Chengdu: Sichuan wenyi chubanshe, 1986), 341. All these sources record moving stories about exile communities.

39 Dai, *Jiusi yisheng,* 228–31.

40 Ibid., 172.

41 "Zhongyang wenhuabu kaochazu xiang 853 changdangwei huibao qingkuang" [The inspection panel of the Ministry of Culture: Records of briefing session with Farm 853 Party committee], May 1959, Farm 853 Archives.

42 For instance, He Chunlin of Farm 853 not only confessed his own historical skeletons but also disclosed Liu Si's "reactionary remarks" to farm authorities. See Bawusan nongchang dangwei, "Guanyu zaidiao youpai fenzi maozi gongzuo zongjie baogao" [Final report regarding the delabelling of rightists], December 22, 1959, Farm 853 Archives.

43 Ding Cong, artist, interview, Beijing, August 20, 2002; Huang, *Mahuatang waiji,* 37; Liu, *Chuntian de yu qiutian qing,* 124–25; Yin, *Huishou canyang yi han shan,* 75.

44 Li, *Ren zai xuanwo,* 299; Ni, *Chensi ji,* 75; Yin, *Huishou canyang yi han shan,* 76.

45 Huang, *Mahuatang waiji,* 47; Dai, *Jiusi yisheng,* 189–90.

46 Dai, *Jiusi yisheng,* 139, 172–73. Dai Huang revealed the names of two informers on his team, whereas Wu Yongliang, Yin Yi, and Liu Meng merely related cases without referring to anyone by name. For his part, Huang Wu uses informers' nicknames. See Huang, *Mahuatang waiji,* 13, 47. It must be noted, however, that not all the rightist headmen were informers; some were friendly and popular with ordinary rightists. According to Wu Yongliang, his platoon leader Hao Qixin and squad leader Xiao Wang were conscientious and protective headmen as they sometimes ignored heavy work orders from above and at times helped other rightists with their tasks. See Wu Yongliang, *Yuxue feifei: Beidahuang shenghuo jishi* [Floating rain and snow: True stories of life in the Great Northern Wilderness] (Beijing: Zhongguo xiju chubanshe, 2002), 58, 119.

47 Liu, *Lishi zai shenpan,* 345.

48 Dai, *Jiusi yisheng,* 146–47, 166; Wu, *Yuxue feifei,* 100–1. In Tan Tianrong's narrative, the less harsh criticisms made by his fellow rightists were merely statements about

drawing a political line between themselves and Tan and avoiding his bad influence. See Tan Tianrong, university student, interview, Qingdao, June 29, 2004.

49 Bawusan nongchang zhengzhibu [The political department of Farm 853], "1960 nian yinian lai youpai fenzi sixiang qingkuang huibao" [Report on the thoughts of rightists in the year 1960], August 30, 1960, Farm 853 Archives.

50 Zheng Jiazhen, *Zhongguo dongbeijiao* [The northeast corner of China] (Harbin: Heilongjiang renmin chubanshe, 1998), 87.

51 Ibid.; Liu, *Lishi zai shenpan*, 345–46.

52 Dai, *Jiusi yisheng*, 146.

53 Ibid., 255. On Beidahuang army farms, some of those who denounced their friends or campmates felt guilty and came back to apologize afterwards. In a political struggle session, farm cadres designated Xin Ruoping to condemn Dai Huang's "anti-Great Leap" poison; later, Xin came to Dai to extend his apology. See Dai, *Jiusi yisheng*, 147.

54 Chen, *Mengduan Weiminghu*, 126–27. Scathing accusations were also widespread in other labour camps. On Zhenlai labour farm, where Hu Xianzhong was interned, when rightist prisoner Liu used a piece of newspaper that happened to have Mao's portrait on it to wrap shoes, his campmate reported him, attesting that by this act Liu had shown his "inveterate hatred" of Chairman Mao. See Hu Xianzhong, university student, interview, Changchun, September 23, 2002.

55 Wu, *Bitter Winds*, 159, 203–4. This story is also recorded by Meng Bo. See Xiao Ke et al., *Wo qinli guo de zhengzhi yundong* [Political campaigns that I have experienced] (Beijing: Zhongyang bianyi chubanshe, 1998), 116–23. According to Meng, some of those who actively joined in the beating had previously suffered at the hands of Guo and Wang.

56 Philip F. Williams and Yenna Wu, *The Great Wall of Confinement: The Chinese Prison Camp through Contemporary Fiction and Reportage* (Berkeley: University of California Press, 2004), 128.

57 Cong, *Zouxiang hundun*, 57. In contrast to the uneasy relationships among their peers, banished intellectuals were generally treated kindly by rural people. During his years of labour under supervision, Cong found that the peasants with whom he worked were more affable than he had expected, never taking advantage of their seemingly superior political status when dealing with the hapless intellectuals. See Cong, *Zouxiang hundun*, 40. Tan Tianrong recalls that, when he had completed his term of labour re-education and was sent back to his native place, a mountain village in Hunan Province, the locals neither discriminated against him nor disturbed his physics research. See Tan Tianrong, "Meiyou qingjie de gushi" [Stories without plot], unpublished essay, 3.

58 Yin, *Huishou canyang yi han shan*, 40. Wang Shuyao believes that, when one confessed those of one's "wrongdoings" that involved group activity, one inevitably exposed others; however, this was not necessarily true of "throwing stones at those in dire straits." See Wang Shuyao, *Yanyuan fengyu zhu rensheng* [My turbulent life and times at Beijing University] (Washington: The Laogai Research Foundation, 2007), 186–87.

59 Wu Yue, journal editor, interview, Beijing, October 5, 2002.

60 Cong, *Zouxiang hundun*, 54–57.

61 Chen, *Mengduan Weiminghu*, 104. Dai, *Jiusi yisheng*, 188, 238. Ni, *Chensi ji*, 77. Wang, *Yanyuan fengyu zhu rensheng*, 287–88, 314–15. Chen Fengxiao recalls that a considerable numbers of cases of physical abuse in Xingkaihu *laogai* branches were perpetrated by cell bosses.

62 Dai, *Jiusi yisheng*, 172.
63 Xingkaihu changshiban, *Xingkaihu nongchang shi* [A history of Xingkaihu Farm] (Mishan: n.p., 1988), 44; Liu, *Mirror*, 197.
64 Liu, *Mirror*, 275–76. Xiao et al., *Wo qinli guo de zhengzhi yundong*, 76–77. For information about the Socialist Education Movement, see Jonathan D. Spence, *The Search for Modern China* (New York: W.W. Norton, 2013), 531–34.
65 Chen, *Mengduan Weiminghu*, 126–27.
66 Williams and Wu, *Great Wall of Confinement*, 115.
67 Huang, *Mahuatang waiji*, 56; Wu, *Yuxue feifei*, 7.
68 Dai, *Jiusi yisheng*, 186.
69 When Wu Ningkun and his fellow inmates were requested to harvest rice overnight on the eve of Chinese Full Moon Day, in his sorrow at not being able to reunite with his family he took comfort in lines from a poem by Song Dynasty poet Shu Shi. See Wu, *Single Tear*, 90–91.
70 Liu, *Mirror*, 247.
71 Ni, *Chensi ji*, 76; Chen, *Mengduan Weiminghu*, 110–11.
72 Wu, *Yuxue feifei*, 135.
73 Huang, *Mahuatang waiji*, 11–15.
74 Dai, *Jiusi yisheng*, 174.
75 Chen, *Mengduan Weiminghu*, 106–7. See Chapter 3 for details on Chen's acts of violence against that troublemaker.
76 Wu, *Bitter Winds*, 158.
77 Ibid., 140. According to Wu, Lu had also refused to help a fellow prisoner (who suffered from haemorrhoids) with his work assignment. Lu reasoned: "We all eat the same food. I won't do someone else's job." See Wu, *Bitter Winds*, 143.

CHAPTER SIX: END WITHOUT END

Epigraph: Wu Ningkun, *A Single Tear: A Family's Persecution, Love and Endurance in Communist China* (New York: Atlantic Monthly Press, 1993), 341.
1   See Zhongyang wenxian yanjiushi, ed., *Jianguo yilai zhongyao wenxian xuanbian* [Selected collection of important documents since the establishment of the People's Republic of China] (Beijing: Zhongyang wenxian chubanshe, 1996), vol. 12: 528.
2   Even Mao had a degree of concern over the problems caused by the Great Leap Forward (e.g., regarding excessive centralization of farmlands, inflated production figures, food shortages, etc.). That was why he held the Conference of Lushan in July 1959, initially intending to discuss these problems. See Frank Dikötter, *Mao's Great Famine: The History of China's Most Devastating Catastrophe, 1958–1962* (New York: Walker, 2010), chap. 12, for Mao's initial agenda for the Conference of Lushan and his abrupt change.
3   See Xiao Donglian, *Qiusuo Zhongguo: Wenge qian shinian shi* [The search for China: The ten years of history prior to the Cultural Revolution] (Beijing: Hongqi chubanshe, 1999), vol. 1: 237; Ye Yonglie, *Fan youpai shimo* [The whole story of the Anti-Rightist Movement] (Xining: Qinghai renmin chubanshe, 1995), 568. Both sources point to the CCP's attempt to relax internal tension and to create a pleasant atmosphere for National Day. Ye also draws a link between Mao's initiative and a traditional Chinese practice of declaring amnesty at time of major celebrations.

4 See Zhongyang wenxian yanjiushi, ed., *Jianguo yilai zhongyao wenxian xuanbian*, vol. 5: 12, 529. Implementing Mao's instruction, the PRC central government released thirty-three high-ranking prisoners of war (Aisin Gioro Puyi included) by December 1959, and provincial authorities remitted the sentences of 12,082 counter-revolutionary offenders (*fangeming fan*) and criminal offenders (*xingshi fan*). See Ma Qibin et al., eds., *Zhongguo gongchandang zhizheng sishi nian* [The Chinese Communist Party: Forty years in power] (Beijing: Zhonggong dangshi ziliao chubanshe, 1989), 174.

5 See Zhongyang wenxian yanjiushi, *Jianguo yilai zhongyao wenxian xuanbian*, vol 12: 572–73.

6 Xiao, *Qiusuo zhongguo*, vol 1: 237. The names of these individuals were published in the *People's Daily*, December 5, 1959. The majority of them, including Fei Xiaotong, Pan Guangdan, Xu Zhucheng, and Pu Xixiu, were influential intellectuals in the fields of science, arts, and the mass media.

7 Hu Ping, *Chan ji: 1957 kunan de jitan* [Allegorical words: The bitter sacrificial altar, 1957] (Guangzhou: Guangdong luyou chubanshe, 2004), 549. A document issued by the CCP central authorities on September 17, 1960, indicated that around forty thousand people had had their hats removed, or 9 percent of all rightists. See "Zhonggong zhongyang tongyi zhongyang zuzhibu he zhongyang tongzhanbu guanyu youpai fenzi gongzuo jidian yijian de baogao" [The authorization of the CCP Central Committee regarding several suggestions by the central organization department and the central united front department regarding the work of rightists], September 17, 1960, in Song Yongyi, ed., *The Chinese Anti-Rightist Campaign Database (1957–)* (Hong Kong: The University Services Centre for China Studies at the Chinese University of Hong Kong, 2010).

8 Bawusan nongchang zuzhike [Organization section of Farm 853], "Dui benchang youpai fenzi zai maozi de gongzuo jihua" [The working plan to delabel rightists on our farm] October 20, 1959, Farm 853 Archives.

9 Bawusan nongchang dangwei [Farm 853 Party committee], "Guanyu zaidiao youpai fenzi maozi gongzuo de zongjie baogao" [Final report regarding the delabelling of rightists] December 22, 1959, Farm 853 Archives.

10 Bawuling nongchangshi bianxie bangongshi, *Bawuling nongchangshi* [History of Farm 850] (Hulin, Heilongjiang: n.p., 1986), 31; Yunshan nongchang shizhi bangongshi, *Yunshan nongchangshi* [History of Yunshan Farm] (Jiamusi: n.p.,1995), 5; Dai Huang, *Jiusi yisheng: Wo de youpai licheng* [A narrow escape from death: My experience as a rightist] (Beijing: Zhongyang bianyi chubanshe, 1998), 168; Wang Zheng, "Meng hui huangyuan," in *Lishi zai shenpan* [Retrial by history], ed. Liu Meng (Chengdu: Sichuan renmin chubanshe, 1996), 343–44; Wu Yongliang, *Yuxue feifei: Beidahuang shenghuo jishi* [Floating rain and snow: True stories of life in the Great Northern Wilderness] (Beijing: Zhongguo xiju chubanshe, 2002), 108–9. According to Wu, during the stay of the central inspection team, many rightists tried hard to perform well in their daily work in order to impress the team leaders.

11 Bawusan nongchang dangwei [Farm 853 Party committee], "Guanyu zaidiao youpai fenzi maozi gongzuo de zongjie baogao"; Yin Yi, *Huishou canyang yi han shan* [The setting of the sun over the mountain] (Beijing: Shiyue wenyi chubanshe, 2003), 71–72; Yu Shanpu and Yang Congdao, "Beidahuang liuren mingdan" [List of names of Beidahuang exiles]. Unpublished note, author's collection. According to Yu and Yang, among more than two hundred rightists sent from central civilian organs to Yunshan, only three had their hats removed in 1959.

12 Bawusan nongchang dangwei, "Guanyu zaidiao youpai fenzi maozi gongzuo de zongjie baogao."

13 Ibid.

14 See Zhang Zhicai, *Yongyuan zai chulian* [In love forever] (Beijing: Jiefangjun wenyi chubanshe, 1992), 332–33; Yao Lan and Deng Qun, *Bai Congxi shenbian de zhonggong mimi dangyuan* [The underground Chinese Communist Party member working with Bai Chongxi] (Beijing: Zhonggong dangshi chubanshe, 1998), 258–59.

15 Dai, *Jiusi Yisheng,* 267–68. Yin, *Huishou canyang yi han shan,* 95–96.

16 "Zhonggong zhongyang tongyi zhongyang zuzhibu he zhongyang tongzhanbu guanyu youpai fenzi gongzuo jidian yijian de baogao" [The authorization from the Chinese Communist Party Central Committee for several suggestions by the Central Organization Department and the Central United Front Department regarding the work of rightists], September 17, 1960, in Song, *Chinese Anti-Rightist Campaign Database.*

17 Yu and Yang, "Beidahuang liuren mingdan."

18 Dai, *Jiusi yisheng,* 244–47.

19 Yu and Yang, "Beidahuang liuren mingdan"; Dai, *Jiusi yisheng,* 253–56, 265–66. A story from Dai tells how a rightist in Yunshan was too sick to attend the hat removal meeting. When his campmates told him that it had just been announced that his hat had been removed, he burst into laughter, cried in delight, and then died. Dai also tells a story about how a rightist died on the train for Beijing after being released.

20 Yang Congdao, military technician, interview, Beijing, July 11, 2004; Dai, *Jiusi yisheng,* 252.

21 Yu and Yang's "Beidahuang liuren mingdan" documents valuable information about the job reassignments of many rightists. Some were at first recalled to their original work units in Beijing but were later relocated to other provinces.

22 For the Sino-Soviet split, see Jonathan D. Spence, *The Search for Modern China* (New York: W.W. Norton, 2013), 523–28.

23 Mishan xianzhi bianweihui, *Mishan xianzhi* [Gazetteer of Mishan County] (Beijing: Zhongguo biaozun chubanshe, 1993), 146; Liu Junying, retired labour camp cadre, interview, Beijing, July 16, 2004.

24 Xingkaihu changshiban, *Xingkaihu nongchang shi* [A history of Xingkaihu Farm] (Mishan: n.p., 1988), 45.

25 Wu Ningkun, *A Single Tear: A Family's Persecution, Love and Endurance in Communist China* (New York: Atlantic Monthly Press, 1993), 109; Peter Liu, *Mirror: A Loss of Innocence in Mao's China* (Philadelphia: Xlibris, 2001), 248. For the transfer of *laogai* convicts, see *Xingkaihu nongchang shi,* 404. Some female inmates were transferred from Xingkaihu to the women's labour team of Beiyuan Farm in northern Beijing. See Niu Weina, *Cuowei: Wo he wojia jidai zhishifenzi de gushi* [Disjunction: The stories of intellectuals in my clan] (n.p.: Printed in Los Angeles, 2003), 148.

26 Liu, *Mirror,* 248; Xingkaihu changshiban, *Xingkaihu nongchang shi,* 404.

27 Liu, *Mirror,* 249; Liu Junying, interview.

28 See Zhonggong zhongyang, "Guanyu zaidiao youpai maozi de renyuan de gongzuo fenpei he shenghuo daiyu de guiding" [Regulations on the work assignment and remuneration of individuals who have had their rightist hats removed], November 2, 1959, in Song, *Chinese Anti-Rightist Campaign Database*; Wang Keqin, military officer, interview, Beijing, July 18, 2004.

29 "Mudanjiang nongkenju zhengzhibu wenjian" [Document of the political department of the Mudanjiang Land Reclamation Bureau], no. 37, 1962, Farm 853 Archives.

30 Wang Keqin, interview.

31 See Hua Min, *Zhongguo da nizhuan: Fanyou yundong shi* [China's great reversal: A history of the Anti-Rightist Campaign] (New York: Ming-ching chubanshe, 1996), 395.

32 Chen Erzhen, engineer, interview, July 18, 2004. Like Chen, some remaining rightists managed to work in their fields of expertise to a limited degree. During his service as a language arts teacher in an elementary school, ex-military playwright Shen Mojun worked with local people to collect war hero stories. The result of his effort was a well-known play, *Red Lantern* (*Hongdeng ji*), which, as a "revolutionary model play," gained huge popularity during the Cultural Revolution. See *Bawuling nongchang shi*, 36; Dai, *Jiusi yisheng*, 249–50.

33 When interviewed, neither Chen Fengxiao nor Yin Jiliang was able to recall the transfer of these people. However, Hui Peilin noticed that, on the livestock farm where she worked, three Christian believers among around one hundred female *laojiao* inmates were sent to the interior. See Hui Peilin, journalist, interview, Beijing, July 19, 2004.

34 Chen, *Mengduan Weiminghu*, 112.

35 Nancy B. Tucker, *Taiwan, Hong Kong, and the United States, 1945–1992: Uncertain Friendships* (New York: Twayne, 1994), 43.

36 Yin Jiliang, journalist, interview, Beijing, October 3, 2002; Chen, *Mengduan Weiminghu*, 112–13.

37 Xingkaihu changshiban, *Xingkaihu nongchang shi*, 409.

38 Ibid., 46–47. Heilongjiang, with its sprawling labour reform facilities and its remote geographical location, is still functioning as an important region for China's *laogai* regime in the post-Mao period. Harry Wu estimates that there are fifty-two labour camps in post-Mao Heilongjiang. See Harry Wu, *Laogai: The Chinese Gulag* (Boulder, CO: Westview Press, 1992), 150. According to the transferred inmates, the most notorious labour farms include Changshuihe Farm (in Bei'an), Hada Farm (in Mudanjiang), Yanjiagang Farm (in Harbin), Wulan Farm (in Zhalaite), Suiling Farm (in Suiling), and Yinhe Farm (in Gannan).

39 Chen, *Mengduan Weiminghu*, 135, 165; Yin Jiliang, interview; Hui Peilin, interview.

40 For this movement during the Cultural Revolution, see Thomas P. Bernstein, *Up to the Mountains and Down to the Villages: The Transfer of Youth from Urban to Rural China* (New Haven, CT: Yale University Press, 1977).

41 For detailed information about Qinghe Farm, see Wu, *Laogai*, app. 3, 218–23. Peter Liu, too, provides useful description in Liu, *Mirror*, 251.

42 Shortly after the Xingkaihu inmates, Harry Wu was transferred to Qinghe from a labour mine in Yanqing, and Cong Weixi was transferred from Tucheng Detention Centre, both located north of Beijing. See Harry Wu, *Bitter Winds: A Memoir of My Years in China's Gulag* (New York: John Wiley and Sons, 1994), 98–99; Cong Weixi, *Zouxiang hundun* [Going towards chaos] (Beijing: Zhongguo shehui kexue chubanshe, 1998), 153.

43 Wu, *Single Tear*, 127. Han Dajun, who was put on the same branch farm as Peter Liu, recalls: "We were taken by truck to Branch 3, which was encircled by a tall wall reinforced by electric barbed wire and four watch towers, one at each corner. A row of one-storey cells had been built close to the wall and accommodated the *laogai* teams, *laojiao* teams, and juvenile teams. In Qinghe, we entered the worst famine period, which was

marked by our receiving sixteen to eighteen *jin* of sweet potato flour as monthly ration, without food oil or vegetable." Han Dajun, scientist, interview, Beijing, July 5, 2004.

44 As Wu Ningkun recalls, the *laojiao* inmates originally "hoped that Qinghe state farm's close proximity to the national capital would bring more humane treatment and better food," as well as "better hopes of release." See Wu, *Single Tear*, 109, 127. Some, such as Han Dajun, hoped that it would be easier for their families to visit them. See Han Dajun, interview.

45 Liu, *Mirror*, 252–53.

46 Wu, *Single Tear*, 136.

47 Peter Liu describes how, to save energy, the surviving inmates killed time in the winter of 1962 in a cold, silent cell after a meagre dinner: "Each climbed up to his part of the long wooden bed the length of the room, leaned against the wall, tucked each hand in the opposite sleeve, his feet wrapped in the quilt, and closed his eyes. This was the posture the two dozen of us remained in from 5 to 9 p.m. ... I was one of these seated statues ... I was aware that time was passing while my life was being drained away. I knew that we all were aware of this." See Liu, *Mirror*, 257.

48 Liu, *Mirror*, 254–55; Cong, *Zouxiang hundun*, 141.

49 Liu, *Mirror*, 255.

50 "Gong'anbu guanyu qingli laodong jiaoyang de youpai fenzi de tongzhi" [Circular on cleaning up labour re-education rightists], put out by the Ministry of Public Security, November 9, 1961; Zhonggong zhongyang tongzhanbu, "Guanyu quanguo tongzhan gongzuo huiyi de baogao" [Report of the National Conference for United Front Work], May 28, 1962. Both located in Song, *Chinese Anti-Rightist Campaign Database*.

51 For instance, Peng Zhen, mayor of Beijing and a CCP Politbureau member, is said to have raised an idea: to build the capital into a pure, crystal-like city, drained of all dregs of society. See Harry Wu, *Laodong jiaoyang yu liuchang jiuye* [Re-education through labour and forced job placement] (Washington: The Laogai Research Foundation, 2004), 81. Ex-rightist Xu Ying believes that the relocation of her family to Anda County, Heilongjiang Province, was based on this scheme. See Xu Ying, journalist, interview, Beijing, July 19, 2004.

52 Han Dajun, interview; Liu, *Mirror*, 254; Xiao Ke, et al., *Wo qinli guo de zhengzhi yundong* [Political campaigns that I have experienced] (Beijing: Zhongyang bianyi chubanshe, 1998), 82.

53 Due to the prolonged hunger in Qinghe, rightists were so frail that, when they were relocated to Tuanhe, many could hardly get off the train because of their swollen legs. Some, such as Tan Tianrong, were carried out of the train on stretchers. See Xiao et al., *Wo qinli guo de zhengzhi yundong*, 143.

54 Ibid., 70–71, 144–46.

55 Dai, *Jiusi yisheng*, 325–26.

56 Liu, *Mirror*, 313–14. Tan Tianrong, university student, interview, Qingdao, June 29, 2004. In December 1969, Harry Wu and another twelve hundred forced job placement inmates were transferred from Qinghe to Wangzhuang Coal Mine in Shanxi Province. See Wu, *Bitter Winds*, 233. Tan considers the years from 1969 to 1979 as the most fruitful period he had ever experienced before rehabilitation since there was no government official or police cadre coming to bother him, and his time for research was guaranteed as long as he did some light agricultural work. See Tan Tianrong, interview.

57 Zhonggong zhongyang, "Guanyu zaidiao youpai maozi de renyuan de gongzuo fenpei he shenghuo daiyu de guiding"; Zhongyang tongzhanbu, zhongyang zuzhibu, zhong-yang xuanchuanbu, "Guanyu quanguo gaizao youpai fenzi gongzuo huiyi de baogao" [Report of the National Conference on the work of reforming rightists], September 27, 1961. Both in Song, *Chinese Anti-Rightist Campaign Database*.

58 All of these three documents are located in Song, *Chinese Anti-Rightist Campaign Database*.

59 Zhonggong zhongyang tongzhanbu, "Guanyu quanguo tongzhan gongzuo huiyi de baogao," in Song, *Chinese Anti-Rightist Campaign Database*.

60 Regarding the term "five black elements," or *heiwulei*, see Lowell Dittmer and Chen Ruoxi, *Ethics and Rhetoric of the Chinese Cultural Revolution* (Berkeley: Center for Chinese Studies, University of California, 1981), 59.

61 Xin Suwei, *Ding Cong zhuan* [A biography of Ding Cong] (Beijing: Zhongguo gongren chubanshe, 1993), 194–98, 203–4, 209–10; Ding Cong, artist, interview, Beijing, August 20, 2002.

62 Li Hui, *Ren zai xuanwo: Huang Miaozi yu Yu Feng* [People in the eddy: Huang Miaozi and Yu Feng] (Jinan: Shandong huabao chubanshe, 1998), 333–34.

63 Dai Huang wrote that it was his frequent disputes with and defiance of the farm cadres at the Yunshan Branch of Farm 850 that invited his poor political appraisal. See Dai, *Jiusi yisheng*, 203–4, 252, 263.

64 Ibid., 273.

65 Wu, *Yuxue feifei*, 10–11. Liu Meng and Yin Yi were both relocated to Inner Mongolia, with Liu becoming a telecommunications worker and Yin a bookstore worker. Liu recalls that his colleagues included more than ten rightists transferred from Beidahuang army farms. See Liu Meng, *Chuntian de yu qiutian qing* [The whisking of rain in spring, the clearing of skies in autumn] (Beijing: Zhongguo gongren chubanshe, 2003), 175, 189–90; Yin, *Huishou canyang yi han shan*, 110–11.

66 Bawusan nongchang zhengzhibu [Political department of Farm 853], "1960 nian yinian lai youpai fenzi sixiang qingkuang huibao" [Report on the thoughts of rightists in the year 1960], August 30, 1960, Farm 853 Archives.

67 Ding Ling's case was mainly handled by the Writers Association of China, which was headed by her foe Zhou Yang. Because of this, even her patron Wang Zhen was unable to decide her political lot. Chen Ming, editor, interview, August 19, 2002; Ding Ling, *Fengxue renjian* [The blizzard world] (Xiamen: Xiamen daxue chubanshe, 1987), 123.

68 Zheng Xiaofeng, *Ding Ling zai Beidahuang* [Ding Ling in the Great Northern Wilderness] (Wuhan: Hubei renmin chubanshe, 1989), 29–30; Ding Ling, "Jianjue chedi gaizao, zhengqu zaori huidao geming de wenyi dajiating lai" [Conduct determined and thorough reform, in order to return to the big family for revolutionary art and literature], August 10, 1960, in Song, *Chinese Anti-Rightist Campaign Database*. See Chen Ming, interview.

69 Ding Ling frequently said that living among the masses gave her life meaning and made her feel better during the years of persecution. When she revisited Tangyuan Farm after rehabilitation, she avoided talking about hardship and suffering but kept mentioning how the masses had given her warm spiritual support during the most difficult years. See Zheng, *Ding Ling zai Beidahuang*, 61, 67.

70 Zheng, *Ding Ling zai Beidahuang*, 84, 88–89.

71 See Zhang Yongquan, "Ding Ling wannian xintai tanxi," in *Zuoyou shuo Ding Ling* [Commenting on Ding Ling from the left and the right], ed. Wang Hong (Beijing: Zhongguo gongren chubanshe, 2002), 231–32.

72 In his early 1962 speeches, Mao promoted notions such as "telling the truth," "developing people's democracy," and "letting people air their different opinions" (see, for instance, his speech on January 30, 1962, in *Mao Zedong wenji*, vol. 8: 289–311), which contributed to a short political relaxation. This relaxation ended, however, in September when Mao changed his mind and came up with the slogan: "The concept of class struggle must be stressed every year, every month and every day." He also condemned "the wind to reverse verdicts (*fan'an feng*)." See Ma, *Zhongguo gongchandang zhizheng sishinian*, 222.

73 Dai, *Jiusi yisheng*, 276–83.

74 Ibid., 304–44.

75 Cao Shuji, "An Overt Conspiracy: Creating Rightists in Rural Henan, 1957–1958," in *Maoism at the Grassroots: Everyday Life in China's Era of High Socialism*, ed. Jeremy Brown and Matthew D. Johnson, 77–101 (Cambridge: Harvard University Press, 2015).

76 See Ye, *Fan youpai shimo*, 577. As Ye points out, during the Cultural Revolution ex-rightists were often called "hatless rightists" or "delabelled rightists" (*zhaimao youpai*); and those who were politically unreliable but not labelled were called "escaped rightists" (*louwang youpai*).

77 Wu, *Yuxue feifei*, 12; Liu, *Chuntian de yu qiutian qing*, 237; Ding, *Fengxue renjian*, 124–30; Ni, *Chensi ji*, 108–10.

78 . Yu Zhen, *Nie Gannu xingshi dang'an* [Penal files on Nie Gannu] (Hong Kong: Mingbao chubanshe, 2009), 52–64; Zhou, *Nie Gannu zhuan*, 234–39; Niu Han and Deng Jiuping, eds., *Yuan shang cao: Jiyi zhong de fan youpai yundong* [Grass on the plains: The Anti-Rightist Campaign in memory] (Beijing: Jingji ribao chubanshe, 1998), 307.

79 Ding, *Fengxue renjian*, 124–26.

80 During the first two years of the Cultural Revolution, the five black elements were often in extreme danger of being murdered. In Daxing County, Beijing, for instance, 325 people who belonged to the five black elements, along with their families, were executed. This included the complete extermination of twenty-two households within less than a week. See Xiao, *Wo qinli guo de zhengzhi yundong*, 100–1.

81 See Zhou, *Nie Gannu zhuan*, 234. In Linfen Prison and Jishan Transit Prison, Shanxi Province, where the elderly received special care, Nie was able to take time to go over the major works of Karl Marx and Friedrich Engels. See Niu and Deng, *Yuan shang cao*, 296–300.

82 Ding, *Fengxue renjian*, 155; Chen Ming, editor, interview, July 5, 2004.

83 For the death of Huang Shaoxiong, see Zhang, *Wangshi bingbu ruyan*, 73–75. After being badly insulted and tortured by the Red Guards, the ex-rightist and French literature specialist Fu Lei and his wife hanged themselves in their home in September 1966. See Ye, *Fanyou pai shimo*, 493.

84 Hu, *Chan ji*, 585–87; Niu and Deng, *Jingli lu*, 466–67. According to the documentary *Xunzhao Lin Zhao de Linghun* [Searching for the spirit of Lin Zhao] made by Hu Jie, a Chinese independent filmmaker, Lin Zhao wrote more than 200,000 words of protest in prison, some of which a warden managed to leak to the outside.

85 Hu, *Chan ji*, 591; Chen Fengxiao, "Wufa wangque de jiyi" [Unforgettable memories], unpublished essay, 5. Tan Chanxue, *Qiusuo: Lanzhou daxue youpai fangeming jituan an*

jishi [Investigation: The true stories of the case of a rightist counter-revolutionary clique at Lanzhou University] (Hong Kong: Tianma chuban youxian gongsi, 2010), 132.

86 "The Instruction of the CCP Central Committee on Total Removal of Rightists' Hats," April 5, 1978, and "The Notification of the CCP Central Committee on Forwarding the Implementation Plan to Totally Delabel Rightists Made by the Central Organization Department, Propaganda Department, United Front Department, Ministry of Public Security, and Ministry of Civil Affairs," September 17, 1978, both in Song, *Chinese Anti-Rightist Campaign Database*. For Hu Yaobang's role in rectification of rightist cases, see Dai Huang, *Hu Yaobang yu pingfan yuan jia cuo an* [Hu Yaobang and redressing unjust, false, and mishandled cases] (Beijing: Xinhua chubanshe, 1998), 142–43; Yang Zhongmei, *Hu Yaobang: A Chinese Biography* (Armonk: M.E. Sharpe, 1988), 134–36.

87 Bo Yibo, *Ruogan zhongda juece yu shijian de huigu* [Recollections of several important policies and events] (Beijing: Zhonggong zhongyang dangxiao chubanshe, 1993), 619. Before the Cultural Revolution, around 300,000 rightists had already had their labels removed. See Xiao, *Qiusuo Zhongguo*, 237.

88 Both 1978 documents refer to the campaign as a "great socialist revolution on political and ideological fronts." Deng Xiaoping, too, declared in March 1980 that "the Anti-Rightist Campaign of 1957 per se was not wrong ... the problem was its excess." See Deng Xiaoping, *Deng Xiaoping wenxuan 1975–1982* [Selected works of Deng Xiaoping, 1975–1982] (Beijing: Renmin chubanshe, 1983), 258.

89 Wu Ningkun recalls that, when he was at first rehabilitated, one of his work unit officials told him that his offences were grave but that, in consideration of his progress in thought reform over the years, the Party had decided to be lenient with him and have his verdict corrected. See Wu, *Single Tear*, 340. Yin Yi and Liu Meng both mention that the "re-evaluation" issued to them contained no word of apology. See Yin, *Huishou canyang yi han shan*, 218; Liu, *Chuntian de yu qiutian qing*, 352.

90 The accounts of the ends of these ex-rightists are based on their recollections or on relevant chapters of their memoirs. For Ding Ling's political activism in the late 1970s and early 1980s, see Zheng, *Ding Ling zai Beidahuang*, 67–69.

91 Wu, *Single Tear*, 341.

92 Ibid., 341–42.

Conclusion

1 According to aggregate statistics released by the Chinese government, for instance, around 12 million urban youths were sent down to rural areas from 1968 to 1975. See Thomas P. Bernstein, *Up to the Mountains and Down to the Villages: The Transfer of Youth from Urban to Rural China* (New Haven CT: Yale University Press, 1977), 2–3.

2 Joel Andreas, *Rise of the Red Engineers: The Cultural Revolution and the Origins of China's New Class* (Stanford: Stanford University Press, 2009), 40.

3 Bo Yibo, *Ruogan zhongda juece yu shijian de huigu*, 1060–61. The population relocated to rural areas and small towns in 1961–62 included not only the rural people who had entered and worked in cities in 1958 and 1959 but also those with "bad" family backgrounds (such as former landlords) and poor political status (such as ex-rightists).

4 Tani Barlow and Gary Bjorge, eds., *I Myself Am a Woman: Selected Writings of Ding Ling* (Boston: Beacon Press, 1989), 43.

5   Merle Goldman, "The Party and the Intellectuals," in *The Cambridge History of China*, ed. Denis Twitchett and John K. Fairbank (Cambridge: Cambridge University Press, 1987), vol. 14: 229, 234–35; Jonathan D. Spence, *The Gate of Heavenly Peace: The Chinese and Their Revolution, 1895–1980* (New York: Viking, 1981), 325–26. As Goldman points out: "Ding Ling's actions epitomized the schizoid nature of most intellectuals in the early days of the regime. She was motivated by a mixture of political opportunism and genuine enthusiasm for the Party in her vigorous implementation of its dictates." See Goldman, "The Party and the Intellectuals," vol. 14: 235.

6   In 1955, Tan, for instance, once participated in supervising Hu Feng's sympathizer Liu Qidi, with whom he was later sent to the same labour camp. See Chen Fengxiao, "Wufa wangque de jiyi" [Unforgettable memories], unpublished essay, 2.

7   Numerous works describe the purging of CCP high leaders and cultural elites during the Cultural Revolution. See, for instance, Roderick MacFarquhar and Michael Schoenhals, *Mao's Last Revolution* (Cambridge: The Belknap Press of Harvard University Press, 2006), 273–84.

8   Liu Binyan's speech, reprinted in *Jiushi Niandai* [The decade of the nineties], Hong Kong, June 1987, 38–40.

Appendix B

1   Xin Suwei, *Ding Cong zhuan* [A biography of Ding Cong] (Beijing: Zhongguo gongren chubanshe, 1993).

2   Ding Cong, for instance, pointed out a number of mistakes in his biography *Ding Cong zhuan*, and he made careful corrections during my personal interview with him in August 2002.

3   For instance, Ding Ling's narrative of her experience in Beidahuang was mild as she intentionally avoided mentioning her physical suffering in her memoir *Fengxue renjian* [The blizzard world] (Xiamen: Xiamen daxue chubanshe,1987).

4   Dai Huang's *Jiusi yisheng: Wo de youpai licheng* [A narrow escape from death: My experience as a rightist] (Beijing: Zhongyang bianyi chubanshe, 1998) was published in 1998 but was not allowed to be reprinted. See Dai Huang, senior journalist, interview, Beijing, July 17, 2004. He Fengming's *Jingli: Wode 1957 nian* [Experience: My 1957] (Lanzhou: Dunhuang wenyi chubanshe, 2006) was condemned by the Gansu Provincial Administration of Press and Publication after it was published in 2006, and the managing editor was forced to engage in self-criticism eight times. See He Fengming, journalist, interview, Beijing, June 7, 2008.

5   Starting in 2001, the Washington-based Laogai Research Foundation has been publishing its Black Series, consisting mostly of *laogai* memoirs. The relevant pieces for this project include *Mengduan Weiminghu* [Broken dreams at Weiming Lake] by Chen Fengxiao, *Yanyuan fengyu zhu rensheng* [My turbulent life and times at Beijing University] by Wang Shuyao, and *Yongyuan de Beidahuang* [The everlasting Beidahuang] by Huang Zhan.

6   Ding Ling, in her *Fengxue renjian*, did not name her rival and persecutor Zhou Yang. However, in an August 19, 2002, interview, her husband Chen Ming clearly indicated that Zhou was the person crucial to Ding's downfall in 1957. Liu Meng, during a personal interview on October 4, 2002, elaborated on the prevalence of stealing among

Beidahuang rightists – something he did not in his memoir *Chuntian de yu qiutian qing*
[The whisking of rain in spring, the clearing of skies in autumn].

7   For instance, Gao Yuansong, an ex-camp official whom I wished to interview, refused
due to the fact that he had been interviewed in early 1990s by Harry Wu. Wu made
considerable use of the information Gao provided in composing *Laogai: The Chinese
Gulag*, and Gao had subsequently received a stern rebuke.

8   Chen Fengxiao told me, when interviewed, that after rehabilitation he tried many times
to request his trial records from the Intermediate Court of Beijing as well as his files
from Xingkaihu, but he was firmly declined.

9   Williams and Wu recognize that, of the four categories of prison writings that figure
in their analysis of the PRC prison camp, the non-fiction (memoirs, diaries, autobiographies, and testimonials) composed by former prison inmates is "perhaps the most
authentic and authoritative in its firsthand description of prison camp regimens and
subculture." See Philip Williams and Yenna Wu, *The Great Walls of Confinement: The
Chinese Prison Camp through Contemporary Fiction and Reportage* (Berkeley: University
of California Press, 2004), 157.

10 Peter Zarrow, "Meanings of China's Cultural Revolution: Memoirs of Exile." *Positions* 7,
1 (1999): 165–91.

11 Paul A. Cohen, *History in Three Keys: The Boxers as Event, Experience, and Myth*
(New York: Columbia University Press, 1997), 64.

12 Wu Yongliang admits that, since the notes that he made about his Beidahuang experience right after the banishment were all burned during the Cultural Revolution, his
memoir is entirely based on his recent recollections. See Wu Yongliang, *Yuxue feifei:
Beidahuang shenghuo jishi* [Floating rain and snow: True stories of life in the Great
Northern Wilderness] (Beijing: Zhongguo xiju chubanshe, 2002), 11–12.

13 Dai Huang and Wu Yongliang were both interned in the same labour farm in
Beidahuang, but their narratives concerning the personalities of their campmates
Jiao Yongfu and Zhang Ji differed considerably.

14 For instance, the memoir of Wu Ningkun (*A Single Tear*).

15 For instance, the memoirs of Ni Genshan (*Chensi ji* [On contemplation]) and Liu Meng
(*Chuntian de yu qiutian qing*).

Bibliography

ARCHIVAL SOURCES

Farm 853 Archives

"Bawusan nongchang guanyu dui youpai fenzi de zhengzhi sixiang he laodong qingkuang de zongjie" 八五三农场关于对右派分子的政治思想和劳动情况的总结
[Final report of Farm 853 regarding political thoughts and labour performance
of rightists]. November 1, 1958, Farm 853 Archives.

"Menglian kugan, zhengqu quanmian dayuejin: 853 nongchang daibiao tuan de
baogao" 猛练苦干, 争取全面大跃进: 八五三农场代表团的报告 [Drilling and
working hard to achieve the all-round Great Leap Forward: The report of the Farm
853 delegation], 1958, Farm 853 Archives.

"Yanjiu youpaidui wenti de jilu" 研究右派队问题的记录 [Records on discussion
of the problems in rightist teams], March 29, 1959. Farm 853 Archives.

"Zhongyang wenhuabu kaochazu xiang 853 changdangwei huibao qingkuang" 中央文
化部考查组向八五三场党委汇报情况 [The inspection panel of the Ministry of
Culture: Records of briefing session with the Farm 853 Party committee]. May 1959,
Farm 853 Archives.

Bawusan nongchang dangwei 八五三农场党委 [Farm 853 Party committee],
"Dui youpai fenzi yinian ling liugeyue gaizao de gongzuo zongjie" 对右派分子一年
零六个月改造的工作总结 [The work summary of the ideological remoulding
of rightists in the past one year and six months]. October 1959, Farm 853 Archives.

Bawusan nongchang zuzhike 八五三农场组织科 [Organization section of Farm 853],
"Dui benchang youpai fenzi zhai maozi de gongzuo jihua" 对本场右派分子摘帽子
的工作计划 [The working plan to delabel rightists on our farm]. October 20, 1959,
Farm 853 Archives.

Bawusan nongchang dangwei 八五三农场党委 [Farm 853 Party committee], "Guanyu
zaidiao youpai fenzi maozi gongzuo zongjie baogao" 关于摘掉右派分子帽子工

作的总结报告 [Final report regarding the delabelling of rightists]. December 22, 1959, Farm 853 Archives.

Bawusan nongchang zhengzhibu 八五三农场政治部 [Political department of Farm 853], "Dui jinhou youpai gaizao gongzuo de yijian" 对今后右派改造工作的意见 [Opinions on the work of remoulding rightists in the future]. July 5, 1960, Farm 853 Archives.

Bawusan nongchang zhengzhibu 八五三农场政治部 [Political department of Farm 853], "1960 nian yinian lai youpai fenzi sixiang qingkuang huibao" 一九六零年一年来右派分子思想情况汇报 [Report on the thoughts of rightists in the year 1960], August 30, 1960, Farm 853 Archives.

Bawusan nongchang zuzhike 八五三农场组织科 [Organization section of Farm 853], "Zai youpai gaizao gongzuo zhong cunzai de jige wenti" 在右派改造工作中存在的几个问题 [On several issues in the work of remoulding rightists], September 16, 1960, Farm 853 Archives.

Bawusan nongchang dangwei 八五三农场党委 [Farm 853 Party committee], "Zhonggong 853 nongchang weiyuanhui guanyu chuli yu chedi qingcha siren wenti de zhishi" 中共八五三农场委员会关于处理与彻底清查死人问题 的指示 [The instructions of the Farm 853 Party Committee on addressing and thoroughly investigating the issue of deaths], March 25, 1961, Farm 853 Archives.

Bawusan nongchang dangwei 八五三农场党委 [Farm 853 Party committee]. "Guanyu 6 ming zhigong, 1 ming laogaifan, 3 ming youpai, 6 ming xiaohai feizhengchang siwang de baogao" 关于六名职工,一名劳改犯, 三名右派, 六名小孩非正常死亡的报告 [Report regarding the abnormal deaths of six workers and staff, one *laogai* convict, three rightists, and six children]. April 7, 1961, Farm 853 Archives.

Mudanjiang nongkenju 牡丹江农垦局 [Mudanjiang Land Reclamation Bureau], "Guanyu 853 nongchang zhigong luanchi sheng baomi zaocheng siwang de tongbao" 关于八五三农场职工乱吃生苞米造成死亡的通报 [Circular on the death of a worker on Farm 853 due to eating raw corn]. April 4, 1961, Farm 853 Archives.

Mudanjiang nongkenju 牡丹江农垦局 [Mudanjiang Land Reclamation Bureau], "Guanyu yansu chuli yu chedi qingcha siren wenti de zhishi" 关于严肃处理与彻底清查死人问题的指示 [Instructions on seriously addressing and thoroughly investigating the issue of deaths], March 6, 1961, Farm 853 Archives.

Mudanjiang nongkenju dangwei 牡丹江农垦局党委 [The Party committee of the Mudanjiang Land Reclamation Bureau], "Guanyu dangqian kenqu gongzuo de jiancha baogao" 关于当前垦区工作的检查报告 [The examination report on the current work of the land reclamation region]. April 6, 1961, Farm 853 Archives.

Mudanjiang nongkenju dangwei 牡丹江农垦局党委 [The Party committee of the Mudanjiang Land Reclamation Bureau], "Guanyu fandui teshuhua de jueyi" 关于反对特殊化的决议 [The decision on anti-privileges], February 25, 1961, Farm 853 Archives.

Mudanjiang nongkenju zhengzhibu wenjian 牡丹江农垦局政治部文件 [The document of the political department of the Mudanjiang Land Reclamation Bureau]. No 37, 1962, Farm 853 Archives.

"Wang Zhen tongzhi gei chang lingdao de xin" 王震同志给场领导的信 [The letter of Comrade Wang Zhen to the farm leaders]. May 29, 1962, Farm 853 Archives.

Shanghai Municipal Archives

Luo Ruiqing 罗瑞卿. "Zai diyici quanguo laogai gongzuo huiyi shang de jianghua" 在第一次全国劳改工作会议上的讲话 [Speech at the first national conference for labour reform work], June 28, 1952, Shanghai Municipal Archives.

Zhonggong zhongyang 中共中央. "Guanyu fazhan junken nongchang de jianyi" 关于发展军垦农场 的建议 [Suggestions on the development of army farms]. March 20, 1958, Shanghai Municipal Archives.

BOOKS AND ARTICLES

Andreas, Joel. *Rise of the Red Engineers: The Cultural Revolution and the Origins of China's New Class*. Stanford: Stanford University Press, 2009.

Applebaum, Anne. *Gulag: A History*. New York: Doubleday, 2003.

Arkush, R. David. *Fei Xiaotong and Sociology in Revolutionary China*. Cambridge: Council on East Asian Studies, Harvard University, 1981.

Ba Jin 巴金. *Suixiang lu* 随想录 [Random thoughts]. Hong Kong: Sanlian shudian, 1979.

Bao Ruo-wang, and Rudolph Chelminski. *Prisoner of Mao*. New York: Penguin Books, 1973.

Barlow, Tani, and Gary Bjorge, eds. *I Myself Am a Woman: Selected Writings of Ding Ling*. Boston: Beacon Press, 1989.

Barmé, Geremie, and John Minford, eds. *Seeds of Fire: Chinese Voices of Conscience*. New York: Noonday Press, 1989.

Bawuling nongchangshi bianxie bangongshi 八五零农场史编写办公室. *Bawuling nongchangshi* 八五零农场史 [A history of Farm 850]. Hulin, Heilongjiang: n.p., 1986.

Bawusan nongchangzhi bianshen weiyuanhui 八五三农场志编审委员会. *Bawusan nongchangzhi* 八五三农场志 [Gazetteer of Farm 853]. Beijing: n.p., 1986.

Beijing dianying zhipian chang 北京电影制片厂. "Guanyu Ba Hong tongzhi zhengzhi lishi wenti de fucha" 关于巴鸿同志政治历史问题的复查 [On reinvestigation of Comrade Ba Hong's political history]. June 12, 1986, author's personal collection.

Beijing shi renmin jianchayuan qisushu – Jingjian (58) fen fanqizi di 454 hao 北京市人民检察院起诉书--京检 (58) 分反起字第 454 号 [Indictment of the People's Procuratorate of Beijing, 1958, procurator file no. 454], author's personal collection.

Bernstein, Thomas P. *Up to the Mountains and Down to the Villages: The Transfer of Youth from Urban to Rural China*. New Haven, CT: Yale University Press, 1977.

Bo Yibo 薄一波. *Ruogan zhongda juece yu shijian de huigu* 若干重大决策与事件的回顾 [Recollections of several important policies and events]. Beijing: Zhonggong zhongyang dangxiao chubanshe, 1993.

Brown, Jeremy and Matthew D. Johnson, eds. *Maoism at the Grassroots: Everyday Life in China's Era of High Socialism*. Cambridge, MA: Harvard University Press, 2015.

Cai Wenhui. *Class Struggle and Deviant Labelling in Mao's China: Becoming Enemies of the People*. Lewiston, NY: Edwin Mellen Press, 2001.

Cao Shuji 曹树基. "An Overt Conspiracy: Creating Rightists in Rural Henan, 1957–1958," in *Maoism at the Grassroots: Everyday Life in China's Era of High Socialism*, ed. Jeremy Brown and Matthew D. Johnson, 77-101. Cambridge: Harvard University Press, 2015.

–. *Zhongguo yiminshi* 中国移民史 [A history of Chinese migration]. Fuzhou: Fujian renmin chubanshe, 1997.

Cheek, Timothy. *Propaganda and Culture in Mao's China: Deng Tuo and the Intelligentsia.* Oxford: Clarendon Press, 1997.

Chen Fengxiao 陈奉孝. *Mengduan Weiminghu: Ershier nian laogai shengya jishi* 梦断未名湖: 二十二年劳改生涯记实 [Broken dreams at Weiming Lake: True stories of my twenty-two years of *laogai* experience]. Washington: The Laogai Research Foundation, 2005.

–. "Wufa wangque de jiyi" 无法忘却的记忆 [Unforgettable memories]. Unpublished essay.

–. "Xingkaihu jishi" 兴凯湖记事 [Stories of Xingkaihu]. Unpublished essay.

Chen Shengxi 陈胜玺 and Zhang Zhenqiang 张镇强, ed., *Mobuqu de lishi jiyi: Nankai wuqi huiyi* 抹不去的历史记忆: 南开五七回忆 [Inerasable memories of history: Recollections of Nankai University, 1957], n.p., 2015.

Cohen, Paul A. *History in Three Keys: The Boxers as Event, Experience, and Myth.* New York: Columbia University Press, 1997.

Cong Weixi 丛维熙. *Zouxiang hundun* 走向混沌 [Going towards chaos]. Beijing: Zhongguo shehui kexue chubanshe, 1998.

Dai Guangzhong 戴光中. *Hu Feng zhuan* 胡风传 [Biography of Hu Feng]. Yinchuan: Ningxia renmin chubanshe, 1994.

Dai Huang 戴煌. *Hu Yaobang yu pingfan yuan jia cuo an* 胡耀邦与平反冤假错案 [Hu Yaobang and redressing unjust, false, and mishandled cases]. Beijing: Xinhua chubanshe, 1998.

–. *Jiusi yisheng: Wo de youpai licheng* 九死一生: 我的右派历程 [A narrow escape from death: My experience as a rightist]. Beijing: Zhongyang bianyi chubanshe, 1998.

Dai Qing 戴晴. *Liang Shuming, Wang Shiwei, Chu Anping* 梁漱溟王实味储安平. Nanjing: Jiangsu wenyi chubanshe, 1989.

–. *Wang Shiwei and "Wild Lilies": Rectification and Purges in the Chinese Communist Party, 1942–1944.* Ed. David E. Apter and Timothy Cheek. Armonk: M.E. Sharpe, 1994.

Deng Xiaoping 邓小平. *Deng Xiaoping wenxuan 1975–1982* 邓小平文选 1975–1982 [Selected works of Deng Xiaoping, 1975–1982]. Beijing: Renmin chubanshe, 1983.

–. *Guanyu zhengfeng yundong de baogao* 关于整风运动的报告 [Report on the rectification movement]. Beijing: Quanguo zhengxie xuexi weiyuanhui yin, 1957.

Dikötter, Frank. *Crime, Punishment and the Prison in Modern China.* New York: Columbia University Press, 2002.

–. "The Emergence of Labour Camps in Shandong Province, 1942–1950." *China Quarterly* 175 (September 2003): 803–17.

–. *Mao's Great Famine: The History of China's Most Devastating Catastrophe, 1958–1962.* New York: Walker, 2010.

–. *The Tragedy of Liberation: A History of the Chinese Revolution, 1945–57.* New York: Bloomsbury Press, 2013.

Ding Ling 丁玲. *Fengxue renjian* 风雪人间 [The blizzard world]. Xiamen: Xiamen daxue chubanshe, 1987.

Dittmer, Lowell, and Chen Ruoxi. *Ethics and Rhetoric of the Chinese Cultural Revolution.* Berkeley: Center for Chinese Studies, University of California, 1981.

Domenach, Jean-Luc. *Chine: L'archipel oublié.* Paris, Fayard, 1992.

Dongbei renda xiaokan 东北人大校刊 [The Northeastern People's University newsletter], 1957, 1958.

Fang Jungui 方君归, ed. *Liu Shaoqi wenti ziliao zhuanji* 刘少奇问题资料专集 [A special collection of materials on Liu Shaoqi]. Taibei: Zhonggong yanjiu zazhishe, 1970.

Fang Lizhi 方励之. *Fang Lizhi zizhuan* 方励之自传 [Autobiography: Fang Li-zhi] Taibei: Tianxia yuanjian chuban gufen youxian gongsi, 2013.

Feng Yidai 冯亦代. *Hui yu ri lu* 悔余日录 [A diary of regrets]. Zhengzhou: Henan renmin chubanshe, 2006.

Forster, Keith. *Rebellion and Factionalism in a Chinese Province: Zhejiang, 1966–1976.* Armonk: M.E. Sharpe, 1990.

Fu Hualing. "Re-Education through Labour in Historical Perspective." *China Quarterly* 184 (2005): 811–30.

Gao Congmin 高崇民. Zhongguo minzhu tongmeng fanyoupai douzheng de jiben qingkuang 中国民主同盟反右派斗争的基本情况 [The basic situation of the anti-rightist struggle in the China Democratic League]. Printed by Minmeng zhongyang bangongting, January 1958.

Gao Hua 高华. *Hongtaiyang shi zenyang shengqi de: Yan'an zhengfeng yundong de lailong qumai.* 红太阳是怎样升起的: 延安整风运动的来胧去脉 [How did the red sun rise: A history of the Yan'an rectification movement]. Hong Kong: Xianggang zhongwen daxue chubanshe, 2003.

Ge Peiqi 葛佩琦. *Ge Peiqi huiyilu* 葛佩琦回忆录 [The memoir of Ge Peiqi]. Beijing: Zhongguo renmin daxue chubanshe, 1994.

Goldman, Merle. *Literary Dissent in Communist China.* Cambridge: Harvard University Press, 1967.

Gonganbu zhengcefalu yanjiushi 公安部政策法律研究室. *Gongan fagui xuanbian* 公安法规选编 [Selected collection of laws and regulations on public security]. Beijing: Qunzhong chubanshe, 1981.

Gottschang, Thomas R., and Diana Lary. *Swallows and Settlers: The Great Migration from North China to Manchuria.* Ann Arbor: University of Michigan Press, 2000.

Guowuyuan fazhiju 国务院法制局, ed. *Zhonghua renmin gongheguo xianxing falu xingzheng fagui huibian* 中华人民共和国现行法律行政法规汇编 [Comprehensive collection of current laws and administrative regulations of the People's Republic of China]. Beijing: Zhongguo falu chubanshe, 1995.

He Fengming 和凤鸣. *Jingli: Wode 1957 nian* 经历: 我的 1957 年 [Experience: My 1957]. Lanzhou: Dunhuang wenyi chubanshe, 2006.

Heilongjiang sheng difangzhi bianweihui 黑龙江省地方志编委会. *Heilongjiang shengzhi guoying nongchang zhi* 黑龙江省志-国营农场志 [Gazetteer of Heilongjiang Province: The state farms volume]. Harbin: Heilongjiang renmin chubanshe, 1992.

Hu Ke 胡可. *Huaishu zhuang* 槐树庄 [Scholar Tree Village]. Shanghai: Shanghai wenyi chubanshe, 1963.

Hu Ping 胡平. *Chan ji: 1957 kunan de jitan* 禅机: 1957 苦难的祭坛 [Allegorical words: The bitter sacrificial altar, 1957]. Guangzhou: Guangdong luyou chubanshe, 2004.

Hu Xianzhong 胡显中. *Yangmou xia de rensheng* 阳谋下的人生 [My life as a pawn in Mao's political game]. Washington: The Laogai Research Foundation, 2008.

Hua Min 华民. *Zhongguo da nizhuan: Fanyou yundong shi* 中国大逆转:反右运动史 [China's great reversal: A history of the Anti-Rightist Campaign]. New York: Ming-ching chubanshe, 1996.

Huang Miaozi 黄苗子. *Huang Miaozi sanwen* 黄苗子散文. [The prose of Huang Miaozi]. Guangzhou: Huacheng chubanshe, 1998.

Huang Wu 荒芜. *Mahuatang waiji* 麻花堂外集 [Additional collection of Mahua Hall]. Guangzhou: Guangdong wenhua chubanshe, 1989.

Huang Zhan 黄湛. *Yongyuan de Beidahuang* 永远的北大荒 [The everlasting Beidahuang]. Washington: The Laogai Research Foundation, 2004.

Jiang Dongping 姜东平. "Weiman riben kaituotuan de zuie lishi" 伪满日本开拓团的罪恶历史 [The evil history of the Japanese pioneer group]. *Zongheng* 纵横4 (1999): 47–49.

Li Caiyi 李才义. *Feng xiaoxiao lu manman* 风萧萧路漫漫 [Soughing wind and endless road]. Guangzhou: Haizhu chubanshe, 2001.

Li Chen 李晨, ed. *Zhonghua renmin gongheguo shilu* 中华人民共和国实录 [Real records of the People's Republic of China]. Changchun: Jilin renmin chubanshe, 1994.

Li Hui 李辉. *Lishi beige: Hu Feng jituan yuan'an shimo* 历史悲歌: 胡风集团冤案始末 [Elegies in history: The wrongful case of the "Hu Feng Clique"]. Hong Kong: Xiangjiang chuban youxian gongsi, 1989.

–. *Ren zai xuanwo: Huang Miaozi yu Yu Feng* 人在漩涡: 黄苗子与郁风 [People in the eddy: Huang Miaozi and Yu Feng]. Jinan: Shandong huabao chubanshe, 1998.

Li Wenhui 李文慧. *Shiji laoren de hua: Wu Zuguang juan* 世纪老人的话:吴祖光卷 [Words of seniors of the century: Wu Zuguang volume]. Shenyang: Liaoning jiaoyu chubanshe, 2000.

Li Zhisui. *The Private Life of Chairman Mao: The Memoirs of Mao's Personal Physician.* New York: Random House, 1994.

Liang Nan 梁南. "Chaosheng zhe" 朝圣者 [The pilgrims], in *Huishou rensheng*, ed. Liu Meng, 1–15. Beijing: Shidai nenyi chubanshe, 1992.

Link, Perry, ed. *Two Kinds of Truth: Stories and Reportage from China.* Bloomington, IN: Indiana University Press, 2006.

Liu Binyan 刘宾雁. *Liu Binyan zizhuan* 刘宾雁自传 [Autobiography of Liu Binyan]. Taibei: Shibao wenhua chuban qiye youxian gongsi, 1989.

Liu Meng 柳萌. *Chuntian de yu qiutian qing* 春天的雨秋天晴 [The whisking of rain in spring, the clearing of skies in autumn]. Beijing: Zhongguo gongren chubanshe, 2003.

–. ed. *Huishou rensheng* 回首人生 [Reflections on our life]. Beijing: Shidai wenyi chubanshe, 1992.

–. ed. *Lishi zai shenpan* 历史再审判 [Retrial by history]. Chengdu: Sichuan renmin chubanshe, 1996.

Liu, Peter. *Mirror: A Loss of Innocence in Mao's China.* Philadelphia: Xlibris, 2001.

Ma Qibin 马齐彬, et al., eds. *Zhongguo gongchandang zhizheng sishi nian* 中国共产党执政四十年 [The Chinese Communist Party: Forty years in power]. Beijing: Zhonggong dangshi ziliao chubanshe, 1989.

MacFarquhar, Roderick, ed. *The Hundred Flowers Campaign and the Chinese Intellectuals.* New York: Octagon Books, 1974.

–. *The Origins of the Cultural Revolution: Contradictions among the People, 1956–1957.* London: Oxford University Press, 1974.

MacFarquhar, Roderick, Timothy Cheek, and Eugene Wu, eds. *The Secret Speeches of Chairman Mao: From the Hundred Flowers to the Great Leap Forward.* Cambridge: Harvard University Press, 1989.

MacFarquhar, Roderick, and Michael Schoenhals. *Mao's Last Revolution*. Cambridge: The Belknap Press of Harvard University Press, 2006.

Mao Zedong 毛泽东. *Mao Zedong wenji dibajuan* 毛泽东文集 第八卷 [Works of Mao Zedong, vol. 8]. Beijing: Renmin chubanshe, 1993.

–. *Mao Zedong xuanji* 毛泽东选集 [Selected works of Mao Zedong]. Beijing: Renmin chubanshe. Vols. 1–4, 1967; Vol. 5, 1977.

McGough, James P. *Fei Hsiao-tung: The Dilemma of a Chinese Intellectual*. White Plains, NY: M.E. Sharpe, 1979.

Mei Jimin 梅济民. *Beidahuang* 北大荒 [The Great Northern Wilderness]. Taibei: Shuifurong chubanshe, 1975.

Mei-Feuerwerker, Yi-tsi. *Ding Ling's Fiction: Ideology and Narrative in Modern Chinese Literature*. Cambridge: Harvard University Press, 1982.

Mishan xianzhi bianweihui 密山县志编委会. *Mishan xianzhi* 密山县志 [Gazetteer of Mishan County]. Beijing: Zhongguo biaozun chubanshe, 1993.

Mühlhahn, Klaus. *Criminal Justice in China: A History*. Cambridge: Harvard University Press, 2009.

Ni Genshan 倪艮山. *Chensi ji* 沉思集 [On contemplation]. Hong Kong: Tianma chuban youxian gongsi, 2005.

Nie Gannu 聂绀弩. *Nie Gannu zixu* 聂绀弩自叙 [Nie Gannu's own account]. Beijing: Tuanjie chubanshe, 1998.

Nieh Hualing, ed. *Literature of the Hundred Flowers*. New York: Columbia University Press, 1981.

Niu Han 牛汉 and Deng Jiuping 邓九平, eds. *Jingji lu: Jiyi zhong de fan youpai yundong* 荆棘路: 记忆中的反右派运动 [The thorny road: The Anti-Rightist Campaign in memory]. Beijing: Jingji ribao chubanshe, 1998.

–. *Liuyue xue: Jiyi zhong de fan youpai yundong* 六月雪: 记忆中的反右派运动 [Snow in June: The Anti-Rightist Campaign in memory]. Beijing: Jingji ribao chubanshe, 1998.

–. *Yuan shang cao: Jiyi zhong de fan youpai yundong* 原上草: 记忆中的反右派运动 [Grass on the plains: The Anti-Rightist Campaign in memory]. Beijing: Jingji ribao chubanshe, 1998.

Niu Weina 钮薇娜. *Cuowei: Wo he wojia jidai zhishifenzi de gushi* 错位:我和我家几代知识分子的故事 [Disjunction: The stories of intellectuals in my clan]. Printed in Los Angeles, 2003.

Ou Jiajin 欧家斤. *Chen Yi pingzhuan* 陈沂评传 [critical biography of Chen Yi]. Beijing: Zhongguo wenlian chubanshe, 2000.

Pohl, J. Otto. *The Stalinist Penal System: A Statistical History of Soviet Repression and Terror, 1930–1953*. Jefferson, NC: McFarland, 1997.

Qian Liqun 钱理群. *Jujue yiwang: 1957 nian xue yanjiu biji* 拒绝遗忘: 1957 年学研究笔记 [Refuse forgetting: Research notes on the subject of 1957]. Taibei: Oxford University Press, 2007.

Red Guard Materials. *Mao Zedong sixiang wansui* 毛泽东思想万岁 [Long live Mao Zedong thought] (a collection of Mao's important speeches). n.p., 1967.

Renmin gongan 人民公安 [People's public security] 1 (1958).

Saunders, Kate. *Eighteen Layers of Hell: Stories from the Chinese Gulag*. London: Cassell Wellington House, 1996.

Seymour, James D. *China's Satellite Parties*. Armonk: M.E. Sharpe, 1987.

Seymour, James D., and Richard Anderson. *New Ghosts, Old Ghosts: Prisons and Labor Reform Camps in China*. Armonk: M.E. Sharpe, 1998.

Shen Zhihua 沈志华. *Sikao yu xuanze: Cong zhishifenzi huiyi dao fanyoupai yundong (1956–1957)* 思考与选择: 从知识分子会议到反右派运动 [Reflections and choices: From the conference on intellectuals to the Anti-Rightist Movement, 1956–1957]. Hong Kong: Xianggang zhongwen daxue dangdai zhongguo wenhua yanjiu zhongxin, 2008.

Smith, Aminda. *Thought Reform and China's Dangerous Classes: Re-Education, Resistance, and the People*. Lanham, MD: Rowman and Littlefield, 2013.

Solzhenitsyn, Aleksandr I. *The Gulag Archipelago, 1918–1956: An Experiment in Literary Investigation*. London: Collins and Harvill Press, 1974–78.

Song Yongyi 宋永毅, ed. *The Chinese Anti-Rightist Campaign Database (1957–)*. Hong Kong: The University Services Centre for China Studies at the Chinese University of Hong Kong, 2010.

Spence, Jonathan D. *The Gate of Heavenly Peace: The Chinese and Their Revolution, 1895–1980*. New York: Viking, 1981.

–. *The Search for Modern China*. New York: W.W. Norton, 2013.

Strauss, Julia. "Paternalist Terror: The Campaign to Suppress Counterrevolutionaries and Regime Consolidation in the People's Republic of China, 1950–1953," *Comparative Studies in Society and History* 44, 1 (2002): 80–105.

Sun Xiaoli 孙 晓 雳. *Zhongguo laodong gaizao zhidu de lilun yu shijian* 中国劳动改造制度的理论与实践 [Theories and practices of China's labour reform system]. Beijing: Zhongguo zhengfa daxue chubanshe, 1994.

Tan Chanxue 谭蝉雪. *Qiusuo: Lanzhou daxue youpai fangeming jituan an jishi* 求索: 兰州大学右派反革命集团案纪实 [Investigation: The true stories of the case of a rightist counter-revolutionary clique at Lanzhou University]. Hong Kong: Tianma chuban youxian gongsi, 2010.

Tan Tianrong 谭天荣. "Meiyou qingjie de gushi" 没有情节的故事 [Stories without plot]. Unpublished essay.

Teiwes, Frederick C. *Politics and Purges in China: Rectification and the Decline of Party Norms, 1950–1965*. Armonk: M.E. Sharpe, 1993.

Thaxton, Ralph. "How the Great Leap Forward Famine Ended in Rural China: 'Administrative Intervention' versus Peasant Resistance," in *Eating Bitterness: New Perspectives on China's Great Leap Forward and Famine*, ed. Kimberley Manning and Felix Wemheuerm, 251–71. Vancouver: UBC Press, 2011.

Thurston, Anne F. *Enemies of the People*. New York: Alfred A. Knopf, 1987.

Tucker, Nancy B. *Taiwan, Hong Kong, and the United States, 1945–1992: Uncertain Friendships*. New York: Twayne Publishers, 1994.

Twitchett, Denis, and John K. Fairbank, eds. *The Cambridge History of China*, vol. 14. Cambridge: Cambridge University Press, 1987.

U, Eddy. "Intellectuals and Alternative Socialist Paths in the Early Mao Years." *China Journal* 70 (2013): 1–23.

Veg, Sebastian. "Testimony, History and Ethics: From the Memory of Jiabiangou Prison Camp to a Reappraisal of the Anti-Rightist Movement in Present-Day China." *The China Quarterly* 218 (2014): 516–17.

Waley-Cohen, Joanna. *Exile in Mid-Qing China: Banishment to Xinjiang, 1758–1820*. New Haven: Yale University Press, 1991.

Wang Fang 王芳, et al., eds. *Dangdai zhongguo de gongan gongzuo* 当代中国的公安工作 [Public security work in contemporary China]. Beijing: Dangdai zhongguo chubanshe, 1992.

Wang Hong 汪洪, ed. *Zuoyou shuo Ding Ling* 左右说丁玲 [Commenting on Ding Ling from the left and the right]. Beijing: Zhongguo gongren chubanshe, 2002.

Wang Mingdi 王明迪, et al. *Zhongguo yuzheng falu wenti yanjiu* 中国狱政法律问题研究 [Studies of legal issues in prison administration in China]. Beijing: Zhongguo zhengfa daxue chubanshe, 1995.

Wang Shuyao 王书瑶. *Yanyuan fengyu zhu rensheng* 燕园风雨铸人生 [My turbulent life and times at Beijing University]. Washington: The Laogai Research Foundation, 2007.

Wang Zhen zhuan bianxiezu王震传编写组. *Wang Zhen zhuan* 王震传 [A biography of Wang Zhen]. Beijing: Dangdai zhongguo chubanshe, 2001.

Wang Zheng 王正. "Meng hui huangyuan" 梦回荒原 [Dreaming back to the wilderness], in *Lishi zai shenpan* [Retrial by history], ed. Liu Meng, 332–49. Chengdu: Sichuan renmin chubanshe, 1906.

Wenche He'en 文彻赫恩. *Kunan de licheng* 苦难的历程 [Difficult journeys]. Washington: The Laogai Research Foundation, 2003.

Whitman, Walt. *Complete Poetry and Selected Prose and Letters*. London: Nonesuch Press, 1964.

Williams, James H. "Fang Lizhi's Big Bang: A Physicist and the State in China," *HSPS* 30, 1 (1999): 49–87.

–. "Fang Lizhi's Expanding Universe," *China Quarterly* 123 (September 1990): 459–84.

Williams, Philip F., and Yenna Wu. *The Great Wall of Confinement: The Chinese Prison Camp through Contemporary Fiction and Reportage*. Berkeley: University of California Press, 2004.

Wu, Harry. *Bitter Winds: A Memoir of My Years in China's Gulag*. New York: John Wiley and Sons, 1994.

–. *Laodong jiaoyang yu liuchang jiuye* 劳动教养与留场就业 [Re-education through labour and forced job placement]. Washington: The Laogai Research Foundation, 2004.

–. *Laogai: The Chinese Gulag*. Boulder, CO: Westview Press, 1992.

Wu, Ningkun. *A Single Tear: A Family's Persecution, Love and Endurance in Communist China*. New York: Atlantic Monthly Press, 1993.

Wu Yongliang 吴永良. *Yuxue feifei: Beidahuang shenghuo jishi* 雨雪霏霏: 北大荒生活纪实 [Floating rain and snow: True stories of life in the Great Northern Wilderness]. Beijing: Zhongguo xiju chubanshe, 2002.

Wu Zuguang 吴祖光. *Wu Zuguang xuanji* 吴祖光选集 [Selected works of Wu Zuguang]. Shijiazhuang: Hebei renmin chubanshe, 1995.

Xiao Donglian 肖冬莲. *Qiusuo Zhongguo: Wenge qian shinian shi* 求索中国:文革前十年史 [The search for China: The ten years of history prior to the Cultural Revolution]. Beijing: Hongqi chubanshe, 1999.

Xiao Ke 萧克, et al., *Wo qinli guo de zhengzhi yundong* 我亲历过的政治运动 [Political campaigns that I have experienced]. Beijing: Zhongyang bianyi chubanshe, 1998.

Xie Guozhen 谢国桢. *Qingchu liuren kaifa dongbei shi* 清初流人开发东北史 [A history of the colonization of the northeast by exiles in the early Qing]. Taibei: Kaiming shudian, 1969.

Xin Suwei 辛述威. *Ding Cong zhuan* 丁聪传 [A biography of Ding Cong]. Beijing: Zhongguo gongren chubanshe, 1993.

Xingkaihu changshiban 兴凯湖场办. *Xingkaihu nongchang shi* 兴凯湖农场史 [A history of Xingkaihu Farm]. Mishan: n.p., 1988.

Yan Peng 阎鹏. "Pan Hannian zai Tuanhe nongchang" 潘汉年在团河农场 [Pan Hannian in Tuanhe Farm], *Zongheng*, 10 (1998): 24–30.

Yang Bin 杨宾. *Liubian jilue* 柳边记略 [Notes from the willow palisades]. Taibei: Guangwen shuju, 1968.

Yang Congdao 杨崇道. "Bawuling Yunshan xumuchang liuren feizhengchang siwang mingdan" 八五零云山畜牧场流人非正常死亡名单 [The list of the abnormal deaths in the Yunshan Branch, Farm 850]. Unpublished note, author's collection.

Yang Kuisong 杨奎松. "Baifenbi yu kuodahua: jiejidouzheng zhili moshi de jingyan he jiaoxun" 百分比与扩大化: 阶级斗争治理模式的经验和教训 [Percentage and magnification: Experiences and lessons from the class struggle-based administrative model]. Unpublished essay, obtained in 2015.

Yang Xianhui 杨显惠. *Gaobie Jiabiangou* 告别夹边沟 [Farewell Jiabiangou]. Shanghai: Shanghai wenyi chubanshe, 2003.

–. *Woman from Shanghai: Tales of Survival from a Chinese Labor Camp.* New York: Pantheon Books, 2009.

Yang Zhongmei. *Hu Yaobang: A Chinese Biography.* Armonk: M.E. Sharpe, 1988.

Yao Lan 姚蓝 and Deng Qun 邓群. *Bai Congxi shenbian de zhonggong mimi dangyuan* 白崇禧身边的中共秘密党员 [The underground Chinese Communist Party member working with Bai Congxi]. Beijing: Zhonggong dangshi chubanshe, 1998.

Ye Yonglie 叶永烈. *Fan youpai shimo* 反右派始末 [The whole story of the Anti-Rightist Movement]. Xining: Qinghai renmin chubanshe, 1995.

Yin Yi 殷毅. *Huishou canyang yi han shan* 回首残阳已含山 [The setting of the sun over the mountain]. Beijing: Shiyue wenyi chubanshe, 2003.

Yu Shanpu 于善埔, and Yang Congdao 杨崇道. "Beidahuang liuren mingdan" 北大荒流人名单 [List of names of Beihahuang exiles]. Unpublished note, author's collection.

Yu Zhen 寓真. *Nie Gannu xingshi dang'an* 聂绀弩刑事档案 [Penal files on Nie Gannu]. Hong Kong: Mingbao chubanshe, 2009.

Yue Daiyun, and Carolyn Wakeman. *To the Storm: The Odyssey of a Revolutionary Chinese Woman.* Berkeley: University of California Press, 1985.

Yunshan nongchang shizhi bangongshi 云山农场史志办公室. *Yunshan nongchangshi* 云山农场史 [A history of Yunshan Farm]. Jiamusi: n.p., 1995.

Zarrow, Peter. "Meanings of China's Cultural Revolution: Memoirs of Exile." *Positions* 7, 1 (1999): 165–91.

Zhang Jie 张洁. *Wu Zuguang beihuan qu* 吴祖光悲欢曲 [Wu Zuguang: Vicissitudes of life]. Chengdu: Sichuan wenyi chubanshe, 1986.

Zhang Linchi 张林池, et al., eds. *Dangdai Zhongguo de nongken shiyie* 当代中国的农垦事业 [Land reclamation in contemporary China]. Beijing: Zhongguo shehui kexue chubanshe, 1986.

Zhang Xiaofeng 张晓风. "Hu Feng anjian yu youpai xuesheng" 胡风案件与右派学生 [Hu Feng's case and student rightists]. Unpublished essay.

Zhang Yihe 章怡和. *Wangshi bingbu ruyan* 往事并不如烟 [Do not let bygones be bygones]. Beijing: Renmin wenxue chubanshe, 2004.

Zhang Yunpeng 张云鹏. "Zhuangzai wuqi, beizai wuqi" 壮哉五七, 悲哉五七 [Glories and tragedies of 1957], in *Mobuqu de lishi jiyi: Nankai wuqi huiyi* [Inerasable memories of history: Recollections of Nakai University, 1957], ed. Chen Shengxi and Zhang Zhengiang, 25–31. n.p., 2015.

Zhang Zhicai 张志才. *Yongyuan zai chulian* 永远在初恋 [In love forever]. Beijing: Jiefangjun wenyi chubanshe, 1992.

Zheng Jiazhen 郑加真. *Zhongguo dongbeijiao* 中国东北角 [The northeast corner of China]. Harbin: Heilongjiang renmin chubanshe, 1998.

Zheng Xiaofeng 郑笑枫. *Ding Ling zai Beidahuang* 丁玲在北大荒 [Ding Ling in the Great Northern Wilderness]. Wuhan: Hubei renmin chubanshe, 1989.

Zhonggong zhongyang 中共中央. "Guanyu zaidiao youpai maozi de renyuan de gongzuo fenpei he shenghuo daiyu de guiding" 关于摘掉右派帽子的人员的工作分配和生活待遇的规定 [Regulations on the work assignment and remuneration of individuals who have had their rightist hats removed]. November 2, 1959, in Song, *Chinese Anti-Rightist Campaign Database*.

Zhonggong zhongyang, guowuyuan 中共中央, 国务院. "Guanyu zai guojia xinji renyuan he gaodeng xuexiao xuesheng zhong de youpai fenzi chuli yuanze de guiding" 关于在国家薪给人员和高等学校学生中的右派分子处理原则的规定 [Stipulations on the principles for dealing with the rightists among state employees and college students]. December 12, 1957, in Song, *Chinese Anti-Rightist Campaign Database*.

Zhonggong zhongyang tongyi zhongyang zuzhibu he zhongyang tongzhanbu guanyu youpai fenzi gongzuo jidian yijian de baogao 中共中央同意中央组织部和中央统战部关于右派分子工作几点意见的报告 [The authorization of the Chinese Communist Party Central Committee of several suggestions of the Central Organization Department and the Central United Front Department regarding the work of rightists]. September 17, 1960, in Song, *Chinese Anti-Rightist Campaign Database*.

Zhonggong zhongyang tongzhanbu 中共中央统战部. "Guanyu quanguo tongzhan gongzuo huiyi de baogao" 关于全国统战工作会议的报告 [The report on the national conference for united front work]. May 28, 1962, in Song, *Chinese Anti-Rightist Campaign Database*.

Zhonghua renmin gongheguo gongan falu quanshu bianweihui 中华人民共和国公安法律全书编委会, ed. *Zhonghua renmin gongheguo gongan falu quanshu* 中华人民共和国公安法律全书 [Comprehensive collection of laws on public security in the People's Republic of China]. Changchun: Jilin renmin chubanshe, 1995.

Zhongguo qingnian chubanshe 中国青年出版社, ed. *Zai fan youpai douzheng zhong xiqu jiaoxun: Ji dang de hanwei zhe he qingnian de bailei* 在反右派斗争中吸取教训: 记党的捍卫者和青年的败类 [Drawing lessons from the Anti-Rightist Campaign: On defenders of the Party and the degenerates among the youth]. Beijing: Zhongguo qingnian chubanshe, 1957.

Zhongguo jianyu shi bianxie zu 中国监狱史编写组. *Zhongguo jianyu shi* 中国监狱史 [A history of prisons in China]. Beijing: Qunzong chubanshe, 1986.

"Zhongyang shi ren xiaozu guanyu fangeming fenzi he qita huaifenzi de jieshi ji chuli de zhengce jiexian de zanxing guiding" 中央十人小组关于反革命分子和其他坏分子解释及处理的政策界限的暂行规定 [Interim provision of the central

ten-member panel regarding policy demarcations concerning the definition and
treatment of counter-revolutionaries and other bad elements], March 10, 1956.
中共天津市委五人小组翻印 [Printed by the five–member panel of the Chinese
Communist Party's Tianjin Committee].

Zhongyang wenxian yanjiushi 中央文献研究室, ed. *Jianguo yilai zhongyao wenxian xuanbian* 建国以来重要文献选编 卷七至卷十三 [Selected collections of important
documents since the establishment of the People's Republic of China, vols. 7–13].
Beijing: Zhongyang wenxian chubanshe, 1993–1996.

Zhongyang wenxian yanjiushi 中央文献研究室, ed. *Zhou Enlai nianpu 1949–1976*
周恩来年谱 1949–1976 [The chronicle of Zhou Enlai, 1949–1976]. Beijing:
Zhongyang wenxian chubanshe, 1997.

Zhou Hongxing 周红兴. *Ai Qing zhuan* 艾青传 [A biography of Ai Qing]. Beijing:
Zuojia chubanshe, 1993.

Zhou Jianqiang 周健强. *Nie Gannu zhuan* 聂绀弩传 [A biography of Nie Gannu].
Chengdu: Sicuan renmin chubanshe, 1987.

Zhou Liangpei 周良沛. *Ding Ling Zhuan* 丁玲传 [A biography of Ding Ling]. Beijing:
Shiyue wenyi chubanshe, 1993.

Zhu Zheng 朱正. *1957 nian de xiaji: Cong baijia zhengming dao liangjia zhengming*
1957 年的夏季:从百家争鸣到两家争鸣 [The summer of 1957: From a hundred
schools of thought contending to two schools of thought contending]. Zhengzhou:
Henan renmin chubanshe, 1998.

Index

accidental deaths, 13, 23–24, 115, 237n12, 238n16
accidental dissidents, 23–24
active counter-revolutionaries, 33, 35, 82, 88–90, 106, 133, 156, 169, 181. *See also* counter-revolutionaries
agricultural workers: accidental deaths, 13, 237n12; labour management, 70; manual labour, 58–59, 114–15; present-day production units, 186; status on farms, 56–57
Ai Qing (poet): denunciation, 149; favourable treatment, 75, 79; first days in exile, 56; memoir literature, 197, 226n36; type of rightist, 29, 51
Anti-Party clique, 147, 151
anti-reform element and anti-Party element, 24, 26, 39, 98, 105, 153
Anti-Rightist Campaign (1957/1958): absurdity of, 19–22; censorship, 213n26; government policy, 3–5, 184; identification of rightists, 17–19; issues, 256n88; motives, 10, 14, 15, 215n9; post-campaign experience, 3–4, 14–16; psychological impact, 159–60, 191–93; social and political ramifications, 188–93; suicide as protest, 135; victim rehabilitation,

181–83, 256n89; victim statistics, 216n16. *See also* banishment; Chinese Communist Party (CCP); labelling; rightists
archives (official sources), 186, 200–6
army farms. *See* labour camps and farms
art and education troupes, 12, 57, 79, 102, 123–24
artists, 43–44, 65, 79, 154, 175, 225n26

Ba Hong (movie director), 43, 84, 124, 128, 242n74
Banbuqiao Detention Centre, 82, 180, 235n88, 238n18
banishment: camp choice, 51, 223n8; comparative perspective, 5, 10–14; government policy guidelines, 45–47, 49; not sent to borderlands, 5, 211n3, 212n6; political offenders, 82–110; pre-banishment denunciation, 146–50; psychological impact, 191–93; Qing dynasty, 212n9; reasons, 28–45; social and political ramifications, 188–93. *See also* Anti-Rightist Campaign (1957/1958); rightists
Beidahuang (the Great Northern Wilderness): about, 6, 52–55, 224n15; asking to go, 53–55; Beijing rightists,

Contemporary Chinese Studies

Glen Peterson, *The Power of Words: Literacy and Revolution in South China, 1949–95*

Wing Chung Ng, *The Chinese in Vancouver, 1945–80: The Pursuit of Identity and Power*

Yijiang Ding, *Chinese Democracy after Tiananmen*

Diana Lary and Stephen MacKinnon, eds., *Scars of War: The Impact of Warfare on Modern China*

Eliza W.Y. Lee, ed., *Gender and Change in Hong Kong: Globalization, Postcolonialism, and Chinese Patriarchy*

Christopher A. Reed, *Gutenberg in Shanghai: Chinese Print Capitalism, 1876–1937*

James A. Flath, *The Cult of Happiness: Nianhua, Art, and History in Rural North China*

Erika E.S. Evasdottir, *Obedient Autonomy: Chinese Intellectuals and the Achievement of Orderly Life*

Hsiao-ting Lin, *Tibet and Nationalist China's Frontier: Intrigues and Ethnopolitics, 1928–49*

Xiaoping Cong, *Teachers' Schools and the Making of the Modern Chinese Nation-State, 1897–1937*

Diana Lary, ed., *The Chinese State at the Borders*

Norman Smith, *Resisting Manchukuo: Chinese Women Writers and the Japanese Occupation*

Hasan H. Karrar, *The New Silk Road Diplomacy: China's Central Asian Foreign Policy since the Cold War*

Richard King, ed., *Art in Turmoil: The Chinese Cultural Revolution, 1966–76*

Blaine R. Chiasson, *Administering the Colonizer: Manchuria's Russians under Chinese Rule, 1918–29*

Emily M. Hill, *Smokeless Sugar: The Death of a Provincial Bureaucrat and the Construction of China's National Economy*

Kimberley Ens Manning and Felix Wemheuer, eds., *Eating Bitterness: New Perspectives on China's Great Leap Forward and Famine*

Helen M. Schneider, *Keeping the Nation's House: Domestic Management and the Making of Modern China*

James A. Flath and Norman Smith, eds., *Beyond Suffering: Recounting War in Modern China*

Elizabeth R. VanderVen, *A School in Every Village: Educational Reform in a Northeast China County, 1904–31*

Norman Smith, *Intoxicating Manchuria: Alcohol, Opium, and Culture in China's Northeast*

Juan Wang, *Merry Laughter and Angry Curses: The Shanghai Tabloid Press, 1897–1911*

Richard King, *Milestones on a Golden Road: Writing for Chinese Socialism, 1945–80*

David Faure and Ho Ts'ui-P'ing, eds., *Chieftains into Ancestors: Imperial Expansion and Indigenous Society in Southwest China*

Yunxiang Gao, *Sporting Gender: Women Athletes and Celebrity-Making during China's National Crisis, 1931–45*

Peipei Qiu, with Su Zhiliang and Chen Lifei, *Chinese Comfort Women: Testimonies from Imperial Japan's Sex Slaves*

Julia Kuehn, Kam Louie, and David M. Pomfret, eds., *Diasporic Chineseness after the Rise of China: Communities and Cultural Production*

Bridie Andrews, *The Making of Modern Chinese Medicine, 1850–1960*

Kelvin E.Y. Low, *Remembering the Samsui Women: Migration and Social Memory in Singapore and China*

Jiayan Zhang, *Coping with Calamity: Environmental Change and Peasant Response in Central China, 1736–1949*

Alison R. Marshall, *Cultivating Connections: The Making of Chinese Prairie Canada*

Ruoyun Bai, *Staging Corruption: Chinese Television and Politics*

Christopher G. Rea and Nicolai Volland, eds., *The Business of Culture: Cultural Entrepreneurs in China and Southeast Asia, 1900–65*

Eric Hyer, *The Pragmatic Dragon: China's Grand Strategy and Boundary Settlements*

Norman Smith, ed., *Empire and Environment in the Making of Manchuria*

Lloyd L. Wong, ed., *Trans-Pacific Mobilities: The Chinese in Canada*

Jennifer Y.J. Hsu, *State of Exchange: Migrant NGOs and the Chinese Government*